S-Barclw

Love you lots

Kat

x x

The Secret History of the
Royal Court of England

Dedication

*Bruno Miguel Jorge (o meu amigo em Lisboa),
a teacher, and most importantly, friend!*

The Secret History of the Royal Court of England

The Scandalous Chronicle of the Georgian Monarchy

Olivia Serres

A New Edition Edited by Stephen Basdeo,
With an introduction by Rachael Gillibrand

PEN & SWORD
HISTORY

First published in Great Britain in 2022 by
Pen & Sword History
An imprint of
Pen & Sword Books Ltd
Yorkshire – Philadelphia

ISBN 978 1 39901 582 0

Typeset by Mac Style
Printed in the UK by CPI Group (UK) Ltd, Croydon, CR0 4YY.

Pen & Sword Books Limited incorporates the imprints of Atlas,
Archaeology, Aviation, Discovery, Family History, Fiction, History,
Maritime, Military, Military Classics, Politics, Select, Transport,
True Crime, Air World, Frontline Publishing, Leo Cooper, Remember
When, Seaforth Publishing, The Praetorian Press, Wharncliffe
Local History, Wharncliffe Transport, Wharncliffe True Crime
and White Owl.

For a complete list of Pen & Sword titles please contact

PEN & SWORD BOOKS LIMITED
47 Church Street, Barnsley, South Yorkshire, S70 2AS, England
E-mail: enquiries@pen-and-sword.co.uk
Website: www.pen-and-sword.co.uk

Or

PEN AND SWORD BOOKS
1950 Lawrence Rd, Havertown, PA 19083, USA
E-mail: Uspen-and-sword@casematepublishers.com
Website: www.penandswordbooks.com

Contents

Introduction to The Secret History of the Court of England

Rachael Gillibrand

A contemporary engraving of Olivia Serres.

In April 1838 the *Quarterly Review* denounced the publication of a new edition of a book titled *The Secret History of the Court of England* for, according to that reviewer, the book was

> [...] nothing but an amplified reprint of libels, equally atrocious and absurd, which have long been in clandestine circulation.[1]

The Secret History of the Court of England was actually a revised and expanded reprint of an earlier anonymously written, short one volume work titled *The Authentic Records of the Court of England for the Last Seventy Years* (1832), published by J. Phillips. The *Authentic Records* was so controversial that the Duke of Cumberland, owing to the numerous accusations of crime and corruption levelled at him in the book, pursued a case of criminal libel through the courts. More serious than mere defamatory libel, criminal libel could have seen the publisher incarcerated.[2] Phillips quickly fled to France but he was tried and convicted in absentia and copies of the *Authentic Records* were no longer published.[3]

The publisher William Henry Stevenson then revised and expanded the *Authentic Records* into two volumes and gave it the title of the *Secret History*, and Stevenson avoided prosecution by taking out those passages which offended the Duke of Cumberland. The book might have been forgotten about were it not for the remarks upon the *Secret History* in the *Quarterly Review* in 1838. To its contemporaries, the book was famous (or perhaps infamous) for its portrayal of the British monarchy as corrupt, immoral, and inconsiderate of the needs of what the author refers to as 'the productive classes'. In fact, the allegedly libellous nature of the book led the *Quarterly Review* to assume that it could only have been marketed by women who, under the cover of darkness, would go covertly from door to door offering copies of 'Lady Anne Hamilton's Journal' for the price of one guinea per volume.[4]

Other reviewers were not quite so harsh or concerned as the *Quarterly Review*. The editor of *The Monthly Magazine*, George W.M. Reynolds—who went on to publish his own fictional exposé of royal life in *The Mysteries of the Court of London* (1849–56)—stated that whilst much of the book 'is palpably untrue, wicked, and absurd […] we must not wilfully and blindly condemn the whole because we do not *wish* to believe it'.[5] Nevertheless, contemporary literary institutions agreed (at least publicly) that the book was, either in whole or in part, an exercise in defamation.

This opinion of the book, as being untrue and slanderous, is particularly interesting in relation to its 'preface'. Here, as you will see, the author professes to be an impartial and unbiased observer of the events discussed, claiming that any negative remarks or accusations were, 'not intended as any disparagement to the private characters or virtues of those statesmen whose talent was great and well cultivated'. Nevertheless, the fact that the book appears to have been modelled on *The Secret History of the Court of Justinian*, written by Procopius in c. 550-558 CE

Title page of the fourth issue of G.W.M. Reynolds's *Mysteries of the Court of London*, in which George IV visits the house of a young and virtuous maiden in order to seduce her. (*Stephen Basdeo Collection*)

(as well as the contents of the book itself) suggests otherwise. Just as Procopius expresses a disillusionment with Emperor Justinian and his wife Theodora, seeking to expose the private lives of the Emperor and his inner circle, so too does the author of *The Secret History of the Court of England* express a sense of discontent with George III, George IV, their ministers, and courtiers, exclaiming 'Oh! England, how hast thou been cursed by debt and blood through the impotency and villainy of thy rulers!' But who, then, was this discontented author of *The Secret History*?

The work itself would suggest that its author was Lady Anne Hamilton (1766–1846), courtier and lady-in-waiting to Caroline, Princess of Wales. However, despite the work being published under her name, Lady Anne Hamilton claimed that this was without her knowledge or sanction. In fact, her life was so upturned by the *Secret History*, that she retired to France in order to avoid public speculation.[6] The *Quarterly Review* jumped to her defence, claiming that 'she is entirely innocent of any share in these volumes so audaciously imputed to her'.[7] Instead, it has been suggested that the *Authentic Records* and *Secret History* was written by a woman, referred to in Lady Anne's letters as 'S. W.', who had gained Lady Anne's confidence (and access to her papers) in the aftermath of Princess Caroline's death. Whilst the exact identity of this 'S. W.' remains unknown, it is strongly assumed that these initials refer to Olivia Serres, *nee*. Wilmot. In her early life, Serres was a landscape painter and author of several romantic literary works; however, she became better known as a royal imposter who, in 1817, claimed to be the daughter of Henry Frederick (Duke of Cumberland and brother of George III) and a Mrs. Payne.[8]

Whoever the author, *The Secret History* provides a fascinating (if not impartial) insight into the contemporary gossips, affairs, and accusations surrounding the courts of George III and his son, George IV. Setting personal tales of deceit, illness, corruption, and murder against events well known to history (such as the American War of Independence, the French Revolution and deeds of Napoleon, or the Irish Rebellion), *The Secret History* is, as *The Monthly Magazine* suggested in 1838, a work of 'too extraordinary a nature to be silently passed over'.[9]

Note on the Text

The *Secret History* was published several times during the nineteenth century. Several printers in the United States released versions of it—Americans were big fans of sensational tales of English court life—and G.W.M. Reynolds's publisher John Dicks released a "People's Edition" of it the 1880s. There have been editions published in the twenty-first century by some print-on-demand publishers but these books are often little better than photocopies, with certain words obscured due to the poor quality of the scans. So I felt it was time for a new edition of this interesting source that would be legible.

The text presented here is taken from the 1832 two-volume edition of William Henry Stevenson's *Secret History of the Court of England*. All of the original spelling, syntax, and punctuation has been retained.

The illustrations that accompany this version were not originally part of the original edition published by Stevenson but have been added by me for the benefit of the modern reader to help them become better acquainted with the people who feature in this history book.

Stephen Basdeo

COMPLETE.

SECRET HISTORY

OF THE

COURT OF ENGLAND.

BY THE
RT. HON. LADY ANNE HAMILTON.

*** *This is a faithful reprint of a work which produced an extraordinary sensation on its first appearance fifty-one years ago, and was speedily suppressed. It is the same, too, for which the sum of a Thousand Pounds was offered in New York about nine years ago.*

LONDON: JOHN DICKS, 313, STRAND.

Price One Shilling.

John Dicks' cheap 6d paperback "People's Edition" of the *Secret History of the Court of England* published c.1884 and featuring an image of Lady Anne Hamilton on the front cover. Dicks was also George W.M. Reynolds's business partner and publisher of Reynolds's *The Mysteries of the Court of London* (1849–56) which was inspired by Serres's *Secret History*.

Secret History of the Court of England

From the Accession of George the Third to the Death of
George the Fourth
Including, among other important matters,
Full particulars of the Mysterious Death of the Princess Charlotte

Of meaner vice and villains, sing no more,
But monsters crown'd, and Crime enrobed with Power!
At Vice's high imperial throne begin,
And boldly brand such prodigies of sin;
With pregnant phrase, and strong impartial verse,
The crimes of lords and crimes of kings rehearse!

Written by Olivia Serres
"Lady Anne Hamilton"

To the Reader

The source from whence this Work proceeds will be a sufficient guarantee for the facts it contains. A high sense of duty and honor has prompted these details which have for many years been on the eve of publication. It will be worthy of the perusal of The Great because it will serve as a mirror, and they who do not see themselves, or their actions reflected, will not take offence at the *unvarnished Picture*—it may afford real benefit to the Statesman and Politician, by the ample testimony it gives, that when *Justice is perverted*, the most lamentable consequences ensue; and to that class of Society whose station is more humble, it may unfold the designing characters by whom they have so frequently been deceived. *They only* are competent to detail the scenes and intrigues of *a Court*, who have been most intimately acquainted with it, and it must at all times be acknowledged, that it is a climate not very conducive to the growth of Virtue, not very frequently the abode of Truth—yet although its atmosphere is so tainted, its giddy crowd is thought enviably happy. The fallacy of such opinions is here set forth to public view, by one who has spent much of her time in *the interior of a Court*, and whose immediate knowledge of the then passing events, give ability to narrate them faithfully. Many, very many, facts are here omitted, which hereafter shall appear, and there is little doubt, but that some general good may result from an unprejudiced and calm perusal of the subjects subjoined.

Preface

How far the law of Libel (as it now stands) may affect us is best to be ascertained by a reference to the declaration of Lord Abingdon, in 1779, and inserted, verbatim, at page 69 of this "Secret History." The following Pages are intended as a benefit, not to do injury. If the facts could not have been maintained proper methods ought to have been adopted to have caused the most minute enquiry and investigation upon the subject. Many an Arrow has been shot, and innumerable suspicions entertained from what motive, and by whose hand the bow was drawn, yet here all mystery ceases, and an open avowal is made:—Would to Heaven for the honor of human nature that the subjoined documents were falsehoods and calumniations invented for the purpose of maligning character, or for personal resentments—but the unusual corroboration of *events*, *places*, times, and persons, will not admit the probability. In the affair of the ever lamented Death of the Princess Charlotte, the three important Letters commencing at page 329 are of essential importance, and deserve the most grave and deliberate enquiry—for *the first time* they *now* appear in print. The subjects connected with the Royal Mother are also of deep interest. The conduct of the English Government towards Napoleon is introduced, to give a true and impartial view of the *reasons* which dictated such arbitrary and unjust measures enforced against that *Great Man*, and which will ever remain a blot upon the British Nation. These unhandsome derelictions from honorable conduct could alone be expressed by those who were well informed upon *private subjects*. Respect for the illustrious Dead has materially encouraged the inclination to give publicity to scenes, which were as revolting in themselves as they were *cruel* and *most heart-rending* to the Victims: throughout the whole, it is quite apparent that certain Persons were obnoxious to the Ruling Authorities, and the sequel will prove, that *the extinction* of such Persons was resolved upon, let the means and measures to obtain that object be what they might. During this period we find those who had long been opposed in Political sentiments, to all appearance perfectly reconciled, and adhering to that party from whom they might expect the greatest honors and advancement in the State. We need only refer as proofs for this, to the late "Spencer Percival," and "George Canning"—who to obtain preferment joined the confederations formed against an unprotected Princess, and yet who previously had been the most strenuous defenders of the same Lady's cause.—Well may it be observed that Vanity is too powerful,

> The Seals of Office glitter in their eyes,
> They leave the truth, and by their falsehoods rise.

These remarks are not intended as any disparagement to the private characters or virtues of those statesmen whose talent was great and well cultivated, but to establish the position which it is the object of this work to show that Justice has not been fairly and impartially administered when the requirement was in opposition to the Royal wish or the administration.

Within these volumes will also be found urgent remonstrances against the indignities offered to the people of Ireland, whose forebearance has been great, and whose sorrows are without a parallel, and who merit the same regard as England and Scotland.—Much is omited relative to the private conduct of persons who occupy *high stations*, but should it be needful, it shall be published, and all the correspondence connected therewith. It is true much honor will not be derived from such explanations, but they are forthcoming if requisite.

The generality of readers will not criticise severely upon *the diction* of these prefatory remarks; they will rather have their attention turned to the truths submitted to them, and the end in view,—*that end* is for the advancement of the best interests of Society—to unite more closely each member in the bonds of friendship and amity, and to expose the *hidden causes* which for so long a period have been barriers to concord, unity, and happiness

MAY GOD DEFEND THE RIGHT

Volume One

The secret history of the Court of England, during the last two reigns, will afford the reflecting mind abundant matter for regret and abhorrence. It has, however, been so much the fashion for historians to speak of kings and their ministers in all the fulsome terms of flattery, that the inquirer frequently finds it a matter of great difficulty to arrive at truth. But, fearless of consequences, we will speak of facts as they *really occurred*, and only hope our readers will accompany us in the recital with feelings, unwarped by party prejudice, and with a determination to judge the actions of kings, lords, and commons, not as beings of a *superior order*, but as *men*. Minds thus constituted will have little difficulty in tracing the origin of our present evils, or of perceiving

How many that *command* should be COMMANDED!

We commence with the year

1761,

about which period George the Third was pressed by his ministers to make choice of some royal lady, and demand her in marriage. They urged this under the pretext, that such a connexion was indispensably necessary to give stability to the monarchy, to assist the progressive improvements in morality and religion, and to benefit all artificers, by making a display at court of their ingenious productions. His majesty heard the proposal with an aching heart; and, to many of his ministers, he seemed as if labouring under bodily indisposition. Those persons, however, who were in the immediate confidence of the king, felt no surprise at the distressing change so apparent in the countenance of his majesty, the cause of which may be traced in the following particulars:

The unhappy sovereign, while Prince of Wales, was in the daily habit of passing through St. James' street, and its immediate vicinity. In one of his favourite rides through that part of town, he saw a very engaging young lady, who appeared, by her dress, to be a member of the Society of Friends. The prince was much struck by the delicacy and lovely appearance of this female, and, for several succeeding days, was observed to walk out alone. At length, the passion of his royal highness arrived at such a point, that he felt his happiness depended upon receiving the lady in marriage.

Every individual in his immediate circle, or in the list of the Privy Council, was very narrowly questioned by the prince, though in an indirect manner, to ascertain who was most to be trusted, that he might secure, *honorably*, the possession of the object of his ardent wishes. His royal highness, at last, confided his views to his next brother, Edward, Duke of York, and another person, who were the only witnesses to the *legal* marriage of the Prince of Wales to the before-mentioned lady, Hannah Lightfoot, which took place at Curzon-street Chapel, May Fair, in the year 1759.

This marriage was productive of *issue*, the particulars of which, however, we pass over for the present, and only look to the results of the union.

Engraving of George III, published by Richard Bentley in 1844. (*Stephen Basdeo Personal Collection*)

Shortly after the prince came to the throne, by the title of George the Third, ministers became suspicious of his marriage with the quakeress. At length, they were informed of the important fact, and immediately determined to annul it. After innumerable schemes how they might best attain this end, and thereby frustrate the king's wishes, they devised the "Royal Marriage Act," by which every prince or princess of the blood might not marry or intermarry with any person of less degree. *This act, however, was not passed till thirteen years after George the Third's union with Miss Lightfoot*, and therefore it could not render such marriage *illegal*.

From the moment the ministry became aware of his majesty's alliance to the lady just named, they took possession of their watch-tower, and determined that the new sovereign should henceforth do even as their will dictated; while the unsuspecting mind of George the Third was easily beguiled into their specious devices. In the absence of the king's beloved brother, Edward, Duke of York, (who was then abroad for a short period) his majesty was assured by his ministers that no cognizance would be taken at any time of his late unfortunate amour and marriage; and persuaded him, that the only stability he could give to his throne was demanding the hand of the Princess Charlotte of Mecklenburgh Strelitz. Every needful letter and paper for the negotiation was speedily prepared for the king's signature, which, in due course, each received; and thus was the foundation laid for this ill-fated prince's *future malady*!

Who can reflect upon the blighted first love of this monarch, without experiencing feelings of pity for his early sorrows! With his domestic habits, had he only been allowed to live with the *wife of his choice*, his reign might have passed in harmony and peace, and the English people now been affluent, happy, and contented. Instead of which, his unfeeling ministers compelled him to marry one of the most selfish, vindictive, and tyrannical women that ever disgraced human nature! At the first sight of the German princess, the king actually shrunk from her gaze;

for her countenance was of that cast that too plainly told of the nature of the spirit working within.

On the 18th of September, the king was *obliged* to subscribe to the formal ceremony of a marriage with the before-named lady, at the palace of St. James. His majesty's brother Edward, who was one of the witnesses to the king's first marriage with Miss Lightfoot, was now also present, and used every endeavour to support his royal brother through the "trying ordeal," not only by first meeting the princess on her entrance into the garden, but also at the altar.

In the mean time, the Earl of Abercorn informed the princess of the *previous* marriage of the king, and of the then existence of his majesty's wife; and Lord Harcourt advised the princess to well inform herself of the policy of the kingdoms, as a measure for preventing much future disturbance in the country, as well as securing an uninterrupted possession of the throne to her issue. Presuming, therefore, that this German princess had hitherto been an open and ingenuous character, (which are certainly traits very rarely to be found in the mind of a German of her grade) such expositions, intimations, and dark mysteries, were ill calculated to nourish honorable feelings, but would rather operate as a check to their further existence.

To the public eye, the newly-married pair were contented with each other;—alas! it was because each feared an exposure to the nation. The king reproached himself that he had not fearlessly avowed the only wife of his affections; the queen, because she feared an explanation that the king was guilty of *bigamy*, and thereby her claim, as also that of her progeny, (if she should have any) would be known to be illegitimate. It appears as if the result of these reflections formed a basis for the misery of millions, and added to that number millions then unborn. The secret marriage of the king proved a pivot, on which the destiny of kingdoms was to turn.

At this period of increased anxiety to his majesty, Miss Lightfoot was disposed of during a temporary absence of his brother Edward, and from that time no *satisfactory* tidings ever reached those most interested in her welfare. The only information that could be obtained was, that a young gentleman, named Axford, was offered a large amount, to be paid on the consummation of his marriage with Miss Lightfoot, which offer he willingly accepted.

The king was greatly distressed to ascertain the fate of his much-beloved and legally-married wife, the quakeress, and entrusted Lord Chatham to go in disguise, and endeavour to trace her abode; but the search proving fruitless, the king was again almost distracted.

Every one in the queen's confidence was expected to make any personal sacrifice of feeling whenever her majesty might require it;

Miss Hannah Lightfoot. (*Licensed under Wikimedia Commons*)

and, consequently, new emoluments, honors, and posts of dignity, were continually needful for the preservation of such unnatural friendships. From this period, new creations of peers were enrolled; and, as it became expedient to increase the number of the "privy cabal," the nation was freely called upon, by extra taxation and oppressive burdens of various kinds, to supply the necessary means to support this vile system of bribery and misrule!

We have dwelt upon this important period, because we wish our countrymen to see the *origin of our overgrown national debt*,—the real cause of England's present wretchedness.

The coronation of their majesties passed over, a few days after their marriage, without any remarkable feature, save that of an additional expense to the nation. The queen generally *appeared* at ease, though she seized upon every possible occasion to slight all persons from whom she feared any state explanation, which might prove inimical to her wishes. The wily queen thought this would effectually prevent their frequent appearance at court, as well as cause their banishment from the council-chamber.

A bill was passed this year to fix the civil list at the annual sum of EIGHT HUNDRED THOUSAND POUNDS, payable out of the consolidated fund, in lieu of the hereditary revenue, settled on the late king.

Another act passed, introduced to parliament by a speech from the throne, for the declared purpose of giving additional security to the independence of the judges. Although there was a law then in force, passed in the reign of William the Third, for continuing the commissions of judges during their good behaviour, they were legally determined on the death of the reigning sovereign. By this act, however, their continuance in office was made *independent* of the royal demise.

Twelve millions of money were raised by loans this year, and the interest thereon agreed to be paid by an additional duty of three shillings per barrel on all strong beer or ale,—the sinking fund being a collateral security. The imposition of this tax was received by the people as it deserved to be; for every labourer and mechanic severally felt himself insulted by so oppressive an act.

The year

1762

was ushered in by the hoarse clarion of war. England declared against Spain, while France and Spain became opposed to Portugal, on account of her alliance with Great Britain. These hostilities, however, were not of long duration; for preliminaries of peace were signed, before the conclusion of the year, by the English and French plenipotentiaries at Fontainbleau.

By this treaty, the original cause of the war was removed by the cession of Canada to England. This advantage, if *advantage* it may be called, cost this country *eighteen millions of money*, besides the loss of *three hundred thousand men*! Every friend of humanity must shudder at so wanton a sacrifice of life, and so prodigious an expenditure of the public money! But this was only the commencement of the reign of imbecility and Germanism.

On the 12th of August, her majesty was safely delivered of a prince. Court etiquette requires *numerous witnesses* of the birth of an heir-apparent to the British throne. On this occasion, however, her majesty's *extraordinary delicacy* dispensed with a strict adherence to the forms of state; for only the Archbishop of Canterbury was allowed to be in the room. But there were *more powerful* reasons than *delicacy* for this unusual privacy, which will hereafter appear.

On the 18th of September following, the ceremony of christening the royal infant was performed by the Archbishop of Canterbury, in the great council-chamber of his majesty's palace, and the young prince was named George Augustus Frederick.

In this year, the city of Havannah surrendered to the English, whose troops were commanded by Lord Albermarle and Admiral Pococke. Nine sail of the line and four frigates were taken in the harbour; three of the line had been previously sunk by the enemy, and two were destroyed on the stocks. The plunder in money and merchandize was supposed to have amounted to *three millions sterling*, while the sum raised by the land-tax, at four shillings in the pound, from 1756 to 1760 inclusive, also produced *ten millions of money*! But to what purpose this amount was devoted remained a profound secret to those from whom it was extorted.

In the November of this year, the famous Peter Annet was sentenced by the Court of King's Bench to be imprisoned one month, to stand twice in the pillory within that time, and afterwards to be kept to hard labour in Bridewell for a year. The reader may feel surprised when informed that all the enormity this man had been guilty of consisted in nothing more than writing the *truth* of the government, which was published in his "Free Inquirer." The unmerited punishment, however, had only this effect: it made him glory in suffering for the cause of liberty and truth.

1763

was a continuation of the misrule which characterized the preceding year.

In May, Lord Bute resigned the office of First Lord of the Treasury, and the conduct of the earl became a question of much astonishment and criticism. He was the foundation-stone of *Toryism*, in its most arbitrary form; and there cannot be a doubt that his lordship's influence over the state machinery was the key-stone of all the mischiefs and miseries of the nation. It was Lord Bute's opinion, that all things should be made subservient to the *queen*, and he framed his measures accordingly.

The earl was succeeded by Mr. George Grenville. Little alteration for the better, however, was manifested in the administration, although the characters and principles of the

John Stuart, Earl of Bute by an anonymous painter. (*Licensed under Wikimedia Commons*)

new ministers were supposed to be of a liberal description; but this may possibly be accounted for by the Earls of Halifax and Egremont continuing to be the secretaries of state.

In this memorable year, the celebrated John Wilkes, editor of "The North Briton," was committed to the Tower, for an excellent, though biting, criticism on his majesty's speech to the two houses of parliament. The queen vigorously promoted this unconstitutional and tyrannical act of the new government, which was severely censured by many members of the House of Commons. Among the rest, Mr. Pitt considered the act as an infringement upon the rights of the people; and, although he condemned the libel, he said he would come at the author fairly,—not by an open breach of the constitution, and a contempt of all restraint. Wilkes, however, came off triumphantly, and his victory was hailed with delight by his gratified countrymen.

In the midst of this public agitation, the queen, on the 16th of August, burdened the nation with her second son, Frederick, afterwards created Duke of York, *Bishop of Osnaburgh*, and many other *et ceteras*, which produced a good round sum, and, we should think, more than sufficient to support this Right Reverend Father in God, at the age of—*eleven months*!

Colonel Gréme, who had been chiefly instrumental in bringing about the marriage of the Princess Charlotte of Mecklenburgh with the King of England, was this year appointed Master of St. Catherine, near the Tower, an excellent *sinecure* in the *peculiar gift of the queen*!

The most important public event on the continent was, the death of Augustus, third King of Poland, and Elector of Saxony, who had lately returned to his electoral dominions, from which he had been banished for six years, in consequence of the war. Immediately after his demise, his eldest son and successor to the electorate declared himself a candidate for the crown of Poland, in which ambition he was supposed to be countenanced by the Court of Vienna; but he fell a victim to the small-pox, a few weeks after his father's death.

During the year

1764,

much public anxiety and disquietude was manifested. Mr. Wilkes again appeared before a public tribunal for publishing opinions not in accordance with the reigning powers. The House of Commons sat so early as seven o'clock in the morning to consider his case, and the speaker actually remained in the chair for *twenty hours*, so important was the matter considered.

About the end of this year, the king became much indisposed, and exhibited the first signs of that mental aberration, which, in after years, so heavily afflicted him. The nation, in general, supposed this to have arisen from his majesty's anxiety upon the fearful aspect of affairs, which was then of the most gloomy nature, both at home and abroad. Little, indeed, did the multitudes imagine the *real* cause; little did the private gentleman, the industrious tradesman, the worthy mechanic, or the labourer, think that their sovereign was living in splendid misery, bereft of the

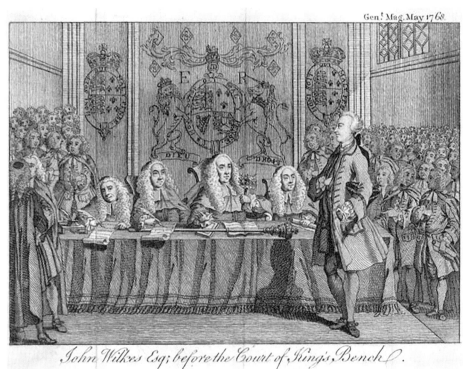

Gen! Mag. May 17 68

John Wilkes Esq; before the Court of King's Bench.

John Wilks before the Court of the King's Bench. (*British Library*)

dearest object of his solicitude, and compelled to associate with the woman he all but detested!

Nature had not formed George the Third for a king; she had not been profuse to him either in elegance of manners, or capacity of mind; but he seemed more fitted to shine in a domestic circle, where his affections were centred, and in that sphere only. But, with all hereditary monarchies, *an incompetent person has the same claim as a man adorned with every requisite and desirable ability*!

In this year, Lord Albermarle received TWENTY THOUSAND POUNDS as *his* share in the Havannah prize-money; while *one pound, two shillings, and six-pence* was thought sufficient for a corporal, and *thirteen shillings and five-pence* for a private! How far this disbursement was consistent with *equity*, we leave every honest member of society to determine.

In December, a most excellent edict was registered in the parliament of Paris, by which the King of France abolished the society of Jesuits *for ever*.

Early in the year

1765,

the queen was pressingly anxious that her marriage with the king should again be solemnized; and, as the queen was then pregnant, his majesty readily acquiesced in her wishes. Dr. Wilmot, by his majesty's appointment, performed the ceremony at their palace at Kew. The king's brother, Edward, was present upon this occasion also, as he had been on the two former ones.

Under the peculiar distractions of this year, it was supposed, the mind of the sovereign was again disturbed. To prevent a recurrence of such interruptions to the royal authority, a law was passed, empowering his majesty to appoint the *queen*, or *other member of the royal family*, assisted by a council, to act as regent of the kingdom. Although his majesty's blank of intellect was but of short duration, it proved of essential injury to the people generally. The tyrannical queen, presuming on the authority of this bill, exercised the most unlimited sway over national affairs. She supplied her own requirements and opinions, in unison with

Charlotte of Mecklenburg-Strelitz, Queen Consort to George III. (*Frontispiece from* Court and Private life in the Time of Queen Charlotte, *1887*)

her trusty-bought clan, who made it apparent that these suggestions were offered by the king, and were his settled opinions, upon the most deliberate investigation of all matters and things connected therewith!

During the king's indisposition, he was most passionate in his requests, that the *wife of his choice* should be brought to him. The queen, judging her influence might be of much consequence to quell the perturbation of her husband's mind, was, agreeably to her own request, admitted to the solitary apartment of the king. It is true he recognised her, but it was followed by extreme expressions of disappointment and disgust! The queen was well acquainted with all subjects connected with his majesty's unfortunate passion and marriage; therefore, she thought it prudent to stifle expressions of anger or sorrow, and, as soon as decency permitted, left the place, resolving thenceforth to manage the helm herself.

On the 31st of October, his majesty's uncle, the Duke of Cumberland, died suddenly at his house in Upper Grosvenor-street, in the forty-fifth year of his age; and on the 28th of December, his majesty's youngest brother, Prince Frederick William, also expired, in the sixteenth year of his age.

On December 1st,

1766,

his majesty's sister, Matilda, was married to the King of Denmark, and the Duke of York was proxy on the occasion. Soon afterwards, his royal highness took leave of his brother, and set out on a projected tour through Germany, and other parts of the continent. The queen was most happy to say "Adieu," and, for the first time, felt something like ease on his account.

The supplies granted for the service of this year, although the people were in the most distressed state, amounted to *eight millions, two hundred and seventy-three thousand, two hundred and eighty pounds*!

In the year

1767,

the noble-minded and generous Duke of York was married to a descendant of the Stuarts, an amiable and conciliating lady, not only willing, but anxious, to live without the splendour of royal parade, and desirous also of evading the flatteries and falsehoods of a court.

In August, the duke lived very retired in a chateau near Monaco, in Italy, blessed and happy in the society of his wife. She was then advancing in pregnancy, and his solicitude for her was sufficient to have deeply interested a heart less susceptible than her own. Their marriage was kept from public declaration, but we shall refer to the proofs hereafter. In the ensuing month, it was announced that (17th September) the duke "died of a malignant fever," in the twenty-ninth year of his age, and the news was immediately communicated to the King of England. The body was said to be embalmed, and then put on board his majesty's ship Montreal, to be brought to England. His royal highness was interred on the evening of November 3rd, in the royal vault of King Henry the Seventh's Chapel.

The fate of the duke's unfortunate and inconsolable widow, and that of the infant, to whom she soon after gave birth, must be reserved for its appropriate place in this history.

The high price of provisions this year occasioned much distress and discontent, and excited tumults in various parts of the kingdom. Notwithstanding this, ministers attempted to retain every tax that had been imposed during the late war, and appeared perfectly callous to the sufferings of the productive classes. Even the land-tax, of four shillings in the pound, was attempted to be continued, though contrary to all former custom; but the country gentlemen became impatient of this innovation, and contrived to get a bill introduced into the House of Commons, to reduce it to three shillings in the pound. This was carried by a great majority, in spite of all the efforts of the ministry to the contrary! The defeat of the ministers caused a great sensation at the time, as it was the first money-bill in which any ministry had been disappointed since the revolution of 1688! But what can any ministers do against the wishes of a determined people? If the horse knew his own strength, would he submit to the dictation of his rider?

On account of the above bill being thrown out, ministers had considerable difficulty in raising the necessary supplies for the year, which were estimated at *eight millions and a half*, including, we suppose, secret-service money, which was now in great demand.

The king experienced a fluctuating state of health, sometimes improving, again retrograding, up to the year

1768.

In his speech, in the November of this year, his majesty announced, that much disturbance had been exhibited in some of the colonies, and a disposition manifested to throw aside their dependence upon Great Britain. Owing to this circumstance, a new office was created, under the name of "Secretary of State for the Colonies," and to which the Earl of Hillsborough was appointed.

The Earl of Chatham having resigned, parliament was dissolved. Party spirit running high, the electioneering contests were unusually violent, and serious disorders occurred. Mr. Wilkes was returned for Middlesex; but, being committed to the King's Bench for libels on the government, the mob rescued Wilkes from the soldiers, who were conducting him thither. The military were ordered to fire on the people, and one man, who was singled out and pursued by the soldiers, was shot dead. A coroner's inquest brought this in *wilful murder*, though the higher authorities not only acquitted the magistrates and soldiers, but actually returned *public thanks* to them!

At this period, the heart sickens at the relations given of the punishments inflicted on many private soldiers in the guards. They were each allowed only four-pence per day. If they deserted and were re-taken, the poor delinquents suffered the dreadful infliction of five hundred lashes. The victims thus flagellated very seldom escaped with life! In the navy, also, the slightest offence or neglect was punished with inexpressible tortures. This infamous treatment of brave men can only be accounted for by the fact, that officers in the army and navy either bought their situations, or received them as a *compensation* for some SECRET

William Pitt, Earl of Chatham.

SERVICE performed for, or by the request of, the queen and her servile ministry. Had officers been promoted from the ranks, for performing *real* services to their country, they would have then possessed more commiseration for their brothers in arms.

We must here do justice to the character of George the Third from all intentional tyranny. Many a time has this monarch advocated the cause of the productive classes, and as frequently have his ministers, urged on by the *queen*, defeated his most sanguine wishes, until he found himself a mere cipher in the affairs of state. The king's simplicity of style and unaffected respect for the people would have induced him to despise the gorgeous pageantry of state; he had been happy, indeed, to have been "the real father of his subjects." His majesty well knew that the public good ought to be the sole aim of all governments, and that for this purpose a prince is invested with the regal crown. A king is not to employ his authority, patronage, and riches, merely to gratify his own lusts and ambition; but, if need require it, he ought even to sacrifice his own ease and pleasure for the benefit of his country. We give George the Third credit for holding these sentiments, which, however, only increased his regrets, as he really had *no power to act*,—that power being in the possession of his queen, and other crafty and designing persons, to whose opinions and determinations he had become a perfect slave! It is to be regretted that he had not sufficient nerve to eject such characters from his councils; for assuredly the nation would have been, to a man, willing to protect him from their vile machinations; but once subdued, he was subdued for ever.

From the birth, a prince is the subject of flattery, and is even caressed for his vicious propensities; nay, his minions never appear before him without a mask, while every artifice that cunning can suggest is practised to deceive him. He is not allowed to mix in general society, and therefore is ignorant of the wants and wishes of the people over whom he is destined to reign. When he becomes a king, his counsellors obtain his signature whenever they desire it; and, as his extravagance increases, so must sums of money, in some way or other, be extorted from his suffering and oppressed subjects. Should his ministers prove ambitious, war is the natural result, and the money of the poor is again in request to furnish means for their own destruction! Whereas, had the prince been associated with the intelligent and respectable classes of society, he might have warded off the evil, and, instead of desolating war, peace might have shed her gentle influence over the land. Another barbarous custom is, the injunction imposed upon royal succession, that they shall not marry only with their equals in birth. But is not this a violation of the most vital interests and solemn engagements to which humanity have subscribed? What unhappiness has not such an unnatural doctrine produced? Quality of blood ought only to be recognized by corresponding nobility of sentiments, principles, and actions. He that is debarred from possessing the object of his virtuous regard is to be pitied, whether he be a king or a peasant; and we can hardly wonder at his sinking into the abyss of carelessness, imbecility, and even madness.

In February,

1769,

the first of those deficiencies in the civil list, which had occurred from time to time, was made known to parliament, by a message in the *name* of the unhappy king, but who only did as he was ordered by his ministerial cabal. This debt amounted to five hundred thousand pounds, and his majesty was tutored to say, that he relied on the *zeal* and *affection* of his faithful Commons to enable him to discharge it! The principal part of this money was expended upon wretches, of the most abandoned description, for services performed *against* the welfare of England.

The year

1770

proved one of much political interest. The queen was under the necessity of retiring a little from the apparent part she had taken in the affairs of state; nevertheless, she was equally active; but, from policy, did not appear so. Another plan to deceive the people being deemed necessary, invitations for splendid parties were given, in order to assume an appearance of confidence and quietness, which her majesty could not, and did not, possess.

In this year, Lord Chatham publicly avowed his sentiments in these words: "Infuse a portion of health into the constitution, to enable it to bear its infirmities." Previous to making this remark, his lordship, of course, was well acquainted with the causes of the then present distresses of the country, as well as the sources from whence those causes originated. But one generous patriot is not sufficient to put a host of antagonists to flight. The earl's measures were too mild to be heeded by the minions of the queen then in power; his intention being "to persuade and soften, not to irritate and offend." We may infer that, had he been merely a "party man," he would naturally concur in any enterprise likely to create a bustle without risk to himself; but, upon examination, he appears to have loved the cause of independence, and was willing to support it by every personal sacrifice.

About this time, the Duke of Grafton resigned his office of First Lord of the Treasury, in which he was succeeded by that disgrace to his country, Lord North, who then commenced his long and disastrous administration. Dr. Wilmot was a friendly preceptor to this nobleman, while at the university; but it was frequently a matter of regret to the worthy doctor, that his lordship had not imbibed those patriotic principles which he had so strongly endeavoured to inculcate; and he has been known to observe, that Lord North's administration called for the most painful animadversions, inasmuch as he advocated the enaction of laws of the most arbitrary character.

Mr. Wilkes, previous to the meeting of the Commons in January, was not only acquitted, but had damages, to a large amount, awarded him; and the king expressed a desire, that such damages should be paid out of his privy purse. The Earl of Halifax, who signed the warrant for his committal to the Tower in 1763, was finally so disappointed that he offered

Contemporary engraving of the Duke of Grafton. (*From a facsimile in the author's collection*)

his resignation, though he afterwards accepted the privy seal.

It was during this year, that the celebrated "Letters of Junius" first appeared. These compositions were distinguished as well by the force and elegance of their style as by the violence of their attacks on individuals. The first of these letters was printed in the "Public Advertiser," of December the 19th, and addressed to the king, animadverting on all the errors of his reign, and speaking of his ministers in terms of equal contempt and abhorrence. An attempt was made to suppress this letter by the strong arm of the law; but the effort proved abortive, as the jury *acquitted* the printer, who was the person prosecuted. Junius (though under a feigned name) was the most competent person to speak fully upon political subjects. He had long been the bosom friend of

Lord North, the Prime Minister who lost the American Colonies. (*From a facsimile in the author's collection*)

the king, and spent all his leisure time at court. No one, therefore, could better judge of the state of public affairs than himself, and his sense of duty to the nation animated him to plead for the long-estranged rights of the people; indeed, upon many occasions, he displayed such an heroic firmness, such an invincible love of truth, and such an unconquerable sense of honor, that he permitted his talents to be exercised freely in the cause of public justice, and subscribed his *addenda* under an envelope, rather than injure his prince, or leave the interests of his countrymen to the risk of fortuitous circumstances. We know of whom we speak, and therefore feel authorized to assert, that in his character were concentrated the steady friend of the prince as well as of the people.

Numerous disquisitions have been written to prove the identity of Junius; but, in spite of many arguments to the contrary, we recognize him in the person of the Rev. James Wilmot, D.D., Rector of Barton-on-the-Heath, and Aulcester, Warwickshire, and one of his majesty's justices of the peace for that county.

Dr. Wilmot was born in 1720, and, during his stay at the university, became intimately acquainted with Dr. Johnson, Lord Archer, and Lord Plymouth, as well as Lord North, who was then entered at Trinity College. From these gentlemen, the doctor imbibed his political opinions, and was introduced to the first society in the kingdom. At the age of thirty, Dr. Wilmot was confidently entrusted with the most *secret affairs of state*, and was also the bosom friend of the Prince of Wales, afterwards George the Third, who at that time was under the entire tutorage of Lord Bute. To this nobleman, Dr. Wilmot had an inveterate hatred, for he despised the selfish principles of Toryism. As soon as the Princess of Mecklenburgh (the late Queen Charlotte) arrived in this country in 1761, Dr. Wilmot was introduced, as the *especial friend* of the king, and this will at once account for his being chosen to perform the second marriage-ceremony of their majesties at Kew palace, as before related.

A circumstance of rather a singular nature occurred to Dr. Wilmot, in the year 1765, inasmuch as it was the *immediate* cause of the bold and decisive line of conduct which he afterwards adopted. It was simply this: the doctor received an anonymous letter, requesting an interview with the writer in Kensington Gardens. The letter was written in Latin, and sealed, the impression of which was a Medusa's head. The doctor at first paid no attention to it; but during the week he received four similar requests, written by the same hand; and, upon the receipt of the last, Dr. Wilmot provided himself with a brace of pocket pistols, and proceeded to the gardens at the hour appointed. The doctor felt much surprised when he was accosted by—*Lord Bute!* who immediately suggested that Dr. Wilmot should assist the administration, as *her majesty* had entire confidence in him! The doctor briefly declined, and very soon afterwards commenced his political career. Thus the German princess always endeavoured to inveigle the friends of the people.

Lord Chatham had been introduced to Dr. Wilmot by the Duke of Cumberland; and it was from these associations with the court and the members of the several administrations, that the doctor became so competent to write his unparalleled "Letters of Junius."

We here subjoin an incontrovertible *proof* of Dr. Wilmot's being the author of the work alluded to:

This is a facsimile of the doctor's hand-writing, and must for ever set at rest the long-disputed question of "Who is the author of Junius?"

The people were really in need of the advocacy of a writer like Junius, for their burdens at this time were of the most grievous magnitude. Although the country was not in danger from foreign enemies, in order to give posts of command, honor, and emolument, to the employed sycophants at court, our navy was increased, nominal situations were provided; while all the means to pay for such services were again ordered to be drawn *from the people*!

1771

was productive of little else than harassing distresses to the poor labourer and mechanic. At this period, it was not unusual to tear the husband from the wife, and the parent from the child, and immure them within the damp and noisome walls of

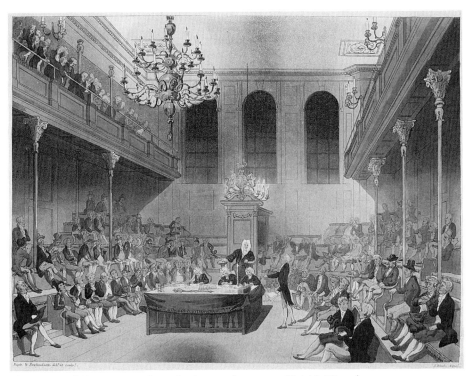

The House of Commons in the early nineteenth century. (*British Library*)

a prison, to prevent any interposition on the part of the suffering multitudes. Yes, countrymen, such tyranny was practised to ensure the *secrecy of truth*, and to destroy the wishes of a monarch, who was rendered incompetent to act for himself.

Various struggles were made this year to curb the power of the judges, particularly in cases relating to the *liberty of the press*, and also to destroy the power vested in the Attorney-General of prosecuting *ex-officio*, without the intervention of a grand jury, or the forms observed by courts of law in other cases. But the boroughmongers and minions of the queen were too powerful for the liberal party in the House of Commons, and the chains of slavery were, consequently, rivetted afresh.

A question of great importance also occurred this year respecting the privileges of the House of Commons. It had become the practice of newspaper writers to take the liberty, not before ventured upon, of printing the speeches of the members, under their respective names; some of which in the whole, and others in essential parts, were spurious productions, and, in any case, contrary to the standing orders of the House. A complaint on this ground having been made by a member against two of the printers, an order was issued for their attendance, with which they refused to comply; a second order was given with no better success. At length, one of the printers being taken into custody under the authority of the speaker's warrant, he was carried before the celebrated Alderman John Wilkes, who, regarding the caption as illegal, not only discharged the man, but bound him over to prosecute his captor, for assault and false imprisonment. Two more printers, being apprehended and carried before Alderman Wilkes and the Lord Mayor, Crosby, were, in like manner, discharged. The indignation of the House was then directed against the city magistrates, and various measures adopted towards them. The contest finally terminated in favor of the printers, who have ever since continued to publish the proceedings of parliament, and the speeches of the members, without obstacle.

In this year, the marriage of the Duke of Cumberland with Mrs. Horton took place. The king appeared electrified when the matter was communicated to him, and declared that he never would forgive his royal brother's conduct, who, being informed of his majesty's sentiments, thus wrote to him: "Sire, my welfare will ensure your own; you cannot condemn an affair there is a *precedent for, even in your own person!*"—alluding to his majesty's marriage with Hannah Lightfoot. His majesty was *compelled* to acknowledge this marriage, from the Duke of Cumberland having made a confidant of Colonel Luttrell, brother of Mrs. Horton, with regard to several important state secrets which had occurred in the years 1759, 1760, 1761, 1762, and 1763.

This Duke of Cumberland also imbibed the *family complaint of* BIGAMY; for he had been married, about twelve months previous, to a daughter of Dr. Wilmot, who, of course, remonstrated against such unjust treatment. The king solemnly assured Dr. Wilmot that he might rely upon his humanity and honor. The doctor paused, and had the courage to say, in reply, "I have once before relied upon the promises of your majesty! But"—"Hush! hush!" said the king, interrupting him, "I know what you are going to say; but do not disturb me with wills and retrospection of past *irreparable injury.*"

The death of the Earl of Halifax, soon after the close of the session in this year, caused a vacancy; and the Duke of Grafton returned to office, as keeper of the privy seal. His grace was a particular favourite with the queen, but much disliked by the intelligent and reflecting part of the community.

The political atmosphere bore a gloomy aspect at the commencement of

1772,

and petitions from the people were sent to the king and the two houses of parliament, for the repeal of what they believed to be unjust and pernicious laws upon the subject of religious liberty. Several clergymen of the established church prayed to be liberated from their obligation to subscribe to the "Thirty-nine Articles." But it was urged, in opposition to the petitions, that government had an undoubted right to establish and maintain such a system of instruction as the ministers thereof deemed most suitable for the public benefit. But expedience and right are as far asunder, in truth, as is the distance from pole to pole. The policy of the state required some *new source* from whence to draw means for the *secret* measures needful for prolonging the existence of its privacy; and it was therefore deemed expedient to keep politics and religion as close together as possible, by enforcing the strictest obedience of all demands made upon the clergy, in such forms and at such times as should best accord with the political system of the queen. In consequence of which, the petitions were rejected by a majority of 217 boroughmongers against 71 real representatives of the people!

An act, passed this session, for "Making more effectual provisions to guard the descendants of the late king, George the Second, from marrying without the approbation of his majesty, his heirs, and successors, first had and obtained," was strenuously opposed by the liberal party in every stage of its progress through both houses. It was generally *supposed* to have had its origin in the marriage contracted but a few months before by the Duke of Cumberland with Mrs. Horton, relict of Colonel Horton, and daughter of Lord Irnham; and also in a private, though long-suspected, marriage of the Duke of Gloucester to the Countess-dowager of Waldegrave, which the duke at this time openly avowed. But were there not *other* reasons which operated on the mind of the *queen* (for the poor king was only a passive instrument in her power) to force this bill into a law? Had she not an eye to her husband's former alliance with the quakeress, and the Duke of York's marriage in Italy? The latter was even more dangerous to her peace than the former; for the duke had married a descendant of the Stuarts!

Lord Chatham made many representations to the king and queen of the improper and injudicious state of the penal laws. He cited an instance of unanswerable disproportion; namely, that, on the 14th of July, two persons were publicly whipped round Covent Garden market, in accordance with the sentence passed upon them; but mark the difference of the crimes for which they were so punished: one was for stealing a bunch of radishes; the other, for debauching his own niece! In vain, however, did this friend of humanity represent the unwise, unjust, and inconsistent tenour of such laws. The king was anxious to alter them immediately; but the queen was decided in her opinion, that they ought to be left entirely to the pleasure and opinion of the *judges*, well knowing *they* would not disobey her will upon any point of law, or equity, *so called*. Thus did the nation languish under the tyrannical usurpation of a *German* princess, whose disposition and talents were much better calculated to give laws to the brute creation than to interfere with *English* jurisprudence!

In November of this year, it was announced that the *king* earnestly desired parliament should take into consideration the state of the East India Company. But the king was ignorant of the subject; though it was true, the *queen* desired it; because she received vast emoluments from the various situations *purchased* by individuals under the denomination of cadets, &c. Of course, her majesty's will was tantamount to law.

The Earl of Chatham resolved once more to speak to the queen upon the state of things, and had an audience for that purpose. As an honest man, he very warmly advocated the cause of the nation, and represented the people to be in a high state of excitement, adding, that "if they be repelled, they must be repelled by force!" And to whom ought an unhappy suffering people to have had recourse but to the throne, whose power sanctioned the means used to drain their purses? The queen, however, was still unbending; she not only inveighed against the candour and sentiments of the earl, but requested she might not again be *troubled* by him upon *such subjects*! Before retiring, Lord Chatham said, "Your majesty must excuse me if I say, the liberty of the subject is the surest protection to the monarch, and if the prince *protects the guilty, instead of punishing them, time will convince him, that he has judged erroneously, and acted imprudently."*

The earl retired; but "his labouring breast knew not peace," and he resolved, for the last time, to see the king in private. An interview was requested, and as readily granted. "Well, well," said the king, "I hope no bad news?" "No bad news, your majesty; but I wish to submit to your opinion a few questions." "Quite right, quite right," said the king, "tell me all." The earl did so, and, after his faithful appeal to the king, concluded by saying, "My sovereign will excuse me, but I can no longer be a party to the deceptions pawned upon the people, as I am, and consider myself to be, amenable to God and my conscience!" Would that England had possessed a few more such patriots!

This year will ever be memorable in history as the commencement of that partition of Poland, between three contiguous powers,—Russia, Austria, and Prussia,—which has served as an example and apology for all those shameful violations of public right and justice that have stained the modern annals of Europe. The unfortunate Poles appealed in vain to Great Britain, France, and Spain, and the States-general of Holland, on the atrocious perfidy and injustice of these proceedings. After some unavailable remonstrances, the diet was compelled, at the point of the bayonet, to sign a treaty for the formal cession of the several districts which the three usurpers had fixed upon and guaranteed to each other. The partitioning *legitimates* also *generously* made a present of an *aristocratic* constitution to the suffering Poles.

In the year

1773,

commercial credit was greatly injured by extensive failures in England and Holland. The distress and embarrassment of the mercantile classes were farther augmented by a great diminution in the gold coin, in consequence of wear and fraud,—such loss, by act of parliament, being thrown upon the holders!

At this time, the discontents which had long been manifest in the American colonies broke out into open revolt. The chief source of irritation against the mother country was the impolitic measure of retaining a trifling duty on tea, as an assertion of the right of the British parliament to tax the colonies.

The year

1774

bore a gloomy and arbitrary character, with wars abroad and uneasiness at home. The county of Nottingham omitted to raise their militia in the former year, and in this they were fined two thousand pounds.

Louis the Fifteenth of France died this year of the small-pox, caught from a country girl, introduced to him by Madame du Barré to gratify his sensual desires. He was in the *sixty-fourth* year of his age, and in the fifty-ninth of his reign. The gross debaucheries into which he had sank, with the despotic measures he had adopted towards the Chamber of Deputies in his latter years, had entirely deprived him of his appellation of the "Well-beloved." Few French sovereigns have left a less-respected memory.

1775

was also a year of disquiet. The City of London addressed the throne, and petitioned against the existing grievances, expressing their strong abhorrence of the measures adopted towards the Americans, *justifying their resistance*, and beseeching his majesty to dismiss his ministers. The *invisible power of the queen*, however, prevented their receiving redress, and the ministers were retained, contrary to all petition and remonstrance. Upon these occasions, the king was obliged to submit to any form of expression, dictated by the minister, that minister being under the entire controul of the queen; and though the nation seemed to wear a florid countenance, it was sick at heart. Lord North was a very considerable favourite with her majesty; while his opponents, Messrs. Fox and Burke, were proportionately disliked. The Duke of Grafton now felt tired of his situation, and told the queen that he could no longer continue in office; in consequence of which, the Earl of Dartmouth received the privy seal.

The Americans, in the meantime, were vigorously preparing for what they conceived to be inevitable—*a war*. Various attempts, notwithstanding, were made by the enlightened and liberal-minded part of the community to prevent ministers from continuing hostilities against them. That noble and persevering patriot, Lord Chatham, raised his warning voice against it. "I wish," said he, "not to lose a day in this urgent, pressing crisis; an *hour now lost in allaying ferments in America, may produce* YEARS OF CALAMITY! Never will I desert, in any stage of its progress, the conduct of this momentous business. Unless fettered to my bed by the extremity of sickness, I will give it unremitted attention; I will knock at the gates of this *sleeping and confounded ministry*, and will, if it be possible, rouse them to a sense of their danger. The recall of your army, I urge as necessarily preparatory to the restoration of your peace. By this it will appear that you are disposed to treat amicably and equitably, and to consider, revise, and repeal, if it should be found necessary, as I affirm it *will*, those violent acts and declarations which have disseminated confusion throughout the empire. *Resistance to these acts was necessary*, and therefore just; and your vain declaration of the *omnipotence of Parliament*, and your *imperious* doctrines of the *necessity of submission*, will be found equally *impotent to convince or enslave America*, who feels that tyranny is equally intolerable, whether it be exercised by an individual part of the legislature, or by the collective bodies which compose it!"

How prophetic did this language afterwards prove! Oh! England, how hast thou been cursed by debt and blood through the impotency and villany of thy rulers!

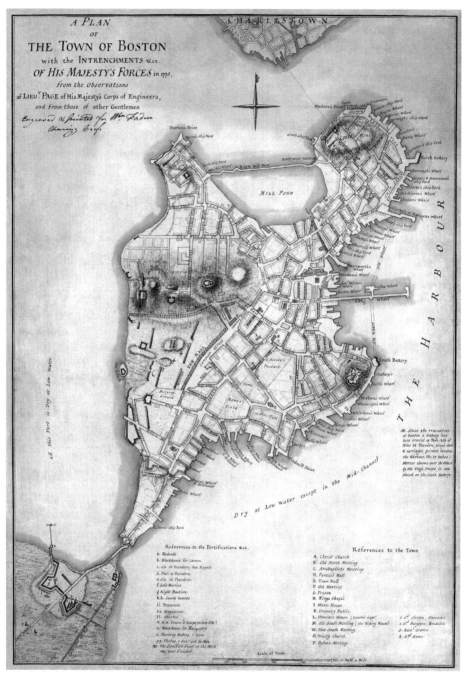

A map of the town of Boston, MA in the late eighteenth century. (*British Library*)

In the year

1776,

the Earl of Harcourt was charged with a breach of privilege; but his services for the *queen* operated as a sufficient reason for rejecting the matter of complaint.

So expensive did the unjust and disgraceful war with America prove this year, that more than *nine millions* were supplied for its service! In order to raise this shameful amount, extra taxes were levied on newspapers, deeds, and other matters of public utility. Thus were the industrious and really productive classes imposed upon, and their means exhausted, to gratify the inordinate wishes of a German princess, now entitled to be the cause of their misery and ruin. The queen knew that war required soldiers and sailors, and that these soldiers and sailors must have *officers* over them, which would afford her an opportunity of *selling commissions* or of bestowing them upon some of her *favourites*. So that these things contributed to her majesty's *individual* wealth and power, what cared she for the increase of the country's burdens!

It is wonderful to reflect upon the means with which individuals in possession of power have contrived, in all ages and in all countries, to controul mankind. From thoughtlessness and the absence of knowledge, the masses of people have been made to contend, with vehemence and courageous enterprise, against their own interests, and for the benefit of those mercenary wretches by whom they have been enslaved! How monstrous it is, that, to gratify the sanguinary feelings of *one* tyrant, thousands of human beings should go forth to the field of battle as willing sacrifices! Ignorance alone has produced such lamentable results; for a thirst after blood is never so effectually quenched as when it is repressed by the influence of *knowledge*, which teaches humility, moderation, benevolence, and the practice of every other virtue. In civilized society, there cannot be an equality of property; and, from the dissimilarity in human organization, there cannot be equality in the power and vigour of the mind. All men, however, are entitled to, and ought to enjoy, a perfect equality in civil and political rights. In the absence of this just condition, a nation can only be partially free. The people of such a nation exist under unequal laws, and those persons upon whom injuries are inflicted by the partial operation of those laws are, it must be conceded, the victims of an authority which they cannot controul. Such was, unhappily, the condition of the English people at this period. To prevent truth from having an impartial hearing and explanation, the plans of government were obliged to be of an insincere and unjust character. The consequences were, the debasement of morals, and the prostitution of the happiness and rights of the people. But Power was in the grasp of Tyranny, attended on each side by Pride and Cruelty; while Fear presented an excuse for Silence and Apathy, and left Artifice and Avarice to extend their baneful influence over society. British courage was stifled by arbitrary persecutions, fines, and imprisonment, which threatened to overwhelm all who dared to resist the tide of German despotism. Had *unity* and *resolution* been the watch-words of the sons of Britain, what millions

The leading men of the American Revolution. (*British Library*)

of debt might have been prevented! what oceans of blood might have been saved! The iniquitous ministers who dictated war with America should have suffered as traitors to their country, which would have been their fate had not blind ignorance and servility, engendered by priests and tyrants, through the impious frauds of church and state, overwhelmed the better reason of the great mass of mankind! It was, we say, priestcraft and statecraft that kindled this unjustifiable war, in order to lower human nature, and induce men to butcher each other under the most absurd, frivolous, and wicked pretences. Englishmen, at the commencement of the American war, appear to have been no better than wretched captives, without either courage, reason, or virtue, from whom the queen's banditti of gaolers shut out the glorious light of day. There were, however, some few patriots who raised their voices in opposition to the abominable system then in practice, and many generous-hearted men who boldly refused to fight against the justified resistance of the Americans; but the general mass remained inactive, cowardly inactive, against their merciless oppressors. The queen *pretended* to lament the sad state of affairs, while she did all in her power to continue the misrule!

At the commencement of

1777,

the several states of Europe had their eyes fixed on the contest between this country and the colonies. The French government assisted the Americans with fleets and armies, though they did not enter into the contest *publicly*. Queen Charlotte still persevered in her designs against America, and bore entire sway over her unfortunate husband. The country, as might be expected, was in a state of great excitement, owing to the adoption of measures inimical to the wishes and well-being of the people. The greater power the throne assumed, the larger amounts were necessarily drawn from the people, to reward fawning courtiers and borough proprietors.

This year, thirteen millions of money were deemed needful for the public service, and the debts of the civil list a *second* time discharged! At this time, the revenue did not amount to eight millions, and to supply the consequent deficiency, new taxes were again levied upon the people; for ministers carried all their bills, however infamous they might be, by large majorities!

In May, Lord Chatham again addressed the "peers," and called their attention to the necessity of changing the proceedings of government. Although bowed down by age and infirmity, and bearing a crutch in each hand, he delivered his sentiments, with all the ardour of youth, in these words: "I wish the removal of accumulated grievances, and the repeal of every oppressive act which have been passed since the year 1763! I am experienced in spring hopes and vernal promises, but at last will come your equinoctial disappointment."

On another occasion, he said, "I will not join in congratulation on misfortune and disgrace! *It is necessary to instruct the throne in the language of truth!* We must dispel the delusions and darkness which envelop it. I am old and weak, and at present unable to say more; but my feelings and indignation were too strong to permit me to say less." Alas! this patriot stood nearly alone. In his opinion, the good of the people was the supreme law; but this was opposed to the sentiments of the hirelings of state and their *liberal* mistress.

As a last effort, the earl resolved to seek an audience of the queen, and the request was readily complied with. The day previous to his last speech, delivered in the House of Lords, this interview took place. His lordship pressed the queen to relieve the people, and, by every possible means, to mitigate the public burdens. But, though her majesty was gentle in her language, she expressed herself positively and decisively as being adverse to his views; and took the opportunity of reminding him of the *secrecy of state affairs*. As Lord Chatham had once given his solemn promise never to permit those secrets to transpire, he resolved faithfully to keep his engagement, though their disclosure would have opened the eyes of the public to the disgraceful proceedings of herself and ministers. The noble earl retired from his royal audience in much confusion and agitation of mind; and on the following day, April the 7th, went to the House, and delivered a most energetic speech, which was replied to by the Duke of Richmond. Lord Chatham afterwards made

Charles Lennox, 3rd Duke of Richmond. (*From a facsimile in the author's collection*)

an effort to rise, as if labouring to give expression to some great idea; but, before he could utter a word, pressed his hand on his bosom, and fell down in a convulsive fit. The Duke of Cumberland and Lord Temple caught him in their arms, and removed him into the prince's chamber. Medical assistance being immediately rendered, in a short time his lordship in some measure recovered, and was removed to his favourite villa at Hayes, in Kent. Hopes of his complete restoration to health, however, proved delusive, and on the 10th of May,

1778,

this venerable and noble friend of humanity expired, in the seventieth year of his age.

The news of the earl's death was not disagreeable to the queen; and she thenceforth determined to increase, rather than decrease, her arbitrary measures. Ribbons, stars, and garters, were bestowed upon those who lent their willing aid to support her system of oppression, while thousands were perishing in want to supply the means.

Manchester, Liverpool, Glasgow, and Edinburgh, this year, were servile enough to raise regiments at their own expense; but the independent and brave citizens of London, steady to their principles, that the war was *unjust*, refused to follow so mean an example!

The year

1779

exhibits a miserable period in the history of Ireland. Her manufactures declined, and the people became, consequently, much dissatisfied; but their distresses were, at first, not even *noticed* by the English parliament. At length, however, an alarm of *INVASION* took place, and ministers allowed twenty thousand Irish volunteers to *carry arms*. The ministers, who before had been callous to their distresses, found men in arms were not to be trifled with, and the Irish people obtained a *promise* of an extension of trade, which satisfied them for the time.

Large sums were again required to meet the expenses of the American war, and, the minister being supported by the queen, every vote for supplies was carried by great majorities; for the year's service alone *fifteen millions* were thus agreed to. As the family of the king increased, extra sums were also deemed requisite for each of his children; and what amounts could not be raised by taxation were procured by *loans*,—thus insulting the country, by permitting its expenditure to exceed its means of income to an enormous extent.

Many representations were made to Lord North, that public opinion was opposed to the system pursued by ministers; but he was inflexible, and the generous interpositions of some members of the Upper House proved also unavailing. The independent members of the Commons remonstrated, and Mr. Burke brought forward plans for the reduction of the national expenditure and the diminution of the influence of the crown; but they were finally rejected, though not until violent conflicts had taken place, in which Lord North found himself more than once in the minority.

About this time, Mr. Dunning, a lawyer and an eminent speaker, advocated, in a most sensible manner, the necessity of taking into consideration the affairs of Ireland; but ministers defeated the intended benefit, and substituted a plan of their own, which they had previously promised to Ireland; namely, to permit a free exportation of their woollen manufactures. The unassuming character of that oppressed people never appeared to greater advantage than at this period, as even this resolution was received by them with the warmest testimonies of joy and gratitude.

There cannot be a doubt, that if the Irish had been honestly represented, their honor and ardour would have been proverbial; but they have almost always been neglected and insulted. The queen had taken Lord North's advice, and acquainted herself with the native character of the Irish, by which she became aware that, if that people generally possessed information, they would prove a powerful balance against the unjust system then in force. At this time, there was not an Irishman acquainted with any *state secrets*; her majesty, therefore, did not fear an explanation from that quarter, or she dare not have so oppressed them.

To provide for the exigencies of state, twelve millions of money, in addition to the former fifteen millions, were required this year; and thus were the sorrows of a suffering people increased, and they themselves forced to forge their own chains of oppression!

Numerous were the prosecutions against the press this year; among the rest, Mr. Parker, printer of "The General Advertiser," was brought before the "House of Hereditaries," for publishing a libel on one of its *noble* members. That there were a *few* intelligent and liberal-minded men in the House of Lords at this time, we do not wish to deny. The memorable speech of Lord Abingdon proved his lordship to be one of these, and, as this speech so admirably distinguishes *PRIVILEGE* from *TYRANNY*, we hope to be excused for introducing it in our pages. We give it in his lordship's own words:

> "My Lords,—Although there is no noble lord more zealously attached to the privileges of this House than I am, yet when I see those privileges interfering with, and destructive of, the rights of the people, there is no one among the people more ready to oppose those privileges than myself. And, my lords, my reason is this: that the privileges of neither house of parliament were ever constitutionally given to either to combat with the rights of the people. They were given, my lords, that each branch of the legislature might defend itself against the encroachments of the other, and to preserve that balance entire, which is essential to the preservation of all.
>
> "This was the designation, this is the use of privilege; and in this unquestionable shape let us apply it. Let us apply it against the encroachments of the crown, and not suffer any lord (if any such there be) who, having clambered up into the house upon the ladder of prerogative, might wish to yield up our privileges to that prerogative. Let us make use of our privileges against the other house of parliament, whenever occasion shall make it necessary, but not against the people. This is the distinction and this the meaning of privilege. The people are under the law, and we are the legislators.

If they offend, let them be punished according to law, where we have our remedy. If we are injured in our reputations, the law has provided us with a special remedy. We are entitled to the action of *scandalum magnatum*,—a privilege peculiar to ourselves. For these reasons, then, my lords, when the noble earl made his motion for the printer to be brought before this House, and when the end of that motion was answered by the author of the paper complained of giving up his name, I was in great hopes that the motion would have been withdrawn. I am sorry it was not; and yet, when I say this, I do not mean to wish that an inquiry into the merits of that paper should not be made. As it stands at present, the noble lord accused therein is the disgrace of this House, and the scandal of government. I therefore trust, for his own honor, for the honor of this House, that that noble lord will not object to, but will *himself* insist upon, the most rigid inquiry into his conduct.

"But, my lords, to call for a printer, in the case of a libel, when he gives up his author (although a modern procedure) *is not founded in law*; for in the statute of Westminster, the 1st, chapter 34, it is said, 'None shall report any false and slanderous news or tales of *great men*, whereby any discord may arise betwixt the king and his people, on pain of imprisonment, *until they bring forth the author.*' The statutes of the 2d of Richard the Second, chapter 5, and the 14th of the same reign, are to the same effect. It is there enacted, that 'No person shall devise, or tell any *false* news or lies of any lord, prelate, officer of the government, judge, &c., by which any slander shall happen to their persons, or mischief come to the kingdom, upon pain of being imprisoned; and where any one hath told false news or lies, and cannot produce the author, he shall suffer imprisonment, and be punished by the king's counsel. Here, then, my lords, two things are clearly pointed out, to wit, the person to be punished, and what the mode of punishment is. The person to be punished is the author, when produced; the mode of punishment is by the king's counsel; so that, in the present case, the printer having given up the author, he is discharged from punishment: and if the privilege of punishment had been in this House, the right is barred by these statutes; for how is the punishment to be had? Not by this House, but by the king's counsel. And, my lords, it cannot be otherwise; for, if it were, the freedom of the press were at an end; and for this purpose was this modern doctrine, to answer modern views, invented,—*a doctrine which I should ever stand up in opposition to, if even the right of its exercise were in us.* But the right is not in us: it is a jurisdiction too summary for the freedom of our constitution, and incompatible with liberty. It takes away the trial by jury; which king, lords, and commons, *have not a right to do*. It is to make us accusers, judges, jury, and executioners too, if we please. It is to give us an executive power, to which, in our legislative capacities, we are not entitled. It is to give us a power, which even the executive power itself has not, which the prerogative of the crown dare not assume, which the king himself cannot exercise. My lords, *the king cannot touch the hair of any man's head in this country, though he be guilty of high treason, but by means of the law. It is the law that creates the offence; it is a jury that must determine the guilt; it is the law that affixes the punishment; and all other modes of proceeding are* ILLEGAL. Why then, my lords, are we to assume to ourselves an executive power, with which even the executive power itself is not entrusted? I am aware, my lords, it will be said that this House, in its capacity of a court of justice, has a right to call for evidence at its bar, and to punish the witness who shall not attend. I admit it, my lords; and I admit it not only as a right belonging to this House, but as a right essential to every court of justice; for, without this right, justice could not be administered. But, my lords, was this House sitting as a court of justice (for we must distinguish between our judicial and our legislative capacities) when Mr. Parker was ordered to be taken into custody, and brought before this House? If so, at whose suit was Mr. Parker to be examined? Where are the records? Where are the papers of appeal? Who is the plaintiff, and who the defendant? There is nothing like it before your lordships; for if there had, and Mr. Parker, in such case, had disobeyed the order of this House, he was not only punishable for his contumacy and contempt, but every magistrate in the kingdom was bound to assist your lordships in having him forthcoming at your lordship's bar. *Whereas, as it is, every magistrate in the kingdom is bound, by the law of the land, to release Mr. Parker, if he be taken into custody by the present order of this House.* Nothing can be more true, than that in our judicial capacity, we have a right to call for evidence at our bar, and to punish the witness if he does not appear. The whole body of the law supports us in this right. But, under the pretext of privilege, to bring a man by force to the bar, when we *have our remedy at law; to accuse, condemn, and punish that man, at the mere arbitrary will and pleasure of this House, not sitting as a court of justice, is tyranny in the abstract. It is against law; it is subversive of the constitution; it is incompetent to this House*; and, therefore, my lords, thinking as I do, that this House has no right forcibly to bring any man to its bar, but in the discharge of its proper functions, as a court of judicature, I shall now move your lordships, 'that the body of W. Parker, printer of the General Advertiser, be released from the custody of the Gentleman Usher of the Black Rod, and that the order for the said Parker, being brought to the bar of this House be now discharged.

"Before I sit down, I will just observe to your lordships, that I know that precedents may be adduced in contradiction to the doctrine I have laid down. But, my lords, *precedents cannot make that legal and constitutional which is, in itself, illegal and unconstitutional.* IF THE PRECEDENTS OF THIS REIGN ARE TO BE RECEIVED AS PRECEDENTS IN THE NEXT, THE LORD HAVE MERCY ON THOSE WHO ARE TO COME AFTER US!!!

"There is one observation more I would make, and it is this: *I would wish noble lords to consider, how much it lessens the dignity of this House, to agitate privileges which you have not power to enforce. It hurts the constitution of parliament, and, instead of being respected, makes us contemptible. That privilege which you cannot exercise, and of right too, disdain to keep.*"

If the country had been blessed with a majority of such patriots as Lord Abingdon, what misery had been prevented! what lives had been saved!

Early in the year

1780,

meetings of the populace took place in various parts of the kingdom, and ministers were boldly accused of having prodigally and wastefully spent the public money; while petitions were presented, praying "for a correction of abuses in the public expenditure." Riots in many parts of England were the consequences of unjustly continuing wars and taxation, and several hundred people were killed and wounded by the military; while many others forfeited their lives on the scaffold for daring to raise their arms against tyranny. Lord George Gordon was also committed to the Tower on a charge of high treason; but no jury of his countrymen could be found to consider his undaunted attempt to *redress the people's grievances as treasonable*, and he was, consequently, *honorably acquitted*! The influence of her majesty, however, kept a minister in office, though contrary to the sense of the wisest and best part of the community; and a ruinous war was still permitted to drain the blood and money of the many.

War might probably be considered by those in power a *legal trade*; but was it not continued for the untenable purpose of avarice? We think it was. There did not appear to be any rational hope for reform or retrenchment, while men versed in corruption were so enriched, and had an almost unlimited sway over the councils of

John Seymour Lucas's depiction of the Gordon Riots. (*From a late nineteenth-century reproduction*)

the reigning authority. Popular commotion was dreaded; yet the ministers could not be prevailed upon to dispel the cause of anxiety by conciliatory measures,—by a timely redress of grievances, by concession of rights, and by reformation of abuses. If they had done so, they would have given satisfactory evidence that government had no other object in view than faithfully to discharge their duty, by adopting such plans as would really benefit mankind, and furnish means to secure the comfort and happiness of all men.

An engraving of Prince George, later the Prince Regent, then George IV.

In the meantime, much distress was imposed upon the unfortunate king, by the increasing and uncontroulable prodigality of some of his children, especially of George. The queen would not hear of anything to his discredit, and thus what little of family enjoyment remained was ultimately destroyed.

The unrestrained predilection of this youthful prince now became habitual pursuits, and excesses of the most detestable description were not unknown to him. Within the circle of his less nominally illustrious acquaintance, every father dreaded the seduction of his child, if she possessed any personal charms, while the mother feared to lose sight of her daughter, even for a moment. It is not in our power to give an adequate idea of the number of those families whose happiness he ruined; but we well, too well, know the number was infamously great. The country gave him credit for being liberal in political principles, and generously disposed for reform. But little of his *real* character was then known; his faults, indeed, were named as virtues, and his vices considered as *gentlemanly exploits*, so that his dissembled appearance was received, by those unacquainted with him, as the sure and incontestable mark of a great and noble soul. But, before our pages are concluded, we fear we must, in duty, prove him a widely-different character! It is true, his acquaintance with political characters was chiefly amongst "the Whigs;" it may also be added that those "Whigs," so particularly intimate with this prince, did not gain much by their connexion with him, but finally became as supine and venal as himself. They determined that, as the heir-apparent, he should not be allowed to suffer any deterioration of greatness, and the principles and practices of so mighty an individual were considered by them to constitute a sufficient patent for continual imitation.

At this period, Mr. Dunning moved his famous resolution to the House, with unbending firmness and uncompromising fidelity. He said, "The influence of the crown has increased, is increasing, and ought to be diminished." It was carried by a majority of 233 against 215; but a second resolution, which was to give effect to the first, was lost by a majority of fifty-one votes.

In the year

1781,

William Pitt, the second son of the late Lord Chatham, delivered his first speech in the Commons, in favour of the bill introduced by Mr. Burke, on the subject of reform.

Lord North brought forward the budget on the 7th of March, containing the various items needful for the service of the year. The amount so calculated was *twenty-one millions of money*!—twelve of which were to be raised by loans, the terms being very high. From this bold imposition upon the public purse and credit, the ministry were much lowered in public opinion.

During this year, the brave General Washington struck that decisive blow which afterwards gave liberty to his countrymen. He kept General Clinton at New York, in constant

Edmund Burke. (*British Library*)

alarm; and then suddenly appeared before York Town in full force, and obtained a grand victory over Lord Cornwallis, who was there with his army. The American war consequently became more unpopular than ever, and shortly after the meeting of parliament, in March,

1782,

a resolution was moved, and *passed without a division*, declaring that the House of Commons would consider as enemies to his majesty and the country all who should advise the prosecution of offensive war in North America!

Shortly after, Lord North resigned, and the Marquis of Rockingham was placed at the head of the new administration. Amongst the promotions at this time, was *Mr. Dunning!* who, at *her majesty's request*, was created Baron Ashburton, and also Chancellor of the Duchy of Lancaster.

A treaty of peace was now entered into with General Washington, and Sir Guy Carleton was deputed to conduct the happy affair.

In the beginning of July, the unexpected death of the Marquis of Rockingham threw the whole cabinet into extreme disorder; and another resignation of ministers took place, on which occasion Mr. Pitt was constituted "Chancellor of the Exchequer," *although only twenty-three years of age*! Lord Shelburne accepted the office of premier, at the request of the king, which gave great offence to Mr. Fox and the Duke of Portland, who resigned. The country was little benefitted by this change, as the money required for the service of the year was more than twenty-four millions, of which thirteen had to be raised by loans.

In November, the provisional articles of peace were signed at Paris between the Commissioners of England and those of the United States.

The Shelburne party were obliged to retire in

1783,

having, by their arbitrary measures, drawn upon themselves general displeasure throughout the country.

Much surprise was created at the unexpected coalition of Lord North and Mr. Fox, which was the natural result of the pressing case of the prince, to whom the queen had confidentially entrusted his father's breach of the law, in the solemnization of his marriage with herself. The queen, in fact, used the prince's influence to prevail upon Mr. Fox to join Lord North, as he was well informed upon all the circumstances of the king's first marriage. Although the political sentiments of these gentlemen were opposed, it was represented as a safe line of conduct, to ensure the tranquillity of the kingdom. Thus, again, was every portion of truth sacrificed to the WILL of the *queen*.

This year, the king agreed that the heir-apparent should receive fifty thousand pounds per annum, and sixty thousand pounds to equip him suitably to his dignity. In the meantime, it became a public fact, that the prince had so deeply involved himself in debt as to be mean enough to resort, through the medium of others, to borrow money (of various amounts) of his tradespeople!

Before the conclusion of the year, the *Whig and Tory* ministry were ejected, to the entire satisfaction of nearly every individual in the nation, who despised such an unholy alliance of opposite principles.

A nineteenth-century engraving of William Pitt the Younger.

Mr. Pitt was now made "First Lord of the Treasury," which was a change very satisfactory to her majesty, as, from the youth of the new "premier," she augured her likely influence over the political hemisphere to be increased. It was well known that her majesty did not like any of the prince's associates, more especially Messrs. Fox and Sheridan. Mr. Burke was not supposed to be so informed upon all subjects; and, though much in the necessary confidence of the prince, the queen presumed it was chiefly in procuring pecuniary accommodations. It was not until an after period, that the *whole truth* was stated to her by the prince.

New taxes alone could furnish means for the immense additional annuities now imposed upon the country; and thus were sums for every succeeding year's demand increased.

At this period, the Prince of Wales and his next brother were associated in dissipation of every kind. Their love of gaming was proverbial, and their excess of indulgence in voluptuousness soon exhausted the income allowed them by the country. Their caprices were various, but those of the prince was most strikingly evinced in his abruptly declining his engagements with the celebrated Mrs. Robinson. His usual plan was, when fascinated by the appearance of a new object, to exert every nerve to possess it. Presents, accompanied by the highest eulogiums, and protestations of eternal love and constancy, were always pressed upon the acceptance of the intended victim; and thus, by apparent devotion and unconquerable passion, many were the delusions he practised, and the outrages he committed, upon the unsuspecting virtue of woman.

Had a plebeian committed but *one* act similar to those in which the prince was so frequently the principal character, his *life* must have atoned for his fault, and a destitute family, in consequence, been plunged into distraction. But, because the prince was of such high-reputed family, he must, forsooth, be accounted a *noble-minded gentleman*; and, instead of exposition and punishment, the venal and hired press of the day launched out into the most fulsome eulogiums of his *graceful, all-attracting elegance of style and manners*, without even speaking of the *infamy* of his amours, intrigues, and debaucheries! Some writers, alas! are so fearful of speaking the truth, lest they should offend the *side they have espoused*, or the inclinations and political principles of those by whom they are likely to be read, that they almost persuade themselves there is a sort of *impropriety* in presenting facts in their proper colours! But is it not beneath the dignity of the press to act in so cowardly a manner?

In the year

1784,

(notwithstanding the dreadfully enormous weight of the "national debt," borrowed by the ministers upon nominal annuities, for which large interest was given) the king was again solicited to assist the prince, in order that his debts might be discharged. This request was refused, and Messrs. Fox and Sheridan advocated the subject to no purpose.

During this year, much public display of talent was made in the House. Mr. Pitt was now fully and entirely in her majesty's "confidence," and he well knew if "the system" were to be continued, war must be carried on, and oppression would increase rather than decrease. While engaged in a private interview with the queen, upon various state subjects, Mr. Pitt submitted his opinion upon the extravagance and improper pursuits of the prince, adding, "I much fear, your majesty, in his delirium of debauchery, *some expressions may escape him, to the injury of the crown!*"

Charles James Fox.
(*British Library*)

"No," answered the queen, "he is too well aware of the *consequences to himself*, if that transpired; so on that point I can rely upon him." "Is your majesty aware," said Mr. Pitt, "that at this time the prince is engrossed by a fair beauty? and I believe, from good authority I may say, intends to marry her! He is now so much embarrassed, that, at the suggestion of his trusty friend, Sheridan, he borrows large amounts from a Jew, who resides in town, and gives his bonds for much larger amounts than he receives; by this means, he is actually involved in debt to the amount of above a million of money; and the interest and principal must, some day, be *honourably* discharged, or else he must never ascend the throne; as the dishonour would cause him eternal disgrace, if not an abdication." Truly, this was a fine picture of England's future monarch!

In the year

1785,

Mr. Pitt caused prosecutions to be issued and enforced to check the rising spirit of the Irish, as they appeared determined to press hard until they received reform in the representation; and, in order to divert the exasperated feelings of the people of England, as he stood deeply pledged to the reformers, "*as a man and a minister*," to bring in "a bill to amend the representation of the people," he moved, April 18th, for leave to bring it forward for the consideration of the House. His plan was to transfer the right of election from thirty-six rotten boroughs to the counties and principle unrepresented towns, *allowing a pecuniary compensation to the owners of the disfranchised boroughs*, and to extend the right of voting for knights[1] of the shires to copyholders. This minister suffered his motion to be negatived by 248 against 194! Had there been honesty on the part of the minister towards the people, unfettered by any *state secrets*, he would have been prepared to meet the numerous opposers; but he found himself unable to serve the cause of liberty and slavery at the same time, and so, to save his word of promise, he did bring in "the bill," when he well knew it was impossible to carry it under the then existing corruptions!

In the farce here played, under the management of that youthful renegade,— Pitt, we have a fair specimen of the way in which the English have been treated. But there is a time rapidly approaching when the supporters of despotism cannot thus delude their countrymen. The whole nest of court sycophants, however, seem determined rather to see England reduced to a state of the most grievous bondage than imagine one of their own ill-gotten acres endangered, or the least of their absurd and exclusive privileges called in question. But are such creatures, their *imagined* interests, and affected opinions, to triumph over the views of the most virtuous patriots and wisest men of the present age? Forbid it, Justice!

The year

1786

was ushered in under some peculiar circumstances of distress and alarm. The king was evidently declining in health, and strong signs of imbecility were apparent. He positively refused to see the prince upon the subject of his debts, and was otherwise much distracted at the recollection of various impositions upon the public, which might have been avoided, if, in the moment of necessity, he had explained himself fully to the nation, and pressed for an amelioration of all *unnatural* and *uncivilized* acts of parliament, detrimental to the peace, welfare, and happiness of the sovereign and the subject.

In July, the prince was so beset with appeals from his numerous creditors, that, partly to silence them, and partly to induce the House to pay his long-standing arrears of borrowed money, he announced his intention to give up his establishment, and, out of his annual income of fifty thousand pounds, to reserve ten thousand, and appropriate forty thousand for the benefit of his creditors.

In the early part of this year, the prince *was married* to Mrs. Fitzherbert. Messrs. Fox, Sheridan, and Burke were present upon the occasion, as also were some of the relatives of the bride. After the ceremony, Mr. Fox handed them into a carriage, and they drove to Richmond, where they spent some days. In the interim, the queen was made acquainted with the marriage. Her majesty requested an audience with the prince, which was immediately complied with. The queen insisted on being told if the news of his marriage were correct. "Yes, madam," replied he, "and not any force under heaven shall separate *us*. If his majesty had been *as firm* in acknowledging *his marriage*, he might *now* have enjoyed life, instead of being a misanthrope, as he is. But I beg, further, that *my* wife be received at court, and proportionately as your majesty receives her, and pays her attention, from this time, so shall I render my attentions to your majesty. The lady I have married is worthy of all homage, and my very confidential friends, with some of my wife's relations, only, *witnessed* our marriage. Have you not always taught me to consider myself *heir* to the first sovereignty in the world? where then will exist any risk of obtaining a ready concurrence from the House in my marriage? I hope, madam, a few hours reflection will satisfy you that I have done my duty in following this impulse of my inclinations, and therefore I wait your majesty's commands, feeling assured you would not wish to blast the happiness of your favourite prince." The queen presumed it would prove her best policy to signify her acquiescence to the prince's wishes, and the interview terminated without any further explanation or remonstrance; nevertheless, the substance of the interview was immediately communicated to Mr. Pitt. The extravagant expenditure of the prince, at this period, was so increased, that he frequently promised *cent. per cent.* for advances of cash!

The Duke of Richmond, this year, proposed to erect *fortifications* all over England! Monstrous as this attempt to enslave the country must appear, the power of Pitt brought the division of the

Richard Brinsley Sheridan.
(*British Library*)

House of Commons on the bill exactly *even*, so that the speaker was obliged, by his conscience, to give his casting vote *against* so traitorous an affair! The establishment of a sinking fund was next brought forward; and, on a surplus of taxes appearing, amounting to NINE HUNDRED THOUSAND POUNDS, new taxes were levied on the plea of making up this sum *ONE MILLION*, which, with compound interest, was to be invariably applied to the *reduction of the national debt.*

In the year

1787,

the queen received the wife of the prince (Mrs. Fitzherbert) *in the most courteous manner in public*! The mental illness of the king became now apparent to those around him, but it *was not spoken of publicly.*

In April, Mr. Newnham, member for the city of London, gave notice that he should bring forward a motion, the intent of which was, "To address the king, in order to procure his approbation to relieve the Prince of Wales from all embarrassments of a *pecuniary* nature," to which he hoped the House would *cordially* agree. This announcement created much conversation, as well it might; and Mr. Newnham was earnestly solicited to withdraw his motion, lest its results should do injury to the state, and be productive of other inconvenience and mischief. The minister (Pitt) said, "*that if Mr. Newnham persevered in pressing his motion upon the notice of the House, he should be driven to make disclosures of circumstances, which otherwise he believed it to be his imperative duty to conceal.*" Mr. Rolle (member for Devonshire) considered that an investigation of this matter involved many questions of consequence, which would affect both church and state. Messrs. Fox and Sheridan, with some other *private* acquaintances of the prince, were bold in their language, and replied, that "the prince did not fear any investigation of his conduct; and that respect or indulgence, by an affected tenderness or studied ambiguity, would be disagreeable to the wishes and feelings of his royal highness!"

A few days after this debate, Mr. Fox called the attention of the House to the strange and extraordinary language used by Mr. Rolle, saying, "that he presumed those remarks were made in reference to the base and malicious calumny which had been propagated out of doors by the enemies of the prince, in order to *depreciate* his character, and injure him in the opinion of the country!" Mr. Rolle replied to this

Maria Fitzherbert, Prince George's paramour, based upon a portrait by Jean Condé.

by saying that, "though the marriage could not have been accomplished under the formal sanction of the law, yet if it existed *as a fact*, it ought to be satisfactorily cleared up, lest the most alarming consequences should be the result." Mr. Fox, in reply, said, "that he not only denied the calumny in question, with respect to the effect of certain existing laws, but he also denied the *marriage in toto*," adding, "though he well knew the matter was illegal under every form of statute provided, yet he took that opportunity to assert, *it never did happen*." Mr. Rolle again asked, "Do you, Sir, speak from DIRECT OR INDIRECT AUTHORITY?" Mr. Fox replied, "FROM DIRECT AUTHORITY." The House was now anxious that Mr. Rolle should express his satisfaction; but he positively and determinately refused, "as he wished every member of the House to JUDGE for himself!" Now mark the result. Mr. Sheridan (the bottle-companion of the prince) rose and declared warmly, "that if Mr. Rolle would not be satisfied, or put the matter into some train for his further satisfaction, his opinion was, the House ought to resolve, that it was seditious and disloyal to propagate reports injurious to the prince." But notice Mr. Pitt's reply, who rose, and protested against an attack upon the freedom of speech in that House. Mr. Pitt, indeed, could do no less than *stop the inquiry*; for if it had proceeded to any greater length, the LEGITIMACY of the prince might have been *doubted*!!!

The prince again sought advice to shield himself from his various opponents, whose impertinent, yet honest expressions, might prove an alloy to his character, and render void all his pretensions to even *common honesty*! His royal highness *deigned* to consult some persons of consequence, but he could not receive any advice equal to his wishes. At length, he saw the queen, and partly explained his difficulties and debts, concluding his remarks by these *threatening* words: "Unless the king suggests *HIS DESIRE* for the payment of these debts, I will *EXPLAIN* all this STATE MYSTERY; and I would receive a shot from a musket, in preference to the galling insults which I well know the *kingdoms* infer *from these shameful arrears*." Again the *state secrets* operated! Again was TRUTH to be hidden in a napkin! The prince retired from the audience; but the queen was no sooner disengaged than Mr. Pitt was announced and introduced. The interview was short, but decisive, and the minister departed on a mission to the prince at Carlton House. There he promised that his royal highness should immediately receive means to discharge his debts, and accordingly, on the very next day, a message was laid before the House, and an address voted to the king, to request him to grant out of the "civil list" the sum of one hundred and sixty-one thousand pounds, to discharge the debts of George, called Prince of Wales, with an additional sum of twenty thousand pounds to finish the repairs of Carlton Palace. When this infamous proposition was made, distress and wretchedness were at an alarming height! But the king was more an object of pity than of blame. Royalty, to him, was a deceitful bauble. Those who beheld it at a distance saw nothing but greatness, splendour, and delight; but, could they have examined it closely, they would have found toil, perplexity, and care, its constant companions.

The king was now fast exchanging the bloom of youth for the languor of age. He knew his duty was to repress calumny and falsehood, and to support innocence and truth; and not only to abstain from doing evil, but to exert himself in every way to do good, by preventing the mischiefs evil counsellors might devise. Yet the *state secrets* kept him from acting as his heart dictated, and his mind soon lost all its vigour!

The prince, from this time, was sure of the attainment of his wishes, if within the power of the queen to bestow; and, from this conquest, he gave loose rein to the impetuous desires of his wayward inclinations. Splendid fêtes were given, money was lavished upon the most insignificant and indecorous occasions; virtue openly insulted, in every possible shape; and the man, who was expected shortly to reign over the destiny of millions, was frequently exhibited to his friends as an UNPRINCIPLED LIBERTINE, a NOTORIOUS GAMESTER, and an UNGRATEFUL SON! But the rank of royal distinction, and the means he possessed to gratify his lusts (being devoid of all positive integrity upon many points) were sufficient causes of excuse in the estimation of himself and his minions! His graceful bow and ensnaring address led many good-natured people into a belief that he was really an honest man and a gentleman!

From the commencement of the year

1788,

the king's health again declined. His mind appeared full of gloomy apprehensions and forebodings; sometimes he uttered the most incoherent language; then, dissolving in tears, would ask after the health of the several members of his family, and especially of his youngest daughter, to whom he was more particularly attached. This state of aberration was, however, strictly concealed from the public as long as possible by the queen. Here, again, mark her German policy! Fearing she could not much longer conceal the king's indisposition, she determined to consult her favourite minister, and they resolved upon a proposition to give to the *queen's* care the charge of his majesty's person, presuming that step was finally needful, as by its adoption *only* could she retain an opportunity of exercising *complete controul over her afflicted husband*! On the reassembling of parliament, therefore, the project of the queen was brought forward by Pitt, who, possessing a decided majority, passed what resolutions he pleased. He contended, in opposition to Fox, that the Prince of Wales had no more right to the regency *than he had*! The debates upon this subject were long and warm; but Pitt and the queen finally triumphed. The care of the king's person and the disposition of the royal household was to be committed to her majesty, who would, by this means, be vested with the patronage of *four hundred places*, amongst which were the great offices of lord-stewart, lord-chamberlain, and master of the horse! These "loaves and fishes" offered the queen a fine opportunity of exercising her tyranny, and further increasing her power!

Let us here digress a little, to reflect upon the *enviable* state in which her majesty was placed at this period.

Behold, then, the Queen of England, in the enjoyment of health, surrounded with all the luxuries of life, knowing the *intricacies* of STATE INFAMY, and anxious to hold the reins of government in her own hands, constantly closeted with the minister—ALONE! his years not half so many as those of his royal mistress! See her confiding in his secrecy, submitting her opinions for his decision, and knowing that herself and her family are in his power! The man, who, after this retrospect, pronounces there never was a *false step*, or a *deviation from rectitude*, we venture to say is but very little acquainted with humanity! It is also well known to more than one or two individuals, that the Prince of Wales dared to *jest* with her majesty upon the occasional *private* interviews she held with this minister; and his royal highness was once seriously sent from her presence, in consequence of a TRIFLING DISCOVERY he made. It therefore seemed the more requisite that the *appearance* of a rigid decorum must exist at court; consequently, if any lady had been known to violate those bounds, she must be excluded from royal favour, and never again enter the precincts of the palace! Her majesty, it will be perceived from this, knew how to put on the garb of virtue, if she possessed it not! Our love of impartiality, however, obliges us to give an instance contrary to the general edict of the queen. Her majesty was made fully acquainted with Mrs. Fitzherbert's history, and therefore knew that this lady had been left a widow—twice; and that she afterwards accepted the *protection* of the Marquis Bellois, which intimacy was of considerable duration. Yet, as soon as the prince *married her*, she was a general visitant at court, and received the most especial and unlimited polite attentions from the queen. Let this example suffice to shew her majesty's *scrupulous* delicacy!

In March,

1789,

the king was declared convalescent, so as to be able to resume his duties, and defeat those air-drawn schemes of power, which his queen was about to assume.

The insulted sovereign thus freed the people, for a time, from the artful stratagems and devices arising from the charnel house of oppression.

It is certain, that his majesty was free from all *violent* paroxysms, and generally manifested a quiet and unobtrusive disposition in all things. But then this was the *utmost* of his improvement. Reason's empire was fatally shook, and the recollection of the past incapacitated him for forming an opinion either upon the present or the future.

The queen, in the mean time, resolved not to be entirely debarred of her prospects

Early nineteenth-century engraving of William Wilberforce. (*Stephen Basdeo Collection*)

of patronage; for, under the specious disguise of kingly authority, her majesty gave appointments and honours to the hirelings around her, and carried "majorities" whenever she pleased.

It was not deemed prudent that the king should open the House in person; therefore, the chancellor delivered the speech in the name of his majesty.

During this session, Mr. Wilberforce pleaded ably for the abolition of West Indian slavery, though to very little advantage.

Some excesses of an unhappy description were practised by the Duke of York; but they were passed over without any public punishment or parental rebuke, although a family of high respectability suffered the loss of their only daughter, a most beautiful and accomplished girl, nearly twenty years of age! She was a victim of the duke's sensuality, and destroyed herself by poison soon afterwards,—such were the extreme sentiments of honor and virtue entertained by her. Some of her family yet live to mourn her loss and regret the privileges of royalty!

In this year a revolution broke out in France, and innumerable lives were lost. The opposite views which Burke and Fox took of this event dissolved the friendship that had so long existed between them.

In February,

1790,

the printer of "The Times" newspaper was fined ONE HUNDRED POUNDS for a libel on the Prince of Wales, and the like sum for a libel on the *equally-illustrious* seducer, the Duke of York. If a verdict had been given otherwise, royalty would have been humbled!

In this year, also, a most remarkable occurrence transpired. A very respectable clergyman was induced to marry two persons upon an extreme emergency, without their obtaining a license or the publishing of banns. The clergyman was tried at Leicester for this offence, and sentenced to be *transported for fourteen years*! Many appeals were made, in a quiet and peaceable manner, to the judge. Expostulations upon the disproportion of the punishment were also made by various classes of society; but, alas! *the happiness of the subject was destroyed*, while the higher authorities remained not only unimpeached, but defended!

During this session, the House was solicited to supply extra sums for the expenditure of the *secret service*, to which, however, many voices were raised in opposition. The prince and his former friends and companions were now apparently in a state of disunion, as each one appeared dissatisfied with the other.

A nineteenth-century reproduction of Frederick, Duke of York.

Mr. Fox proved the most unremitting member of the House in the discharge of his duties, opposing the increase of the national debt, and the imposition of new taxes. The salary of the speaker of the House of Commons, however, was advanced to six thousand pounds, remonstrance proving of no avail.

About this time, the prince and two of his brothers became so embarrassed by their imprudent conduct, that they found it expedient to resort to some measure for the attainment of means to satisfy the clamorous demands of their creditors. Jews and money-brokers were tried, but to no effect; and their last resource seemed to be by obtaining the amount desired upon their respective or joint bonds. Every likely person was solicited to grant the loan; yet, after a long and mortifying attempt, all their endeavours proved fruitless. A large interest was offered, and had the parties been persons of indubitable integrity, many of their countrymen would have gladly lent their money upon such terms; but former inaccuracies paved the way for future misgivings. At length the sum was furnished, from foreign houses chiefly,—the amount of which was ONE MILLION!!! The princes received nearly half a million immediately, and the other portion was to be paid according to the stipulation,— the interest being fixed at *six per cent*. This interest, however, was not paid upon its becoming due; consequently there was a suspicion of unfair dealing; but of this subject we must treat anon.

A trifling dispute with Spain this year cost the country THREE HUNDRED THOUSAND POUNDS!

The year

1791

was a period of continual debate and of harassing vexation, both at home and abroad. In the mean while, the prince was engrossed in his pursuits of pleasure, ever searching after variety in every possible shape. Such also were the pursuits of his royal brothers.

It now becomes our painful duty to speak of the FEMALES of this *"ILLUSTRIOUS FAMILY."*

It is one of the unnatural distinctions of royalty, and which is often fatal to the happiness of society, that *their ways are not the ways of the other sons and daughters of humanity*. Though royal blood is not of itself considered a barrier against marriage, the very few persons that are eligible to marry a king's daughter, besides the unsurmountable difficulties which religion opposes to such unions, makes them almost amount to absolute exclusion.

It would argue a callous heart not to feel the force of the above reflection, while speaking of the royal daughters of Queen Charlotte. They were at this period in the bloom of youth, in all the glowing exuberance of health, but from the real enjoyment of which the miserable etiquette of regal splendour, and the feigned prudery of their mother, debarred them. In the full meridian of their state, possessing every exterior advantage calculated to excite vulgar envy and admiration, these royal ladies were less blessed, in reality, than the daughters of peasants, who were free to marry the men of their choice. When this secluded state of royalty is considered, the reflecting mind will feel disposed to exercise charity and forbearance; but the subjects of our present notice partook of *rather more* of female frailty than ought to have been allowed. We have heard, indeed, of the most desperate excesses committed by *royal* ladies, and are ourselves acquainted with an *accoucheur*, who officiated under a circumstance of a lamentable kind,—independent of the birth of Captain Garth! Alas! were the crimes of the court of Charlotte but painted in their true colours, how would Virtue blush!—how would Honesty be abashed!—how would Credulity be staggered! The slightest deviation from honor in a tradesman's daughter is generally punished by eternal disgrace! For the present, we must leave these very painful reflections; though we fear *truth* will compel us to renew the subject.

The revenue was, as usual, unequal to meet the extravagancies of the royal family, and so was added every succeeding year an increase to the already immense "NATIONAL DEBT."

The queen became now much disturbed by the dissatisfaction so generally expressed by all classes of society, and she therefore resolved to give the minister her opinion upon the subject. Mr. Pitt accordingly presented himself, and was received with courteous attention. The queen expressed her fears of an ill *ultimatum*, unless some plan could be proposed to satisfy the desires of the people. After various propositions were made and rejected, it was deemed prudent to resist any and every motion which might be made in the Commons for reform in the state of the representation, and to rule over the people by *force*, if found needful.

The House met early in the year

1792,

and the king announced the marriage of his second son, Frederick, with a daughter of the King of Prussia. In March, Mr. Pitt proposed to settle thirty thousand pounds per annum upon their royal highnesses! The Opposition remonstrated, but the motion was finally carried.

Much interest was excited upon the subject of the slave trade; and Mr. Wilberforce urged the abolition of it in very warm and generous language. Mr. Pitt was eloquent on this occasion, and pleaded, most animatedly, in favour of its entire abolition; but the minister *was not sincere.* A series of resolutions were ultimately agreed upon, and sent up to the Lords for their concurrence.

The Duke of Clarence and future King William IV as depicted in *The Mirror of Literature* (1828).

The Duke of Clarence now commenced his parliamentary career, by violently declaiming against the abolition of slavery and its advocates. This caused it to be delayed, and the guilt of Britain increased.

The queen *appeared* vexed at this circumstance, as she had imagined such a concession would have given great satisfaction, without decreasing her influence at home.

In a private conversation with an illustrious person, some days after this defeat, Mr. Wilberforce said, "He did not believe the queen or the minister were *truly desirous* of the abolition of slavery; for, if it had been intended by them to be carried, they would have secured it in the Upper House."

After thus trifling with the wishes of the people, it appeared probable that dissatisfaction might arise amongst the middle classes of society; to provide against which, the establishment of a new police for Westminster was proposed and carried.

The year

1793

commenced with the usual aspects, and power appeared to have had a hardening influence upon the minds of statesmen. The crisis seemed near, that some salutary and healing measure of reform in the state of the representation must be adopted; for it was imprudent any longer to be silent on the subject. Mr. Grey, therefore, moved the question in the House, on the 30th of April, and was supported ably by Mr. Erskine and others; but the minister (Mr. Pitt) repelled the motion, and spoke as warmly for its withdrawal as he had formerly spoken in its defence, and of its necessity. The result was prejudicial to the rights and privileges of free-born men; the motion was dismissed, and a royal proclamation issued against all seditious writings and correspondences,—plainly proving that the crown needed the aid of *spies and informers*, in order to continue its baneful and injurious influence over a deluded and degraded people! Thus was an attempt to obtain justice defeated by a combination of overbearing tyranny and oppression; and thus was the "state automaton" moved at pleasure by the secret springs of court intrigue and infamy, regulated by the queen! One extreme generally leads to another, and so by degrees the freedom of the constitution was changed to tyrannical fetters, under the assumed title of "*improvements in our code of laws*," whilst distress continued, and expostulation, as usual, proved fruitless.

Mr. Pitt, at this time, through a private channel, communicated his desire to see Mr. Canning, who of course promptly attended. The premier complimented Mr. Canning on his reputation as a scholar and a speaker, and stated, that, if he concurred in the policy which government was then pursuing, arrangements would be made to bring him into parliament. These few words will briefly explain to future generations the manner of introducing members to parliament by this minister.

Previous to this *honourable* offer, Mr. Canning belonged to what was then termed "the opposition faction," and among those who were the *most violent* in their opinions, *he* had been considered and spoken of as their *protégé*. But a seat in parliament from the hands of a prime minister, who, however haughty and reserved in his general manners, had perhaps, for that very reason, a peculiar power in fixing himself in the minds of those whom he wished to please, was a tempting offer to a young man, conscious of superior talent, but rendered by his situation in life agreeably alive to such flattering and powerful notice. Our readers will hardly feel surprised, then, at his after vacillating conduct, which we shall have occasion frequently to notice.

The Prince of Wales now veered in his political expressions, and deserted his former acknowledged principles, in obedience to the wishes of the *queen*. The other male branches of the royal family were revelling in the vortex of voluptuousness; and so expensive were their amours and gallantries, in addition to their gambling transactions, that they were continually involved in debt, and, for momentary relief, borrowed sums of every person willing to run the risk of a loan, or afraid to incur the royal displeasure.

The king was ignorant of the most dishonorable transactions in which his sons were so deeply involved; what he did know was sufficient to make him miserable. Their supplies and income were to an enormous extent; yet his majesty was aware that the Duke of York's horses and carriage were seized, while going down Piccadilly, and his royal highness obliged to walk home!

Declaration of hostilities was announced between Great Britain and France, and the year's supply amounted to TWENTY MILLIONS. To provide this enormous sum, extra taxes were again levied upon the people.

We enter upon the year

1794,

with sorrow and indignation, as it was the commencement of an all-important era in national affairs. The king beheld the critical state of the empire with much sorrow and disquietude. The extravagant and imprudent conduct of his sons also acted as a canker upon his heart. In vain did he endeavour to represent to them, that to be worthy of holding their rank in such a great nation, they ought to lay aside the follies which had so long been practised by them; and as earnestly, yet as vainly, did he press them to retire from the society of voluptuous acquaintances, with whom he too well knew they were so deeply involved, in various ways.

At this period of our history, we are grieved to record the tyrannical acts of government, in apprehending a number of persons on the charge of *treason*. Some of our readers will, doubtless, recollect the glorious acquittal of Hardy, Tooke, and Thelwall; but there were others, less fortunate. We would rather have been Claudius or Caligula, Nero, Tiberius, or the *Christian*, blood-stained Constantine, than the man who, in cold blood, could deliberately sign a warrant against those patriotic martyrs, Muir, Skirving, Margarot, Palmer, and Gerald, whose only *crime* consisted in having *supported Mr. Pitt's own original system of reform*!

Our readers, at this distance of time, will reflect with amazement and indignation, that on the 8th of February, 1794, the four first-named citizens, without a moment's previous notice, were surprised in their beds by the Newgate ruffians, chained and handcuffed like the vilest felons, and thus conveyed to Woolwich, where they were sent on board a transport ready to receive them. A few hours afterwards, the vessel dropped down the river; but, during the short interval it remained at Woolwich, all communication was cut off between them and their friends! Even the wife of Margarot was denied admission to him! Such were the positive orders of that illiberal and corrupt minister,—Mr. Henry Dundas.

Let us hope that the day is for ever past when men can be thus treated for merely giving vent to their complaints and sufferings. It is the prerogative of affliction to complain, more sacred and natural than any titles or immunities which *privileged* persons enjoy! And whenever *force* is employed against *argument and reason*, though the contest may be unequal, depend upon it that the cause of *TRUTH* will *ULTIMATELY PREVAIL*!

At this period, the Prince of Wales was involved in more than SIX HUNDRED THOUSAND POUNDS, beside bonds and bills, signed by him, to a very enormous amount; and, finding himself unable to procure any further sums, he applied to the queen for assistance in this extremity. Her majesty referred him to his father, and pressed him to yield to any advice which the king might suggest, or any plan he might recommend.

A time was appointed for an interview, and the father and son entered upon these very distressing and dishonorable transactions. After much deliberation, the king observed, "that it was utterly impossible to ask parliament for any relief, as it was all the minister could now do to keep the wheels of state in motion; and, even to do that, it required *immense loans* to be raised, to make up the deficiency of the year's current expenses." As a last resource, the king proposed that the prince should MARRY, and that a lady of royal birth be selected, as agreeable to the inclinations of the prince as possible. Upon such an event, the minister would, no doubt, furnish means for his liberation, and a sufficient income for the additional expenses attendant upon such an alliance. The prince received the opinion of his father with varied sensations, and requested time to think upon the proposition, when he would announce the result of his cogitations.

Alas! how much are kings to be pitied! If their principles and intentions be virtuous, what difficulties have they to surmount, what sorrows to endure! This was a trying period for George the Third: on the one hand, he saw the impropriety and cruelty of marriage merely for state policy, and more particularly so in the present instance, as he considered the prince's marriage with Mrs. Fitzherbert solemn and binding in the sight of heaven, though certainly in direct opposition to the *law* of the country, which was *in operation at the time it was solemnized*. On the other hand, it appeared that a royal marriage was an event that would give great satisfaction to the people, and might, perhaps, reclaim the prince from those considerable errors and obnoxious pursuits in which he was so deeply entangled; for he associated with some of the most unprincipled characters, of whom any person of morality or *common decency* would certainly have been ashamed.

Here again the gewgaw of royal parade was intended to entrap the admiration of the ignorant. The vain pomp and pageantries of courts and the splendour of fortune have ever been an *ignis fatuus* to seduce the people to their ruin. They have, alas! too often served as an useful shelter to every excess of folly, every enormity of crime; while the deepest distresses and the most urgent wants have not been allowed as an extenuation for the slightest transgression, though committed to satisfy the craving exigencies of famished nature! Had a *private* individual acted as this prince was about to do, would he not have become an outcast from his family, and would not the whole world have abandoned him? Yet, although the prince's example was ten thousand times more contagious, all the breaches of faith of which he had been guilty scarcely received the slightest animadversion! But so it was; common interest united even those who were disunited by particular discordances, and the *seeming* harmony of the royal family may undoubtedly be inferred to have arisen from their equal interest in the success of the piece. Their private differences were apparently lost in the immensity of the SECRETS by which the state chain was rivetted, as if it were by adamant.

We must not suppose his majesty was all this time ignorant of the situation of his nephew, the only child of his brother Edward; so far from that being the case, he had caused him to be brought up privately, and was regular in the discharge of the yearly expenses incurred on his account at Eton. The queen presumed that her children were safely seated, so long as the king's *first* marriage should be concealed, and therefore did not bestow many thoughts upon the happiness or misery, fortune or misfortune, life or death, of this MUCH-INJURED YOUTH! Does not nature revolt at this barbarity, this secret unfeeling conduct of the queen? What mother could know a similar case, and not afford all the generous tenderness of sympathy to mitigate the losses this *orphan* had sustained, not only of fortune, but of the fostering care of both his parents?

The complicated wickedness of the court seemed now nearly approaching its climax. Deception had been added to deception, until, to complete the delusion, another victim must necessarily be added, in the person of the Princess Caroline of Brunswick!

After conferences with Mrs. Fitzherbert, the queen, and a few others, closely interested in the affair, had taken place, the prince acquainted his father with his submission to the royal will, and requested to know whom his majesty would recommend for his bride. The king suggested his niece, the daughter of his sister, the Duchess of Brunswick, for whose acceptance he urged the prince to send his miniature, and other formalities, usual on such occasions. *The prince, with apparent vivacity, acquiesced*; but his majesty thought that his son's language wanted sincerity.

The evening was spent in revelry and debauchery by the prince and his companions, and his royal highness swore "I will marry the Princess of Brunswick, which," said he, "will be no marriage at all, and desert her, of which I will give her timely notice." The miniature was painted *flatteringly*, and the following letter from the prince accompanied it to his intended wife:

Copy of a letter written to the Princess Caroline of Brunswick, by
George Prince of Wales.

1794.

"Madam,

"The king my father, whom I highly respect and esteem, has just announced to me that your hand is destined for me. I am obliged, by the imperious force of circumstances to own, that this intelligence has thrown me into despair, and my candour does not allow me to conceal my sentiments from you. I hope that when you are acquainted with them, you will aid me in breaking the ties which would unite us only to render us unhappy; and which will be in your power to oppose, since *I* am unable to do so. You, Madam, are adored by your parents; I am aware that they have allowed you the liberty of refusing all the princes who have been proposed to you in marriage; refuse *me* also, I conjure you in the name of pity, to which I know you are no stranger. You do not *know* me, Madam; you therefore can have no cause to lament my loss. Learn, then, the *secret* and *unhappy* situation of the prince whom they wish you to espouse. I cannot love you; I cannot make you happy; my heart has long ceased to be free. She who possesses it is the only woman to whom I could unite myself agreeably to my inclinations. *You* would find in me a husband who places all his affections upon another. If this *secret*, which I name to you in *confidence*, does not cause you to reject me; if ambition, or any other motive of which I am ignorant, cause you to condescend to the arrangements of my family, learn that, as soon as you shall have given an heir to the throne, *I will abandon you*, never to meet you more in public. I will then attach myself to that lady whom I love, and whom I will not leave. Such is, Madam, my last and irrevocable resolution; if you are the victim of it, you will be a *willing victim*, and you cannot accuse me of having deceived you.

"I am, Madam,

"With great truth,

"Your's sincerely,

"George P."

After reading this very curious epistle, the reader may presume that the princess was *indiscreet* in her acceptance of the hand of a prince who so *boldly* professed himself averse to the union; but the following letters of George the Third to herself and her mother, (the king's sister) which accompanied the one of the prince, will afford some explanation of her conduct:

Copy of a Letter to Caroline, Princess of Brunswick,
from her uncle, George the Third.

1794.

"My dearest Niece Caroline,

"It has afforded me very much pleasure to hear, by the means of my son Frederick of York, that you merit my very best regard. I have no doubt you have frequently heard of my very great and affectionate regard for your dear mother, my sister; and I assure you I love her daughter for her sake. I am well persuaded that my dear niece will not refuse the pressing request of myself and her mother with respect to an alliance with my son George, Prince of Wales, which I earnestly desire may be arranged to take place as speedily as possible. I promise, most solemnly promise, that I will be your friend and father upon every occasion, and I entreat you to comply with this ardent desire of my heart, that my agitated mind may once more be composed.

"I have explained to my sister the probable difficulties which my son George may mention; but they must not have any weight in your mind and conclusions. I beg you not to refuse this pressing petition of your most

"Sincere and affectionate

"Uncle,

"George R."

"P. S. Do not delay a reply an hour longer than can be avoided."

"*To Caroline, Princess of Brunswick,*"&c. &c. &c.

Copy of a Letter to the Duchess of Brunswick, from
her Brother, George the Third.

"My Dear Sister,

"I have endeavoured to excite and promote in the mind of my son George a desire to espouse my dear niece Caroline. *This*, I am aware, he will only consent to as a prudent step, by which his debts may be paid. I will trust to your influence with Caroline that she may not be offended with any thing he pleases to say. He may please to plead that he is already married!—and I fear he will resort to any measures rather than an honorable marriage. But as, in my former letters, I have explained my wishes upon this subject, I therefore need not now repeat them. Tell my dear niece she must never expect to find a mother or friend in the queen; but *I will be her friend to my latest breath.* Give me your support, my sister, and prevail upon my niece Caroline at all hazards.

"Your's affectionately,

"George R."

A courier was despatched with these preliminaries of a royal marriage, and the prince again sank into the depths of vice. The queen saw her path was rather difficult, and feared for the consequences; but she resolved to exert every thought to devise the surest plan for future safety. Her majesty did not assist the prince to any extent, because her purse was of the greatest utility to her personal safety, and therefore *promises* were chiefly given to the clamorous and ruined creditors, that, as soon as the prince was MARRIED, all debts would be discharged! The reasons which prompted the parsimony of the queen were obvious to those who knew her plans, though not to the public. She was aware of the slight tenure she held, and the illegality of her marriage; the unaccounted-for death of the king's eldest brother; the uncertainty of the fate of his issue; fears for his future public appeals, and her knowledge of the validity of his claims! Beside all this, the relatives of the legally-married wife of the Duke (Edward) were of more illustrious descent than even the queen herself; and from them she stood in doubt, lest the untimely death of this lady and her husband, the unfortunate Duke of York, as well as the privacy of their offspring, should be brought forward in a public manner, or in any way which might reflect dishonour upon the influence of the crown!

How much has guilt to fear from exposure by TRUTH! *Secrecy* was the ministerial watch-word then in vogue, and though fallacious and destructive, as experience has demonstrated the principle to be, yet the nation was cajoled by its influence, and even induced indirectly to sanction measures the most desperate and ruinous that imagination can depict!

The hireling part of the press, notwithstanding, strove to eternize this awful and barbarous system, and thus assisted the minister to cherish the growth of Ignorance. Indeed, it is an undeniable fact, that the corruption of government pervaded every branch of Mr. Pitt's administration; but surely this minister must have been sometimes afraid that the people would discover the frauds and impositions practised upon them, and demand satisfaction. Mr. Pitt, indeed, was an *apostate*, who, at the beginning of his career, stood forth as the CHAMPION OF THE PEOPLE'S RIGHTS; but no sooner had he gained possession of power, than he at once threw off the mask, deserted his benefactors, who had trusted and exalted him, maintained, with all his might, the utmost stretch of the royal prerogative, owned himself the unblushing advocate of influence and corruption, and the decided enemy of the human race! When we reflect on the obduracy, perfidy, and ingratitude of "this pilot that *gathered* the storm," in whose breast neither shame nor pity seldom found a residence, but as if dead to every noble passion of the soul, he first exhausted the resources of the nation by his imposition of taxes, and then enslaved it by his politics; when we reflect, we say, on the conduct of this man, Sejanus and Rufinus, profligate and cruel as they were, appear angels of light, and we cannot help feeling disgusted with the age that tolerated such a minister! Secure in his parliamentary majorities and the favours of his queen, he imagined the people at large mere nonentities, and set them at defiance, while he must have laughed at their tameness and stupidity! Did he not warmly commend the sentences of proscription, imprisonment, and transportation, passed against his countrymen solely for attempting to procure a reform of grievances, by the very same means which he had himself previously employed? Did he not, when every really-loyal subject in the realm was deploring the disgraces and defeats of the British arms, insult the people with affected serious congratulations on the successes that had been obtained by the allied powers, and the happy change that had taken place in their favour? Yes, reader, these acts may be taken as specimens of the policy of the "heaven-born minister, that weathered the storm," as a certain chancellor once imprudently designated Mr. Pitt.

The courier, bearing the despatches to the Princess of Brunswick, arrived at the court of her father in October, where he delivered his packet, and was entertained with generous and courteous attention. The duke and duchess retired to peruse its contents, which they read with agitation; and Hope and Fear strove tumultuously to gain an ascendency. The king's letter was considered, in a certain degree, explanatory of the follies of the prince, though it did not name any vices; and as it also expressed a *confident opinion*, that, united to a person of amiability and worth, like the princess, all good would ensue, the parents of the princess were inclined to hope for a favourable result from the alliance. The good opinion of the king, their brother, was an extra inducement to the fond and indulgent parents of Caroline to plead in behalf of her acceptance of this offer; and all must admit their conduct to be natural and affectionate.

The letter of the prince was soon after delivered by the duke to his daughter, accompanied by the remark, "I hope my dear Caroline will one day be the happy queen of a free and happy nation. Retire, my child, and, after thinking seriously, decide prudently." The princess retired, and read the strange epistle written by the prince. She knew not, for some considerable time, what to think, or how to decide. At length, after a few hours of rest and enjoyment, the courier departed. He arrived safely at St. James', and delivered the following reply to the Prince of Wales:

Copy of the Reply to George, Prince of Wales, from
Caroline, Princess of Brunswick.

"My Lord and Cousin,

"I cannot express to your royal highness the feelings of surprise which your letter has afforded me, neither can I rely *entirely* upon what it contains; because the accompanying letter of the good king, your father, is so very opposite to its meaning. I thought that the ties of relationship which exist between us would have obliged your royal highness to treat with delicacy and honor the princess whom your king destines for you. For my own part, my lord, I know my duty, and I have not the power or the wish to break the laws which are wished to be imposed upon me. I, therefore, have decided upon obeying the wishes of those who have the right to dispose of my person. I submit, at the same time, to the consequences with which your highness threatens me. But, if you could read *that heart* to which you impart such anguish, you would perhaps have feelings of remorse from this barbarous treatment, in which your royal highness appears to boast. I am now resolved to await from *time* and our *union* the just regard I will endeavour to merit; and I trust that your regret for what you have written will, in some measure, avenge the wrongs you have so wantonly committed. Believe me, my lord, that I shall not cease to offer my prayers for the happiness of your royal highness; *mine* will be perfect if I can contribute to your's.

"I am, for life, your most devoted Cousin,

"Caroline Amelia of Brunswick."

We have given this and the preceding letters solely with a view of forwarding the cause of truth, and shall leave our readers to draw their own inferences as to the propriety or impropriety of the conduct of the parties concerned.

Early in the ensuing year,

1795,

preparations were made, upon a moderate scale, to receive the Princess of Brunswick as the intended wife of the heir-apparent.

The prince was still as *dissolute* as ever, and associated with the very dregs of society, of both sexes. Yet this same personage was about to be allied, according to the outward usages of the church, to a princess of the most opposite principles and sentiments! Many times has he become the *father* of innocent victims, who were doomed to perish in a workhouse, or be consigned to a premature grave! How improbable then was it, that his heart would ever feel affection for the issue of an honourable connexion,—if it may be so called in *this* case,—more particularly when that was the last resource to extricate him from debt and disgrace! Well, indeed, might his companions say, "the princess may hear, in the joyful peal, (after her vows) the surer knell of her happiness." Too well the result proved the truth of their prophetic announcement!

Previous to the arrival of Caroline, it was arranged by the queen that persons of distinction, upon whom her majesty could depend in this instance, should attend her highness, and a selection was made accordingly. The notorious Lady Jersey was one; of her character and intriguing disposition, we need not say more than announce the fact, that her favours had been at the command of the prince for a considerable time. Her disposition was artful and cruel; indeed, unless such qualities had been invested in her ladyship, the queen would not have given her orders in a manner so undisguised and bold. Cruelty and Vice are always inseparable companions.

At length, the princess arrived on these (to her) inhospitable shores. On the 8th of April, the formality of a marriage ceremony took place, at the palace of St. James. The king was particularly attentive to the princess; but not so the queen, who manifested an unbending haughtiness, and sometimes lost sight of etiquette so far, that sarcasm was too evidently visible. The princesses were in too much fear of their mother to bestow any particular attentions on the Princess of Wales, except one of them, who, however, dare not publicly avow her sentiments.

On retiring for the night to Carlton House, the princess was attended only by those invidious characters who had

Lady Caroline Brunswick arrives in Britain, as depicted in *Cassell's History of England*.

deliberately planned her ruin. Several historians have recorded, that, by some inaccuracy or defect in demeanour, the prince received an unexpected impression unfavourable to her royal highness; but such *was not the case*. It is true, that the conduct of the prince was any thing but gentlemanly; though of this little notice was taken. Her royal highness resolved to forbear from any unpleasant complainings, as she was now separated from her much-beloved home and friends. She plainly saw the disadvantage of her change; and, in the disappointment of her heart, frequently deplored her cruel destiny. Many times has she been obliged to witness the various favourites of the prince receiving those attentions and enjoying those smiles which ought to have been hers only.

In a conversation with the prince, shortly after their nuptials, (if such an appellation may be used) her royal highness said, "that, after the candour with which I have explained myself, I certainly feel entitled to the respectful attentions of your highness, and I cannot endure the insults I am continually receiving from your mistresses and coarse associates." This gentle remonstrance was repeated by this "all-accomplished gentleman" when he next met his half-drunken companions, and their infamy was heightened by maliciously abusing this much-injured lady.

The prince's yearly income was augmented at his marriage with his cousin to one hundred and twenty-five thousand pounds, besides having all his debts discharged.

The princess now seldom saw her husband. His nights were spent in debauchery, and he was frequently carried to bed, totally unconscious of all around him. Gaming supplied his leisure hours, and scenes of immorality were the common routine of each succeeding day. Such were the deportment and character of the man, or *monster*, who was to be invested with power over millions of brave, generous, and industrious people! It was impossible for such an one to have retained in his confidence a single upright and conscientious person. The soul sickens at the retrospect; but we must pursue the revolting subject.

The king was, at this time, the only friend in whom the Princess of Wales could repose any confidence, and to him she unburdened herself unreservedly. His majesty was much incensed at the indignation heaped upon the daughter of his sister, and, but for the apparent situation of his niece, he would have recommended severer measures than he then thought prudent.

In opposition to all remonstrance and advice, the prince gradually sunk deeper into the vortex of sensuality, and very frequently expressed himself in high hopes that the princess would soon "BE GOT RID OF." He still remained ignorant of the confidence the princess had reposed in her uncle; and well was it for her he was ignorant of it, as his passion was extreme, and rage might have gained such a pre-eminence as to have induced him to add *another FOUL DEED to his number*.

This fatal year, more than twenty-nine millions were required, eighteen of which were raised by loans! Here may be observed how progressively the "national debt" was incurred, partly for the immoderate extravagance of those who ought to have acted as models for imitation at home, and partly by unjust and destructive wars abroad! until Englishmen became any thing and every thing but a free people. The discontents of the tax-payers were loud and deep; but the ministers heeded them not!

On the 7th of January,

1796,

the Princess of Wales was safely delivered of a daughter, whose birth, in some measure, assuaged the miseries of her forlorn condition. The Duke of Clarence might have very frequently repeated his expressions, delivered in the House of Lords in the preceding June, when he said, "Unless suitable provisions were made for the prince, the Princess of Wales, A LOVELY AND AMIABLE WOMAN, must feel herself torn from her family, (although her mother was the king's sister) removed from all her early connexions," &c. Ah! William Henry, were you prepared to prove this to be a speech in favour of your cousin and sister-in-law? Was it not *only* for the aggrandizement of your spendthrift brother?

To oblige her majesty, the young princess was named Charlotte. But what a different character did the younger Charlotte prove from the elder! Oh! that so sweet a disposition and so noble a mind should have been crushed in the bud, and that, too, by one nearly allied to her by the ties of nature!

Those more immediately about the person of the Princess of Wales were best capable to form an opinion of her maternal tenderness, and of the prince's negligence. The proofs of affectionate solicitude on the part of the mother, contrasted with the indifference of the father, deserve public explanation. The first time the prince saw his child, his countenance was not in the least illuminated by any ray of pleasure, as he contented himself by merely observing, "It is a fine girl." The princess afterwards acknowledged her disappointment, as she had hoped his heart was not entirely debased, or his sense of virtue altogether lost; but this fond, this very natural, hope was doomed to disappointment, and while this desolate lady was nursing her tenderly-beloved child, the prince was walking and riding out, openly and shamelessly, with Mrs. Fitzherbert and Lady Jersey! Would not the poor cottager have felt abashed to hear of his fellow-labourer's similar conduct, even in the most humble station of life, who must, of necessity, be devoid of ten thousand advantages this personage had derived from birth and education? Yes, doubtless; and he who could so act deserved no other appellation than that of a VOLUPTUOUS BRUTE.

It was much to be regretted at this time, that all the very heavy taxation and increase of debt were said to be in consequence of the "king's great predilection for the lavish expenditures of the royal family, and his anxious determination to continue the disastrous war." Such were not his majesty's desires, but exactly the reverse; though, unfortunately, his opinions were always overruled by the queen.

A formal separation took place this year between the Prince and Princess of Wales, and certainly her royal highness deserved much more general sympathy than she then experienced. The nobility appeared uncertain which side to espouse, and therefore, for want of *principle* to do that which their consciences said was right, they fell imperceptibly into error; besides which, it was indispensably necessary, that those who wished to stand well with the queen and prince must withdraw from all intimacy with the Princess of Wales!

The immense amount for the supply this year was above THIRTY-EIGHT MILLIONS!—about twenty of which were raised by loans!

In

1797,

the heavy burdens imposed on the people to supply the insatiate thirst for war, and keep a gorgeous appearance at court, reduced the middle classes of people to want and distraction. While the prince and his fawning courtiers were revelling in every obscenity, and glutting themselves with the prospect which still continued, that to-morrow would be more abundant, thousands,—nay, millions,—in England and Ireland were perishing for want of bread! During this unexampled period of sorrow, the conduct of the ministry proved them to be perfectly indifferent to the distresses of the people. Splendid entertainments, at an immense expense, were frequently given, and the lofty halls of palaces rang with the loud shouts of conviviality and profanity! Such recitals may, to some persons, appear incredible, or too highly coloured; but *we* well know they did occur, though we do not wish to shock the feelings of our readers by entering into the minutiæ of the infamous conduct practised by the Prince of Wales and his courtiers. Well might the prince, in his memorable letter to the princess in the preceding year, say, "Our inclinations are not suited to each other." He was correct; they were not suited; neither did the Princess Caroline ever desire they should be, because General Lee could testify that the prince had *more propensities than propriety suggested*!

In this most pressing and trying case, when the mind of the Princess of Wales was wrought up to the greatest point of agony, she resolved upon an interview with the queen, when her royal highness told her, that Carlton House could no longer be inhabited by her, as the infamous scenes she was too often obliged to witness were of a description so notoriously abominable, that common decency was grossly outraged! Her majesty supported the right of the prince to choose his own associates, and at the same time stated, as her opinion, that it was very disagreeable to the prince to have her in town at all, and it was proper the princess should remove to some distance agreeable to herself, where the prince might not be under the necessity of meeting her, when he had occasion to spend any time at the palace.

It will readily be presumed, the princess left the presence of the haughty queen with a heart full of disappointment and chagrin. Her royal highness found herself surrounded by persons on whose confidence she could not depend; because everyone appeared in awe of the queen. She was also neglected and insulted by the prince, who ought to have been the first to protect her; but the smile of her infant still cheered her gloomy moments.

This was the most disastrous period of the war: the Bank of England stopped payment; mutinies broke out in the army and navy, which were attended by much bloodshed; Ireland was on the verge of rebellion; and the sum required for the year's service amounted to the abominable and increased sum of FORTY-TWO MILLIONS OF MONEY, of which thirty-four millions were raised by loans, and three millions by Exchequer Bills. The premier also proposed to extort seven millions from the people by a new impost, under the name of "the triple assessment!"

The year

1798

presented a continuation of grievances amongst most classes in humble life. Revelry and uproarious riot, however, were ever to be found in the residences of the royal, yet unnatural, husband of the Princess of Wales; and each succeeding year seemed but to *improve* him in all sorts of infamous engagements. He had at his command some of the most desperate and inhuman characters by which society was ever debased. One in particular, M'Mahon, who would at any time seduce a female from her home, under some specious pretence, in order to take her as a prize to his master, whose favour thereby might be secured!

The intrigues of the Duke of York were also of a most abandoned character; and the other brothers *merit* some notice in the "Annals of Infamy!" During Frederick's residence in Germany, he contracted habits and indulged in excesses abhorrent to human nature, and we should be spared much deep humiliation, as Englishmen, if we had not occasion to recur again to these sickening facts; but the recording angel of Truth forbids our silence, and we must not, therefore, disobey her mandate.

1799

will be remembered, and reference made to it, as long as humanity can reflect upon the desolations and calamities occasioned by war. The earth, in many quarters, was covered with "killed and wounded," while the money of the tax-payers paid the *legal assassins*!

In the meantime, the minister at home was racking his brains how new taxes might be levied, to supply the means for the continuation of carnage. Property, liberty,—nay, even life itself, were deemed toys in the hands of Mr. Pitt, whose passions seemed to centre in rapine, enmity, and ambition. His heart was steeled against the cry of the widow and the plaintive sigh of the destitute orphan. The queen's account in the day of retribution must also be rather enormous, for the minister acted in concert with her in this complicated trickery. Mr. Pitt and the queen seemed to think their only part consisted in draining the resources of the people to their last ability, and in refusing all overtures of peace, whatever offers might be made.

This year, France made proposals of peace with these kingdoms, which were *refused*, and war, desolating war, with all its attendant and consequent horrors, still reared its "gory banners" over the principal part of the world!

We will leave the contemplation of this heart-rending subject, and turn to another, scarcely less revolting to humanity,—the conduct of the Prince of Wales,—whose court was generally filled with a host of harlots. His royal highness was anxious to get rid of the princess (his wife) entirely, and most heartily did the queen concur in his wishes. The difficult part of the task was, the consideration and organization of those measures most likely to promote the desired end. The Princess of Wales' letters, addressed to her family in Brunswick, had many times been opened, and, not unfrequently, even *suppressed*! So that her persecutions were now commenced.

The princess was too open and ingenuous in character to obtain the queen's approbation, and therefore, after the several repulses which she had received from her majesty, Caroline was justly incensed at her uncalled-for unprovoked haughtiness, and overbearing manners. The unsuspecting nature of the Princess of Wales, however, prevented her from being aware of the infamous snares laid for her destruction at this period. Her royal highness has many times been heard to say, "Had I been suspicious, pray what should I not have feared? The queen, from the first time I saw her, frowned upon me, and very little I said or did pleased her; so I never thought I was an object of any consequence to her majesty." These were the reasonings of naive, unsophisticated feelings, and well would it have been for the queen if her heart had been equally open, and her language equally candid.

The year

1800

was a continuation of dissension and discord, both at home and abroad. Twice in this year the king's life was attempted; once in Hyde Park, and again, on the same evening, at Drury-lane Theatre; the first being by a ball cartridge, and the latter by a pistol. In the court, the same lavish display as formerly was continued, and the royal means were not curtailed. It was *said*, that the king declined having more than one course served up, but this was merely *nominal*; indeed, if it were as stated, the country did not benefit much by the change, as the allowances to royalty were, in many instances, very much increased, instead of being decreased.

Such was the scarcity of provisions this year, that the generality of the population existed upon a scanty portion of potatoes during the twenty-four hours. Bread was not within the power of the poor to obtain, as the quartern loaf, mixed with all sorts of deleterious ingredients, sold for twenty-one pence!

This year was rendered of immortal memory by the union of Ireland with England, which

The Act of Union between Ireland and Great Britain.

was effected by a profuse distribution of *money* and *titles*. Oh! disgrace to the Irish nation, ye servile few, who could sell your country for selfish ends! To yield up "name and fame," and all that is dear to honesty, for the sake of an "empty sound!"

The amounts required for this and the last year were nearly the same as for 1798.

In the early part of the year

1801,

it was announced that the king had taken a severe cold, while hunting, and, in consequence, was not able to visit the several concerts to which he had previously given the promise of his attendance and patronage; but his indisposition was *mental*, not bodily. His majesty was so exceedingly distressed at the base and unworthy conduct of his son to his niece, the Princess of Wales, that he said frequently, "It is more than a father can bear!" Many times would he order his horse to be brought, and, requesting his attendants not to follow him, pursue his way towards Blackheath, where the princess then resided, sympathizing with her sorrows, and, more especially, in the intended removal of her child; for even at this early period, when the Princess Charlotte was but four years of age, the queen would signify her commands that the child should pass some days with her, either in London or Windsor, whichever happened to be most convenient to her majesty.

Notwithstanding the extreme scarcity of money and the high price of food, the queen and the younger branches of her family continued to give their splendid entertainments, as expense was the last consideration with the royal brood, when it was known the country supplied the means. Oh! John Bull, thy gullibility has, for above half a century, been *more* than proverbial!

On the 29th of October, the king opened the house in person, and announced the conclusion of war. Parliament then adjourned till after the Christmas recess. England now exhibited the effects of an eight years' war; the national debt had been DOUBLED, and internal distress had become general; the poor were in a state bordering on starvation, and commerce had the prospect of every foreign port being shut against it; while the supplies required for the year amounted to nearly FORTY MILLIONS.

The year

1802

was ushered in under the greatest embarrassments. The vitals of the people were nearly destroyed by the enormous taxation they had endured for so many years, and it was doubtless owing to the intolerable load they had sustained, and still expected to have forced upon them, that independent sentiments were proclaimed. They had a right to condemn the usurping power of the queen, for producing all their troubles.

The recess having terminated, the House met. The chancellor came forward to shew that the sovereign's pecuniary affairs were very much in arrear. After introducing his plan of finance, he was obliged to inform the House that certain taxes had been mortgaged by Mr. Pitt, (*who had now resigned*) for which the present minister must provide. To defray this expense, very heavy additional duties were imposed on beer, malt, hops, &c. A considerable addition was also made to the assessed taxes, and upon imports and exports. At this period, the whole of the "funded debt," including the loans of the present year, amounted to *five hundred and forty millions*, and the interest was annually *seventeen millions sterling*!

On the 7th of May, Mr. Nichol moved that an address be presented to his majesty, thanking him for the removal of Mr. Pitt from his councils, when Lord Belgrave rose, and moved an amendment, expressive of the high approbation of that House respecting the character and conduct of the late minister and his colleagues! In the face of all opposition, Lord Belgrave's amendment was carried by more than *four to one*, as also a second motion, by Sir H. Mildmay, "that the *thanks* of the House be given to the Right Hon. Mr. Pitt." This was assurance in perfection! These discussions only seemed to increase Mr. Pitt's popularity, and on the occasion of his next birth-day, Earl Spencer, late first lord of the Admiralty, gave as a toast to the company, "the pilot that weathered the storm," instead of "the pilot who *gathered* the storm!"

In the latter part of this year, much fear was excited, lest hostilities should again arise between France and England, on account of the ascendency of Buonaparte.

At the commencement of the year

1803,

the unhappy king, by the desire of his overbearing wife, directed a message to the House, recommending "the embarrassed state of the Prince of Wales to their attention," and, in consequence, sixty thousand pounds annually were further settled upon his royal highness, to continue for three years and a half. This sum, however, was not half sufficient to meet his lavish engagements; and therefore Mr. Calcraft had the hardihood to move, that "means be granted to enable the prince to resume his state and dignity!" But this inconsistent and insulting motion was "*too bad*," and, in defiance of even the boroughmongers, was negatived.

The supplies voted for the public service this year amounted to above FIFTY-SIX MILLIONS! We really wonder of what materials Englishmen were composed to allow such iniquitous grants.

Ministers again declared war with France, and men and money were in no inconsiderable request. The French Consul possessed himself of Hanover, and threatened an invasion of England, which frightened ministers to put the country in a state of defence. But was not this a political *ruse*?

Mr. Addington was not so popular as his predecessor in the capacity of minister; he had not so much hardihood as Mr. Pitt, and was not calculated to endure the load of obloquy which he received, as he considered himself free from the charge of having destroyed the prospects of his country by the immense debt then contracted; for that was the arrangement of Mr. Pitt. Mr. Addington was merely a *tool* in the hands of others.

Those who knew the intricate and perplexed state of affairs within the court were only able to judge how long Mr. Addington's ministry would continue, and also, WHY it was brought into action. Alas! not merely or intentionally to satisfy the liberal politicians, or to change any part of the long misrule of the former minister. Widely opposite were the motives which proved the main-spring to the meditated result. The queen again intended to press the king for an increase of income, to a serious amount, for her favourite spendthrift, and she asked the minister how it might be best attained. The plan was therefore concerted, and as Pitt dared not so soon again ask for further advances, a new minister *might* be induced to do it, if shielded by the royal message.

Henry Addington, Prime Minister of the United Kingdom between 1801 and 1804. On his elevation to the Peerage he was styled Lord Sidmouth and, between 1812 and 1822, served as Home Secretary.

If such conduct were not juggling and acting with the most abominable treachery and hypocrisy, we must for ever give up our claim to the possession of one iota of common understanding. As we proceed, we will explain to the gentle or indignant reader, whichever he may be, in what way our enormous "national debt," as it is called, was contracted, when we have no doubt that he will be as incensed as ourselves, and will be ready to exclaim, "Was this the policy pursued by that paragon of her sex, Queen Charlotte?—she who was at all times revered for her *piety*, and admired for her inexpressible and *unspotted virtue*!" Yes, reader, the very same; the only difference is, you have formerly beheld her in *borrowed* plumes,—*we* present her in *her own*!

Let us here recur to the consideration of the treatment, exercised against the Princess of Wales by her abominable husband and his vindictive mother. We formerly alluded to some confidential communications made by her to his majesty. The suspicious and mean characters then placed about her person reported to the queen every interview which the king had with his daughter-in-law, and maliciously, represented the imprudence of such an intimacy. From this time, the Prince of Wales *professed* to believe his father was *improperly* interested in the cause of the princess, and spies were placed in various situations, to give notice of all visits the princess received and paid. Notwithstanding, the plotters' most ardent wishes were disappointed, and they could not fix upon any action, which they were able to prove, to affect her honour or virtue. In the meantime, Caroline's only child was removed from her, without the enjoyment of whose endearing society life was a mere blank.

In proportion as the prince was applauded, and the queen supported him, so was the princess abused and insulted. With respect to pecuniary affairs, every honest and upright person saw the strange disproportion in the incomes of the several members of the family; for the princess, who had to keep an entirely distinct and separate establishment at her sole expense, was allowed no more than twenty-two thousand pounds per annum, while the other members, who were chiefly expensive to the king, had their salaries granted without reference to this subject. Yet it was expected that the etiquette of rank should be maintained, and with an equal ostentatious display as if means were proportionately provided to defray such expenses. Although living upon the establishment of the king, the queen's real independent income was fifty-eight thousand pounds a year! Ought we not to ask why the princess was thus neglected and shamefully insulted?—left in debt, and in extreme perplexity of circumstances, for which the family must ever be considered mean and unjust? How was her royal highness to act in such a trying case? If she had retired to *private* life, her enemies would have pronounced her an improper person to retain the high station which she had formerly occupied. If appearances were to be maintained, and royal splendour continued, she must mix with *certain* society, and debt be the inevitable consequence. The princess felt there were points, beyond which a virtuous, insulted female could not shew forbearance; and she, therefore, resolved no longer to endure the galling yoke of oppression, without farther explanation.

We now proceed to the year

1804,

which commenced amidst much political dissension at home, and preparations for increasing desolation abroad.

His majesty's health now became very indifferent, and, in February, an official bulletin announced his malady. It was reported to be a very slight attack; though we are sorry to say it was, to the king, productive of great pain and agitation of mind by the misrule of the queen, and the improprieties of his family! Little did the nation at large imagine that the family of the sovereign (to whose individual income they had so promptly and munificently contributed) were the causes of his acute anxieties! His sons were deeply embarrassed by PLAY, their female connexions chiefly of the most abandoned character, and their engagements in the world, generally speaking, far beyond their powers to discharge. His daughters were also composed of the FRAILTIES of human nature. Born and educated in a court, under the severe tuition of their mother, they believed themselves of superior worth. The pleasures and enjoyments of life were ever waiting for their acquiescence, and their exercise on horseback, attended by *certain* persons, occupying *certain* stations in life, afforded them a variety of opportunities for conversation, in which the *softest subjects* met the ear!

At this period also, the king's already-distracted mind was farther embittered by what he considered the loss of virtue in one of his daughters; and the agony he endured, lest the circumstance should transpire to the public, would defy any language to depict.

After calmness, in some measure, was restored to his majesty's wounded feelings, his health gradually improved, and, on the 29th of March, he was declared to be convalescent.

On the resignation of Mr. Addington, Mr. Pitt again assumed the reins of government, and appointed his *protégé*, Mr. Canning, treasurer of the navy. Why do not the many biographers of this political character explain the reason, if every thing were fair and straightforward, of his quitting office in 1801, because the Catholic question was forbidden to be mentioned, and returning to it in 1804, under an express stipulation that no member of the government should agitate it contrary to the royal inclination? Was the promise that had been given only binding for *three years*? Was Mr. Canning's secession from office a trick? Was his return to it a sacrifice,—a sacrifice of honour and principle,—to the miserable gratification of obtaining *power*? Alas! the public had little to thank Mr. Canning for; but they knew not, at that time, his love of place and pension.

In October, it was said the king and prince were *reconciled*; but the substance of that reconciliation was not made known to the nation. The queen had resolved to oblige her favourite son, and promote his wishes, by finally relieving him from any farther engagements with the princess, his wife; though of the various abominable schemes then in action, the king was kept entirely ignorant.

In this year, the health of Mr. Pitt began to fail; his ardour seemed cooled, and he experienced short intervals of extreme debility and pain.

In the year

1805,

certain existing evils rendered it needful and expedient, in the opinion of the ministry, that the English nation *should fear* an invasion from Buonaparte. We will say WHY they deemed it necessary. Because the burdens of the poor were already immense, and it was requisite to give an *excuse* for stripping thousands of families of their scanty apparel, their few mean and simple articles of furniture, and their humble home, for the purpose of enabling the "hydra-headed monster" of corruption to pursue his unlimited course over this insulted nation! And what could be better to effect this object than alarming the country with the fear of an invasion? The diabolical scheme too fatally succeeded!

In order to strengthen the power of the queen at this period, Mr. Pitt renewed his connexion with Mr. Addington, who was raised to the peerage by the title of *Viscount Sidmouth*, and succeeded the Duke of Portland as president of the council.

The minister, Mr. Pitt, cool as he was on many iniquitous subjects, could not avoid feeling pangs of remorse at the continual impositions he was *compelled* by the queen to make (in various shapes) upon the people. His unbending pride, however, would not permit him to name his uneasiness to her majesty, as he well knew her inflexible temper and disposition would not permit her to receive *any opinion* in preference to her own. He soon resigned his earthly vexation upon this point, as he became so indisposed as not to be able to attend his political affairs, and was obliged to seek for repose in retirement from active life.

At the commencement of the year

1806,

parliament was opened by commission; but the usual address was omitted, on account of the absence of the minister, who, as before stated, was then seriously indisposed.

On the 23rd of January, Mr. Pitt expired, in the forty-seventh year of his age. He was said to have died insolvent. Be this as it may, forty thousand pounds were voted as a plea to discharge his debts, as well as means to defray the expenses of his funeral! Probably this was the best laid-out money of the ministry for some time past. If the occasion had occurred twenty years before, what an immense saving it had produced the country!

The public life of Mr. Pitt will afford no room for praise to the faithful and just historian. When the errors and praises of his biographers shall have lost their force, future generations will behold his character in its native colours. He must then appear either in the light of an ungrateful hypocrite, or submit to the only alternative of being reckoned a man of contracted mind. Even in private life, he was not more amiable nor exemplary. The ministerial system which he had laid down pervaded the internal economy of all his actions. He appeared to imagine true dignity consisted in a coolness and reserve, (probably acquired from his queen) that banished every suitor from his presence; nor did he ever suffer a case of distress, however just or pressing the claims might be, to divert him from the routine of office, or to extort the least relief or comfort from himself. Negligent and careless in his domestic concerns, he never permitted a single ray of generosity to burst forth to animate the general frost of his character. He retained his natural sullenness and reserve; even in the best moments of convivial mirth, he never displayed a flexibility of disposition, or an openness to conviction. Often as he was obliged to submit to the decrees of necessity, whereon he imagined his continuance in office depended, yet he never had the candour to acknowledge the weakness of any measure, originating in himself, that brought on that necessity. But what a departure was this from the principles of his illustrious ancestor, the Earl of Chatham, who would never crouch to the authority of any sovereign or cabinet, when militating against his own more enlightened judgment. He resisted bribery, and generally succeeded in his views, or, if baffled, resigned his office. The son of this nobleman, however, pursued far different maxims, and pertinaciously clung to the douceurs and infamy of office; for *infamous* it most certainly was, to practice measures his own sentiments condemned. Never did man accede to power on more just or noble principles, and never did man forsake those principles with less reserve. He forgot all obligations, and at a happy crisis, when he might have availed himself of the occasion of honorably fulfilling them, in advancing the liberty and happiness of the country, he was eternally launching out into vapid and unmeaning encomiums on the boasted excellencies of the British constitution, instead of adhering to his solemn contract, of exerting all his influence and abilities to reform its blemishes. With all the failings of this minister, his caution and plausibility were admirably calculated to entrap the confidence of the landed and monied interest, and he turned it to the best account, labouring with all his zeal to inculcate a belief of the flourishing state of the national finances, enforcing every circumstance tending to confirm this belief, and concealing every truth that would serve to diminish or destroy it. Will not such a man, then, be regarded by posterity as a time-server and an apostate?

After the death of Mr. Pitt, Mr. Fox joined the ministry; and, at the same time, Lord Sidmouth continued a member of the cabinet! But Mr. Fox did not retain his situation long. His health soon after declined, and he died on the 13th of September following.

Of this great statesman, we may say, "take him for all in all, we ne'er shall look upon his like again." He was an unbending patriot; possessed of great political ability, and loved, as well as advocated, the cause of LIBERTY. Light and shade, however, were mixed in Mr. Fox's picture. He permitted private friendship, in one instance, to over-balance his public duty. We refer to the language used by him in the House of Commons, in April, 1787, which must have been against his conscience. He there *denied* the marriage between the Prince of Wales and Mrs. Fitzherbert, when, in fact, *he assisted at that very marriage*; but, because he had engaged secrecy to the prince, he thought proper to utter a direct falsehood rather than break his promise upon the subject!

Mr. Pitt's death was an unpleasant consequence to the usurping queen, and perhaps impelled the ardour of her determination to get her favourite son's divorce from his injured wife settled as soon as possible. The scheme for this purpose, which seemed most practicable, was the obtaining some document as evidence *against the moral character of the princess.* By the queen's express desire, therefore, Lady Douglas had removed her abode, nearly six years previously, close to Blackheath, and was purposely employed to invent some dishonourable report against the princess.

The Princess of Wales accidentally and innocently (on her part) became acquainted with this lady, and from that period no pains were spared, on the part of Lady Douglas and her husband, to increase that acquaintance, until their diabolical object should be attained. The most assiduous attentions and extravagant pains were used to entrap the generous mind of the princess; but as the object in view proved of a very difficult nature, so did the means for its accomplishment become equally numerous. This intimacy commenced in 1801, and terminated in 1804; and during that period did these base designing slanderers and ungrateful guests, by secret application, obtain an opportunity to vilify, outrage, and insult the princess, in connexion with *nearly* every branch of the royal family, who were too closely united in one general interest not to assist each other.

The only patriotic members, the Dukes of Kent and Sussex, appeared much wrought upon by the specious and abominable fabrication brought forward by these unprincipled, time-serving, and heartless enemies of Caroline. Although their statements and depositions were taken so fully, and examined so closely,— although the prince pursued the subject with such unfeeling barbarity,—yet the princess was acquitted, most honourably acquitted. Indeed, to any rational inquirer, the wickedness of the Douglas statement was, beyond doubt, most palpable. It was full of improbabilities, of contradictions, and absurdities, which well merited punishment. Had a similar insult or a flagrant transgression been offered to the royal family in the person of any *other than the Princess of Wales*, would not the whole royal phalanx, headed by the queen, have arisen in defence of their *illustrious* and *virtuous* house? Nay, would not the insulting falsehoods and infamous assertions have been proved treasonable? Yes, undoubtedly; but, because the injured Princess of Wales was the INTENDED VICTIM OF A CONSPIRACY, although so gloriously acquitted, yet no prosecution of her traducers followed; neither did any branch of the royal family exemplify one pleasurable feeling upon the conclusion of this disgracefully-iniquitous business! Their chagrin was much more evident!

Lord Castlereagh, engraving from Historic Memoires of Ireland (1833).

As if in this year a deluge of sadness and sorrow, in addition to all other trials and injuries, were to fall upon the persecuted Caroline, she had to suffer the heavy and irreparable loss of her father, William, Duke of Brunswick, at the memorable battle of Jena, October 14th, in the seventy-first year of his age.

The character of the venerable Duke of Brunswick is beyond praise; "his NAME shall be his *monument*!" If at any period the Princess of Wales needed the kind and soothing balm of friendship, it was at this trying juncture. Her friends were few in number, and their friendship was of an evanescent description. They sometimes professed their readiness to serve her, and eulogised her greatness of mind and talent; yet, when brought to the point by public opinion and inquiry, they very generally expressed their sentiments *equivocally*, or with some portion of hesitation calculated to injure, rather than benefit, the cause they professed to serve. Mr. Canning and Mr. Whitbread were two of these *particular* kind of friends, as our after history will abundantly testify.

How wretched must have been the Princess Charlotte at this period, who was nearly deprived of all communication with her affectionate mother, and without one friend to whom she could freely speak of her sorrows and anxious wishes!

The year

1807

commenced with selfish men in office, who contrived selfish measures for the continued purposes of corruption.

The king now became very imbecile; and the queen and the Prince of Wales intimidated him from acting honourably towards the Princess of Wales, as he had so committed himself by his fatal act of BIGAMY. As his mind became proportionately depressed by the perplexities of his situation, so did his conduct become more influenced as they desired it; until, at length, he proved a mere automaton, to be moved at their pleasure!

In any case of vital importance to character, delay is dangerous; because it causes suspicion, suspicion begets mistrust, and so on do these injurious sentiments proceed, until, ere the time of trial arrives, the injured party has suffered unjustly in a two-fold way. Thus it was in the case of the unfortunate Caroline. To oblige the queen, his majesty postponed seeing his daughter-in-law as long as it suited the views of the designers against her happiness.

From the active part which Mr. Perceval had taken in defence of the princess, especially in his book, which made much noise in the world at this time, the queen thought it prudent to advise his being accommodated with office. She made her will known to the prince, who was very happy to concur in the suggestion, but only feared an obstacle in Mr. Perceval's *rigid virtue*. This, however, was not insurmountable, and Mr. Perceval was made "Chancellor of the Exchequer;" Mr. Canning, "Secretary for Foreign Affairs;" and Lord Castlereagh, "Secretary for the Department of War and the Colonies." Thus were two of the former advocates of the Princess of Wales enlisted under the banners of her most deadly enemies! As to the *honor* they derived from their base desertion of the cause of innocence, we leave our readers to judge.

The Prince of Wales, at this juncture, made no secret of his diabolical intentions; for we well know that he has frequently raised the goblet to his lips, and drank "TO THE SPEEDY DAMNATION OF THE PRINCESS." It was very perceptible that the royal party were well aware of the injustice practised towards the princess; but, charity being a virtue of little worth in their ideas, they resolved to carry their plans into execution, no matter at what cost.

The least the late *friends* of the princess could do was, to remain *silent*; but human beings can articulate sounds, and be oppositely communicative with their optical faculties. An individual, who accepts *place* amongst those whom he formerly professed to despise, renders himself an object of suspicion, if not of detestation.

For the present, we abstain from further remarks upon these two late principal friends of the persecuted Princess of Wales.

Upon hearing of the Duke of Brunswick's death, the king could do no less than solicit the duchess, his sister, to visit England. As

Joseph Nollekens bust of Spencer Perceval, completed after 1812. Perceval served as Prime Minister between 1809 and 1812, and he has the distinction of being the only British Prime Minister to have been assassinated. (*Licensed under Wikimedia Commons*)

the country around her was in a deplorable state, and feeling desirous to see her daughter, she determined to accept the invitation, and arrived at the house of the Princess of Wales, at Blackheath, on the 7th of July, in one of her royal highness' carriages.

The injured Caroline was so overpowered at this interview as to cause the duchess much serious disquiet; for she plainly saw that her daughter had great cause for sorrow, the particulars of which she was yet ignorant. The princess afterwards appeared soothed; and this short interview, cheered by a fond mother's presence, proved a solace to her lacerated heart.

The king went from Windsor to see his sister, and the queen also from St. James' Palace; the Princess Charlotte, and several other members of the family, paid their respects to the duchess.

Thus, though common or decent attention was refused the daughter, while mourning over her early misfortunes and recent losses, yet, when her mother arrived, some little regard must be paid to *etiquette*, although the daughter *was to receive the visiters*. But so it was. Poor Queen Charlotte, how hard it was for her to vouchsafe or condescend to let fall one smile upon Caroline!

After the opportunity this visit afforded the Princess Charlotte, the mother and daughter were of necessity explicit, and they mourned over the seeming hard destiny each was doomed to experience.

During the remainder of this year, the king became more and more incapacitated for business of any sort; he could not even distinguish any object by either its colour or size, and was led from one place to another as if in the last stage of blindness. The long-continued distractions of his mind, and the anxiety yet remaining, caused his rational moments to be most gloomy. His favourite daughter was incurably diseased with a scrofulous disorder, from which she suffered dreadfully, and nature seemed fast declining. Throughout the whole of his family, the poor monarch had but little gratification, as every individual composing it was separately under her majesty's controul. To have contradicted *her* order or command would have been attended with no very pleasant consequences. Her *look* was sufficient to frighten every one into obedience!

We now enter upon the year

1808,

in which the session of parliament was opened by commission, on the 21st of January, the king's indisposition preventing him from going in person.

At this period, a very strong sensation was excited against the continuance of the pension list. The productive classes ascertained, in a very correct way, how the fruits of their industry were devoured. In consequence of which, they felt themselves imposed upon in the highest degree; but resolved to try rational entreaty and petition ere they resorted to acts of violence. The number of these dissatisfied classes, in every large town, was immensely great, and they only needed *system* to obtain, by their SIMPLE PETITION, what they so much desired; but the authorities knew

A satirical print depicting Mary Ann Clark, the Duke of York's mistress, selling offices of state to various people in order to fund hers and the Duke's lavish lifestyle. After this print was published in 1809 the Duke of York was forced to resign from the army. (*Library of Congress*)

the incapacitated state of the sufferers, in the absence of that *system*, and therefore very ungenerously refused their appeal.

In March, the City of London (John Ansley, mayor) petitioned both Houses for parliamentary reform, and the abolition of sinecure places and pensions; but they received the expense attendant upon their exertions for their reward, and the mortification of the ministers' apathy for their satisfaction. Popular indignation, however, is not so easily allayed; for, though extreme appearances may for a time be concealed, they will eventually break forth with ten-fold force. The public reasoned upon a rational ground, and was fully aware that their strength was spent to support *enemies*. Their resolve to petition for freedom was the dictate of an unerring and fixed principle, ever inherent in the breast of man. The blandishments of folly, and the encouragement given to imposition, have rendered the industrious and honest citizen a prey to the lordlings of arbitrary power; and so long as he can assist to supply means whereby their cravings may be satisfied, so long do they seem to suppose he lives to a sufficient purpose. Under these circumstances, the oppressed classes were perfectly justified in making a stand against farther innovation; and also in resisting the intolerable injustice in force against them. Still the administration continued inexorable to the pressing prayers and miserable condition of the people. The political disease, however, was rapidly advancing to a crisis.

Similar distress and dissatisfaction existed at the commencement of the year

1809,

provisions were dear, and labour scarce; yet an additional sum was required for the state, to uphold its *secret* machinations, and pervert the ends of justice.

It will be remembered that, in this year, the celebrated Mrs. Mary Ann Clark, formerly a mistress of the Duke of York, appeared at the bar of the House of Commons, as evidence against him. Mr. Wardle, with an intrepidity worthy of the cause in which he was engaged, took upon himself the awful responsibility of preferring those serious charges against the duke, which it were unnecessary for us here to repeat. The public officers of the king volunteered their services to rescue his royal highness from public odium by denominating the proceeding as a *conspiracy*! In spite, however, of every artifice which a knowledge of the law enables bad men to practice to defeat the ends of justice, there were exposed to public view scenes of the grossest corruption, of the most abandoned profligacy, of the most degrading meanness, and of the most consummate hypocrisy. The contagion had reached every department of the state; nor was the church exempted from its baneful influence. It was fully proved that, not only subordinate situations, but even deaneries and bishoprics (which had been supposed to be the rewards of piety and learning) were applied for to his royal highness, through the intervention of his mistress! A great majority of the boroughmongers, of course, acquitted the duke from these charges, and talked of voting an address of thanks to him for the manner in which he discharged his official duties. Fortunately, however, the mode of investigation adopted enabled every man in the kingdom to judge for himself. Englishmen, for once, spoke out, and the duke was compelled to resign. This step on the part of the *illustrious* debauchee prevented further exposure, and saved him from the severe and heavy weight of being *voted out of office*, and degraded! Behold, then, reader, what the principles of Pitt achieved! That minister always persuaded the male branches of the family, that the queen's protection (through the medium of the minister) would prove at all times a sufficient retreat and asylum, in case of complaint or *refractory sensation* of the people at their frequent derelictions from duty and honor.

The fluctuations of the public funds was an opportune chance for speculation, and the queen's love of money induced her to turn her sources of information to the best account; she therefore acted in concert with her broker, and immediately, upon any rise taking place, she "sold out," and when gloom overspread the market, she "bought in." By this speculation alone, the Duke of Kent acknowledged that his mother realized *four hundred thousand pounds*! At the same period, her majesty had another excellent speculation in hand; namely, the profits arising from the sale of cadetships for the East Indies. Dr. Randolph and Lady Jersey were the chief managers of these affairs, though her majesty received the largest portion of the spoil. Dr. Randolph himself acknowledged, that the queen had realized *seventy thousand pounds* upon this traffic alone! In one transaction with a candidate for a cadetship, an enormous premium was required, and the applicant was very much incensed, as it appeared to him to be nothing less than a bold imposition. He expostulated; but Dr. Randolph made short of the affair by refusing any further communication upon the subject. For once, Dr. Randolph forgot his own interest, as also the *public character* and *safety* of his royal mistress. The gentleman, shortly afterwards, was visiting a friend in Paris, when the conversation turned upon the English constitution, and the immense revenues of the kingdom. The friend spoke in raptures upon the liberal feelings and generous provisions exercised and provided towards, and for all, aspirants to honor. At length, the visiter could no longer conceal his mortification and chagrin, and he candidly explained every particular of his correspondence with Dr. Randolph, in which her majesty's name was as freely introduced as the doctor's. The astonishment and surprise of his friend were great indeed, and he recommended him *to publish the whole affair* in France, and circulate it through the surrounding kingdoms. A printer was sought for, who required a certain time to determine the risk he should run in the undertaking; this was accordingly granted, and the parties separated. As soon as the person intended to be employed found the consequence attached to it, he communicated the important information to a solicitor, of some eminence, in London, to whom he had formerly been known. The affair was subsequently made known to the queen's youngest son, and by him the queen was fully acquainted with the probability of public exposure. An overwhelming infamy she well knew would be inseparably attached to it. Her majesty had been accustomed to deception, but hitherto she had not feared detection; but the moment of her fancied security was the moment most likely to prove fatal to her existence as a queen.

The Duke of Kent was unremitting in his exertions to obtain a settlement of this nefarious affair, and *twenty thousand pounds* were actually paid for the *correspondence*, and *two thousand pounds* given by the queen (through the medium of the duke) to the person who effected the settlement of the business, under the provision "that that business might never transpire to the public." His royal highness was too well aware of the general disposition of the queen, and her avaricious character, not to *affect satisfaction* at the high price her majesty paid for silencing this unpleasant affair. It may be inferred, that if the queen had committed herself by such flagrant acts of injustice as these, there might be many more dishonourable transactions of a minor description, occurring nearly at the same period. Yes, the inference is correct, for her majesty was truly born and bred a German!

We will relate another instance of Queen Charlotte's ungenerous conduct. She had the superintendence of the education of her daughters, as far as related to the choice of their preceptors. Her majesty appointed a very clever and scientific gentleman, who resided in London, to teach herself and the six princesses—geography, astronomy, arithmetic, and the nature of the *funds*. Besides which, he was asked, as a *favour*, to settle the very deranged accounts of the princesses. This accomplished and worthy gentleman also held of Princess Elizabeth a bond for ten thousand pounds. After dancing attendance upon these *illustrious* individuals for twenty-six years, without receiving any remuneration, though he had frequently pressed for payment of his long-standing account, he again solicited a settlement with the queen; but, as he only received abuse of an unmeasured description for his pains, he determined to maintain himself and his large family out of the profits of his private scholars, leaving the royal debt as a provision for his children after him. His expenses were considerable in attending the royal family, as he was always obliged to go full dressed in a bag and silk stockings, to hire carriages to go down to Windsor, to live at an inn, and to sleep there, if they chose to take lessons the two following days, by which he was also often obliged to neglect and disoblige his private scholars. For all this attendance, he received *no remuneration whatever*; and Queen Charlotte had the heart to say, "I think you have had remuneration sufficient by your youngest son receiving a pension of eighty pounds a year for teaching the younger princesses only writing!" The preceptor, however, still claimed *his remuneration*, and was, at last, referred to the lawyers, who required him to produce proofs of every lesson he gave, the day and the hour, for twenty-six years! To their astonishment, he produced his diary, and such clear accounts, that there was no contradicting them. But as lawyers are never at a loss how to gain their ends, they next required him to declare, upon oath, the name of each particular servant that had let him in during the twenty-six years! This he could not do; and her majesty, not to be behind the lawyers, advised they should plead the statute of limitation! The lawyers, however, persuaded *her most excellent majesty* that such a proceeding would be against her interest. After being harassed about in this manner for a considerable time, the old, care-worn, broken-hearted master was most injuriously persuaded to suffer the business to be decided by *one* arbitrator only, instead of trusting to the laws of his country. The poor old gentleman never held up his head afterwards, but always used to say he should leave all his family beggars, which, alas! proved too true. He shortly after died at his house in Manchester-street. He was a very worthy and an exceedingly clever man. On one occasion, Mr. Pitt sent for him to solve some difficulty in the finances of the country, for which none of the ministers could account. He instantly set them all right by showing that such an error was *possible* to occur, though it very seldom did occur.

Besides the claims upon Queen Charlotte, the worthy preceptor had a bill against the Princess Charlotte for eight hundred pounds. On applying to the Prince of Wales for this money, he refused to pay it, and referred him to the king, who was then quite deranged! The Princess of Wales knew all these particulars, and told her daughter, the Princess Charlotte, the desperate state of the poor man's family. Her royal highness spoke to her uncle, the Duke of York, about it, who persuaded her that the venerable master was an *old rogue*, who had robbed the princesses and all the family, and her royal highness chose to believe him. That he was a scientific man, his books and valuable mathematical instruments bore ample testimony. These were sold after his death for eight thousand pounds, which went to discharge his debts.

George Canning, who held various government positions in the early nineteenth century before becoming Prime Minister in 1827, is depicted here in a nineteenth-century engraving based upon a painting by Richard Evans.

Many other instances might be recorded to prove the unfeeling and barbarous behaviour of the queen; but this alone must be sufficient to convince our readers how totally unfit her majesty was to reign over a *free people*.

In the September of this year, Lord Castlereagh sent a challenge to Mr. Canning, which was accepted; but the effects of the duel were not *very serious*, though it subsequently led to the resignation of both. It is hardly worthwhile, perhaps, to recur to this now-forgotten, and always, as far as the public were concerned, insignificant business. Lord Castlereagh acted as a vain and high-spirited man, who fancied his confidence betrayed, his abilities called in question, and, like an Irishman, saw but a short vista between an offence and a duel. Mr. Canning, equally high-spirited, felt that he had got into a disagreeable business, and that the fairest escape from it would be to fight his way out. Lord Castlereagh's conduct, when we think of a sober and wise statesman, is ridiculous. Mr. Canning's, when we picture to ourselves a high-minded and frank-hearted gentleman, in spite of the *plausibility* of explanations, is displeasing.

The wretched policy of this year required *fifty-four millions of money* to support it.

1810

was ushered in under distressing and unsatisfactory circumstances. The royal family were divided amongst themselves, and every branch seemed to have a separate interest. Under these circumstances, it was not a matter of surprise that *truth* was now and then elicited; for it is a veritable saying, that "when rogues fall out, honest men are gainers."

The king was at this time labouring under a severe attack of mental aberration: the situation of the country, his children, and his own peculiar sorrows, made impressions on his mind of the most grievous description.

In a former work of ours, called "The Authentic Records of the Court of England," we gave an account of the extraordinary and mysterious murder of one Sellis, a servant of the Duke of Cumberland, which occurred this year. In that account, we did what we conceived to be our duty as historians,—we spoke the TRUTH! The truth, however, it appears, is not always to be spoken; for his royal highness instantly commenced a *persecution* against us for a "malicious libel." We say *persecution*, because almost every person is aware, that filing a criminal information against an individual can be done only with a view of *preventing the exposure of truth*, which, though such procedure be according to English law, cannot be reconciled with the original intention of law, namely—to do *justice* both to the libelled and the libeller! In America, no such monstrosities disgrace the statute-book; for there, if any person be accused of *scandalum magnatum*, and can prove the truth of what he has stated, he is honorably acquitted. Yet as we are not in America, but in England,—the boasted *land of liberty*,—we must, forsooth, be seized as *criminals*, merely because we wish to institute an inquiry into the circumstances of the murder of an individual, whose assassin, or assassins, have hitherto escaped the slippery hands of justice! We are no cowards in regimentals, nor did we make our statement with a view of slandering the royal pensioner. We would have willingly contended with his royal highness in a court of law, if he had had the courage to have met us on *fair grounds*. At the time we write this, we know not what the judgment of Lord Tenterden,—we beg his lordship's pardon, we should have said *the court*,—may be; but, whatever the punishment awarded, we hope to meet it with that fortitude which never fails to uphold a man "conscious of doing no wrong!" If the Duke of Cumberland, however, imagines he can *intimidate* us from speaking the *truth* OUT OF COURT, he has mistaken us. We are not, as we said in our first work, to be prevented from doing whatever we conceive to be our duty. Though it may not be in our power to prove *who* was the murderer, the very suspicious circumstances attending the death of poor Sellis fully warrant renewed inquiry.

Passing over the various reports in circulation at the time of the murder, we proceed to notice the very contradictory evidence brought forward at the inquest. That we may not be accused of partiality, we take the report of this *judicial* proceeding from that Tory organ, "The Morning Post," which, it will be observed, deals out its abuse with no unsparing hand on the poor murdered man, whom it calls by the *charitable* appellation of *villain*, and sundry other hard names, which had better suited the well-known characters of other persons, who acted a prominent part in this foul business. After a few unmeaning preliminaries had been performed,

"Mr. Adams addressed the jury, and informed them of the violent attack that had been made upon the Duke of Cumberland; and that there was very *little doubt but it was done by the deceased*. He stated, the circumstances had been fully investigated by the *privy council* on Thursday, and that the depositions of the numerous witnesses *had been taken before Mr. Justice Read*, which he should read to them; after which the witnesses would be called before them, and the depositions would also be read to them, when they would have an opportunity of altering or enlarging, and the jury could put any question to them they thought fit."

In this address, some of the privileges of royalty are explained. Because the murder had been committed in a palace, the privy council must examine the witnesses *before* they may be allowed to meet the jury, and their depositions taken by a justice, under the influence of the suspected party. The coroner may then tell the jury that there was very *little doubt* of the deceased person having attempted his master's life, and afterwards cutting his own throat to avoid detection. Merciful heaven! can this be called an impartial administration of justice? Are such *careful* proceedings ever adopted in the case of a poor man? To be sure, the jury were told they might *ask any question they thought fit*; but is it to be supposed that, after the INQUIRIES they had undergone, the witnesses would let slip any thing likely to criminate themselves or their royal master?

"The first affidavit that was read was that of his royal highness the Duke of Cumberland, which stated, that about half-past two o'clock on Thursday morning he received two violent blows and cuts on his head; the first impression upon his mind was, that *a bat had got into the room, and was beating about his head*; but he was soon convinced to the contrary by receiving a third blow. He then jumped out of bed, when he received several more blows; from the *glimmering light afforded from a dull lamp in the fire-place, and the motion of the instrument that inflicted the wounds, they appeared like flashes of lightning before his eyes. He made for a door near the head of his bed*, leading to a small room, to which the assassin followed him, and cut him *across his thighs*. His royal highness not being able to find his alarm-bell, which there is no doubt the *villain* had concealed, called with a loud voice for Neale (his valet in waiting) several times, who came to his assistance; and *Neale*, together with his royal highness, alarmed the house."

The blows of the assassin must have indeed been *slight* to resemble "a bat beating about the head of his royal highness;" but we cannot understand how the *cut of a sword* can bear any *similarity* to the beating of a little animal, like a bat! Poor Sellis, however, was but a *little man*, and his weak arm might be still more enfeebled by the consciousness of his ingratitude in attacking so *kind and liberal a master*! Sellis had been the duke's page, or valet, for more than five years, in daily, nay, almost hourly, personal communication with him; and it must, therefore, appear very strange, if Sellis was really the assassin, that his master did not *recognise him*! If the room was so dark that the duke could not *see the person* attacking him, it is singular that the *assassin could see to strike his royal highness*, as he did by "cutting him across his thighs, after he was out of bed!" As the supposed murderer followed the duke, who thought it best to take to his heels, we think his royal highness should have stated whether he meant his thighs in *front* or *behind*; but, of course, an examination of the *scars* would soon set this matter at rest! They would, no doubt, be found *behind*, as it is *unreasonable* to suppose that, in a *dark room*, the *pursuer* could have cut at the *pursued* in front. The Duke of Cumberland is a field-marshal, and a BRAVER man, IT IS SAID, never entered the FIELD; but *in a dark room*, with a man little more than half his weight, it would have been *cowardly* to *fight*, particularly as his royal highness might, IF HE HAD SO WISHED, have taken the weapon out of Sellis' hand, and broken it about his head. No! no! the Duke of Cumberland knew what was due to his honour better than to take so *mean* an advantage of a *weak* adversary, and therefore *coolly* endeavoured to ring his bell, that a more *suitable* antagonist might be procured in his valet *Neale*!

"Cornelius Neale, sworn.—He said he was valet to the Duke of Cumberland, and that he was in close waiting upon his royal highness on Wednesday night, and slept *in a bed in a room adjoining the duke's bed-room*. A little before three o'clock, he heard the duke calling out, 'Neale, Neale, I am murdered, and the murderer is in my bed-room!' He went immediately to his royal highness, and found him bleeding from his wounds. The duke told him the door the assassin had gone out at; he armed himself with a poker, and asked if he should *pursue* him. The duke replied '*no*,' but to *remain with him*. After moving a few paces, he stepped upon a *sword*; and, *although in the dark*, he was convinced it was *covered with blood*; it proved to be the *duke's own regimental sword. The duke and witness then went to alarm the house, and got a light from the porter.* The duke was *afraid the murderer was still in his bed-room.* His royal highness was obliged to lean upon him from the loss of blood, and he gave directions that no person should be let out of the house. They called up the *witness' wife*, who is the housekeeper, and told *her* to call *Sellis*. He then returned with the duke to his bed-room. At that time the duke was very faint from the great loss of blood. Upon examining the premises they found, in a second adjoining small room, a pair of *slippers with the name of Sellis on them*, and a dark lantern. The key of the closet was in the inside of the lock, and, to his knowledge, the key had not been in that state for *ten years*. He had reason to believe the wounds of the duke had been given by a sword. Sellis took out the duke's regimentals some time since, and put them by again, but left out the *sword upon a sofa for two or three days*. It is the same sword which he trod upon, and it was in a bloody state.

"The foreman of the jury, (Mr. Place, of Charing Cross) asked the witness if he thought the deceased had any reason to be dissatisfied with the duke. He replied, on the contrary, he thought Sellis had more reason to be *satisfied than any other of the servants*; his royal highness had stood godfather for one of his children, the Princess Augusta godmother. The duke had shown him *very particular favour* by giving him apartments for his wife and family, with coals and candles.

"A juryman asked him if he ever heard the deceased complain of the duke. The witness asked if he was obliged to answer that question. The coroner informed him he must. He then stated that about two or three years since the duke advanced their board wages from 10*s*. 6*d*. a week to 14*s*., but at the same time took off 3*s*. 6*d*., allowed for travelling. After this regulation was adopted, a paper was drawn up by the steward for the servants to sign, expressing their satisfaction at the regulation, which the deceased *refused* to sign, and said, 'he'd be d—d if he did, and none but blackguards would sign it.' The steward told him the duke said he must sign it, *or his wife and family must quit the apartments he had given them*, as the rest of the servants had signed it. He had never heard the deceased *complain* since. Within the last year, the *duke and royal family had been extremely kind to him*. He had never given him an *angry word*, although he had often made use of very *bad language to him*; if he did, he never answered him. The deceased was of a very malicious disposition. He would never be *contradicted*, if he began a subject, for which reason he never wished to have any conversation with him. He frequently quarrelled with Mr. Paulet, one of the duke's servants, and fought with the steward at Kew. Lately the deceased had a bad cold, and the duke was so very *kind* towards him in consequence, that he took him *inside the carriage* to Windsor. Sellis dressed the duke on Wednesday night. *He had no doubt but Sellis intended that he should be charged with being the murderer, to get him out of the way*."

This Neale's evidence ought to be received with great caution. He slept in the next room to the duke, and when called upon for his assistance, stated his wish to pursue the murderer with a poker; but was prevented by his master's "fear of being left alone!" In this *courageous* offer of Neale, however, he trampled upon a *sword*, which, although in *total darkness, he was* CONVINCED *was* COVERED WITH BLOOD!! We have no intention to dispute *Neale's knowledge of this*, or that "it was his master's own regimental sword!" There have been so many wonderful people who could see AS WELL IN THE DARK AS IN THE LIGHT, and describe the minutest particulars of an article as well with their EYES SHUT AS OPEN, that we ought not to be surprised at anything! Notwithstanding, many persons WERE SURPRISED at the sagacity of Neale, not only in this, but in many other particulars. If the duke, "covered with gore, accompanied this servant to alarm the house," the traces of blood on the doors, &c., leading to *Sellis' room*, might be very *naturally accounted for*! They, however, thought it better not to call Sellis THEMSELVES, but sent Neale's wife to do it!!! Although the duke pointed out to his *confidential man* the door through which the villain had ESCAPED, his royal highness "felt afraid the murderer was STILL in his bed-room," which we have *no reason to doubt*! "A pair of slippers were left in an adjoining room, with the name of Sellis upon them." That Sellis left them there, however, is rather IMPROBABLE;

because it is natural to suppose he would, if HE had been the murderer, have gone to his master's room WITHOUT SLIPPERS, or shoes of any kind, to make as little noise as possible. This circumstance, we are inclined to think, was a *planned affair*, though badly executed; for we know that these slippers were placed the *wrong way*,—a fact which will be hereafter proved. Through the whole of Neale's evidence, not a word was said to show that Sellis had the *least motive* for murdering either the duke or himself. On the contrary, "Sellis had every thing to expect from his master's living."

In concluding our remarks upon Neale's evidence, we point the attention of our readers to the last sentence: "He had no doubt but Sellis intended that he (Neale) should be charged with being the murderer, to get him out of the way!" Now, as there was not the slightest evidence to bear Neale out in this malicious assertion, we think, FOR HIS OWN SAKE, he had much better have kept the expression to himself. Some of our readers may not be aware of the *cause* Sellis had given this fellow-servant to hate him; but the following letter, addressed to B. C. Stephenson, Esq., written by Sellis a few months before his death, will elucidate this matter a little:

"St. James', July 9th, 1809.

"Sir,—I am extremely anxious to know his royal highness' decision concerning the evidence produced before you against Mr. Neale, and I beg you, Sir, to have the goodness to relieve me from this most disagreeable suspense. If I may, Sir, judge from appearance, either his royal highness is not acquainted with what has been proved, or his royal highness has entirely forgiven him. Should the former be the case, Sir, I hope you will have the goodness to acquaint his royal highness to the full extent of the roguery of this man; and here it may be necessary to say, that the witnesses you have examined are all of them ready to take their oaths in a court of justice, and there to assert what they have already said before you. But, Sir, should his royal highness have forgiven him, then I must be under the most disagreeable necessity to beg his royal highness to have the goodness to dispose of me as his royal highness may think proper, so that I may not have the mortification to live and act in the same room with a man I have *convicted as a rogue, and with whom no human being is able to live on friendly terms.* Had it been his royal highness' pleasure to have had this business in a court of justice, the man would have been *transported at least for seven years*; and what I am going to communicate to you now is, I believe, transportation for life. I have been told, Sir, that Mr. Neale cheats his royal highness in everything he buys; in two different articles I have already ascertained this to be a fact; on the toothpicks he gains fifty per cent., by charging eighteen pence for that for which he only pays one shilling, and on the soap he charges two shillings for that which he pays eighteen pence, and should his royal highness wish me to proceed with these discoveries, it will be found that the *dishonesty of this man has no bounds*! The evidence you have taken, Sir, and what I have communicated to Major Thornton, with which also you must be acquainted, you must be satisfied, that this man is as *great a villain as ever existed*; NO OATH OR PROMISE IS BINDING WITH HIM; and he relates alike that which he must have sworn to keep sacred in his bosom, as he will a most trifling thing; and slanders and THREATENS WITH PUBLIC EXPOSURE AND LARGE DAMAGES HIS BENEFACTOR and only maker of his fortune, just as he would one of his own stamp. Sir, to serve his royal highness, I have always thought it as my greatest honour, and to serve him in any situation that his royal highness may be pleased to place me, shall always be the greatest pride of my life; but no longer can I live with this monster. I have, Sir, served his royal highness for nearly twelve years, and would rather forego all my wishes and pretensions, and beseech his royal highness to allow me permission to look out for another place. To your goodness I trust, Sir, that you will lay my case before his royal highness, and acquaint me with his royal highness' pleasure.

"I have the honour to be, Sir,

"Your most obedient and most humble servant,

"J. SELLIS."

B. C. Stephenson, Esq."

In this letter, enough is set forth to make us receive the evidence of Neale with *caution*, if not to render him *unworthy of belief altogether*. *Why* the Duke of Cumberland retained Neale in his service *after* his peculating tricks had been discovered, and *after the* THREAT he held out against his royal master, we must leave our readers to discover.

"The jury proceeded to examine the bed-room of the royal duke, which they found in a most distressing and horrible state. It could not be discovered what his royal highness' *nightcap* was made of, it being completely *soaked in blood*; the first blow given his royal highness was providentially prevented from proving fatal, from the duke wearing a *padded ribbon bandage round his cap, and a tassel, which came in contact with the sword*; the *bed-clothes generally were blooded; the paper of the room, the prints and paintings, the door at the head of the bed* (through which his royal highness endeavoured to make his escape) was *cut with the sword* at the time the *villain was cutting at the duke*, and the dark assassin must have *followed* his royal highness to the door of an anti-room, which was *also spotted with blood*."

Supposing Sellis to be the *villain* here meant, the wretched means he took to accomplish the end in view were so inadequate, that it were quite impossible for him to have done all the bloody work so minutely related, from the *position in which the parties were placed*. The duke was in a modern *high bed*, his *head well protected* with "a padded ribbon bandage," the only vital part of him that was above the bed-clothes, and the *curtains drawn around him*. Sellis was *not taller than the level of the bed-clothes*, and yet he chose a SWORD to attack his *recumbent master*!!! In a contest so unequal, the duke *might* have annihilated Sellis in a minute.

"The jury then proceeded to the room where the corpse of the deceased *villain* remained. They found it with the whole of the body (except the head and feet) covered with blood; the razor which did the deed in a bloody state. The deceased's *neckcloth was cut through in several places. The drawers, wash-hand basin-stand, and the basin, were also bloody.*"

To some people, such a state of the room may appear any thing but convincing of the *guilt of Sellis*; yet, to such *sensible* men as were on the jury, *all* confirmed the verdict afterwards recorded. *Sellis*, from his neckcloth having been "cut through in several places," blood being sprinkled in all parts of the room, and an appearance of some one having WASHED THEIR HANDS IN THE BASIN, MUST have been his own murderer, and consequently the assassin of the Duke of Cumberland!

"After the examination of the rooms, the jury proceeded to the investigation of the witnesses.

"Thomas Jones, a surgeon and apothecary, of the Strand, said he had attended the Duke of Cumberland's household since the year 1803. He knew the deceased well. *He never saw him in a low or desponding way.* The last time he had seen him was on Monday evening; he observed he was not very well, from a cold. He had seen him on the Sunday previous, when he was very anxious for the state of his child, having lately lost one. On Tuesday the child got better. He observed nothing particular about him for six weeks past, when he complained of a pain in his chest. *He never complained to him of harsh treatment from the duke.* He attended him four or five years since for a pain in his chest, which he said was brought on by riding on horseback. He understood he lived very happy with his wife. His wife told him it was of no use his sending physic for the pain in his chest, for he would not take it. *He never observed any symptoms of derangement in him.*"

It will here be perceived, that Sellis was neither *deranged*, nor had the slightest cause for attempting his own life, or that of his master. Is it not singular, that Mr. Jones mentioned nothing about the wound in Sellis' throat, or the *methodical position* in which the murdered man was found? Was he permitted to examine the body? If he was not, dark suspicion must ever attend upon those who refused *any* medical man such a privilege; and if he did view it, why not have given his opinion of the matter? But this affords another proof of the unfairness of the proceedings on this inquest.

"Ann Neale, the housekeeper, said she was called up at about three o'clock on Thursday morning by her husband; at the same time she heard the duke saying, 'I am murdered.' She got up with all possible speed, and saw the duke bleeding very much in the valet's room: *she went with several others to the door of the deceased, to call him; she found it fastened on the inside*, and no answer was given to their calls. *She and other servants went to another door, which opened to his room*; as they approached the door, they heard a noise, as if a man was gargling water in his throat. The porter entered first, and he exclaimed, '*Good God! Mr. Sellis has cut his throat.*' He was a very *obstinate and quarrelsome man. He would not bear contradiction, not even from the duke.* His royal highness and Princess Augusta stood (by proxy) to his last child. *The duke was very partial to him*, and allowed his family to sleep in the house. His royal highness allowed him to ride in his carriage with him, when travelling, since his illness. The Princess Elizabeth gave his wife two pieces of muslin lately. The Princess Augusta made her a present of several articles of value. The principal acquaintance the deceased had was a Mr. Greville, a servant to the Duke of Cambridge, and Mr. and Mrs. Dupree, wax-chandlers. About three weeks since, he told her Mrs. Marsh, the housekeeper to the Royal Cockpit, was dead, and that he should speak to the duke to give the place to his wife; and if he did not succeed with Lord Dartmouth for that, he should apply to him to get his wife a sinecure, as he had asked his royal highness to get him a messenger's place, but he supposed the duke did not like to part with him. She asked him about a week since if he had succeeded. And he replied, he had not yet. He and his family were in so much favour, that every court-day, when the queen came to dress at the duke's apartments for the drawing-room, Sellis' wife and children were had down for the queen and princess to see them. On the last drawing-room the child the princess stood for was had into the queen's private apartments. A special privilege was granted to Sellis of a bell being permitted to be put up, to ring him to the duke from his family's apartments. The deceased would quarrel with people sooner than give up a point."

This woman's description of the door of Sellis' room being fastened inside was, doubtless, thought to be a very clever affair. Guilt, however, generally betrays itself; for, instead of *bursting open the door* so secured, "she, and other servants, went to another door, which opened to his room," and which door *WAS NOT FASTENED INSIDE*! Now would not the first impulse of every person, *unconscious of crime*, in such a peculiar situation as this woman was placed, have rather suggested the breaking open of Sellis' door than going round to another? If both doors had been secured, the thing would have appeared a little more consistent.

"Benjamin Smith, porter to the Duke of Cumberland, said, that about a quarter before three o'clock, he was called up by the duke and Neale, who said his royal highness had been murdered. He got up, armed himself with a sword, and then called to the soldiers on guard not to suffer any person to go out of the house. He then went to call the deceased, but receiving no answer, *he went to his family's apartments, and called through the key-hole.* A child answered he was sleeping at the duke's. He then, with several of his fellow-servants, *went to Sellis' apartments again*, when, *on hearing the noise in his throat, he supposed somebody else was murdered in the house.* When he first saw the duke, he was covered with blood, and Neale said the duke was murdered. There had not been any quarrel between any of the servants and Sellis, to his knowledge."

This was the porter described by the last witness as having exclaimed, "*Good God! Mr. Sellis has cut his throat!*" There is, however, a little difference between *his own statement and that of Mrs. Neale*; such as his going "to his family's apartments" after "receiving no answer from Sellis," and then "returning to Sellis' apartment, when, on hearing the noise in his throat, he supposed *somebody else was murdered*!" If this man thought that Sellis *cut his own throat*, as stated by Mrs. Neale, what did he mean by saying, "he supposed SOMEBODY ELSE WAS MURDERED?" Do not the porter's own words imply, that *Sellis had been murdered*, and *not* that he had *murdered himself*? Yet the jury *saw no discrepancy in the evidence*!!!

> "Matthew Henry Grasham, a servant of the duke's, said he armed himself with pistols upon his being called up. *He was not able to find his way to Sellis' apartments by the* REGULAR *door*, but found his way to *another*, when he and his two fellow-servants were afraid to enter the room on account of the groans and noise in the throat of the deceased, although he had two pistols, and another had a sword. He had been so much frightened ever since, that he had not been able to visit the room where the body lay. *He considered Sellis a civil, well-behaved man.* He seldom heard Neale and Sellis speak together; did not suppose he ever heard them exchange ten words together. The last time the duke went to Windsor, he took Sellis inside the coach, because he would not expose him to the morning air. He never observed Sellis to be low spirited; he did not appear so well lately as in general, in consequence of his having a cold."

This witness, it appears, although terribly alarmed, was unable to find out the *regular* door to Sellis' apartments, but found his way to another, *more difficult of access*. Now, without denying the truth of this statement, it seems rather singular that he should not have gone the way he *knew best*; but, from his cowardly nature, he probably followed Mrs. Neale, who appeared to know the EASIEST WAY OF GAINING ADMITTANCE TO THE CHAMBER OF HORROR. Grasham also added his testimony to almost all the other witnesses as to the *amiable character* of the murdered Sellis, as well as proving his perfect *sanity*.

> "Mr. Jackson, a surgeon.—He had examined the body of the deceased; he found the windpipe completely divided; *he had seen larger wounds done by a man's own hands*; the arteries on both sides were completely separated; he had no doubt but they were done by a razor, or sharp instrument; the wound was five or six inches wide, and an inch and a half deep. *He had no other wound in his body*, and had no doubt but his throat being cut was the cause of his death."

This was the only medical gentleman allowed to give evidence as to the state of the murdered man's wounds. We are totally unacquainted with Mr. Jackson, and cannot, therefore, be actuated by any malice towards him; neither do we wish to accuse him with *interested* motives when he made the above statement. But *Justice* asks, why was not the opinion of six medical men, *at least*, recorded on this very momentous head? *We* will, however, tell the reader *why*. One or two other professional persons DID examine the body of poor Sellis, and, if they had been ALLOWED TO GIVE THEIR OPINION, would assuredly have convinced every honest man of the *IMPOSSIBILITY* of Sellis being *HIS OWN MURDERER*. One of these, Dr. Carpue, has frequently been heard to say, that "the head of Sellis was nearly severed from his body, and that EVEN THE JOINT WAS CUT THROUGH!!!" Dr. Carpue has also stated, that "no man could have the power to hold an instrument in his hand to cut ONE-EIGHTH of the depth of the wound in the throat of Sellis!"

> "Sergeant Creighton, of the Coldstream regiment of Foot Guards, said, in consequence of the alarm of the duke being murdered, he went with several men into the house; when they came to the deceased's room, the servants were afraid to go in on account of the noise; he in consequence took the candle from them. He found the deceased dead, with his throat cut, and a razor about *two yards from the bed*; the deceased was quite dead, but not cold; the blood was then running and frothing out of his neck. He did not *appear to have struggled with any person, but had his hands quite straight down by his side.* The deceased had on pantaloons and stockings."

Notwithstanding part of this man's evidence was *suppressed*, we have here sufficient to prove that Sellis was *not* his own murderer. No man, after cutting his head nearly off, could possibly throw a razor "TWO YARDS FROM HIS BED!"[2] A man, in the agonies of death, would rather have *grasped the deadly instrument in his hand*; for this circumstance has almost always been observed in those persons committing suicide. Further than this, however, the witness states, "he did not appear to have *struggled* with any person, but had his HANDS QUITE STRAIGHT DOWN BY HIS SIDE." Every man, who will not *abjectly resign his reason*, cannot deny that such a position of the hands was contrary to the NATURAL STRUGGLES OF A DYING MAN, and that it was quite impossible for Sellis to have so SYSTEMATICALLY LAID OUT HIS OWN BODY! But the *suppressed evidence* of this sergeant, which afterwards appeared in "The News," fully proved that the first impression of the duke's servants was, that Sellis had been murdered, and not that he had murdered himself! For Creighton says,

> "On entering the house, accompanied by another sergeant, and two or three soldiers, he met two servants, who told him that the Duke of Cumberland had been *wounded* and that *Sellis was murdered*!"

This witness also corroborated some other important points, for instance:

> "On the floor before the bed lay a white neckerchief, *cut in several places*. On the opposite side of the room was a wash-hand basin, with some water in it, which looked as if some person had been *washing blood in it*! *The curtains were sprinkled with blood, as well as several parts of the room*; at that time it was *broad day-light*."

When we ask *why* the "Morning Post" thought it *prudent* to omit this and much other important evidence, we could give the *because*; but our readers will easily understand it!

"James Ball, a footman, said, upon the alarm being given, he inquired of a female servant what was the matter. She informed him the duke was murdered. He went down to the porter with all possible speed, who desired him to *call Sellis*, which he did, but could not gain admittance; he went to the *other door*, when he saw the deceased with his throat cut on his bed; the sight was so shocking, he drew back and almost fainted. *His wife since told him he ate a hearty supper, shook hands with her, and bid her good night at parting.* He never quarrelled with the deceased. He understood the origin of the quarrel between Sellis and Neale was Neale's taking a newspaper out of Sellis' hand. The duke was particularly partial to Sellis, and behaved better to him, he thought, than to any other servant. Sellis and Neale were obliged frequently to be in the same room together, but he never observed any thing particular between them. *Sellis was a very sober man. If he was not at the duke's apartments upon his business, he was sure to be found with his family.* The duke continued his kindness to the last. *He had heard Sellis say he could never be friendly with a man (meaning Neale) who had treated him as he had done.* Sellis used some years since to ride in the carriage with the duke, but since a box has been made to the carriage he was ordered by the duke to ride there. He objected to that, saying it shook him very much."

This servant, like most of the others, was ordered to call Sellis, and his evidence, in this particular, seems merely a REHEARSAL of the rest. The corroboration which Ball here gave of the excellent character of Sellis had been sufficient, one would think, for any jury to have acquitted the poor fellow of any participation in the attempt upon the duke, or with being his own murderer. In Ball's evidence, also, the dislike which Sellis entertained towards Neale is again set forth, and which, in our opinion, goes far to prove the occasion of it, which we have before explained. Neale, in his evidence, attempted to turn this dislike to his own advantage, by charging Sellis with the attack upon his master, and with endeavouring to fix the crime upon him (Neale) out of revenge! "A guilty conscience needs no accuser,"—a saying perhaps never better exemplified!

"Thomas Creedy, a private in the Coldstream Regiment of Guards, who was on duty, and the *first man who entered the room of Sellis*. The servant being afraid, he trembled so much that he let the *candle fall*, but he caught it up, and prevented it from *going out*. After seeing Sellis' throat cut, and hearing robbers were in the house, he looked under the bed. *He did not see a coat in the room*, (which is very small) although there *was a blue one belonging to Sellis, with blood on the left cuff, and blood on the side*. He observed a wash-hand basin *with blood on the sides, and blood in some water*. The deceased did not appear to have struggled with any one; *his head was against his watch at the head of the bed*."

This was one of the soldiers who accompanied Sergeant Creighton; but whether the sergeant or this man was the "first who entered the room of Sellis," is not exactly clear. Creighton, in his evidence, says "IT WAS BROAD DAY-LIGHT," and, therefore, why CANDLES were required is rather difficult to comprehend! Yet, notwithstanding the *smallness of the room*, "he did not see a coat, although (as he himself confidently states) there was a blue one, belonging to Sellis." How could this witness know it belonged to Sellis, whom he probably never saw alive? As to "*blood being on the left cuff and on the side*," what proof did he adduce of this, for *he himself never saw the coat at all*? He, however, observed a wash-hand basin, in the very suspicious state described by other witnesses, and gave the additional evidence of Sellis' head being "against his watch at the head of the bed;" indeed, the poor man's head only HUNG BY A SMALL PIECE OF SKIN, and his murderers had therefore placed it in *that position* to keep it from *falling off altogether*! Is it not monstrous, then, that men could be found so lost to honor as to record a verdict of *felo de se*?

> "John Probert and John Windsor, two privates in the Guards, said they were on duty opposite the duke's house at the time of the alarm, and were *positive no person went out of the house after the alarm was given*."

The evidence of these men merely shew, *that Sellis was murdered by some one belonging to the house*, which we see no reason to dispute.

> "Thomas Strickland, under butler to his Royal Highness the Duke of Cumberland, said he saw the deceased in the duke's bed-room about ten minutes before eleven o'clock on Wednesday night; *he was surprised at seeing him there*, supposing him to be in close waiting upon the duke. The deceased appeared to have a *shirt in his hand*; he looked very earnest at him, but had a *smile on his countenance. He went to take a cupfull of light drink for the duke to take in the night, which it was his duty to do. He never heard Sellis speak disrespectfully of the duke*."

No satisfactory reason is here given *why* this man should have felt *surprised* at seeing Sellis in the bed-room of his master; for Sellis was there only in the performance of his *duty*, which the *witness acknowledged*. How ardently have those connected with this black affair endeavoured to fix the odium upon the murdered man! Yet how futile, to all *reasonable men*, must appear their observations! Sellis, with a "shirt in one hand," and "a cup of light drink" in the other, in the Duke of Cumberland's bed-room, ought not to have created surprise in any one, knowing the peculiar *situation which Sellis filled in the household of his royal highness*! Did Strickland *really* feel *surprised*, or was he *anxious to say so*? But, it will be observed, that even this witness confessed "he never heard Sellis speak disrespectfully of the duke." Can it, then, be believed, *he* was guilty of the attack upon his royal master?

> "Sarah Varley, housemaid to the Duke of Cumberland, said she put two bolsters into the closet in the second anti-little room adjoining on Wednesday night, they being only put upon his royal highness' bed for ornament in the day-time; there was *no lantern in the closet at the time she put them there, and*

the dark lantern found in the closet is like one she had seen on the deceased's dressing table. There was no sword or scabbard when she put the bolster there."

The dark lantern, sword, &c., were not in the closet when this woman went there to put away the bolsters. Well, what of that? Might they not have been put there *afterwards?* As to "the dark lantern found in the closet being like one she had seen on the deceased's dressing table," proves nothing against Sellis, even if this lady had *positively sworn* to its being *the same*. It were very easy to place a lantern in *Sellis' room*, and *afterwards remove it to the aforesaid closet!* But we have little doubt that *more than one* dark lantern might have been found on premises where so many *secret* deeds had been done! To have made this matter better evidence, why did not some kind friend write *the name of Sellis on the lantern*, similar to the *plan adopted with the slippers?* Such a scheme might have brought the *very* scrupulous jury to their verdict *three hours sooner*, at least!

> "James Paulet, a valet to the duke, first saw his royal highness in his room with Neale holding him up. The duke told him he was murdered, and the murderers must be in his room. The witness replied, he was afraid they should be all murdered, on seeing all the doors opened. The duke insisted they should both stay with him. *His royal highness repeatedly called for Sellis.* In a short time after, some person called at the door that *Sellis was found murdered. The duke appeared very anxious for the safety of Sellis*, and as soon as Surgeon Home had dressed *his* wounds, he sent him to attend to *Sellis*. Mr. Home *soon* returned, and said *there was no doubt but that the man had killed himself. Sellis cautioned him not to be friends with Neale.* He complained to him of the duke's making him ride in a *dickey*, as it shook him much, and riding backwards made him ill. Sellis, however, had the carriage altered to go easier, without asking the duke's leave, at Windsor, and he had appeared content with it ever since. Sellis often talked about leaving the duke's service, saying, *he could not remain in the family if Neale did.* He urged him to the contrary, reminding him how kind the duke was to him and his family."

The duke's anxiety for the services of his faithful valet, Sellis, manifested itself by his royal highness *repeatedly calling for him*. "Some person called at the door that Sellis was found *murdered*,"—another proof that the *first* impression of the servants was the *true one!* Indeed, TRUTH is ever uppermost in the mind; but ARTIFICE requires *time to mature its plans.* We are sure that our readers WILL ADMIRE, with us, the "ANXIETY of his royal highness for the SAFETY of Sellis;" for, as soon as his wounds were dressed, the duke sent HIS OWN SURGEON to attend Sellis! Where shall we look for greater CARE or CONDESCENSION than this? How truly fortunate was the duke in being blessed with so *expeditious* and so *penetrating* a surgeon! "Mr. Home *soon* returned, and said there was no doubt that the man had killed himself!" Oh, talented man! who could perceive, *at a glance*, that "the man had killed himself!" Dr. Carpue must never more pretend to a knowledge of surgery, when his opinion can be set aside by a *single glance* of a man of such eminence in his profession as Mr. Home! As to the joint in his neck being cut through, Mr. Home easily accounted for. What! a man cut his own head off, and wash his hands afterwards! The further testimony of Paulet only proves the dislike which Sellis entertained for Neale, and the caution he gave to all the other servants to avoid him.

> "The widow of the deceased was examined. Her appearance and evidence excited the *greatest compassion and interest*; it tended to *prove he was a good husband, not embarrassed in his circumstances, and that he had parted with her in the usual way, without any suspicion on her part of what he had in contemplation*."

Well, even this admission of the substance of the poor woman's evidence is sufficient to throw discredit upon the jury, who, "after deliberating for upwards of an hour, returned a verdict of *felo de se*." As Mrs. Neale's evidence, however, "excited the greatest compassion and interest," "The Post," acting impartially, ought to have printed it at length, as tending to prove how little the *interest* of Sellis was involved in his master's murder, and how wholly unprepared the poor woman must have been to find her husband accused of committing such a deed. For instance:

> "She never heard him complain of the treatment he received from his royal highness; but, on the contrary, was highly gratified by the kindness he and other branches of the royal family had shewed him, particularly the present of muslin which witness had received from the queen, and Princess Augusta, standing godmother to his child. He was not embarrassed in his circumstances, for she did not know of any debt he owed, but one to the apothecary. Since the birth of their last child, about eight months ago, he never spent an evening out, but was always with his family, when not employed with the duke. He belonged to no club or society. During his illness, he was sometimes giddy, but never took the medicines that were prescribed him by the surgeon, saying that regular living was the best medicine. He sometimes talked of leaving the duke's service, on account of his disputes with Neale; but she remonstrated with him on his imprudence in entertaining such a wish, when they had a good house and plenty of coals and candles allowed them. The subject was not mentioned within the last two years. After supper on Wednesday, he mixed a glass of brandy and water, which he made her drink, as she was troubled with spasms in the stomach. He partook of a little of it, shook hands, and wished her a good night, and *she never saw him more cheerful*. He took some clean linen away with him, and said he would bring home the dirty linen *on the following morning*. She said he was a tender father and an affectionate husband."

Let every unbiased individual read this, and then judge of the monstrous and unnatural verdict returned by the jury! Some further statements were given to us by a gentleman who received the communication, a few years back, from Mrs. Sellis herself:

"The heart-broken widow said, that she had been brought up from a child in the service of the Princess Augusta, and that he had been many years in that of the Duke of Cumberland. Their marriage had, therefore, taken place under the special sanction of their royal master and mistress. They had one child, a daughter, to whom the princess condescended to stand godmother, and it was the practice of the parents, on the return of every birth-day, to present the child in her best array to her royal godmother, who always distinguished her by some little present as a token of recognition. The birth-day of the child was a few days *after* the death of the father; and the widow represents the conversation which occurred between her and her husband on the evening of his death as consisting, among other things, in consultations as to the cap and dress in which the child should be presented to the princess; so little did he appear to have in view the event which followed. He was accustomed to spend all the time not required on his attendance on his master with her, to whom he was in the habit of communicating every little incident in which he was concerned that he thought might be interesting to her. On the night in question, he was just as usual, nothing in his conversation or manner betokening the *least agitation*, much less the contemplation of the *murder of his master*, on whose favour, as she says, their whole hopes for subsistence and comfort depended. According to her account, he was habitually civil, sober, frugal in his little expenses, and attentive to his duties. His wife and his child appeared the whole world to him; and the poor woman declared, that when he parted from her, but a few hours before the dreadful catastrophe occurred, *the committal of a wrong towards the duke appeared as improbable a proceeding from him as the destruction of her and her child*. In fact, the one was involved in the other; for when these circumstances came to our knowledge a few years ago, she represented herself as in temporary want and distress."

It was, however, thought PRUDENT to pension Mrs. Sellis and her *mother*, who offered her remarks *very freely* about this mysterious transaction. They were both privately sent out of the country, (it is believed to Germany) but, with all our efforts, we have not been able to ascertain where they now reside, as their evidence had much assisted us in proving the statements made in our work, entitled "The Authentic Records," &c.

The public appeared much dissatisfied with the verdict of the jury, and one or two publications spoke rather openly regarding the impropriety and suspicious nature of the whole proceeding, throwing out some dark insinuations against the royal duke. In order to counteract this, Sir Everard Home, the *extraordinary man* whose *perceptive* faculties are described on the inquest by the name of *Mr. Home*, published the following declaration relative to it:

"Much pains having been taken *to involve in mystery the* MURDER *of Sellis*, the late servant of his royal highness the Duke of Cumberland, I feel it a public duty to record the circumstances respecting it that came within my own observation, which I could not do while the propagators of such reports were before a public tribunal.

"I visited the Duke of Cumberland upon his being wounded, and found my way from the great hall to his apartment by the traces of blood which were left on the passages and staircase. I found him on the bed, still bleeding, his shirt deluged with blood, and the coloured drapery, above the pillow, sprinkled with blood from a wounded artery, which puts on an appearance that cannot be mistaken by those who have seen it. This could not have happened had not *the head been lying on the pillow when it was wounded.* The night ribbon, which was wadded, the cap, scalp, and skull were obliquely divided, so that the pulsation of the arteries of the brain were distinguished. While dressing this and the other wounds, report was brought that *Sellis was wounded, if not* MURDERED. His royal highness desired me to go to him, as I had declared his royal highness out of *immediate danger.* A second report came, that Sellis was dead. I went to his apartment, *found the body lying on his side on the bed,* without his coat and neckcloth, the throat cut *so effectually* that he could not have survived *above a minute or two. The length and direction of the wound were such as left* NO DOUBT *of its being given by his own hand. Any struggle would have made it irregular.* He had not *even changed his position*; his hands lay as they do in a person who has fainted; they had *no marks of violence upon them; his coat hung upon a chair, out of the reach of blood from the bed; the sleeve, from the shoulder to the wrist, was sprinkled with blood, quite dry, evidently from a wounded artery*; and from such kind of sprinkling, the arm of the assassin of the Duke of Cumberland could not escape!

"In returning to the duke, I found the doors of all the state apartments had marks of bloody fingers on them. *The Duke of Cumberland, after being wounded, could not have gone any where but to the outer doors and back again, since the traces of blood were confined to the passages from the one to the other.*"

"EVERARD HOME."

We regret, with Sir Everard Home, that "so much pains should have been taken to involve in mystery the murder of Sellis," but such pains were taken in the PALACE, AND NOT BY THE PUBLIC! Sir Everard's description of the matter, however, is only calculated to involve it in still greater mystery and contradiction! For instance, "he found the body lying on his *side* on the bed, the throat so *effectually* cut that he could not have survived above a *minute or two!*" How a man could cut his throat so *effectually,* when *lying on his side,* for "HE HAD NOT EVEN CHANGED HIS POSITION," is rather a puzzling matter to people of common sense! yet Sir Everard says, "*the length and direction of the wound were such as left* NO DOUBT OF ITS BEING GIVEN BY HIS OWN HAND!" In a conversation we had with Mr. Place, the foreman of the jury, a few weeks since, that gentleman informed us "*the man lived* TWENTY MINUTES *after his throat was cut!!!*" We do not mean to say that Mr. Place's knowledge of this matter is to be put in competition with that of Sir Everard Home; but Mr. Place urged this circumstance to us as confirmatory of

St James's Palace in the early nineteenth century, from an engraving in E.W. Brayley's *The Beauties of England and Wales* (1814).

Sellis having murdered himself. It is, therefore, very extraordinary that Sir Everard Home did not set the talented foreman right upon this all-important point, as it might have been the means of producing a *widely-different verdict*! With regard to "the hands having no marks of violence upon them," we can only say that such an account is contrary to the report of other persons who *saw them* as well as Mr. Home; for both his hands and wrists BORE EVIDENT MARKS OF VIOLENCE! The desire which Sir Everard manifests, in this account, to bring proof against Sellis for an attempt to assassinate his master has more of *zeal* than *prudence* in it; for, in speaking of the blood said to be found upon Sellis' coat, the learned doctor asserts it to be "just such kind of sprinkling, the arm of the assassin of the duke could not escape!" How ridiculous must such an observation as this appear to any man, possessed of common understanding! Sellis was reported to have used a SWORD in this pretended attempt upon his master's life, *the length of which and the position of the duke* would render it next to impossible for *any blood of the duke's to reach him*! The worthy knight further says, when speaking of the matters in Sellis' room, "his coat hung upon a chair, *out of the reach of blood from the bed*;" but several witnesses upon the inquest stated that "blood was found all over the room, and the hand-basin appeared as if some person had been washing blood in it." What is the reason, then, why blood might not have been sprinkled upon the *coat* of the murdered man as well as "upon the curtains, on several parts of the floor, and over the wash-basin?" *Why* did Sir Everard Home omit to mention these important particulars in his attempt to explain away the "mystery of the murder of Sellis?" His description of the dreadful wounds of his royal master are also rather at variance with the idea the *duke himself gave of them*, "THE BEATING OF A BAT ABOUT HIS HEAD!!" The skilful surgeon concludes his statement by saying, "The Duke of Cumberland, after being wounded, could not have gone any where but to the outer doors and back again, since the traces of blood were confined to the passages from the one to the other;" when it will be observed in *Neale's evidence*, that "the duke and witness went to alarm the house, and got a light from the porter!!!" Now we may naturally suppose the *porter slept at some distance from the duke*, and therefore either Sir Everard Home or Neale must have made a *slight mistake* in this particular; for we cannot accuse two such *veritable* personages with *intentionally contradicting each other*!!

Having now carefully and dispassionately examined all the evidence brought forward to prove Sellis an assassin and a suicide, we proceed to lay before our readers a few particulars tending to confirm an opposite opinion.

Mr. Jew, then in the household of the duke, and who probably is now alive, (information of which fact might be ascertained by application to the King of Belgium) *was inclined* to give his deposition upon this subject, in the following terms, alleging, as his reason, the very severe pangs of conscience he endured, through the secrecy he had manifested upon this most serious affair.

Deposition

"I was in the duke's household in May, 1810; and on the evening of the 31st, I attended his royal highness to the opera;—this was the evening previous to Sellis' death. That night it was my turn to undress his royal highness. On our arriving at St. James', I found Sellis had retired for the night, as he had to prepare his master's apparel, &c., and to accompany him on a journey early in the morning.

"I slept that night in my usual room; but Neale, another valet to the duke, slept in an apartment very slightly divided from that occupied by his royal highness. A few days previous to this date, I was commanded by my master to lay a sword upon one of the sofas in his bed-chamber, and I did so. After undressing his royal highness, I retired to bed. I had not long been asleep, when I was disturbed by Neale, who told me to get up immediately, as my master the duke was nearly murdered! I lost no time, and very soon entered his royal highness' bed-room. His royal highness was then standing nearly in the middle of the chamber, apparently quite cool and composed, his shirt was bloody, and he commanded me to fetch Sir Henry Halford, saying, 'I am severely wounded.' The sword, which a few days before I had laid upon the sofa, was then lying on the floor, and was very bloody. I went with all possible haste for Sir Henry, and soon returned with him. I stood by when the wounds were examined, none of which were of a serious nature or appearance. That in his hand was the most considerable.

"During this period, which was *nearly two hours*, neither Neale nor Sellis had been in the *duke's room*, which appeared to me a very unaccountable circumstance. At length, when all the bustle of dressing the wounds (which were very inconsiderable) was over, and the room arranged, the duke said, 'Call Sellis!' I went to Sellis' door, and, upon opening it, the most horrific scene presented itself: Sellis was lying perfectly straight in the bed, the head raised up against the head-board, and nearly severed from the body; his hands were lying quite straight on each side of him, and upon examination I saw him weltering in blood, it having covered the under part of the body. He had on his shirt, his waistcoat, and his stockings; the *inside* of his hands were perfectly clean, but on the outside were smears of blood. His watch was hanging up over his head, *wound up*. His coat was carefully folded inside out, and laid over the back of a chair. A razor, covered with blood, was lying at a distance from his body, but too far off to have been used by himself, or to have been thrown there by him in such a mutilated condition, as it was very apparent death must have been immediate after such an act.

"The wash-basin was in the stand, but was *HALF FULL OF BLOODY WATER*! Upon examining Sellis' cravat, it was found to be cut. The padding which he usually wore was covered with silk and quilted; but, what was most remarkable, both THE PADDING AND THE CRAVAT WERE CUT, as if some person had made an attempt to cut the throat with the cravat on; then, finding the woollen or cotton stuffing to impede the razor, took it off, in order more readily to effect the purpose.

"During the time the duke's wounds were being dressed, the deponent believes Neale was absent, in obedience to arrangement, and was employed in laying Sellis' body in the form in which it was discovered, as it was an utter impossibility that a self-murderer could have so disposed of himself.

"Deponent further observes, that Lord Ellenborough undertook to manage this affair, by arranging the proceedings for the inquest; and also that every witness was previously examined by him; also, that the FIRST JURY, being unanimously dissatisfied with the evidence adduced, as they were not permitted to see the body in an undressed state, positively refused to return a verdict, in consequence of which, they were dismissed, and a SECOND jury summoned and empannelled, to whom, severally, a special messenger had been sent, requesting their attendance, and each one of whom was directly or indirectly connected with the court, or the government. That, on both inquests, the deponent had been omitted, and had not been called for to give his evidence, though it must have been known, from his personal attendance and situation upon the occasion, that he must necessarily have been a most material witness. The second jury returned a verdict against Sellis, and his body was immediately put into a shell, and conveyed away *a certain distance* for interment. The duke was *privately* removed from St. James' Palace to Carlton House, where his royal highness manifested an impatience of manner, and a perturbed state of mind, evidently arising from a conscience ill at ease. But, in a short time, he appeared to recover his usual spirits, and being hurt but in a very trifling degree, he went out daily in a sedan chair to Lord Ellenborough's and Sir William Phipps', although the daily journals were lamenting his very bad state of health, and also enlarging, with a considerable expression of sorrow, upon the magnitude of his wounds, and the fears entertained for his recovery!"

The further deposition of this attendant is of an important character, and claims particular consideration. He says,

"I was applied to by some noblemen shortly after this dreadful business, and very strongly did they solicit me to make a full disclosure of all the improper transactions to which I might have been made a party upon this solemn subject. I declined many times, but at length conceded, under a binding engagement that I should not be left destitute of comforts or abridged of my liberty; and, under special engagements to preserve me from such results, I have given my deposition."

(Signed) "JEW."

The fact of *two juries being summoned* has been *acknowledged by the coroner*, in his affidavit before the Court of King's Bench in April last. The affidavit of this gentleman, however, contains so many *errors*, that we here introduce an exposition of it, as given by the talented D. Wakefield, esq., in shewing cause against the rule being made absolute in the case of "Cumberland *v.* Phillips."

"Mr. Wakefield said it would be in the recollection of the court, that this was a rule obtained by Sir Charles Wetherell, for a libel contained in a publication relating to his royal highness the Duke of Cumberland. He would not read the alleged libel in detail now, but confine himself first to the affidavit of Samuel Thomas Adams, the coroner who had held the inquest on Sellis. It was necessary that he should read the affidavit, as he had to offer several remarks upon it."

The learned counsel then read the affidavit, as follows:

In the King's Bench.

"Samuel Thomas Adams of No 9 Davis street Berkeley square in the County of Middlesex solicitor maketh oath and saith that he hath seen a certain book or publication entitled "The Authentic Records of the Court of England for the last Seventy Years" purporting to be published in London by J. Phillips 334 Strand 1832 and that in the said book or publication are contained the following statements or passages which this deponent has read that is to say—"

[Here the deponent, *lawyer-like*, set out the whole of the pretended libel, as published in the "Authentic Records," for the purpose of putting us to all the expense and trouble possible.]

"And this deponent further saith that he was coroner for the verge of the King's Palace at St. James's in the month of June one thousand eight hundred and ten before whom the inquest on the body of Joseph Sellis referred to in the aforesaid passages extracted from the said book or publication was held and that it is not true as stated in the aforesaid passages that Lord Ellenborough undertook to manage the affair by arranging the proceedings upon the said inquest or that every witness or as this deponent believes any witness was previously examined by the said Lord Ellenborough or that the first jury for the reasons in the aforesaid passages alleged or for any other reasons refused to return a verdict in consequence of which they were dismissed and a second jury summoned and empannelled to whom *severally a special messenger had been sent* requesting their attendance and each of whom was directly or indirectly connected with the court or the government. And this deponent further saith that it is not true that any person was omitted as a witness whose evidence was known or could be suspected to be material but on the contrary this deponent saith that when the death of the said Joseph Sellis was notified to him he as such coroner as aforesaid was required to hold an inquest on the body of the said Joseph Sellis and that it being required by a statute passed in the twenty-third year of Henry the Eighth chapter twelve that in case of death happening in any of the king's palaces or houses where his majesty should then happen to be and in respect of which death an inquest should be necessary that the jury on such inquest should be composed of twelve or more of the yeoman officers of the king's household to be returned in the manner therein particularly mentioned he this deponent in the first instance issued as such coroner as aforesaid an order that a jury should be summoned composed of the said yeoman officers of the king's household pursuant to the directions of the said statute. But this deponent saith that believing it to be important that the cause and circumstances of the death of the said Joseph Sellis should be investigated in the most public and impartial manner *he took upon himself the responsibility of not complying with the strict letter of such statute as aforesaid and countermanded the first order as aforesaid for summoning such jury in conformity to the said statute and instead thereof directed a jury to be summoned consisting of persons not being yeomen officers of the king's household* but living at a distance from and totally unconnected with the palace of St. James's And this deponent further saith that thereupon his agent as this deponent has been informed and believes took the summoning officer to Francis Place of Charing Cross man's mercer and that the said Francis Place then mentioned to the agent of this deponent the names of many persons fit and eligible to compose such jury and out of such persons so summoned by the officer as aforesaid an impartial jury was formed of which jury the said Francis Place was foreman And this deponent saith that before such jury so summoned and duly sworn he as coroner proceeded on the first day of June one thousand eight hundred and ten to hold an inquest on the body of the said Joseph Sellis And this deponent further saith that the court which under other circumstances would have been a close one he this deponent directed to be thrown open to the public and all persons without distinction And this deponent believes the same was done and that all persons without distinction were admitted into such court amongst whom were many reporters for the newspapers who attended for the purpose of taking and did take notes of the proceedings and of the depositions of the witnesses examined upon such inquest And this deponent further saith that at the commencement of the said inquest the several informations on oath of the principal witnesses taken on that and the preceding day by John Reid Esquire the then chief magistrate of the police were read over and handed to the said jury to enable them the better to examine such witnesses respectively and such witnesses were respectively resworn before this deponent as coroner and permitted to make any addition to their evidence so given before the magistrate as aforesaid and that each and every of such witnesses had full opportunities of making any addition to such testimony which they thought proper And this deponent further saith that all the circumstances of the case as far as they could be collected were carefully and impartially scrutinized by the said jury and that all the evidence which could be collected and brought forward and that every person was called before the said jury and examined as a witness and no person was omitted to be called and examined who would have been or who it could be supposed would have been a material witness And this deponent further saith that in the course of the inquiry the said jury proceeded to the apartment where the body of the said Joseph Sellis had been first discovered and was then lying and did then carefully view examine and inspect the body of the said Joseph Sellis and all the other circumstances deemed by them necessary to be examined into and ascertained in any way touching the death of the said Joseph Sellis And this deponent further saith that he locked the doors of the apartment in which the body of the said Joseph Sellis was found and did not permit the same to be inspected nor the state and position of the said body to be disturbed, from the first discovery of such body in the aforesaid apartment until the same was inspected by the said jury And this deponent further saith that on the conclusion of the investigation the said jury immediately and unanimously returned a verdict that the said Joseph Sellis voluntarily and feloniously as a *felo de se* murdered himself And this deponent further saith that the proceedings upon the said inquest were in all respects regular *except* as to the jury not consisting of the yeoman officers of the king's household and that such proceedings were themselves conducted in the most fair open and impartial manner and that the verdict so found by the jury as aforesaid was a just true and honest verdict and that there is not the smallest ground for supposing or alleging any thing to the contrary thereof.[3]

"SAM^L. THO^S. ADAMS."

"*Sworn in Court the eighteenth day of April 1832—By the Court.*"

"The first remark he had to submit to the court in this case was, that a person who applied for an extraordinary remedy by criminal information, must deny all the charges contained in the libel. The rank of the illustrious individual in this case made no difference with respect to that point. Now the court would find, by the affidavit of Mr. Adams, the coroner, that one of the main parts of this alleged libel, so far from being contradicted, was SUBSTANTIATED,—he alluded to the fact of there having been TWO JURIES summoned to inquire into the circumstances relating to the death of Sellis. He did not mean to say that that fact formed any justification for the publication of the libel; but the fact itself was certainly extremely important, and Mr. Adams' affidavit contained the reasons why the mode pointed out by the act of parliament for summoning juries in such cases had been departed from. The fact of there having been two juries summoned was no doubt sufficient to induce any person to believe that there was some reason for that proceeding, which was not apparent on the face of it. Mr. Adams had described the manner in which the jury were summoned. He said he sent the summoning officer to Mr. Place, man's mercer, of Charing-cross; but Mr. Place was not the coroner for the verge of the King's Palace, and had no authority to act. He would leave it to the court to form their own opinion, whether or not this departure from the usual course was or was not for the purpose of obtaining an IMPARTIAL TRIAL. The affidavit showed that Mr. Adams had flown in the face of the act of parliament, and the statement in the Authentic Records, that there had been a second inquest, was CORROBORATED by that affidavit. Mr. Adams had referred to the act of parliament, as being that of the 23rd of Henry VIII., whereas it was that of the 33rd of Henry VIII.: that was no doubt a trifling circumstance, but it tended to show the manner in which Mr. Adams performed the duties of his office. Mr. Adams had stated that summonses had been drawn up for summoning TWO JURIES, but those for summoning the FIRST were not used; but the reason he gave was most unsatisfactory. He had no right to send to Mr. Place, and Mr. Place had no right to act as coroner; and he (Mr. Wakefield) submitted that the court ought to require an affidavit from Mr. Place to corroborate what Mr. Adams had stated. He believed it would not be difficult to show that the inquest might be quashed, as being illegal; and it certainly might have been quashed if Sellis had had any goods, which would have been subject to an extent at the suit of the crown. At all events, Mr. Adams might have been prosecuted for a breach of duty. There was another point which, though of a trifling nature, he would take the liberty of adverting to, in order to show that the inquest was illegal. By the 28 Henry VIII. c. 12, the jury in cases of this description were to be summoned from the verge of the court. Now this applied to the court sitting at Whitehall; but at the time in question the court was sitting at St. James'. The summoning, therefore, was clearly not good, and the jury, consisting of Mr. Place's junta, could not legally hold an inquest on the body of Sellis."

Four other mistakes, also, in the coroner's affidavit were pointed out by *Mr. Place* himself in a letter to the public.

1. Mr. Adams says, "he issued an order to summon a jury of persons of the king's household, but that he rescinded the order, and summoned a jury

of persons who lived at a distance, and were wholly unconnected with St. James' Palace." Mr. Adams must by these words mean that he summoned a jury from the only place to which his power extended; namely, "the verge of the court,"—a small space, and from amongst the few tradesmen who resided within its limits. *I never before heard that he had issued any order to summon a jury of persons of the king's household.*

2. Mr. Adams says, that his "summoning officer applied to Francis Place, of Charing Cross, for the names of persons who were eligible to compose a jury, and that out of such persons an impartial jury, of which Francis Place was the foreman, assembled on the 1st of June, 1810." Mr. Adams probably speaks from memory, and is, therefore, incorrect. He might, to be sure, have instructed his officer to apply to me; but, if he did, it was a STRANGE PROCEEDING. The officer was in the habit of summoning juries within the verge, and must have known much better than I did who were eligible. The jurors could not have been indicated by me, since, of seventeen who formed the inquest, five were wholly unknown to me, either by name or person; and amongst the seven who did not attend, there were probably others who were also unknown to me. The number of persons liable to be summoned is so small, that it has been sometimes difficult to constitute an inquest, and there is no room either for choice or selection.

3. Mr. Adams says, "the depositions of the witnesses were taken by John Read, the then chief police magistrate, and were read to the witnesses, who were severally asked if they had any thing to add to them." This, if left as Mr. Adams has put it, would imply negligence on the part of an inquest which was more than usually diligent and precise. The depositions were read, but not one of them was taken as the evidence of a witness. Every person who appeared as a witness was carefully and particularly examined, and the order in which the evidence was taken, and the words used, differ from the depositions; the evidence is also much longer than the depositions. Both are before me. The inquest examined seven material witnesses, who had not made depositions before Mr. Read.

4. Mr. Adams says "the jury *immediately* and *unanimously* returned a verdict that the deceased, Joseph Sellis, voluntarily and feloniously murdered himself." The jury of seventeen persons were every one convinced that Sellis had destroyed himself, yet two of them did not concur in the verdict,—one, because he could not believe that a sane man ever put an end to his own existence; and another, because he could not satisfy himself whether or no Sellis was sane or insane.

FRANCIS PLACE.

Charing Cross, April 19, 1832.

The very morning this letter was published, we called on Mr. Place, who repeated the substance of it to us, adding that Sir Charles Wetherell had sent a person to him for his affidavit, which he REFUSED in a letter to the learned knight, condemning the whole proceeding of criminal information. Mr. Place read a copy of this letter to us, and promised he would publish it if ever a *sufficient reason* presented itself. It was an admirable composition, and did credit to the liberality of the writer's opinions.

As to the affidavits of the Duke of Cumberland and Neale, they contain nothing but what other people in similar situations would say,—*they deny all knowledge of Sellis' murder, and of unnatural conduct.* Whoever thought of requiring them to *criminate themselves?* But affidavits, from interested persons are not worth much. The notorious Bishop of Clogher, for instance, exculpated himself in a criminal information by an affidavit, and the result was, the man who published the *truth* of that *wretch* groaned in a jail!!! Sir Charles, therefore, had no occasion to boast of the Duke of Cumberland's *charitable* mode of proceeding against us by *criminal information*, instead of commencing an *ex-officio* action; for in neither of these modes of procedure does

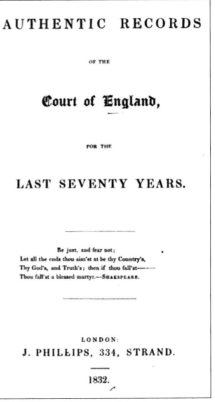

The title page to *The Authentic Records of the Court of England* (1832).

the *truth* or *falsehood* of the charge form an object of consideration. We are, therefore, *prevented* by the Duke of Cumberland and his adherents from proving the *truth* of the statements we made in "The Authentic Records" *in a court of law*; but where resides the *power* that shall rob us of the glorious LIBERTY OF THE PRESS? We are the strenuous advocates of the *right to promulgate* TRUTH,—of the right to scrutinize public actions and public men,—of the right to expose vice, and castigate mischievous follies, even though they may be found in a *palace!* The free exercise of this invaluable privilege should always be conceded to the HISTORIAN, or where will posterity look for *impartial information?* In this character only did we publish what we believed, and *still believe*, to be the *truth* in our former work of "The Authentic Records," and which we have considerably enlarged upon in our present undertaking, merely for the purpose of fulfilling our sacred duty, and not with the idea of slandering any man! If the Duke of Cumberland had proved our statement *false*, we would have freely acknowledged our error, as every man ought to do who seeks fairly and honorably to sustain a noble function in the purity of its existence. We know there are writers who seek, not to enlighten, but to debase; not to find amusement, but to administer poison; not to impart information, either political, moral, or literary, but to indulge in obscenity,—to rake up forgotten falsehoods, and disseminate imputed calumnies! To such, the sanctuary of private life is no longer inviolable; the feelings of the domestic circle are no longer sacred; retirement affords no protection, and virtue interposes no defence, to their sordid inroads. Upon offences like these, *we* would invoke the fiercest penalties of the law. The interests of society demand it, and the rights of individuals claim it! But our strictures and exposures are of a widely-different character,—not if they were *false*,—but because their TRUTH must be apparent to every unbiassed individual in this mighty empire! With this conviction alone we stated them, and even Sir Charles Wetherell himself said we "seemed to have no other motive in stating them only for the purpose of stating them!" We are not disposed to comment upon this part of the learned counsel's speech, as it proves all we want to prove regarding our motives.

This year was not less remarkable for the king's family sorrows than for public grievances. His majesty was nearly childish and blind. The queen dreaded the ascendency of the popular voice in favour of the Princess of Wales, and the Princess Charlotte exhibited a resolute spirit, which it was feared would end to the unhappiness of the puissant queen. The Princess Amelia suffered under indescribable sorrows, both bodily and mental, which ultimately terminated her earthly career on the 2nd of November.

Many representations were made to the public of the numerous visits made to the Princess Amelia by the king, and their affecting final interview. We believe we may, with truth, say those representations were erroneous; for the king's malady was of too serious a nature to admit of any new excitement, and the peculiar regard he entertained for this daughter would not allow his hearing of her sufferings in any shape, without feeling the most acute pain.

The Prince of Wales also still pursued the most dissipated rounds of pleasure, making his very name hateful to every virtuous ear. The house of royalty, indeed, seemed divided against itself.

General historians say that the year

1811

was not marked by any very particular events of much interest, either to kings or kingdoms; yet we must differ from them in this opinion, inasmuch as, at its commencement, the Prince of Wales was appointed *Regent*, and the king's person confided to the care of the queen, conjointly with archbishops, lords, and other adherents of her majesty.

The session was opened on the 12th of February; and the speech, delivered by commission, in the name of the regent, expressed *unfeigned sorrow* at the king's malady, by which the exercise of the royal authority had devolved upon his royal highness. It also *congratulated* parliament and the country on the success of his majesty's arms, by land and sea, and did not forget to beg for further SUPPLIES,— *so much required.*

Let us here inquire the cause that prevented the *amiable* regent from opening the session in person. Had his mistresses detained him too late in the morning? or had they played a *designed part* with him, to prove their superior domination? or had he been in his most privately-retired apartments, *conversing with a few of the male favourites of his household in* ITALIAN? If either of these do not give the true reason of his absence, we may be sure to ascertain it upon inquiry of the vintner or faro-table keeper. Here the different *degrees* of morality, contrived by custom and keeping the people in ignorance, are well illustrated!

The queen was much at Windsor at this period, she being obliged, by etiquette, to hear the bulletins issued by the physicians concerning his majesty's health, or her *affection* for the afflicted king would not have produced so great a *sacrifice* on her part.

In this year, the disgraced Duke of York was restored to his former post of commander-in-chief; although, but a short period before, he was found guilty of being privy to, if not actually and personally, disposing of situations in the army, by which traffic, very large amounts had been realized by one of his royal highness' mistresses.

The money required for this year's supply amounted to *fifty-six millions*! The distress in all the manufacturing districts, notwithstanding, was of the heaviest nature; while, instead of ministers devising means to relieve the starving poor, oppressive enactments were substituted.

Let it not here be supposed that we are condemning any constitutional enactment of government. We only wish to see the interests of the poor a little more regarded, instead of laws being made solely with a view of aggrandizing the wealthy, whose eyes already stand out with fatness. Is it not evident that the men at this period in power were resolved to continue their system of corrupt administration, in despite of all remonstrance and opposition? A long course of oppression had apparently hardened them, and so far steeled their hearts against the petitions of the suffering nation, that they actually seemed to delight in increasing the heavy burdens which already preyed upon the vitals of the community.

Our readers may probably be aware that the visits of the Princess Charlotte to her mother were always "few and far between;" but at this period, the interviews became so uncertain and restricted, that they could not be satisfactory either to the mother or the daughter. Some of the attendants always remained in the apartment with them, *by the regent's command*, to witness the conversation. For some time, the princess contrived to write *privately* to her mother, and obtained a confidential messenger to deliver her communications. This was ultimately suspected, and, after a close scrutiny, unfortunately discovered, and immediately forbidden. Her royal highness was now in her fifteenth year, in good health, and possessing much natural and mental activity. It was not very probable, therefore, that the society of FORMAL LADIES, every way disproportionate to herself in years and taste, could be very agreeable to her, more especially when she knew that these very ladies were bitter enemies to her adored mother. If the Princess Charlotte had been allowed to associate with natural and suitable companions, the very decisive feature of her character would have rendered her the brightest ornament of society; but this was not permitted, and England has great cause to mourn that she was not more valued by her father and grandmother.

The elegant and accomplished Dr. Nott was now selected for the Princess Charlotte's preceptor, and he ardently exerted himself to improve the mind of his royal pupil. The very superior *personal*, as well as mental, qualifications of the reverend gentleman, however, soon rendered him an object of *peculiar interest* to the youthful princess. The ardency of her affections and the determinate character of her mind were well known to her royal relatives. They, therefore, viewed this new connexion with considerable uneasiness, and soon had occasion to suspect that her royal highness had manifested too much solicitude for the interest of her friend and tutor!

The Duke of York first communicated his suspicions on this subject to the regent, and the prince immediately went to Windsor (where the queen then was) to inform her majesty of his fears, and to consult what would be the most proper and effectual measures to take. Her majesty was highly incensed at the information, and very indignantly answered, "My family connexions will prove my entire ruin." Her majesty, accompanied by the prince, drove off directly for London, and the Princess Charlotte was commanded to meet her grandmother in her chamber. With her usual independent readiness, the princess obeyed the summons, and was ushered into the presence of the haughty queen.

After some considerable period of silence, her majesty began to ask what particular services Dr. Nott had rendered, or what very superior attractions he possessed, to engage the attentions of her royal highness in such an unusual degree, as was now well known to be the case. Her royal highness rose up, and in a tone of voice, not very agreeable to the queen, said, "If your majesty supposes you can subdue me as you have done my mother, the Princess of Wales, you will find yourself deceived. The Reverend Mr. Nott has shown me more attentions, and contributed more to my happiness in my gloomy seclusion, than any person ever did, except my mother, and I ought to be grateful to him, and I WILL, whether it pleases your majesty or not!" The queen saw her purpose was defeated in the attempt to intimidate her grand-daughter, and therefore, in a milder manner, said, "You must, my dear, recollect, I am anxious for your honour and happiness; you are born to occupy the highest station in the world, and I wish you to do so becoming the proud character of your royal father, who is the most distinguished prince in Europe." The queen had scarcely concluded her sentence, when her royal highness burst forth, in the most violent manner, and with an undismayed gesture, said, "Does your majesty think I am always to be under your subjection? Can I believe my royal father *so great and good*, when I have so long witnessed his unremitted unkindness to my neglected mother? Neither do I receive much attention from the prince; and my uncle of York is always preaching to me about virtue and submission, and your majesty well knows *he does not practise either*! Mr. Nott practises every amiability which he enjoins, and I esteem him exceedingly *more than I do any other gentleman*!" The queen was quite vexed at the unbending disposition manifested by the princess, and desired her to retire, and reflect upon the improper conduct of which she had been guilty, and, by humility and contrition, to make a suitable atonement.

While walking out of the room, the princess appeared in deep thought, and more tranquil; her majesty, imagining it to be the result of her own advice, said, "The Princess Charlotte will never want a friend if she abide by her grandmother's instructions, and properly maintain her dignity of birth." Her royal highness returned to her former situation before the queen, and exclaimed, "What does your majesty mean?" "I mean," replied the queen, "that you must not condescend to favour persons in *low life* with your confidence or particular respect; they will take advantage of it, and finally make you the tool to accomplish their vile purposes." "Does your majesty apply these remarks to the Rev. Mr. Nott?" hastily replied the princess. "I do," said the queen. "Then hear me, your majesty; I glory in my regard for Mr. Nott. His virtues are above all praise, and he merits infinitely more than I have to give; but I resolve, from this moment, to give him all the worldly goods I can; and your majesty knows that, by *law*, I can make a will, though I am but little more than fifteen; and my library, jewels, and other valuables, are at my own disposal! I will now, without delay, make my will in his favour, and no earthly power shall prevent me. I am sorry your majesty prefers *vicious and wicked characters, with splendid titles*, to virtuous and amiable persons, destitute of such empty sounds!" The princess left the room, and the queen was more disturbed than before the interview.

The regent was soon made acquainted with the result, and recommended that no further notice should be taken of the matter, hoping that the princess would change her intention upon a more deliberate survey of the subject. But in this opinion, or hope, his royal highness was disappointed; for the princess that day signed a *deed*, whereby she gave *positively* to her friend and preceptor, Dr. Nott, her library, jewels, and all private property belonging to her, and delivered this instrument into his hand, saying, "I hope you will receive this small token as a pledge of my sincere regard for your character, and high estimation of your many virtues. When I am able to give you greater testimonies of my friendship, they shall not be withheld." We need hardly say that the divine was *delighted* at the great attention and unexpected generosity of her royal highness. He was more; for his heart was subdued and affected.

A considerable period elapsed after this circumstance, when the queen was resolved to recover the *deed* at all hazards, as she feared, if the validity of such an instrument were ever acknowledged, royalty would suffer much in the estimation of the public. All the queen's deceptive plans, therefore, were tried; but failed. The prince, at length,

Princess Charlotte of Wales, as depicted in G.W.M. Reynolds's *Mysteries of the Court of London*. (*Stephen Basdeo Personal Collection*)

offered a large amount as a remuneration, and finally persuaded the doctor to give up the deed! Of course a good living was also presented to him, on his retiring from the situation in which he had so long enjoyed the smile and favour of his royal pupil.

The Princess Charlotte was mortified, beyond expression, at this unexpected conduct on the part of her father and grandmother, and was not very sparing in her expressions of dislike towards them. Mr. Perceval (who was then premier) was requested by the prince to see her royal highness, and to suggest *any* terms of reconciliation between the princess and the queen; but he could not succeed. "What, Sir!" said her royal highness, "would you desire me to *appear what I am not*, and to meet her majesty as if I believed her to be my sincere friend, when I know I am hated for my dear mother's sake? No, Sir! I cannot do as you desire; but I will endeavour to meet her majesty at all needful opportunities with as much gentleness of manners as I can assume. What indignities has not the queen offered to my persecuted mother? You well know, Sir, they have been unmerited, and if her majesty insults the Princess of Wales again in my presence, I shall say, 'your majesty should regulate your family affairs better, and teach lessons of virtue to your *daughters*, before you traduce the characters of other ladies!' You, Sir, are the regent's minister, and in his confidence, so I may venture to give you my candid opinion, and I do not consider that, by doing so, I exceed the bounds of propriety. Will you, therefore, oblige me by announcing to the prince, my father, that I am unalterably devoted in heart to my mother, and while I wish to be a dutiful child to my father, I must not even be that at the expense of principle and honourable sentiments. My grandfather always had my respect and pity."

It is scarcely necessary to say, that Mr. Perceval retired with evident symptoms of disappointment and chagrin. He immediately communicated the result of his interview to the regent and the queen, who declined making any further remonstrance, lest the princess should imagine they feared her, or were at all intimidated by her bold decisions.

In this year, Lord Sidmouth moved to bring in a bill to alter the "Toleration Act." His lordship stated, that this bill was calculated to serve the interests of religion, and promote the prosperity of the Church of England! But Lord Sidmouth, for once, was disappointed. The sensation excited throughout the country was of an unprecedented description; for, within forty-eight hours, no less than three hundred and thirty-six petitions against it were poured into the House of Lords! and

The Duke of Wellington. (*Stephen Basdeo Personal Collection*)

the House was presented, on the second reading, with five hundred more! It was consequently abandoned.

The supplies voted for the public and *private* services were FIFTY-SIX MILLIONS!

At the close of this year, the poor were perishing for want; yet the court became more splendid than ever! The ill-fated sovereign was as imbecile and as weak as an infant, and his representative a profligate ruler. What a condition for England!

War still raged at the commencement of

1812.

We will not, however, record the scenes of devastation and horror consequent from it; neither will we eulogize Lord Wellington for the *victories* he obtained. Much rather would we shed a tear at the remembrance of the slaughtered victims to kingly or ministerial ambition. Who that believes in the immortality of the soul can think of these horrid engagements without shuddering at the immense and inexpressible accountability of the destroyer? It would be utterly impossible to give an idea of the number of WIDOWS and ORPHANS who have had to mourn the consequences of *splendid* victories, as a *wholesale murdering of soldiers* are denominated. How many *ducal coronets* have been purchased at the expense of human existence! Rather should our brows never be encircled than at such an unnatural price!

On the 13th of February, the restrictions formerly in force against the prince regent terminated; and, properly speaking, it may be declared, *he then assumed the kingly power*. One hundred thousand pounds were voted for him, *professedly* to meet the expenses attendant upon his assumption of the regal authority.

This was a moment of triumph to the queen, and the sequel will prove that her majesty took especial care to turn it to her own account. The Duke of York was fully reinstated as "Commander-in-Chief," and, therefore, ready ways and means presented themselves to her majesty. The regent engaged that the queen should have the continued sanction of his name and interest, in all the various ways she might require. Accordingly, it was soon arranged, that *her majesty should receive an additional sum of ten thousand pounds per annum* FOR THE CARE OF HER ROYAL HUSBAND'S PERSON!

We cannot pass by this shameful insult to the nation without making an observation upon so *unnatural* an act. If the queen were the kind and affectionate wife she had so very frequently been represented to be, could she have allowed herself to receive an immense payment for merely doing her *duty*? But a more selfish woman, and a more unfeeling wife, never disgraced humanity, as this wicked acceptance of the public money fully testifies.

An additional nine thousand pounds annually were also granted to each of the princesses, whilst places and pensions were proportionally multiplied. In the case of Colonel M'Mahon, upon whom a private secretaryship had been conferred, much very unpleasant altercation took place in the House of Commons; but *bribery* effected that which argument proved to be *wrong*. It was a well-known fact, indeed, that this individual was nothing more than a pander to the regent's lust, to which infamous engagements and practices we shall hereafter refer.

On the 11th of May, as Mr. Perceval was entering the lobby of the House of Commons, he received a shot in his left breast, and, after staggering a few paces, fell down and expired. The assassin was tried on the 15th and executed on the 18th of the same month. He defended his conduct on the ground of having received much injury from the government, who had denied redress of his grievances, and, therefore, thought he had only done an act of justice in taking away the life of a member of so callous an administration.

Agreeably to the regent's message, fifty thousand pounds were voted for the use of Mr. Perceval's family, and two thousand annually to be paid to his widow. In case of her demise, however, the same amount was to be continued annually to such male descendant as might at that time be the heir, for the term of his life.

Let us here inquire into the services which Mr. Perceval had rendered his country to warrant ministers in this lavish expenditure upon his family, one of whom now frequently intrudes his crude notions in the House of Commons. Mr. Perceval had been for a long period the *pretended friend* of the ill-fated Princess of Wales. "The Book" which he arranged, and which had been printed, but not published, in 1807, giving the particulars of the "Delicate Investigation," improperly so called, *was bought up* in 1809, and as much as fifteen hundred pounds GIVEN *for a single copy*. The rancour and malice of the unprincipled enemies and calumniators of the open-hearted Princess of Wales had been much exposed by Mr. Perceval, and by his apparent generous and manly defence in her royal highness' favour, the storm materially abated. After a long period, she was again received at court, and acknowledged *innocent* of the charges preferred by her assailants. Apartments were given to her at Kensington Palace, and it appeared very probable that her wishes would finally be completed, in the restoration of her beloved daughter to her society. But mark the ensuing change. Mr. Perceval was chosen by the regent to assist in his councils; and as no man can serve two causes at the same time, Mr. Perceval deserted the princess, and became the servile minister of the prince! Surely there must be something supernatural in the smile of royalty, when, in some instances, principle and conscience have fallen subdued before it! We know for an *incontrovertible* fact, that but a few months before Mr. Perceval's acceptance of office, he delivered his sentiments concerning the Princess of Wales to a particular friend, in these words:

"I am decidedly friendly to the Princess of Wales, because I am well satisfied and assured her royal highness is a much-injured lady. I am also convinced her mother-in-law had conceived an inveterate dislike to her before she arrived in this country, on account of the objections preferred by the prince against any connexion, except that which his royal highness had already formed. From these unhappy circumstances, I am obliged to believe, that the sufferings of her highness are unmerited on her part, and very much increased by the dictatorial behaviour of her majesty."

At another interview with the same person, the following question was put, unreservedly, to Mr. Perceval: "Do you, Sir, think her royal highness has been deserving of the persecutions she has endured, by any deviation from virtue and propriety?" "I do not think the princess guilty," earnestly rejoined Mr. Perceval, "and I am fully satisfied, in my own mind, that if there had not existed ungenerous intentions on the part of the royal family, the affair would long since have sunk into silence. There is a gaiety and levity about her royal highness which is not usual with the *English* ladies generally; but, with all the exterior frivolity of the princess, when she chooses to be lively, *I would prefer her infinitely to the professedly-modest and apparently-reserved of the sex in high life*. I believe the princess to be playful, and incautiously witty, in her deportment; but *I prefer that to secret intrigue and infamous practices*."

We leave our readers to judge whether this simple declaration was not honourable to the princess, and whether it does not correspond with every speech delivered by this gentleman in his public and private defence of her royal highness. Humanity, however, is weak, and the ingratiating attentions of the prince were too powerful to be resisted by Mr. Perceval. At his royal command, Virtue, Goodness, and Truth, assumed the garb of Vice, Infamy, and Falsehood. "Oh, blasting privilege of sovereignty! The bare scent of thy perfume spreads desolation to society; changes man, the noblest of God's works, into a monster; and the consequences of thy *unnatural existence* will most probably produce the engine to be used for *thine own destruction*!"

Shortly after the untimely death of Mr. Perceval, Lord Liverpool was appointed first lord of the Treasury; Mr. Nicholas Vansittart, chancellor of the Exchequer; and Lord Sidmouth, secretary of state for the home department.

On the 17th of June, Mr. Vansittart brought forward his budget,—the amount of the supplies required being more than sixty-two millions. Certainly this was not a very exhilarating or agreeable prospect to the nation of the retrenchments intended by the new ministry; but notwithstanding the divisions on the subject, it finally received the sanction of parliament. Had it not been for the corrupt state of the representation, can we suppose it possible that such a sum would have been permitted to be drawn from the starving multitudes, when there existed such pecuniary distress in the manufacturing and commercial districts, unequalled in former years?

Lord Liverpool, from an engraving in *Memoirs of the Public Life and Administration of the Right Honourable, the Earl of Liverpool* (1827).

The new parliament met for business on the 30th of November, and one of its first acts was, to grant the sum of one hundred thousand pounds to Lord Wellington for the part he had taken in legal slaughter!

It may, with propriety, be submitted here, how large a grant would have been made to any man who should have presented a *plan for the comfortable and honourable maintenance of the perishing millions?* We fear any patriot, who had dared to press such a scheme would have soon been consigned to a damp and dreary dungeon, charged with disaffection to the monarch, or commanded, under *certain protection*, to set sail for another country; and, if permitted to reach the destined shore, there to be received and treated as one of the most infamous of the human race! But in these days, the *will* of the regent, supported by the queen, was supreme law. There was not one who ventured to *insult his dignity* by speaking to him TRUTH!—not one *dared* to stem the torrent of his royal displeasure! It is true that, when Lord Liverpool first entered office, he once *hinted* to his royal master the general voice of dissatisfaction which the people expressed; but the imperious regent commanded silence upon all such subjects, and desired Lord Liverpool never again to meet his highness, unless under a positive resolve not even to give the most distant hint at matters so very disagreeable to the royal ear, and which were of *no considerable importance!* His lordship proved himself wanting in fortitude to set an example to courtiers, and the principle of his mind was, consequently, bartered for the *pleasure* of being the *slave* of a haughty prince, who had "relinquished Justice, and abandoned Mercy!"

We must here refer to a most interesting circumstance with respect to the Princess of Wales. Her royal highness was well aware of the bonds, *still in existence*, given by the Princes George, Frederick, and William, to the firm of Perigoux and Co., of Paris, which were to the amount of several hundred thousand pounds, as we have before named; and, in an open and friendly conversation with Messrs. Whitbread and Perceval, the princess said, "The regent and the royal dukes engaged in those bonds are perfectly aware they deserve severe exposure. Their action was not only wicked, but their intention also; as every person in any way acquainted with their concerns must be sure they undertook to pay more than their means would ever permit, seeing how deeply the country was in debt, and that the revenue did not then meet the annual amount required. And," emphatically added the princess, "if the world did but *know of the* LIVES SACRIFICED *in this affair, to preserve the good reputation of these princely brothers, I suppose royalty would not gain much in the estimation of good people by the exposure!*"

The substance of this conversation soon afterwards transpired to the Prince of Wales. There cannot be a doubt that his royal highness was *afraid*, but he resolved not to *appear so*; and from that period, he and the queen were the unalterable and bitterest enemies of the princess, both publicly and privately. So, then, for the simple expression of *truth*, to those who were already in possession of the whole affair, was an injured princess to be pursued by the hounds of destruction until her capture should be accomplished. The prince sought an immediate divorce; but as the former attempts on this ground, in the year 1806, had failed, there appeared great difficulty in the attainment of his object. The former charges and gross calumnies were declared false, and Lady Douglas had been shunned by all good and strictly-honourable society; for, except where she was received in compliment to the queen, her invitations were, indeed, but very few. The old story was again resorted to, and as Mr. Perceval was now no more, a bold attempt was resolved on, as the last resource, to obtain the desired end.

Mr. Whitbread communicated to the Princess of Wales the scheme then forming against her honour, and that the ministry were favourable to the wishes of the regent. Her royal highness stood amazed at this unexpected information. "What!" said the princess, "is not the Prince of Wales satisfied with the former abuses he has poured upon me? Is he so abandoned, being heir-apparent, as to risk his life, or engage the vengeful disposition of the nation, in the punishment due to the crimes he has committed against me? *If the generous English people were informed of half the sufferings I have endured since my arrival in this country, they would never be induced to yield obedience to the commands of a prince whose virtues are not the least balance to his* VICES! But," continued her royal highness, "I will go down to Windsor, and request an interview with the queen." Mr. Whitbread remonstrated, and at last the princess consented to write, and ask an audience. A courier was despatched with it, and the *verbal* reply of her majesty was, "She would see the Princess of Wales, provided her royal highness was at Windsor Castle by *eight o'clock in the evening.*"

Not a moment was to be lost; the carriage was announced in a few minutes, and the princess, attended by only one lady, entered it. "Drive quickly," said her royal highness. It was only half-past seven when the princess was announced. Her royal highness was received in courtly style and unbending manner by her majesty, who, in her usual way, inquired "the cause which gives me the pleasure of a visit, so very unexpectedly, from the Princess of Wales?"

"Madam," answered her royal highness, "I am quite sensible of your surprise at my hasty request and appearance; but as I am tired of hearing the false reports in such general circulation in the court, I am resolved to ask your majesty in person, if I am likely to experience any renewal of those bitter persecutions which, in former years, were agitated to my horror and surprise. I am well aware the regent would not enter upon such a business, unless he had your majesty's sanction and countenance, as well as assistance. Is it because Mr. Perceval is dead, that your majesty thinks me so unprotected as to fall immediately a prey to my base enemies?—if so, your majesty will be in the wrong; for although Mr. Perceval forsook my interest when he engaged himself in confidence to the regent, my husband, I never shall forget the gratitude I owe him for former benefits, and his letters speak volumes of truths, which it was entirely impossible for him to name or attest, unless his mind had been duly influenced by the solid foundation upon which his opinion was fixed."

Her majesty appeared vexed and astonished; then, assuming that hauteur for which she was so remarkable, said, "I do not know, princess, that I am under any necessity to answer your question, as it seems to me improper to do so. The prince regent has an unquestionable right to choose his ministers and counsellors, and also to engage their attentions and services *for any purpose his royal highness may please*, and therefore I decline to answer any interrogatory upon the subject. Your royal highness must be aware this interview and conversation is very unpleasant to me, and I hope, in future, you will not put me to the very disagreeable task of refusing you an audience, or of permitting one, under similar circumstances. I must, therefore, desire your royal highness will take some refreshment in the adjoining room, and I wish you a very good evening."

It hardly need be told that the insulted Caroline did not stay to partake of the proffered *hospitality* of this German princess. To be injured by the son, and insulted by the mother, was as much as human feeling could endure, and the princess reached her home in a state of mind little short of distraction. On the following morning, one of the royal dukes called upon the princess, and told her, he was informed of her journey to Windsor by an express from his mother, and also stated his opinion that no measures of an unpleasant nature were in agitation. The princess hastily answered, "Do you think I was not fully satisfied of the regent's intention upon the subject before I resolved to visit the queen? You forget, prince, that I am an injured lady. You know I was brought into this country to afford money to pay my intended husband's enormous debts, and to give him means to live in the greatest splendour with his numerous mistresses! I am deprived of the society of my only child! Injurious reports are circulated and received against my honour, and I am not even permitted to exonerate myself from these vile and slanderous imputations, because I am injured by the reigning authority."

The royal duke said, "I beg, my dear cousin, you will not permit the harsh and unfeeling conduct of the queen to operate on your mind. *We all know she is revengeful in the extreme*, but she always *favours George* in everything; and, from her very bitter conduct to you, we are well assured George is meditating some new scheme against you. One thing I promise you: I will abide by you, even presuming anything *disreputable is proved*; and I only beg you will give me your *private* confidence, that I may be prepared for the worst."

Her royal highness, hastily rising, said, "Sir, if you intended to insult me, I feel it such; but if, from unguarded or not well-considered language, you have so very improperly expressed yourself, then I am not captious to place any ungenerous meaning upon your words! If my rectitude did not rise higher in the scale of truth and uprightness than that of your family, including *both sexes*, I should not have ventured the close and determinate inspection into my conduct at the will or command of my avowed foes! If it were not for my child's sake, I would *satisfy you all* that I am privy to TRANSACTIONS which one day or another will be punished with the vengeance of heaven, and which I solemnly believe to be my duty to explain, though it may even cause 'the cloud-capp'd towers and gorgeous palaces' to fall into one general heap of ruins!"

The duke was almost petrified with the language and manner of the princess, and strongly urged the necessity of *silence* upon any and all of the unfortunate or dishonourable transactions in which the family had been engaged, observing, "Your own welfare depends upon their's, and that is a consideration of positive importance, which I hope your royal highness will justly appreciate!"

This suggestion of the cowardly duke produced the opposite effect to that which was intended; the princess declared that the mean sentiments of the queen had also found way into the minds of her sons, and instead of proving their royal descent by greatness of mind and action, they condescended to suggest self-preservation and self-enjoyments in preference to an open avowal of truth, and an honourable meeting with an enemy. "And," hastily said her royal highness, "is this, Sir, a specimen of the character of the English royal family? What would my ever dear and lamented father have thought of such principles and opinions? Doubtless, he would rather have followed his daughter to the tomb, and have seen her remains deposited with his ancestors, than have had her associated with persons who could sacrifice HONOUR for mean and paltry conveniences. Your royal highness must be well assured, that I am not a stranger to the unfounded and most abominable assertions or suggestions issued against my child's legitimacy; certainly, if I am only the Princess of Wales *nominally*, then my daughter bears a surreptitious title, and if either of us is considered as an obstacle to the interests of the nation, why are not the assertions upon that point made in an honourable and open manner. You well know, Sir, that I would sacrifice anything and everything for the happiness and future prosperity of my child; but I must be fully convinced, that *my* destruction of rights or enjoyments of privileges would not produce the entire annihilation of *her's* also. I must be made to understand that the mother and child have separate interests, and that insults received by one are not dishonourable to the other. I have also another powerful objection to keep silence upon these heart-rending and distracting subjects, which is, Charlotte's deep-rooted aversion to those persons who have insulted me most. This feeling assures my mind that I ought not to shrink from any avowal of truth which I may in justice to this generous nation be called upon to make, and nothing less than my child's safety shall keep me from making a disclosure of the unmerited and most incomparable wicked conduct manifested towards me. If I find that likely to operate against my daughter's happiness, I will forbear; but not upon any other ground."

The determined manner of her royal highness fully satisfied the abashed duke that the sentiments thus boldly expressed were the unalterable principles entertained by the princess, and would only gather energy and force by opposition and remonstrance; he therefore very soon afterwards took his leave, and gave the outline of the conversation to his *august* mother, BY WHOSE EXPRESS WISH THE INTERVIEW HAD TAKEN PLACE.

The queen was posed by the firmness her royal highness had displayed; and, in reply to the communication, said, "I will not be disappointed by this seeming boldness; the princess shall *feel my* POWER. She shall see Charlotte still less; the restrictions shall be enforced with greater severity, and she shall repent of her stupidity. Does the Princess of Wales imagine that I am to submit to *her* opinions upon my conduct, or to *her* abuse of any of my family? *My only fear is that the daughter will prove* AS UNBENDING AND AS DETERMINATELY RESOLUTE *as the mother is*, and I am therefore resolved to separate them as much as possible."

The result proved the queen's indignation and resentful disposition; as, immediately, a council was held upon the subject, and her majesty was positive in her instructions, that the restrictions between the Princess of Wales and her daughter should be more rigidly enforced.

At the commencement of the year

1813,

the princess found her situation more irksome than ever; and she resolved, therefore, to inform the prince regent of the hardships of her case, soliciting his royal highness to inform himself of all or any part of her behaviour or demeanour, to which the queen had made such heavy objections. The following is an exact copy of the letter of her royal highness to the prince:

27th Jan., 1813.

"Sir,

"On the 14th of this month, I transmitted to the hand of your royal highness a letter relative to the cruelty and injustice of my situation, in reference to my beloved child's separation from me, the most heart-rending point upon which you could so severely afflict me. Why does your royal highness refuse to answer my simple, but honest and honourable inquiry? What have I not endured since the moment I became your princess and wife? Heaven only knows, and heaven only can avenge my wrongs. It is now more than seventeen years since I gave birth to your lovely daughter, Princess Charlotte of Wales, at which time I did most certainly hope and also believe, that her royal father's affectionate recollections of her mother would not only revive, but be exemplified. Yet to this time, your royal highness has not evinced one spark of regard to the consort you vowed 'to love and cherish.

"More than this, my lord and husband, you permit her majesty to usurp such extreme authority over me, and insult me in every possible way. Why, my lord, I ask, do you allow these indignities to be imposed upon your cousin and wife, (so called) the mother of the heiress to the throne of these united kingdoms? If I had deserved such treatment, I should most naturally have avoided all scrutiny; but, that I have endeavoured to obtain all possible investigation into my conduct, I need only refer to my several correspondencies with your august father, your brother of York, privy council, &c. &c.

"I cannot conclude without saying, if you refuse me justice, I will leave indisputable proofs to this insulted nation that its generosity has been abused, though, at the same time, I would save *you yourself* from IGNOMINY at the hazard of my liberty. To the queen, I never will bow. Her majesty WAS, IS, and EVER WILL BE, A TYRANT to those she may imagine obstacles in her path. Perhaps her majesty presumes I am not an object of material consequence; but time will develop all these things. If this letter meet not with your royal approbation, I can only regret it, and waiting your reply,

"I am, ever,

"Your faithful and devoted

"CAROLINE."

"P.S. I entreat your royal highness to inform yourself of every part of my conduct which may at any time have been esteemed derogatory; and, while I beg this favour, I trust your royal highness will never again submit to the unprincipled, slanderous, and abominable aspersions cast upon my character. Let me suggest, my lord, that TRUTH MUST PREVAIL, SOONER OR LATER. After the most deliberate, careful, and scrutinizing investigations, I only beg to be punished with the most extreme rigour, if I am found GUILTY; but if free from guilt, I ought to say, I have an indisputable right to be ACKNOWLEDGED SO!"

"To his Royal Highness, the Prince Regent."

This letter was not noticed when the commissioners sat on the 23rd of February; and Lord Liverpool never even mentioned it when communicating with the princess, or when he had the private interview with her royal highness, by the regent's request.

We should not act with justice or honour if we neglected to state this *omission*; because the letter reflected much credit upon the princess, and ought to have been the first read when the council assembled. The result of this new inquiry, however, was what the vindictive queen intended it should be; for the almost-distracted Princess of Wales was refused the natural privilege of intercourse with her only daughter!

In the meantime, every opportunity was gladly embraced to detract the character of the princess. Base inuendos and malicious remarks were incessantly poured forth against her, until her life became one continued scene of sorrow and abuse, caused by those from whom she ought to have experienced protection. Under these imputations, the princess again appealed, by an address to the Speaker of the House of Commons; and, after many inquiries and replies, the subject was dismissed with an acknowledgment, that *"Her royal highness is declared free from all imputation."*

We must not here forget to mention, that Mr. C. Johnstone submitted a motion, on the 5th of March, "to request the prince regent will permit the copy of a certain report, made in 1806, to be laid before the House;" but Lord Castlereagh opposed it, as being *unnecessary*, and the document was consequently refused.

Notwithstanding the disgust manifested by every honest Englishman at the base conduct of Sir John and Lady Douglas, when they preferred their abominable charge against the character of the Princess of Wales in the year 1806, they had the hardihood to present a petition to the House this year *to re-swear to the truth of their former depositions concerning the conduct of the Princess of Wales*! No proceedings, of course, took place in consequence of this attempt still to propagate their calumnies; but a motion was made by Mr. C. Johnstone, a few days afterwards in the House of Commons, "That the petition of Sir John and Lady Douglas ought to be regarded as an audacious attempt to give a colour of truth, in the eyes of the nation, to evidence which they had delivered touching the conduct of her royal highness the Princess of Wales, and which evidence was a foul and detestable endeavour to bring the life and honour of her royal highness into danger and suspicion." This resolution, however, could not be passed, in consequence of the House *not being in possession of the evidence*, which was refused, as we have just stated, by Lord Castlereagh; but many members expressed their agreement with the *sentiments* of the resolution.

What was the *real* reason for not *prosecuting* Sir John and Lady Douglas, after the House had rejected their petition with such indignation, on the motion of Mr. Johnstone, it is not very easy to divine; that alleged by Lord Castlereagh is most certainly not a *satisfactory* one. It has been often insinuated, that if the conspiracy against the life and honour of the Princess of Wales did not originate with her royal relatives, it was certainly fostered and brought to maturity by persons connected with the queen and the prince regent; and the evidence of Bidgood and Cole very much favours that opinion. If the Douglases, and Bidgood and Cole, were the "suborned traducers," to which her royal highness alluded in one of her letters to the prince about this time, the impunity with which the knight and his lady were suffered to continue at large cannot excite surprise. This impunity, the report that Bidgood had received a pension of one hundred and fifty pounds a year, and the direct interference of the Prince of Wales in promoting the inquiry, and in entering his caveat to prevent the princess being received at court, have thrown a suspicious veil around this part of the proceedings, which will not be very soon removed.

On the 23rd of March, the Princess of Wales had to bear another severe stroke of fortune, in the death of her mother, the Duchess of Brunswick, who was interred with much funeral pomp, at Windsor, on the 31st. This melancholy event, following so closely after her late persecutions, was as much as the princess could endure; and had it not been for the sympathetic attentions of one confidant, her royal highness would, no doubt, have sunk under her immense load of sorrow.

In July and August, the princess devoted the greater portion of her time to correspondence with the prince, her husband. Very many of the letters could not, we think, have met the eye of the regent, or answers must have been sent, if only in common courtesy, as the prince knew *his* honour, and also that of his family, were at stake. We have *transcripts of all these letters*; but shall content ourselves with only introducing *the last she wrote to his royal highness previous to her going abroad*. The following is a literal copy of it:

23rd of Aug., 1813.

"Sir,

"I have waited, with most anxious feelings, to receive an acknowledgment of the safe receipt of several important communications which I addressed to you as 'private and confidential.' To this hour I have not received a reply, and I therefore take up my pen for the last time upon this most disagreeable business. To you it is well known, that the good king, your father, has invariably treated me with the most profound respect, and proper attention; and his majesty would have done me more essential service long since, had it not been for the oath he gave to Lord Chatham, to preserve from all *public* investigation the connexion formed in 1759 with the Quakeress.

"I am aware, Sir, that you may say I intrude myself upon your royal notice very frequently; but I think and feel it to be my indispensable duty and privilege. I have lately had an interview with Lord Liverpool; but his lordship cannot serve your royal highness and the persecuted Princess of Wales. I, therefore, shall not submit myself to any further interviews with his lordship, by my own request. As I intend this letter as a *final appeal* and *explanation* to your royal highness, I beg to ask your forbearance and lenity on account of its length and detail.

"Your royal highness has not forgotten how strangely I was allured from my father's court to receive your hand in marriage (the letters of 1794 bear me witness). You cannot have forgotten the kind reception of the king, your father, on my arrival in the metropolis of this empire, and the sarcastic manners of the queen. Two days had scarcely passed after our marriage, when you commanded me to receive Lady Jersey upon all occasions, although your royal highness was too well acquainted with the deep-laid schemes formed by her majesty against me, which were to be put into execution by Lady Jersey; and when I most humbly requested of you, that I might be secluded from all society rather than endure that which was so hateful to me, your royal highness cannot have forgotten the inhuman reply you made me, '*The Princess of Brunswick has answered every purpose I desired, inasmuch as my debts are to be settled, and my income augmented, and I will provide an heir to the throne more worthy of popular regard than any descendant of my father's family could ever prove.*' These, Sir, were words of so heavy and doubtful a character, that from that moment I never forgot them; and from the hour in which my Charlotte was born, I have feared for her health and happiness. How your royal highness could thus insult me, you can best imagine.

"Another most material grievance imposed upon me was, your unnatural remark to Lady Jersey, in my presence, '*that you thought the king* TOO FOND *of the Princess of Wales; and if her royal highness had any children, his majesty would no doubt be the* FATHER, INSTEAD OF THE GRANDFATHER.' Lady Jersey's reply will never be effaced from my memory, while reason holds her empire: '*Yes, my prince, and you deserve it, if ever you notice the Princess of Wales again in the character of a husband or lover.*' Your royal highness may remember I instantly left the room, more deeply insulted and wounded than language can describe. From that time, I was aware of my cruel fate, and I did deeply deplore the necessity which had forced me from the much-loved scenes of my infancy and youthful years.

"The very remarkable request of Mr. Pitt, in 1800, for a private interview with me, was another cause for disquiet to my mind; but I acceded immediately, and he accordingly was admitted. The object of that minister's visit was to solicit my silence upon the subject of the *bondholders, whose fate had caused so great an interest in several countries*, and whose families had been the *victims* of their ready acquiescense to the wishes of the royal princes. '*But*' said Mr. Pitt, '*these affairs are of as much consequence to your royal highness as they are to*

the other members of the royal family; and if matters of this kind are to be canvassed publicly, your royal highness may rest assured that ere long your family will not be permitted to occupy the exalted rank and station they now enjoy. I therefore most earnestly recommend that your royal highness does not name these subjects to any of the anti-ministerial party, who are not at present in possession of the circumstances.'
I do not doubt but Mr. Pitt laid the whole of this conversation before your royal highness, and he must have noticed the very cool and guarded reception I gave him. To have behaved openly to Mr. Pitt was impossible, as I knew too well his avowed hostile feelings against me. But a few days had elapsed after this interview, when I had the pleasure of seeing the good king. I now take the liberty of laying before your royal highness the substance of our conversation. 'My dear daughter,' said his majesty, 'I hear Pitt has paid you a confidential visit,' 'Yes, Sire, he has,' I replied. 'What was the object of it?' 'Upon the subject of the bondholders, your majesty.' *'I hope you made no rash promise?'* said the king; 'None, Sire.' *'Why could not Pitt have called upon you at a more suitable hour, Caroline?'* 'I do not know, Sire; but I plainly saw Mr. Pitt did not think much etiquette was necessary to the Princess of Wales, as *he well knew it was my dinner hour*; and yet I was determined not to refuse myself, as I was perfectly sure the whole of the affair would be reported to the queen.' 'Caroline, my niece,' said the king, 'do not, pray do not, fear Pitt, or any of my family. I will put you in possession of some affairs which will soon silence them all; and before the end of this week I will send you a small parcel of important papers, by the hand of a trusty messenger.'

"Your royal father most scrupulously kept his word, and enclosed me the PROOFS he had named, and promised to send. Many times since then have I informed your royal highness that I was in confidence upon those subjects; but you have never condescended to acknowledge those communications, or expressed one sentiment of obligation for the strict silence I have observed. I have been restrained only from the most ARDENT AND PARENTAL AFFECTION TO MY LOVELY DAUGHTER, or long ere this I would have proclaimed the extent of the wrongs I have endured from some of the illegal and unjust impositions practised upon me and the British nation. Your royal highness knew at the moment you met me at the altar in the palace, that you were already the affianced husband of Mrs. Fitzherbert, and you were well aware that if my uncle, the king, had known of that former circumstance, he would have prevented the left-handed marriage taking place. In this his majesty was deceived, and I have been the victim of your intentional imposition. It has generally been supposed by your royal highness' family connexions, that there was some impropriety or defect by which you received an unfavourable opinion of me in the early part of our fatal marriage; and, in my presence, your royal highness has insulted me by such insinuations, though you well know I was not the OFFENDER, but the OFFENDED!!! Up to this period, I have buried your royal highness' UNNATURAL CONDUCT to me in my own bosom; but if I am to be so injured, and if my character is to be so vilified, I shall EXPLAIN MYSELF TO THE NATION, and think I am performing an imperative duty. Your royal highness cannot have forgotten *the outrage you committed by entering my chamber at Montague House, and your denial of it to the queen, your mother, for the avowed purpose of traducing my honour.* Had I not then been restrained from explanation upon those base designs, by an unalterable love to my *child*, I should have exposed the infamous conduct you manifested towards me.

"I name these things, Sir, to prove to you the inviolable honour I have observed, in despite of all the insults and provocations I have received from your royal highness and the queen, and also from the creatures employed to ruin me in the estimation of this generous English nation. A *time will come when the secrets of my life will be* PUBLISHED TO THE WORLD; *then let the unprejudiced judge.*

"I remain, Sir,
        "Your royal highness' most
                "Faithful wife and cousin,
                        "Caroline P."
"To his Royal Highness, the Prince Regent."

It is more than probable that the confidentially-private and notorious secretary (M'Mahon) was the receiver of these appeals and documents, who, possessing the most unbounded assurance in the ability of his royal master's coadjutors to carry any plan into execution, or to prevent vexatious trouble to any extent, *suppressed them* at the moment when they might have proved of the greatest consequence to her royal highness. We cannot wonder at this, when we take into account the character of this private secretary, who dared to violate the rights of friendship, and break through the most sacred ties of conjugal affection, treating the honourable engagements of persons in general as matters of minor consequence! Were this depraved man now an inhabitant of the earth, we would ask him if his recollection could furnish the *number* of inroads he had made upon the abodes of innocence and beauty, to gratify his royal patron. We could ourselves name several instances; but one will suffice, which we copy from the manuscript of a friend, and the substance of which has been before published.

The private secretary of the prince (M'Mahon) was accustomed to retire for *recreation* to Bath, at certain periods. At the time to which we now advert, he was travelling to that city, and, at Marlborough, a respectable and venerable gentleman, accompanied by two young ladies, took their seats in the stage coach. The courtier was not wanting in attentions, and, in reply to his numerous questions, he soon received the information, "that the gentleman was a *poor* clergyman, residing near Marlborough; that the two young ladies were his daughters, whom he then was accompanying to visit a relation at Bath." M'Mahon's polished manners, added to the fixed determination of sacrificing these ladies to his royal master's desires, had the hoped-for effect, and the deluded party was anxious to cultivate further acquaintance with the stranger. Two days after their arrival, the intriguing secretary wrote and despatched the following letter to the prince:

"(Most Private.)

"Bath, Sunday Evening.

"Sir,—Ever alive to the obtaining possession of any object which may contribute to your royal pleasures, I hasten to inform your royal highness, that chance has thrown me into the company of two most lovely girls, the daughters of an indigent curate, and who, from their apparent simplicity and ignorance of the world, may be soon brought to comply with the wishes of your royal highness. I shall immediately devise some plan by which they may be induced to visit the metropolis, and the remainder of my task will then not be difficult of execution. The prize is too valuable to be lost sight of; the elder of the girls bears some resemblance in her form and make to Hillisberg, although it is evident that the whole fullness of her growth has not yet developed itself. The younger is more of a languishing beauty; but, from the knowledge which I possess of your royal taste, the elder will be the object of your choice.

"I have the honour to remain, &c. &c.

"JOHN M'MAHON."

"To his Royal Highness the Prince Regent, &c. &c."

The intimacy at Bath was cultivated. M'Mahon promised to intercede for the interest of the worthy clergyman, and afterwards engaged to ensure him promotion.

In the midst of explanations, promises, and engagements, M'Mahon was summoned to town by the royal order. Ere he departed, he promised, instantly upon seeing the prince, to lay their case before him, and dwelt in vivid terms upon the effects of such a representation. Within the ensuing fortnight, the clergyman received a letter from him, announcing "that a vicarage was vacant, in the gift of the crown, to which he should receive the presentation." M'Mahon again visited Bath, and recommended the clergyman and family to take up their abode in the metropolis. For this purpose, he had engaged apartments in the house of Mrs. General Hamilton, in Gloucester-place, to which they soon resorted. In the mean time, M'Mahon informed the clergyman that his induction would shortly take place, and that, in the interim, he must employ himself in the most agreeable manner, as also his daughters, in such amusements as the town afforded. Mrs. Hamilton was also pleased to say she would be their conductor and companion upon all occasions. The lady just named was a gay, though *unsuspected*, character. Shortly after this period, at an evening party, M'Mahon introduced Colonel Fox, "a gentleman," he said, "allied to the noblest families, and of an immense fortune."

If our readers should here inquire, *who* was Colonel Fox? we answer,—the Prince of Wales.

We hasten to the conclusion of this most infamous history. The deceived clergyman was informed that he must proceed to a village in Leicestershire, where his induction would instantly take place; and he, therefore, hastily took leave of his daughters, with an assurance that they were in the best society. Indeed, Mrs. Hamilton had evinced such interest and apparent solicitude in their happiness, that his heart was relieved from any doubts for their safety. This amiable father took leave of his children in the most affectionate manner; but little did he imagine that embrace would be the last he should ever receive from them,—yet so it proved. A short time after, early in the day, M'Mahon called upon Mrs. General Hamilton, expressing the necessity of her seeing her solicitor upon some affairs relative to the estate of her deceased husband.

The carriage was ordered, and the secretary promised to remain with the younger, while the elder sister accompanied Mrs. Hamilton. "We will first drive to Taylor's, in Bond-street," said Mrs. Hamilton, "he has some commissions to execute for me," and accordingly they were set down there.

The obsequious shoe-maker requested them to walk into the drawing-room, which they did; and in a few minutes Mrs. Hamilton said, "I will now step down, and transact my business with Taylor." In a short time she returned, saying, "How truly fortunate we are; Colonel Fox has just entered the shop, and, being informed *you* are here, has solicited permission to keep you company until I return from my solicitor's; *you* cannot refuse the request;" and then, without waiting a reply, she left the room. The *pretended* Colonel Fox entered; he professed *eternal love* and *unalterable constancy*; and, within one hour, this lovely, but most unfortunate, female was added to the infamously-swelled list of the prince's debaucheries and cruel seductions. The younger sister *still lives*—a melancholy proof of outraged and insulted honour.

We have given this detail to satisfy the scrupulous portion of society, that the prince merited a thousand-fold more exposure and execration than he ever received.

At this period, Mr. Whitbread was very pressing with the Princess of Wales, advising her to make a tour upon the continent, in order to divert her mind from the provocations she was so frequently called upon to endure. Upon one occasion, he urged the subject with considerable warmth, and his great earnestness surprised her royal highness. With her usual readiness, she said, "I feel sure Mr. Whitbread does not intend any thing disagreeable in these remarks; but, Sir, are you aware that Mr. Canning has been pressing the same opinion upon my notice? and I do not comprehend *why* this suggestion is made by you also. If I go away, shall I not leave my beloved child exposed to the determinate will and caprice of the queen, and others, who, doubtless, will vex her as much as possible? Are you, Sir, *requested* to represent this to me, or is it your private opinion?" Mr. Whitbread replied, "It is *my personal opinion*, and solely to provide against any unhappy effects arising from the queen's displeasure, which," he added, "I well know is unbounded."

On the 27th of May, the princess went to the Opera House. It was her first appearance in public since her triumphant acquittal. Her royal highness was received with considerable acclamations, while even her enemies were compelled to acknowledge "the dignity, delicacy, and feeling, pre-eminently displayed in her behaviour."

On the 30th, the regent gave a grand supper and ball, but the princess was not invited.

The supplies required for the service of this year amounted to upwards of one hundred and twenty millions!

Endless vexations and anxieties attended the Princess of Wales up to the year

1814;

but the public voice cheered her to the ultimate defeat of her base enemies.

The transactions of this year do not reflect much credit upon certain mis-named *illustrious* individuals, and can never fail to excite contempt in the minds of the British people. The Douglas party were promised *rewards*, which they could not obtain, except in a less degree, as it was alleged they had failed in a principal part of their unworthy undertaking; namely, the degradation of the princess, by a full and unlimited verdict against her royal highness, agreeable to the charges they had preferred.

The disappointed queen was indignant, beyond bounds, at the honourable acquittal of the Princess of Wales. "What!" said her majesty, "am I for ever to be disappointed by the adroit talents of the princess, whose very name I hate! It must not be. If she be recognised as an unblemished character, I am well satisfied the odium of the whole proceeding will fall upon *me*; and rather would I prefer death than suffer her royal highness to triumph over me!"

Lord Castlereagh was then consulted by the queen, and he engaged to do his utmost against the princess; and the regent again suggested the idea of her going abroad, when steps, more effectual, might be taken to ruin her character. Lord Castlereagh, therefore, the next day informed the princess, by a note, "that for the present time all interviews with the Princess Charlotte must cease."

On the 7th of January, the Princess of Wales gave an entertainment at Montague House, where a select party was invited, in honour of the Princess Charlotte's birth-day, who had now attained her eighteenth year.

An unexpected event, about this period, gave the Princess Charlotte an interview with her mother for nearly two hours, in which these affectionate relatives enjoyed an undisturbed conversation. The Princess Charlotte was very explicit in her communications to her dear mother on the severity of the queen, during the time she had lately spent with her majesty at Windsor; and, among other observations, remarked, "Her majesty is a tyrant to all around her. If you walk out with the queen," continued the charming and noble princess, "you are sure to be told your pace is disagreeable,—either too quick or too slow. If you feel pleasure in seeing any sweet pretty plant, and express admiration of its several beautiful colours, and its various delicate appearances, you are sure to be told, such observations prove your *want of taste and judgment*. Indeed, my dear mother, I like anybody better than my *disagreeable grandmother*, and I can never permit myself to remain with her so long again. When I am at the castle, I am seldom *allowed to see my grandfather*, the king; and, when I do, he scarcely looks at me, and seems extremely unhappy. When my royal father goes to the castle, he is always with the *queen alone*, and very rarely pays a visit to the king." Such was the ingenuousness of the Princess Charlotte. She would immediately speak the *truth*, and defy all results, rather than act with dissimulation to please or conciliate any one. This was the longest interview which was to fall to the lot of these high-spirited and generous-minded personages. Alas! their destiny might have been pourtrayed by the pen of cruelty, and traced in characters of blood! At parting, the princess most tenderly embraced her mother, and that parent for the moment forgot all her sorrows. But what was her agitation, when her ONLY HOPE was saying, "Farewell!" Agonizing—beyond all expression—agonizing! We must sympathize with such sorrows, and admit the propriety of the remark of the Princess of Wales at this separation, "My life has already been too long, since it has been one continued scene of misfortune!"

The prince regent now paid a visit to the Duke of Rutland, for the avowed purpose of standing sponsor to the young marquis, the duke's son and heir. The preparations for the reception and accommodation of his royal highness were upon the most magnificent scale, which, we are sorry to relate, were little else than thrown away. In the evening, the sparkling goblet was so freely emptied by the royal guest, that he was obliged to be *carried* to the chamber prepared for him. Do not imagine, gentle reader, that we are disposed to dwell ill-naturedly on the mischances of this luckless night; but the prince was unfortunate, and committed such sins and transgressions in this ducal apartment, and IN *the bed* prepared for him, that, at a very early hour, his carriage was ordered, and his royal highness was on the road to London! The domestics at Belvoir Castle were left to relate this very disagreeable incident, and testify that the means required for the *purification* of their master's premises were of no common quality!

However facetiously we may have spoken of this "untoward occurrence," yet we recoil with disgust and indignation from such scenes. How revolting is the reflection that this was the prince invested with *kingly authority*, and to whom so many millions of intelligent beings were looking for the redress of their grievances, and the amelioration of their many miseries!

The king's indisposition increased in the early part of this year, and the over-bearing tyranny of the queen consequently knew no bounds. In May, she addressed several notes to the Princess of Wales to forbid her appearance at the drawing-room, to which her royal highness replied very spiritedly. Some of these letters were afterwards published, but several were suppressed. It was at this time that the prince expressed his unalterable determination "never again to meet the princess, either in public or private," and the queen was the person who communicated his royal highness' unmanly vow to the princess.

About three weeks after this announcement, some illustrious foreigners, who were formerly intimate with the family of the princess, paid her royal highness a visit; and, on the ensuing day, they received her royal highness' invitation to dine with her on that day's night. It was accepted with pleasure; but, only about an hour previous to the appointed time for dinner, an apology was sent, asking pardon for the delay, which was said to be *unavoidable*, as the impediments arose from the COMMANDS OF THE REGENT, which had only been communicated to them a few hours before! Upon Mr. Canning's next visit to the princess, he explained the reason of this shameful conduct, by saying, "that Colonel M'Mahon desired, as a compliment, they would dine at Carlton House that day, and expressed an apology for the *shortness of the invitation*, as the regent had some days before given him his instructions to invite them, but that he (the colonel) had FORGOTTEN IT IN THE HURRY OF BUSINESS. Now," added Mr. Canning, "I know this story to be an invention; for it was only on the very morning of the day appointed by your royal highness that a brother of the regent heard of their intended visit, and informed him of it; and the prince then commanded M'Mahon to invite the party to dine at Carlton House, which they could not refuse, as etiquette would forbid their accepting any engagement in preference to that of the regent." Was there ever a more artful and vindictive piece of business concocted? How worthy was the master of such a scheming servant as M'Mahon!

In June, the allied sovereigns arrived in London, and fêtes and festivals followed in close succession. New honours were conferred upon several persons, who had been leaders in the late war. Lord Wellington was created Marquis of Douro and Duke of Wellington. To support this new dignity, four hundred thousand pounds were granted to him by the boroughmongering majority!

In consequence of the queen's edict, the Princess of Wales was excluded from the drawing rooms, held in honour of the illustrious guests; and this extra piece of persecuting malice sufficiently attested the *littleness* of the minds of her too powerful enemies.

Under these trying circumstances, Mr. Canning and Mr. Whitbread again urged their advice, that it would be better for all parties if the princess absented herself for a period, as the queen was so severe to the Princess Charlotte, in consequence of her regard for her mother. This consideration was enough for the fond parent. "Yes," said her royal highness, "for the sake of my child, I will leave England; I feel assured that my afflicted father-in-law, the king, cannot long survive; he is falling very gradually. But the crisis may be sudden; in that case, you know my situation; and what has been refused to the Princess of Wales cannot, I presume, be refused to the Queen of England! In making this reference, I merely and only mean, that I have hitherto been treated with the most unmerited severity, and the greatest injustice; this, I hope, will not be permitted in the event of my being queen. I name this to satisfy you, as my friends, that whenever I can return to this country with safety to my child, and honour to my few zealous friends, I shall not lose one moment in answering the summons."

On the 4th of June, Lord Castlereagh moved in the committee of the House, that fifty thousand pounds be annually paid to her royal highness the Princess of Wales. Mr. Whitbread offered some very correct and spirited remarks upon the subject, and the motion was agreed to. The princess, in the most generous manner, wrote to the Speaker on the 5th, declining to receive more than thirty-five thousand, adding, as a reason for this, her dislike to increase the already heavy burdens imposed upon the nation.

The ill-natured manner in which this most honourable act was received is best explained in the words of Lord Castlereagh, who, on the 8th, called the attention of the House to the letter of the princess, and concluded by saying, "It is not my duty to vote the public money to a *subject* who is not inclined to receive it." Her royal highness certainly was not much indebted to Lord Castlereagh for his very elegant and noble mention of her name, thus made; and the most dim-sighted person might have easily seen that "if the vessel came safe to shore," a *marquisate* would be the reward of the pilot.

The Princess of Wales at length requested leave of the ministers to go abroad. This was very readily granted; and, after some arrangements for correspondence, her royal highness prepared to depart. A very short interview was permitted with the child of her hopes and affections, while even that was attended by the ladies in waiting. They separated *then—TO MEET NO MORE IN THIS WORLD*!

It was during this affecting interview that her royal highness committed some letters of importance to the care of her noble-minded daughter; and, as it appeared impossible for any *private* conversation to pass between them, a letter accompanied the others, addressed to the Princess Charlotte by her afflicted mother, of which the following is a transcript:

"*Copy of a letter to my dear Charlotte, Princess of Wales.*

"*1814, June 7th.*

"My dearest Child,

"I deposit to your keeping a small parcel, of letters for my much-esteemed friend, Lady *******. I well know her generous disposition will cause her to endure a vast load of sorrow on my account, and, from these documents, the nation may one day *be told*. I must tell you, my dearest child, that in conformity to my father and mother's opinion, I became the wife (so called) of your father. Well do I remember the time when my dear father, the Duke of Brunswick, entered my library, (holding in his hand a letter) saying, 'Caroline, my love, I desire you will give your attention to the request of your most excellent uncle, the King of England, and, without any demur, engage to marry your cousin George. He is undoubtedly the most *elegant man* and the most ACCOMPLISHED GENTLEMAN in Europe. Very unfortunately, this prince has been captivated by the many beautiful ladies surrounding the court; but although he may have committed himself in *formal engagements*, yet the prince is the most ready, desirous, and expectant supplicant for your hand!' I started, and exclaimed, 'What, my dear sire?' The sequel, however, is sufficient. I came to England. I was received heroically by the people, flatteringly by the persons deputed to attend me, and sarcastically by the queen, my aunt; but most pleasantly by the king, my uncle, and the prince, my destined husband. After my marriage with the prince, your father, I soon had occasion to regret my change of situation. However, I strove to conceal my disappointment and chagrin, and appeared as lively as if I had no cause for regret. Speedily after my marriage, I was informed that the prince was not my *legal* husband; that, some time previous to our marriage, he had been united to Mrs. Fitzherbert, and therefore our engagement was null and void! I opened the sorrows of my heart to the good king. 'Ah! Ah!' said his majesty, 'I will befriend you, but my family will prove my ruin. They care not for any thing beside their own ease, and they, sooner or later, will *lose the crown* by such improper conduct. The disposition of my son George is *unrelenting*; but I will tell you, my dear niece, that you may subdue his public injurious mention of your character, if you make use of proper means. My son is so lascivious, that if you would attempt to hide his defects, they would speedily become more apparent.' In the course of conversation, his majesty informed me of the untimely end of his brother Edward, and also of the MARRIAGE and ISSUE of that brother, who, he stated, had been educated for the *church*; and also, that he had frequently seen him during his residence at Eton with no small degree of affection and regret, and had even appointed interviews with the individual under whose care he was placed, to adopt plans for his welfare. I confess, my dear Charlotte, I was quite unprepared for this exposition, and I answered with much warmth, 'Does your majesty mean to say, that his royal highness left issue which has never been acknowledged?' 'I do, indeed,' replied the king, 'and though the affair has been hitherto kept from the public, yet I fancy it will, one day or another, be made known.' My dear Charlotte will conceive how much I felt upon these singular explanations. I long to tell you more upon the subject, but as our confidential messenger is waiting, I must conclude by subscribing myself

"Your very affectionate mother,
"Caroline."

The persecuted wife of the heir-apparent now prepared to leave England. Her royal highness went to Worthing on the 2nd of August, and on the 9th embarked for the Continent, with a heart heavily charged with the most poignant feelings.

The evening of her departure was spent in rioting and drunkenness by the inhabitants of Carlton House, as they had now attained a portion of their dishonourable object, and, in a great measure, relied upon final success. The entertainments given at this period by the "unparalleled prince" were of the most dazzling and costly description. The massive services of richly-chased gold, and the viands served upon them, in addition to every luxurious appendage, were daily superseded by others, still more rare and expensive than the preceding ones. Hundreds of thousands were thus lavished on useless pomp, while, perhaps, a poor tradesman, who had received *the honour* of an order by command of the prince, and had borrowed the larger portion of the means to enable him to execute it, solicited, in the most humble manner, a portion of his debt; but, alas! solicited in vain; and, after daring to press his destitute and ruined condition several times, is probably forbidden ever to ask for the settlement again, but to wait the royal pleasure. His impatient creditors, in the interim, arrest him; he is carried to a prison, and, in the agony of his soul, commits suicide. Many a wife and family of children have thus been reduced to a workhouse, and the greater number of them afterwards thrown upon the town! But—these are some of the privileges of royalty!

The reminiscences of the queen were sometimes rather painful; and, shortly after she had driven her daughter-in-law from the country, symptoms of melancholy were observed. Her physicians, therefore, recommended a change of air; and, in order to amuse her majesty, it was proposed that she should repair to Brighton for a short time, accompanied by the princesses.

The Princess Charlotte, after the departure of her much-beloved mother, appeared very unhappy, and, from that time, saw her father and grandmother as seldom as possible. They well knew she was favourable to her mother's cause, in opposition to theirs, not only from the very great affection which she naturally felt for her mother, but also from the numberless proofs she had observed of the honourable motives by which the conduct of the Princess of Wales had been influenced. To these might be added the opinion of the virtuous part of the nation upon the subject, and the very great respect at all times paid to her royal highness by those persons who were *independent* of the royal family and the government.

Upon her majesty's return to Windsor, she found the king something improved in natural spirits, but desirous not to be troubled with unnecessary visitors. This slight improvement was, however, but of short duration; for, in a few days afterwards, this distressingly-afflicted sovereign relapsed into insensibility, and frequently became very boisterous in his conduct.

The amount required for this year's service was upwards of one hundred and sixteen millions, twenty-seven of which were raised by loans.

The year

1815

commenced under numerous public and private difficulties. The regent found himself in a very unpleasant situation, being under a necessity of increasing the number of the various orders of knighthood, in order to preserve himself a sufficiency of adherents. A strange concatenation of events had also placed the rest of the royal family in an uneasy position. The Duke of Kent, some considerable time before, entered into a positive engagement with a foreign princess, by solemnly promising her marriage; yet, upon requesting his mother's approbation of the choice he had made, how great was his surprise and indignation to find that she would not listen to it! But, hastily snatching up the letter a second time, she said, "It is impossible such things can be permitted; we need money too much in our own family to squander it upon these miserably-poor connexions." This indignant lady quite forgot, or did not wish to remember, her own origin, and the *great wealth* she had brought to this country. Ere this self-important personage had said so much, she should have called to mind the many *noble* acts by which she had been distinguished above all other royal ladies, and ought to have reflected, how many thousands had suffered privations and want to permit her royal self and family to live in splendour, and how many had been privately disposed of to satisfy her inordinate ambition and insatiable thirst for power!

Her majesty had also another mortification to endure in the marriage of her hopeful son, the Duke of Cumberland, with the Princess of Salms. Lord Castlereagh, always happy to take from the people, had the audacity to propose an additional grant to the Duke of Cumberland upon his alliance with a lady so congenial to the taste and talents of his royal highness! The House of Commons, however, opposed this grant, and several members made the most severe, though *just*, remarks upon the character of Ernest Augustus on this occasion.

"Mr. R. Gordon rose, and declared that he could not reconcile it to his sense of duty to allow this motion to pass with a silent vote against it. He was astonished at the observation of the noble lord (Castlereagh) who brought forward this motion last night, that he did not apprehend any opposition, while he agreed with the noble lord that it must be painful to hear any reflections upon the character of the individual referred to, or any comments whatever at all likely to depreciate the consequence of the illustrious family to whom that individual belonged. But ministers alone were to blame in *dragging* the Duke of Cumberland before that House. If any reflections were thrown out against that individual, it was the fault of ministers in *forcing* him upon the consideration of that House. *After what had* NOTORIOUSLY PASSED WITH RESPECT TO THIS INDIVIDUAL, *and his connexions,—after the* RUMOURS *that were afloat upon the subject,—he could not, by any means, concur with the noble lord, that this was not to be regarded as a* PERSONAL *question!*"

"Mr. Bennet said, the Duke of Cumberland, of all the branches of the royal family, was the *only one* who could come to that House, and make an application for money, which he should feel *compelled to oppose!* He appealed to every person in the committee, whether they did not hear, out of that House, *every individual in the country express* ONE UNIFORM FEELING *with respect to that personage,—a feeling decidedly averse from any disposition to concur in such a grant as was now proposed.* It was impossible even to go to what was called *fashionable* society, without hearing the *same feeling of disrespect expressed*!!!"

"Lord Nugent disapproved of the grant proposed, with reference to the time in which, to the manner in which, and to the *person* for whom, the grant was proposed. He differed with his honourable friend who spoke first in the debate, not in his vote, but in that he did not admit public rumour to influence his vote. For his own part, he voted mainly on evidence which could come before the House only by public rumour,—public rumour uncontradicted and unencountered!!!"

"Lord A. Hamilton thought the House was called upon to consider the *merits of the individual* before it assented to this proposition, unless it were assumed that, upon the marriage of any branch of the royal family, the House was bound to grant an additional allowance, without any consideration of the nature of the marriage, which was a proposition too preposterous to be maintained! The intimation, too, which he understood to be authentic, that it was the intention of the Duke of Cumberland not to reside in this country, furnished another argument against the present measure; nay, it was stated that the grant was brought forward upon the *settled condition that his royal highness should fix his residence* ELSEWHERE!"

"Mr. Methuen contended that the House ought to shew, by its vote that night, that it was not inattentive to the *morals* of the country, and that therefore he should oppose the grant, not from the slightest personal motives, but merely in the conscientious discharge of what he conceived to be his duty."

"Sir H. Montgomery said, that when the present bill was first brought into the House, he voted for it, because he thought the proposed sum was no more than what was necessary; but, from what he had heard since, he almost fancied he had done something very wrong! In the present case, however, he really saw nothing which would warrant the House in putting such a *stigma* upon his royal highness as *would be conveyed by refusing the grant*!"

The House of Commons DID REFUSE THE GRANT, though only by a small majority. But this majority was sufficient, according to Sir H. Montgomery, one of his royal highness' *admirers*, to cast a STIGMA on the Duke of Cumberland!

As soon as the Princess of Wales was known to have left Brunswick, and while proceeding to Geneva, persons were despatched from the British Court to watch all the movements and pursuits of her royal highness, and to report accordingly, through agents appointed for the mean purpose. Our country's money was used upon this base business with no sparing hand. Mr. Whitbread, being perfectly aware that these secret contrivances were put into execution, felt more in fear of some evil result to the princess than if she had remained in England. He, as well as many others, knew that assassination was of very frequent occurrence in Italy, and more than once expressed himself anxious to see the princess safely landed again on our shores. But this was not permitted; for, on the 6th of July, this patriot committed suicide, while in a state of mental aberration. He fell a sacrifice to the intensity of his feelings upon several most important subjects.

As a man of firm principles, Mr. Whitbread was justly entitled to the praise of his countrymen. He never allowed himself to be bribed into dishonourable actions; and we cannot, therefore, attribute his unhappy end to the stings of conscience. The man whose life, or a principal portion of it, has been spent in furthering the wily schemes and treacherous plans of others may, very probably, in the midst of enjoying the reward of his villanous conduct, be struck by memory's faithful reflection, and, afraid of exposure, prefer instant death; but the patriot who loves his country, and has largely contributed to the defence of justice and liberty, finding his exertions of no available use, and sick at heart at the insults levied against the oppressed, may be driven by despair to rush into the presence of his Maker by his own act. This latter case, no doubt, applies to the patriot whose untimely end we are now lamenting. It was Mr. Whitbread's glory to be an Englishman,—it is his country's boast that he used his energies for her general benefit. He actively and fearlessly investigated the cause and nature of abuses, was the ready advocate of the oppressed, and the liberal friend of all mankind!

The amount required for the service of this year was one hundred and sixteen millions, which was obtained from the heavily-taxed people, earned by the sweat of their brow, and consequently by robbing their starving families of comforts!

From such oppressive exactions, the present *domineering* Tory Aristocracy has reared its unblushing and hydra head. It was engendered in Deception, brought forth by Infamy, nursed by Indolence, educated by Sovereign Power, and has long lived the life of an Impostor—daring and hardy! We venture to predict, however, that its reign is drawing to a close; for the eyes of the whole nation are now fixed upon it, and its excrescences are discovered! Yes, the monster has outwitted itself, and from its seat will speedily shoot forth the TREE OF LIBERTY. May its fruits prove healing to nations! Merit will then be rewarded, Industry recompensed, Commerce revive, and Tranquillity reign in society. Kings will learn to do justice, sanguinary laws will be abolished; and thus the millennium of Peace and Joy will be established on a basis illustrious and impregnable!

At the commencement of the year

1816,

the intended marriage of the Princess Charlotte of Wales with Prince Leopold of Saxe Cobourg was announced, which had received the sanction of the regent. This intended union appeared to us, for many reasons, highly improper, and too closely allied to the circumstances of George the Third. We knew, for a considerable period before this announcement, that Leopold had been paying the most devoted attentions to a lady of great merit and accomplishments; and, also, that marriage had been promised. We likewise did not believe the prince was a Protestant from conviction, if he professed so to be; and feared that, if finally the husband of the princess, he would only be a convert to our "established religion" from *convenience*, but really and in truth, by inclination and education, a *Catholic*. We do not name the religious sentiments of the prince as any degradation or disqualification to his character as a man or as a prince, but simply to shew that his principles prohibited his entrance, by marriage, into the English royal family; for the royal marriage act expressly declares "such marriages shall be null and void."

While staying at the city of Augsburgh, in the early part of this year, we heard various reports upon the subject in question, and the paper of the day having met our eye, what were our feelings when we read the annexed paragraph!

"Augsburgh, January 10th.

"The Gazette of this city contains the following article, from Vienna, of January 3rd: 'Yesterday was celebrated, in the Cathedral Church of St. Stephen, in the presence of the reigning Duke of Saxe Cobourg, the MARRIAGE of his brother, *Prince Leopold*, with the young and beautiful Countess of Cohaky, according to the rites of the *Catholic* church.'"

In contemplating this circumstance, every honest man must view the conduct of Leopold with indignation. Example is generally considered preferable to precept, and Leopold embraced this opportunity of shewing himself a convert to such doctrine. George the Third committed BIGAMY; his son George did the same; and the remaining Hope of England was destined to be a victim to similar wickedness!

After some formal correspondence, the regent sent a message to both houses of parliament, on the 14th of March, to announce the marriage contract of his daughter, the Princess Charlotte, with his serene highness the Prince Leopold of Saxe Cobourg. Sixty thousand pounds were voted to the illustrious couple, annually; and, in case of *her royal highness' demise*, FIFTY THOUSAND POUNDS PER ANNUM were to be paid to the PRINCE *for his life*. Sixty thousand pounds were also granted for their outfit.

Well may foreigners exclaim, "How generous are the great English people!" Alas! it was not the act of the *people*; but the absolute will of Imbecility, Ignorance, and Impudence, which we shall have further occasion to illustrate.

We must now refer our readers to the former expectation of marriage between the Princess Charlotte and the Prince of Orange. That union was much desired by the regent, because the Prince of Orange had promised unrelenting opposition to the Princess of Wales. As soon as the Princess Charlotte, however, became aware of this, she determinately refused to see the prince again; and we well know that the Duchess of Oldenburgh took every possible opportunity to press Prince Leopold upon her notice. Up to the moment of the marriage, the Princess Charlotte did not hear or know a single word about the *former* serious engagement of her affianced

Princess Charlotte of Wales meets Prince Leopold, from an engraving in *The Life and Memoirs of Her Royal Highness Princess Charlotte of Charlotte of Saxe Coburg Saalféld* (1818).

husband, except the mean and paltry report, that "he had been very voluptuous in his gratifications, and was then desirous of bidding an eternal adieu to those who had formerly led him *astray!*" On the other hand, Charlotte was tired of the overbearing and indiscriminate conduct of her grandmother, the queen; and therefore resolved to free herself from such restraint.

Previous to the marriage, Prince Leopold solemnly promised to fulfil every iota of the Princess Charlotte's wish, with respect to her abused and insulted mother; and further engaged, that he never would permit or allow himself to be made a party, directly or indirectly, to injure the Princess of Wales, or to prevent any correspondence between the daughter and mother, of which her royal highness the Princess Charlotte might approve. But of what signification were the promises of such a faithless man!

The former marriage of the prince was not considered by the queen a sufficient impediment to his union with her grand-daughter; and she used her utmost ability to suppress any representation contrary to the interest of his serene highness. "The Augsburgh Gazettes" were, therefore, bought up at an immense expense, to save the character of this prince from public animadversion, and consequent contempt and hatred.

On the 21st of February, Prince Leopold arrived at the Clarendon Hotel. Lord Castlereagh waited upon his serene highness, and, on the following day, Sir B. Bloomfield arrived from Brighton, with the regent's command to invite the prince to the Pavilion.

Early on the ensuing morning, the prince and Sir B. Bloomfield left town for Brighton; and his serene highness was received with as much warmth and friendship by the regent as if he had been an old acquaintance, or an especial friend in iniquity!

On the 27th, the queen, accompanied by the Princess Charlotte and two of the princesses, arrived at the Pavilion, from Windsor Castle; the interview was short between Leopold and his intended bride. The family resolved that the marriage should take place as soon as possible. The royal ladies returned to Windsor, and the prince remained at Brighton with the regent.

At the time such immense sums were voted for this intended marriage and outfit, large means were also required for the support of our expensive establishments at home, which ought to have prevented any squandering of money upon *foreigners*, for we could never consider Prince Leopold as one of the royal family of *England*.

Mr. Vansittart, however, was very eloquent, *in his way*, in setting forth "the great, the incomparably great" station occupied by this country amongst the nations of the earth! In truth, we will tell the precise state of our *then greatness*. Our jails were crowded with farmers and the best of our tradesmen; our streets and roads swarmed with beggars, nearly dying from filth and want; agriculture languished, and commerce was paralyzed!

After some delay, caused by circumstances not very *honourable* to Prince Leopold, the marriage took place on the 2nd of May; and a very general report obtained credit that Prince Leopold pronounced his responses very tremulously, scarcely articulating his portion of the ceremony. This could hardly be wondered at, as he well knew the sacrifice of honour he was then making, and the inconstancy of his former sacred vows!

We pass over the time between the marriage and when the Princess Charlotte was declared *enceinte*. This occurred twice; but, after one disappointment, the accouchement was expected with all the ardour of English anticipation.

The princess had generally expressed her opinion, that mankind, in reason, policy, philosophy, and religion, were all of one great family; and hence arose her extreme aversion to the pomp and magnificence of the court. Indeed, the princess shewed herself very frequently to the public, and was so free and gracious in her manners, that she appeared in a natural English character, far opposed to the German pompous style.

A circumstance of no inferior import occurred at this period, which gave suspicion to the inquiring spirit of the liberal part of the English nation. This was—the return to office of George Canning! By the Tories, the event was regarded as a last resource; by the Whigs, his accession, under royal favour, was considered a token of victory. Each party was positively assured of an undeviating principle in this gentleman's character; but each one had to learn that the opinion was erroneous.

In this year, died two individuals, who had formerly been the bosom companions of royalty. One of these, Mrs. Jordan, expired on the 5th of July, near Paris, and was buried in the cemetery of St. Cloud; her body was put into a *thin shell, stained black*, with no ornament whatever. Mrs. Jordan had lived in Paris for some time in great privacy and poverty, under the assumed name of Mrs. James. Is not the newly-created Earl of Munster, and one or two other *great* personages, the issue of this unfortunate lady's singular engagement with the prince of some great nation? The other character was Richard Brinsley Sheridan, the favourite companion and devoted servant of the Prince of Wales. Let his scanty means of subsistence be remembered whenever the name of the prince regent is mentioned. Yes, reader, the man who had devoted his highly-improved and naturally-eloquent abilities to the cause of this regent was permitted to die in the course of an arrest!

The sorrows and disappointments which Mrs. Jordan underwent in this world were of the most agonizing description. Oh! why is it tolerated that royalty should be allowed to exercise the prerogative of inflicting the deepest wounds without the possibility of the injured party ever receiving redress? Is it not contrary to all laws, both human and divine, to suppose "the king can do no wrong?" If a prince commit an act of injustice, ought he not to be equally amenable with the peasant to the laws of his country? *We* think so, and hope to see the day when the whole world will acknowledge its justness, and *act* upon its principle.

Upon the retrospect of Mr. Sheridan's life, we are forcibly struck by the ingratitude practised towards him by his royal master. The vices he had contracted were the results of his acquaintance with this "all-accomplished prince," and during the period of his successive debaucheries with him, he frequently added his name to notes of hand, upon sight, or at a longer date, for the prince's extravagancies, or to meet any demand that might be required upon a run of ill luck at the gaming-table. Even the debt for which he was arrested was contracted under the last-mentioned circumstances, and had been paid by a note given *solely* for the regent's use by this unfortunate courtier. As soon as the country became informed of the unkindness Sheridan had experienced, they saw the character of the prince in its true light, forming their opinions from FACTS only, and not from the sophistical meaning given to his actions by the absolute prince himself, or by the parasites in his service. Honest men could not help grieving at the reflection, that the money produced by their labour, and even at the expense of depriving their families of comforts, was being squandered away at gambling-tables, upon unworthy characters, and in unwarrantable undertakings. The indignation caused by the base treatment of Mrs. Jordan and Sheridan manifested itself in several publications of the day, and many facts were elicited relative to these two unfortunate individuals; indeed, there was scarcely a subject in the realm, at all acquainted with their shameful desertion, who did not indulge in some bold expression of disgust and abhorrence at the disgraceful conduct of certain *illustrious* individuals, as being the causes of their multiplied sorrows and sufferings.

There was a time when monarchs and peers would have lived on the meanest food, merely sufficient to sustain human nature, in order to discharge the debts of a faithful servant; and it is well known, that, to reduce the pressure of taxation or impost upon the poorer classes of society, a certain sovereign even pawned his jewels! But, alas! this reign and regency did not present such an endearing feature to the nation; on the contrary, "the regent of blessed memory" would rather have pawned his subjects than have relaxed in his extravagant pleasures!

The marriage of the Princess Mary with her cousin the Duke of Gloucester took place in July, and gave "general satisfaction;" though his royal highness never benefitted the people in any other way than *honouring* them by accepting their bounty!

About this time, a considerable sensation was produced by the re-appearance of Mrs. Fitzherbert in the gay circles of fashion. The public journals noticed such an unexpected circumstance with timid expression, and professed that delicacy prevented any explanatory remarks! Ignorance and Avarice were more probably the obstacles in the way; but it would have better become writers, who pretended to patriotism and independence of character, to have stated unhesitatingly what they *did know* of the intentions of the royal plotters; they certainly might have paid a fine, or endured some imprisonment for speaking the *truth*; yet he who faulters when his country's weal is at stake is unworthy the name of—Briton!

The regent appeared now more determined than ever to procure a divorce from the Princess of Wales, and the means how this might be accomplished were put in active preparation. All the ungenerous and mean expedients hitherto used had been unavailing to produce the desired end. Spies had not succeeded, and a bolder invention had therefore become necessary. At the various courts connected with the "Holy Alliance," the princess had received very little attention; but in every circle where her royal highness appeared, which was uninfluenced by the crown, she was received rapturously, and treated most respectfully.

Previous to the conclusion of this year, a naval captain was offered ten thousand pounds if he could, by any stratagem, obtain PROOF of adulterous intercourse between the princess and any person of rank whatever. The *personage* who made this offer is NOW ALIVE, and if this statement of simple truth meet his eye, surely the blush of shame will die his hardened cheek.

The Baron Ompteda was also employed in this foul and diabolical plot, and, as a reward for his services, he has received a sufficiency from the hard-earned money of the tax-payers of this kingdom. We suggest that it had been quite in character to have presented the same in a purse, with "THE REWARD OF VILLANY" inscribed upon it.

We will here lay before our readers a plain statement of facts, relative to the persecutions which the unfortunate Princess of Wales endured abroad, and which is extracted from an original letter now in our possession:

"For some days past, there have been inserted in several of the papers various pretended extracts of letters from Milan, Munich, and other places, respecting the Princess of Wales, and giving a most erroneous statement of an affair that occurred some months since in her royal highness' family. You may depend upon the following, as being an authentic narrative of the transaction alluded to. An Hanoverian baron was observed to follow the princess' route wherever she went. He was always received by her royal highness with the attentions due to his rank. On the princess' return to Milan from her long voyage, the baron was still there, and paid his respects to her royal highness as usual; but reports having come to the ears of her household, that the baron had made use of expressions in society highly injurious to her royal highness, one of the gentlemen in her suite, an English officer, sent the baron a challenge, and this conveyed, in terms too plain and unequivocal to be misconstrued, that he accused him of 'a most infamous and unmanly return for the kindnesses he had received from her royal highness,' and called upon him to 'meet him at eight o'clock the next morning at Bartassima, (half way between Milan and Como) there to answer for this sacred charge against his honour as a gentleman and a man, who had ever received the most marked hospitality at the hands of the princess, and who had committed the greatest act of hostility against the very first of virtues.'

"This challenge was delivered to the baron by the hands of the Baron Cavalotti, a friend of the English officer. The answer to this direct challenge was an attempt to explain away the charge imputed to him; but an acceptance of the challenge, claiming his right to the choice of weapons, and saying that he would fight in Switzerland, but that his intended second was absent; in two days he would send him to settle the time and place.

"Just at this period, a discharged servant of her royal highness wrote a letter to the chief magistrate of Como, saying that his conscience touched him, and that he was desirous of making a confession of the part he had acted in a treacherous confederacy with the Hanoverian, in whose pay he had been for the preceding ten months, to disclose to him every transaction of the household, to procure false keys to her royal highness' apartments and drawers, &c. &c. This was made known to her royal highness. She treated all that he could have obtained by such insidious means with contempt; and actually took the footman, who had thus acted as a spy upon her actions, again into her service, on his imploring her pardon; but another accomplice was delivered over to the police, to be tried and punished.

"The very next day after this discovery, her royal highness gave a grand entertainment, at which the Governor of Milan and all the principal nobility were present. When the princess communicated the whole affair to the governor, he expressed his indignation at the scandalous conduct, and having learnt that a challenge had passed from one of her gentlemen to the baron, said that certainly that person was unworthy to be treated as a gentleman. The Hanoverian knew nothing of all this; but, according to his promise, sent Count Cantenogh, one of the chamberlains to the Austrian Emperor, to Como, who, having met the British officer, said he was not much acquainted with the Hanoverian who had requested him to be his second in an affair of honour; that he was anxious to have the matter fully investigated; and trusted that, if the baron should prove his innocence of the language imputed to him, the British officer would be satisfied that he had acted hastily. But, in case he was not satisfied, he was further instructed to say, that the baron wished the meeting to be in Germany, on the confines of France, instead of Switzerland, and time could not be convenient to him sooner than three weeks, a month, or more, from that time, as he had to go to Hanover to settle his affairs in the interim. The Englishman then related to Count Cantenogh the disclosures that had been made the day before, and submitted to him whether such behaviour did not render his principal unworthy the support of a man of honour, or to be met as a gentleman. The count declared that he could not be the second of such a person; that he must justify himself from this infamous charge, or choose another friend. With this, the count returned to Milan, and a message was soon after delivered to her royal highness, from the governor, to say that the Hanoverian baron had received orders to quit the Austrian dominions, which he had accordingly done.

"This curious affair made a considerable noise at the time, which was the beginning of November last, and is, we suppose, the foundation of the stories which have lately been circulated and misrepresented."

"In the summer of 1815, another wicked secret plot was formed against the princess, the origin of which it is not difficult to guess. The princess was narrowly watched, and attempts were made to seduce her people; but only one, Piqueur Crade, was so weak as to yield, and to promise Baron O** to conduct him into the apartments of the princess by means of false keys. The plot was, however, discovered, and the piqueur turned away. The man wrote to the Chevalier Tommassia, confessed that he had let himself be seduced by Baron O***** to betray his mistress, and begged for mercy. The princess thought it proper to acquaint the governor, Count Sawrau, with this event, and Baron O***** was forced to leave the dominions of his Majesty the Emperor. Hownham, the princess' private secretary, challenged the baron, but the latter has hitherto put it off. Since this affair, the princess is very cautious, particularly towards Englishmen whom she does not know; but she conceals herself from nobody, only she will not be the object of calumny, and of a shameful *espionage*, of which she has already been the victim. What has happened gives ground to fear still greater enormities.

"An event, which took place at Genoa, has more the appearance of an attempt at *assassination* than robbery. Some armed men penetrated, during the night, into the house of the princess, and almost into her bed-chamber. An alarm being given, one of the servants fired upon these people, and pursued them, but in vain. It is not yet discovered what were their intentions. But let a veil cover all this. Her first master of the horse, Schiavini, has kept a circumstantial account of her journey to the Holy Land. The princess went from Genoa to the island of Elba, thence to Sicily and Barbary, then to Palestine. She visited Jerusalem, Athens, &c., and was every where received with the honours due to her rank.

"By the assistance of several *literati*, she obtained a collection of valuable antiquities, for which object she spared no expense. Wherever the princess appeared, she left behind her grateful recollections by her beneficence. At Tunis, she obtained the freedom of several slaves. The princess is now employed in writing the history of her life, which she will make public when the time comes.

"By this, she will throw great light on many facts which are now involved in obscurity."

We need hardly offer a remark upon the vindictive measures, so fully set forth in this narrative, exercised against the unfortunate Princess of Wales. It will not be difficult for our readers to recognize the REAL INSTIGATORS of the many annoyances she endured; *their names* will be handed down to future generations as the "Oppressors of Innocence," while the finger of Scorn will mark the spot where lies their "SORDID DUST."

The calamitous situation of the nation at this time became truly appalling. Subscriptions were entered into for the purpose of relieving the distresses of the poor, and her majesty's name was put down for the insignificant sum of three hundred pounds! If we were to be prolix in our account of this German lady's *discretionary* liberality, the details, we fear, would not interest our readers. She was only liberal when her own interest was at stake!

Early in

1817,

the queen became indisposed, so much so as to cause alarm amongst her partisans for the issue. It was deemed expedient that the prince regent, who was then at Brighton, should be informed of the circumstance, and the Duke of York set off in the night to convey the intelligence to him. Why a courier could not have been forwarded, we do not pretend to say; but deception and mystery always attended the royal movements. Shortly afterwards, however, her majesty was declared convalescent, and the family were gratified by her recovery, being well assured that her assistance would be of the most essential consequence to the completion of the regent's wishes in the intended divorce.

In February, the "Habeas Corpus Act" was suspended, and, upon *suspicion only*, were Mr. Evans and his son seized and committed to prison on a charge of treason. They observed at the time, with great truth, "Poor devoted England! she cannot be called our country, but our grave!" This was confirmed by Lord Sidmouth, who rendered his every service in this disgraceful business, and was at all imaginable pains to prove, that his master, the regent, was the "Vicegerent of heaven, and had all power upon earth."

The country was now elated by the information that the Princess Charlotte was likely to give an heir to the throne; because the people hoped that her progeny would prove more worthy of a crown than some of the sons of her austere grandmother. Upon this amiable princess, indeed, the English people had long placed their hopes, and they lived in anxious expectation to see the then existing tyranny superseded by a better form of government, under her auspices. In the mean time, every member of the royal family appeared more interested for the health of the queen than for the Princess Charlotte. Her majesty had experienced several relapses; but, after each attack, when she appeared in public, no symptoms of previous indisposition were visible.

Lords Liverpool, Castlereagh, and Sidmouth, and the *accommodating* George Canning, were now the arbiters of the fates of nations; their will was no sooner expressed than it passed into a law; and, while revelling at the festive board with their puissant prince, the country was writhing in the most pitiable condition. Even bread and water were not always within the poor man's grasp, and the starved peasantry of Ireland, in open defiance of military power, were living by stealing and eating raw potatoes, to enable them to eke out their most miserable existence! Under this humiliating condition, their rights and liberties were suspended, and it was made "treason and sedition" to murmur or complain.

When the tyrannical King John oppressed his subjects, and endeavoured to usurp despotic power, the barons assembled around him, and, unsheathing their swords, swore, "The laws of England shall not be changed!" But the days of chivalry were past! Lord Castlereagh was now our dictator, and a standing army of one hundred and forty thousand men, to enforce his vile and unconstitutional measures, destroyed even the chance of emancipation. We may add, in the words of our immortal bard, that his lordship was a *man*,

> "Ay, and a *bold* one, that dare look on that
> Which might appal the devil!"

The galling distresses of the people, at this period of national calamity and misrule, drove them to the commission of violent acts, and the diligence of well-chosen officers and prosecutors, with the partiality of judges, supplied the defect of evidence needful for punishment. The law was actually made a snare, while vice received encouragement and rewards, when on the side of the oppressors. This was not solely confined to the higher tribunals, but was also apparent in almost every inferior court. Indeed, Lord Sidmouth sent a circular letter to all lieutenants of counties, recommending even "justices of the peace to hold to bail persons publishing alleged libels!!!" The whole ministry proved themselves to be uninfluenced by the dictates of *equity*, or those principles of *moderation* which distinguished some of our noble ancestors. Power was every thing with Castlereagh and his associates, assisted by the MITRED HEADS of the "established church," who were ever his zealous friends in the cause of tyranny! Be it, then, our duty to tear the mask of hypocrisy aside, and exhibit the deformity of Power, more especially when disguised under the specious form of PIETY. He who can assume the sanctity of a SAINT, and perform the deeds of a RUFFIAN, will not be spared in our explanations of TRUTH! The title of "Right Reverend Father in God" shall not cause us to be dismayed, if, by their *reverend* works, they prove themselves to be the children of the devil! We are not what *pretended pious* people term INFIDELS; but we detest to see the tools of power endeavour to subdue the nation in the garb of godliness, insulting the *poor* with orders for "general fasts," while they themselves are indulging in the most riotous excesses!

We must now, as honest and fearless historians, record the most cold-blooded and horrible CRIME that was ever perpetrated in this or any other Christian country!

> "'Tis a strange truth. O monstrous act!
> 'Twill out, 'twill out!—I hold my peace, sir? no:
> No, I will speak as liberal as the air!"

We are almost ready to murmur at Providence for permitting some of the assassins to escape from this world without meeting the punishment they merited. One or two, however, still remain to pollute the earth, and upon whom we yet hope to see justice administered!

Every honest heart was full of bitterness and anguish, when it was announced, "The Princess Charlotte is DEAD!" The heavy-tolling bell, the silence of the streets, and the mute astonishment of all who met and parted, exhibited signs of unfeigned sorrow. In an *unexpected* moment, the hopes of this great nation were brought to nought! Her royal highness was England's star of promise,—the beacon which it was expected would light the traveller to escape the quicksands of destruction!

On the 5th of November, at nine in the evening, this exemplary princess was safely delivered of a male child, said to be still born; and although pronounced at that time, by her *accoucheur*, to be doing extremely well, yet, at half-past two on the morning of the 6th, her royal highness expired! Sir Richard Croft announced to Prince Leopold the heart-rending intelligence; and a messenger was instantly sent to the prince regent (to whom a former communication of fearful import had been made) and also to the queen at Bath. All the royal family then in England hastened to London, *report said*, "nearly destroyed with grief."

Special messengers were also despatched with the melancholy information to the Duke of Kent, who was at Brussels, and to the Duke of Cambridge, at Hanover; but the MOTHER of the late princess was entirely *neglected*. Etiquette and respect were attended to in the cases which least required notice, and omitted in the situation which really demanded, in common decency and justice, the most prompt consideration.

The prince regent arrived at Carlton House at four o'clock on the fatal morning, and was informed by Lord Bathurst and the Duke of York of the event. The regent had been, for ten or twelve days, sojourning with the Marquis, or *Marchioness*, of Hertford, at their seat near Sudbury. In contradiction to several either servile or ignorant historians, we fearlessly say that it was not unexpected news to his royal ear! In the course of the ensuing day, a letter was written and delivered to Dr. Sir

She was a nation's hope—a nation's pride,
With her that pride has fled—those hopes have died!

A contemporary print published in 1817 depicting Britannia mourning the death of her beloved princess.

Richard Croft, announcing the prince regent's offer of thanks for the attention paid to the Princess Charlotte, and assuring the doctor that the prince was fully satisfied with his skill and superior merit; concluding with these words: "As it is the *will of Divine Providence*, his royal highness is in duty bound to submit to the decree— *of heaven.*"

Prince Leopold was not so hasty in returning his thanks for the attentions of Dr. Croft, though much better able to judge of the matter than the regent; for *he* was many miles off, and could not *personally* know any thing of the matter.

Notwithstanding the professed deep sorrow and grief of the prince regent, however, we can announce that his royal highness did not permit himself to relax in any pursuit of pleasure, except that of openly exhibiting himself; for, on the ensuing evening, we ourselves were not very distant from Carlton House, and can testify to this fact. He and his brother of York were not in *very great* anguish upon the occasion; they pledged each other in quick succession, until the circumstance which had caused their meeting was entirely forgotten by them. "I drink to the safety of the regent," said the duke, "and *I* to the safety of *York*," retorted the prince. These remarks created irritability, and the prince very warmly replied, to an interrogation of his brother, "What would *you* think if the ghost of Edward Augustus stood at your elbow?"

How very different was the report issued to the world! The daily papers stated that "the extreme sorrow of the regent had produced an unusual sensation of pain in the head of his royal highness." We were not surprised at this announcement; though we had hoped to have heard the royal *heart* was affected upon a review of his past enormities!

We regret to say, that when the Princess Charlotte was in daily expectation of her accouchement, she was not soothed by the attentions of any of her female relatives. It is true they had not, by any former acts of kindness, given her occasion to expect it; but the disrespect shewn to her royal highness was chiefly owing to the affection for, and defence of, her persecuted mother, which, though perfectly *natural* and praiseworthy, displeased certain high and powerful personages. The *queen* (that boasted paragon of goodness!) was one hundred and eight miles distant, and the hearts of all the family seemed as if estranged from virtuous and honourable feelings. Her majesty, with the Princess Elizabeth, left Windsor Castle for Bath, on the morning of the 3rd of October, for the avowed purpose of drinking the

Engraved title page to *Memoirs of Princess Charlotte* (1817) depicting the princess's death.

waters. On the 27th of the same month, the prince regent, accompanied by Sir B. Bloomfield, left London for the seat of the Marquis of Hertford, at Sudbury, in Suffolk. The Duke of Clarence was also absent. It is true that the cabinet ministers, whose presence was required by precedent and state necessity, were in waiting; but how far their services could be agreeable or beneficial to a young female in such a situation, we are at a loss to discover. Alas! *that parent* who ought to have been present, and who would most joyfully have flown on the wings of maternal affection, was denied the privilege. But while the daughter was struggling in the agonies of a cruel death, the mother was a wanderer in a foreign land, and beset with snares laid for her destruction also!

During the pregnancy of the Princess Charlotte, the prince, her husband, was chiefly her companion. Her choice of an *accoucheur* fell upon Dr. Sir Richard Croft, as he was considered the most able and skilful man in his profession. The ladies in attendance upon her royal highness were unfit to render advice or assistance upon any emergency, as neither of them had been a mother. The princess, when in an advanced state of pregnancy, was kept low, and scarcely allowed animal food, or wine, to both of which she had previously been accustomed. Between the fifth and seventh months, her royal highness was bled several times, and still kept upon very low diet. Claremont, the place chosen for the eventful period, was sixteen miles from town, and when any pressing occasion required the attendance of a surgeon or physician from London, the distance caused a considerable delay. Her royal highness' confinement was expected to take place about the end of October, and the period between that time and the final issue was strongly marked by symptoms of approaching labour. Her royal highness was in extreme pain for more than forty-eight hours, yet each bulletin declared, "The princess is doing extremely well." At half-past twelve, A.M. her royal highness became uneasy and very restless; she exhibited much difficulty of breathing, and at half-past two—EXPIRED!

The substance of this detail found its way into the daily journals, and excited, as it was naturally calculated to do, much remark and inquiry. The generally-received opinion was, that the lamented heiress to the crown had been *wantonly* suffered to perish, from the folly of etiquette, or some other unnatural and unexplained cause. We, however, are not bound to surrender our judgment to a journalist, or to subscribe to the opinion of any man less acquainted with a particular subject than ourselves; and, upon this melancholy and tragical event, therefore, we shall dare to give utterance to TRUTH. In doing so, we beg to state that we are not influenced by personal resentment, but, in the discharge of our task, are determined only to award "honour where honour is due."

The labour of the princess was commenced under extreme debility; and, at an early period, it appeared very probable that *surgical* assistance would be finally requisite; yet no provision was made for such assistance! The bulletin of Wednesday morning, eight o'clock, signed by the attending practitioners, was rather doubtfully expressed. The second bulletin, at ten in the evening, was confidently affirmative of the *well-doing* of the royal patient. Dr. Sims affixed his signature to these bulletins, but he had not seen her royal highness since the first pang she had experienced.

How this gentleman could allow his name to be thus affixed to a declaration, of the truth of which he was totally ignorant, we know not; but it was said, by the time-serving press, "that Dr. Sims being unknown to the princess, his appearance in her chamber might have alarmed her." The folly of this excuse is best exposed by supposing that if, at this trying moment, Dr. Croft had been ill, and unfit to attend the princess, would she have been left to perish for lack of assistance? We think not; for this would have given too plain an idea of the expectations of certain parties. The public papers announced that the letter summoning Dr. Sims to Claremont was written on Tuesday morning, yet he did not arrive until Wednesday morning at three o'clock. It was further stated, that the nurse discovered the dreadful change in her royal highness by the difficulty manifested in swallowing her gruel, and that she was so alarmed by this appearance of spasm, that she immediately called the faculty out of their beds, as well as Prince Leopold. Another journalist stated a contrary case. But *we know* that, although some beverage was administered to the princess, it was NOT GRUEL; for her royal highness had a great aversion to gruel, and could never be prevailed on to take it. Soon after her royal highness took the liquid, she was afflicted in a most *unusual way*, though only for a short time. The low state of muscular strength, to which the princess had gradually been reduced, certainly required greater nourishment than was given to her; and in this professional treatment, therefore, the *accoucheur* acted unwisely as well as unskilfully, to say the least of it. That most eminent practitioner, Dr. Thynne, made it an invariable rule, after a protracted birth, to revive the mother, by giving a tea-spoonful of egg, beat up with wine, from time to time. The symptoms of not being able to swallow, and the convulsive action of the body, were plainly indicative of a dying patient; but the real cause of the patient's dying was then a mystery, except to two or three individuals.

The public journals of the day called loudly upon the gentlemen who attended the Princess Charlotte, as her *accoucheurs*, to give all facility for an investigation of their whole mode of treatment, adding, that "if they be conscious that they have acquitted themselves well, they will have no objection to an investigation of their conduct, and cannot consider themselves placed in a worse situation than the captain of a king's ship, who, in the event of the loss of his vessel, is obliged to undergo a trial by court martial." To this and similar appeals, the ministers promptly replied, "that it was *impossible*, after the prince regent had been pleased to express his approbation and award his thanks, as it would seem to *reflect* upon the prince, who alone was endowed with the sovereign power to act in the case." This royal cant-phraseology, however, failed to lull suspicion; for the attending circumstances were of a nature too horrible to be buried in oblivion! If all had been correct, why refuse inquiry, particularly when it was solicited by nine-tenths of the nation?

The queen left Bath on Saturday, the 8th of November, and arrived at Windsor in the evening. The next day, the prince regent went from Carlton House to Windsor to see the queen; but the privacy of the visit did not permit it to be of long duration. We are able to give the particulars of this interview.

Her majesty's mind had been disturbed by the receipt of a letter, from a medical gentleman, upon the subject of the *untimely* death of the Princess Charlotte. No time was to be lost. The prince was requested immediately to see his royal mother; and, on his arrival, her majesty presented him with the letter, the contents of which proved, beyond doubt, that the writer had been an *eye-witness* to some particular events connected with the dissolution of the much-lamented and tenderly-beloved princess.

The letter commenced with the most respectful dedication to royalty, and prayed for an extra extension of candour and patience by her majesty, while the facts of which it was composed were examined and duly considered. The writer then proceeded,—"I am perfectly satisfied your majesty could not be *personally* aware of the case, because of the distance your majesty then was from Claremont; but I submit it to your majesty's good feeling and judgment, if the particulars attendant upon this most lamentable loss ought not immediately to be most strictly inquired into. Refusal to do this, or to permit it being done, will only aggravate the matter, instead of setting the question at rest for ever. The public well know that all was not as it ought to have been,—that something had been neglected or imprudently attempted, that ought to have received a widely-different attention. As a proof that I do not intrude my remarks and remonstrances improperly, or without information upon the nicest points of the case, I will give reasons for my dissatisfaction. From the first moment Sir Richard Croft was placed in attendance upon her royal highness, there was no reason to anticipate or fear any unhappy results. The natural appearances were unequivocally satisfactory. Previous to the delivery, the infant was not supposed to be dead. It was quite unnecessary and unnatural to inform the princess that the child was still-born; such a communication is very seldom made to any female at such a moment. Camphor julaps are very seldom administered to a healthy patient, or where the stomach is sound, immediately after delivery, as the effect would generally be to produce irritation, sickness, and convulsion. Dr. Croft ought not to have retired to bed, presuming that her royal highness was so indisposed as to cause her incessant moaning, *which was really the case*. More than this, your majesty, about noon of the Wednesday, Dr. Croft said, 'I believe the princess might very quickly be delivered by having recourse to an *operation*; but I dare not perform it without the *presence* and *sanction* of her royal father, the prince regent.' I hope (continued the writer) that your majesty will see this plain statement in its own character, and that you will save all future disclosures of an unpleasant nature, by your timely recommendation of the subject to the prince regent, your son. Your majesty may believe I am induced by vindictive motives to offer these remarks; but that would prove an incorrect opinion; and unless your majesty causes a very prompt inquiry to be permitted upon the facts of this case, I fear yourself and family will finally have cause to regret the delay."

The prince was much displeased that any subject should have dared to take such a liberty as to speak or write an unpleasant TRUTH to any of his *noble* family,—more especially to the *queen*. It was an unpardonable transgression; yet, as the gentleman had given his name and address, it was a very delicate affair. The queen had so often witnessed the prostration of the multitudes of fashion's votaries, that she imagined much might be accomplished by commanding an interview, and subduing the voice of inquiry and truth by the splendour of pageantry, and the intoxicating smile of royalty. By her majesty's command, therefore, an interview took place. With her general air of confidence, the queen said, "I presume, Sir, you are the author of this letter?" "I am, please your majesty." "And what," said the queen, "am I to understand from such an unaccountable appeal to me and my family?" "I beg your majesty's pardon personally, as well as previously by letter, but I deemed it my duty to inform your majesty of my information upon the subject in question, and I am very sorry if your majesty does not think it necessary to have the most prudent means used to satisfy the public inquiry." The queen was very gracious, and smiling, said, "I will name your good intentions to the prince regent, and I will not forget them myself; but I can satisfy you, that your opinions upon the subject of your communication to me are incorrect." The gentleman rose, and was about to retire; but the queen had not attained her object. Her majesty, therefore, hastily said, "I trust you are convinced of the impropriety of your former opinions?" "No, please your majesty, I never can change my opinions upon this subject until I lose my principles, and I trust sincerely that I shall never endure such an humiliation while I retain my reason. But," added the gentleman, "your majesty must be well assured that I am acquainted with the greater portion of your family; yea, very intimately acquainted, not indecorously so, but in the discharge of my professional engagements. Your majesty well knows that I saw the lamented Princess Charlotte just before the unhappy event, and also am not ignorant of the constitution of your majesty's *daughters*. I therefore am bold to assert, that the death of her royal highness was not, and is not to be, naturally accounted for! It is true, that I am not known to the world in the capacity of *accoucheur* to your family; but your majesty knows, I have been your trusty and confidential servant upon more occasions than one; and I am now resolved to relinquish the royal favour, if it must be purchased at such an unknown expense."

The queen retired, and so did the heart-stricken gentleman; but their ruminations and consequent determinations were very dissimilar. Her majesty was endeavouring to evade explanation; the gentleman, meditating upon the most prudent plan for adoption to put a period to the agitated feelings of the public.

The reader may imagine that this professional person had been previously selected to render his services to some members of this illustrious family, which was actually the case. He had travelled more than twenty miles in the royal carriage, and had performed the most delicate offices. He knew royalty was not exempt from frailty, and that rank did not preserve its possessors from the commission of crime. Denial of this would prove abortive, for the gentleman LIVES, and would, if called upon, assert the same even at the expense of life. He does not fear the interdiction of a crowned head! neither would he shrink under "a special commission." He wields the two-edged sword of *truth*, and therefore defies the strong arm of power. He has seen enough of the wily snares of courtiers, and has retired from the unhallowed association with feelings of disgust, contempt, and detestation. The adulation of the parasites of royalty is odious to his ear; and, to save the increasing stings of an offended conscience, he is now publicly explicit upon this hateful subject. Despising secrecy and infamy, he openly avows enmity to such characters as are leagued against the peace and happiness of society; and their intentions to perpetuate their unjust, partial, and devastating system, must be checked by the information of those persons who are privy to the cause, as well as to the effects, of their overgrown power.

The day after this unpleasant interview, the queen paid a visit to the king; and, as nearly two months had elapsed since her majesty visited her husband, it was productive of great anxiety on the part of the royal sufferer. The daily papers stated that "his majesty was much improved, and very tranquil, in consequence of the queen having paid him a visit." Does not this neglect of the poor afflicted king reflect disgrace upon her majesty? The wife who forgets her duty to the man she has espoused is undeserving the respect of society. *Who* was Queen Charlotte, that the eyes of the public should be blinded, or their tongues mute, upon this apathy and unfeeling demeanour to the king, her husband, who had raised her from comparative poverty to affluence and greatness? Had similar inattention been manifested by the wife of a peasant, her neighbour's reproach would not have been wanting; but every one seemed afraid of impugning the character of a *queen*, so celebrated for *amiability* and *virtue*! A few days after the interment of the Princess Charlotte and her infant, the queen again went off for the city of Bath! and we assert, without fear of contradiction, that her majesty's eye was never observed to be dim upon this most melancholy occasion. Let the world judge if such unfeeling deportment agreed with her majesty's reported sorrow.

On the 19th of November, the Princess Charlotte and her infant were consigned to the tomb. The Dukes of York and Clarence were supporters to the chief mourner, Prince Leopold; and, after the ostentatious parade of funeral pomp, they retired without much appearance of sorrow. It was said that a king, or prince invested with royal power, could not attend the ceremony, or join in the cavalcade of a funeral. The regent, therefore, was not present at the closing scene of his child's hard destiny. But royalty has many privileges; distinct from the common herd of mankind. It must not, for instance, reside in the same habitation with a corpse, lest its delicately-refined nerves should sustain injury, or be excited to an extreme point of agony!

The body of the unfortunate Charlotte was reported to have been embalmed, but the heart only was extracted; THE INTESTINES WERE NOT REMOVED! This was an unprecedented circumstance, as upon all former occasions this barbarous custom had been permitted. The surgeon who accompanied Prince Leopold from Germany was solicited to say *why* this form had been omitted; and his suspicious reply was, "Neither now, nor at any future time, shall any power on earth induce me to speak one word upon the subject." He was then requested to give into the hand of Prince Leopold a sealed letter upon the subject; this he also positively refused to do, adding, at the same time, "the prince would not receive it." Very shortly afterwards, a letter *was* conveyed into the prince's hand, offering "to communicate certain facts relative to the demise of the late princess, his consort, if he pleased to express his willingness to receive the same." His serene highness never paid attention to that letter.

It was said, at the time of her royal highness' death, that Prince Leopold was so angry with the nurse (Mrs. Griffiths) that he turned her out of the house, without permitting her to stay to attend the funeral. One thing, however, is certain, that she has several sons in different public offices. To one of these, her favourite, she said, (when labouring under the effects of a dreadful illness she had shortly after the princess' death) "I have never kept but one HORRID SECRET from you, which has always weighed upon my mind; but I cannot communicate it, unless I am sure of death the next minute!"

This Mrs. Griffiths certainly knows more about the death of her late royal mistress than she has yet thought proper to communicate; though, in one of her moments of compunction, she confessed to a friend of ours, that the Princess Charlotte had actually been POISONED, and related the way in which she found it out. Mrs. Griffiths stated, that, "after giving her royal highness some BROTH (not gruel) she became dreadfully convulsed; and, being struck with the peculiarity of the circumstance, she examined the cup from which her royal highness had drank. To her astonishment, she there perceived a *dark red sediment*, upon *tasting which*, HER TONGUE BECAME BLISTERED!!!" Mrs. Griffiths immediately asked Dr. Croft what he had administered to the princess; but she received no satisfactory answer. A few hours after this, however, the doctor said sufficient to prove that the princess had been MURDERED! As Mrs. Griffiths is now alive, we challenge her to deny this statement, if incorrect.

The lamented princess was treated most cruelly by all around her, and one of the higher household asserted, that he believed her royal highness was left "two hours in the agonies of death, without any person going near her!" Mrs. Lewis, her waiting woman, has denied this statement; but it is well known, that Mrs. Lewis was placed as a *spy* about her royal highness even from her infancy.

The last time the prince regent was at Claremont, not long before the princess' confinement, a most respectable gentleman heard him say, "A child of the Princess Charlotte shall never sit upon the throne." Did not this speak volumes as to her intended destruction? Surely no one can doubt, after these disclosures, that the Princess Charlotte fell a victim to a vile conspiracy.

The murder of the Princess Charlotte proved the signal for letting loose the hounds of destruction upon her heart-broken mother. On the morning of the second day after her majesty's return to Bath, a lady had a private audience with her. The object of the interview was, to offer the services of her husband (an officer in the navy) in the impeachment and intended destruction of the honour of the Princess of Wales. "What situation does the person occupy?" said the queen. "He is a lieutenant, please your majesty." "What would be deemed a sufficient recompense for his attentions?" said her majesty. "Your majesty's good opinion is all my husband aspires to," said the lady; and, after a few unmeaning expressions of civility, she retired. Lord Liverpool was consulted, and gave his opinion that the person in question could not be implicitly relied on; and a messenger was therefore sent to the gentleman, according to the address left by his wife, declining the offered service; and stating that "her majesty had no unkind or ungenerous feelings towards the

Princess of Wales, and had quite misunderstood the offer, having supposed it to be made under very opposite circumstances." The lady was recommended to the queen's notice by Lord Castlereagh, though doubts were entertained whether the lieutenant might be trusted, as he was believed to be anti-ministerial.

We here relate another fact, relative to the Princess of Wales' persecutors:—A certain personage sought for an interview with an individual whom we will disguise under the name of Captain Rock. "Well," said his royal highness to the captain, "I wish to engage your services; you are well acquainted with Italy; we expect the Princess of Wales will be at Pisa in about three months, and as you have served us before, we suppose you will have no objection to do so again; you shall not want for cash." The offer was accepted, and his royal highness *wrote* this offer upon paper, and a sum was advanced on the evening of the same day. This mean slave of power departed; but, before following the instructions of his royal employer, went off to London, and communicated to Lord Castlereagh his mission, requiring five hundred pounds more, declaring the *written* promise should strictly be enforced, as he had been a loser by his former services. The amount demanded was given. "I assure you, my lord," said the captain, "I will execute my commission well; but I must also be paid well." Lord Castlereagh assented, and this unmanly spy took his leave of England to wait the expected arrival of the princess at Pisa.

These proceedings against her royal highness soon manifested themselves in a commission being appointed at Milan; and rumours were circulated in this country that her conduct was at variance with propriety.

Mr. Leech, a Chancery barrister of some eminence, and who was subsequently elevated to the situation of Vice-Chancellor, and is now Master of the Rolls; Mr. Cook, also a barrister, and a writer of great eminence on the subject of bankruptcy; Mr. Powell, a gentleman of private fortune and connected with the court; a Colonel Brown, the impropriety of whose conduct met with general disapprobation; and Lord Stewart, the cowardly lordling who had repeatedly vilified the character of the princess, and had even personally insulted her, were selected as the individuals proper to conduct an inquiry into the character and conduct of her royal highness, during her residence on the Continent. To Milan they repaired. A person by the name of Vimercati was selected as the Italian agent. Colonel Brown was stationed to assist him. Salaries were of course attached to their respective offices, and each individual had his post assigned him. Vimercati was invested with the greater part of the management of this affair, and the nature of his conduct and proceedings cannot but excite mingled feelings of surprise and horror.

By this commission, witnesses were first obtained, then examined, and re-examined; exorbitant prices were offered to them for their testimony, and threats were made to those who shewed, or pretended to shew, any dislike subsequently to appear to verify their statements. Rastelli, afterwards a witness, was employed as *courier*, and to him was delegated the all-powerful argument of a *long purse*. Dumont, while in the hands of this commission, carried on a correspondence with her sister, (who was still in the queen's service) through the medium of Baron D'Ompteda, (the villain we mentioned a few pages back) for the purpose of obtaining information from her majesty's servants. And Omati was paid by D'Ompteda for stealing papers, for the use of the commission, from his master, who was her majesty's professional agent at Milan. These are facts proved by witnesses whose characters are irreproachable, and whose evidence is as well written as parole.

The year

1818

was a dark and troubled period,—a period of great private distress,—so that the minds of men were bent with more acerbity than usual upon the redress of public grievances. The country, borne down by debt, harassed by taxation, which had no longer for its excuse a monopoly of commerce, looked naturally enough to the source from which these calamities had flowed. They found the theory and the practice of the constitution at variance, and hearing they had a right to be taxed by their representatives, they thought it hard and unjust that over the great majority of those who taxed them they had no controul. Retrenchment and economy were what they required. They considered parliamentary reform would be the means of producing economy and retrenchment. Public meetings in favour of parliamentary reform were, therefore, held, resolutions in favour of it passed, and petitions in favour of it presented to the two houses of parliament; the energies of a free people were roused, and great excitement prevailed. When a country is thus agitated, a minister must resist with vigour, or yield with grace. Unjust and violent demands should be met with resistance; but sober and legitimate requests, with concession. When weakly opposed, they are obtained by immediate violence; successfully refused, they are put off for a day, or postponed for a week or a year; but they are not got rid of. Lord Castlereagh and Mr. Canning, however, were vain enough to think otherwise.

Parliament was opened by commission in January. The speech referred to the continued indisposition of his majesty, and the death of the Princess Charlotte; but without promising an inquiry into the *cause* of her untimely end! An address was voted in the Commons' House, according to custom, though Sir Samuel Romilly was not wanting in his expressions of severe opposition to the course ministers were pursuing. He stated, "that the despotic conduct of the ministry had produced in the minds of the people a determination to withstand any further infringement upon their rights and privileges."

Totally regardless of the sufferings of an over-burdened people, however, and during the very heavy and calamitous sorrows of the middle and lower classes, the chancellor of the Exchequer had the effrontery to move "that one million of money be raised for the purpose of supplying the deficiency of places of worship belonging to the establishment, by building new churches and chapels of ease, where the increase of population rendered it needful." How applicable are the words of Tartuffe to the advocates of this measure! "With one hand, I have encouraged spies, suborned perjury, and committed murders; and with the other, built churches,—*but not with my own money*!" The bill passed, and an extra "plume of worldly-mindedness" was consequently placed in the cap of hypocrisy! Oh! that the pure religion of our

Saviour should be thus perverted! His kingdom was not of this world, neither did he luxuriate in the "good things" of the earth. Did he wear lawn sleeves and a mitre? Did he loll in gaudy carriages, and look down with supercilious contempt on his poorer brethren? Did he require *theatres* for his churches, or *perfumed* divines to preach his gospel? Did he interfere with political matters, and exert his energies to enslave the people? We leave these questions to be answered by those locusts of the land, commonly called *bishops* of the *established* church; at the same time we call upon them to reflect, whether, if hereafter they should feel inclined to recall the opportunity of conciliating the respect of the country, they will not have the misfortune of finding it much too late!

If our readers were to look over the singular parliamentary proceedings at this gloomy period of our history, they would be forcibly struck with the littleness, servility, and the utter want of intellectual calibre, so fully set forth in the characters of those who conducted the solemn mockery of legislation. The most unjust and arbitrary laws were put in force, and the public money allowed to be squandered, without the least inquiry. As a proof of this last remark, we need only mention the fact of *ninety thousand pounds* being voted for the department of the "Master of the Horse," who kept thirty saddle and twenty-eight carriage horses for the use of his majesty, yet the king had never been out of the castle for more than seven years! This disgraceful squandering of money was carried on, too, when honest citizens and affectionate fathers were incapable of providing bread for themselves and families! Indeed, Lord Liverpool seemed resolved to push the country to its utmost verge, by proposing and sanctioning every expensive outlay. He was, with Lords Castlereagh and Sidmouth, the author of many plans to perplex, impoverish, and subdue the people, in which plans the *bishops* most zealously assisted. Every contrivance that had the sanction of the queen was sure to be *well-managed*, till Justice herself was set at open defiance.

Our readers will recollect our former statements respecting the Princess Charlotte, and we think the circumstance we are now about to relate will not operate against the proofs we have adduced concerning her untimely end.

Dr. Sir Richard Croft, the *accoucheur* of that lamented princess, had been engaged to attend the lady of the Rev. Dr. Thackeray, at her house, 86, Wimpole-street, Cavendish-square. Sir Richard went there on Monday, the 9th of February, and remained in attendance until Thursday morning, at eleven o'clock, when, finding his continued presence unnecessary, he went out for a short time to fulfil his other engagements. An apartment on the floor above that occupied by Mrs. Thackeray was appointed for the residence of Sir Richard. In this chamber, there were two pistols belonging to Dr. Thackeray, hanging within the reach of Dr. Croft. Sir Richard retired to bed at half-past twelve, and about one, Dr. Thackeray heard a noise, apparently proceeding from the room occupied by Dr. Croft, and sent a female servant to ascertain the cause; she returned, saying, "the doctor is in bed, and I conceive him to be asleep." A short time after, a similar noise was heard, and the servant was sent again. She rapped at the door, but received no answer. This circumstance created alarm; in consequence of which, the door of his apartment was broken open. Here an awful spectacle presented itself. The body of Sir Richard was lying on the bed, shockingly mangled, his hands extended over his breast, and a pistol in each hand. One of the pistols had been loaded with slugs, the other with ball. Both were discharged, and the head of the unfortunate gentleman was literally blown to pieces.

On the inquest, Doctors Latham and Baillie, and Mr. Finch, proved that the deceased had, since the death of the Princess Charlotte, laboured under mental distress. He had frequently been heard to say, that "this lamentable occurrence weighs heavily on my mind, and I shall never get over it." Mr. Finch said, he was well aware that the deceased had been labouring under derangement of intellect for a considerable time past; and he should not have reposed confidence or trust in him on any occasion since the lamented catastrophe alluded to. The jury returned a verdict, "that the deceased destroyed himself while in a fit of temporary derangement."

During the inquest, the newspaper reporters were denied admission, which circumstance gave rise to various rumours of a suspicious tendency. This was certainly an unconstitutional act; but we will, as honest historians, speak candidly upon the subject. Delicacy to surviving friends must not prevent our detail of facts.

It will appear evident, then, that Sir Richard had not been perfectly sane since the ever-to-be-regretted fatal event at Claremont. Was it not therefore astonishing, that his professional as well as other friends, who were *suspicious*, if not *fully aware*, of the doctor's derangement, should have been silent upon this important point, and have allowed Sir Richard to continue in the exercise of his professional practice? Did they not, by such silence, contribute to the peril of females in the most trying moment of nature's sorrow? The *disinterested* reader will, doubtless, join us in our expressions of indignation at such wanton and cruel conduct.

The letter written to Sir Richard, by order of the prince, proves nothing but the folly of those who advised it. That letter was not calculated to remove any of those suspicions respecting the untimely death of the Princess Charlotte, which rolled like heavy clouds over the intelligent minds of the greater portion of the nation; neither was it likely to hush the spirit of *inquiry*, because its details were evidently meant to prevent any special explanation. The Marquis of Hertford, chamberlain to the regent, well knew, at this period, how to estimate *medicinal cause and effect*!

Presuming my Lord Bloomfield to have been an actor in "the tragedy," we cannot help thinking that his reward was more than adequate to the *services* performed. His pension of twelve hundred pounds per annum was dated December, 1817. What extraordinary benefits had he rendered to this oppressed nation to merit such an income? We ought also to mention, that, after this period, we find his lordship named as "envoy and minister-plenipotentiary in Sweden," for which he received the annual sum of four thousand, nine hundred pounds, and, as colonel of artillery, one thousand and three pounds, making in all the enormous annual sum of seven thousand, one hundred, and three pounds!

These remarks are not intended to wound the feelings of private families; but are made with a view to urge a strict investigation into the cause of the Princess Charlotte's death. We are well aware that many *great* persons have reason to fear the result of such an inquiry, yet the injured ought to have justice administered, even at the "eleventh hour," if it cannot sooner be obtained. Many a murderer has been executed twenty, or even thirty, years after the commission of his crime!

Though at this time ministers had a parliament almost entirely devoted to their wishes, there were a few members of it who vigorously opposed unjust measures, and they could not always carry their plans into execution. The amount solicited for the Duke of Clarence upon his intended marriage with the Princess of Saxe Meiningen is a proof of this; for, although the regent sent a message to the House to accomplish this object, it was at *first* refused, and the duke did not gain his point till a considerable time afterwards.

The Duke of Kent, and father to Queen Victoria, from an engraving by Edward Scriven published in 1834. (*Licensed under Wikimedia Commons*)

In this year, the Duke of Kent was united to a sister of Prince Leopold.

In September, while most requisite to her party, the queen was taken ill. Bulletin followed upon bulletin, and the disorder was reported to increase. Some of the public papers announced, that her majesty had expressed an ardent desire to witness a *reconciliation* between the Prince and Princess of Wales, as she imagined her dissolution was now near at hand. The report, however, was as false as it was unlikely; for, only a month before this period, *spies* had been despatched to obtain witnesses, *of any description*, against the honour of the princess, by which means her enemies hoped to accomplish their most ardent desires. Queen Charlotte's *conscience* was not of a penetrable nature as her bitter enmity to the Princess of Wales continued even to her death!

With her majesty, it had ever been an invariable maxim, that "might constitutes right;" but the reflections of her mind, while surveying the probability of a speedy dissolution, must have been of a complexion too dreary to be faithfully pictured. She,—who had been the arbitress of the fates of nations, whose commands none dared dispute or disobey, and at whose frown numberless sycophants and dependents trembled,—was now about to face the dread enemy of mankind! The proud heart of Queen Charlotte must have been humbled at the thought of meeting HER Judge, who is said to be "no distinguisher of persons."

During her indisposition, the queen seemed much impressed with the idea that she should recover, and it was not till the 2nd of November that the physicians deemed it requisite to acquaint the queen of her danger. The intelligence was given in the most delicate manner possible; yet her majesty exhibited considerable alarm at the information. It was pressingly hinted by the princesses to their mother, that the sacrament ought to be administered; but the queen positively refused the "holy rite," saying, "It is of no use, as I am unable to take it." One of the princesses immediately said, "You do not mean to say that you murdered the Princess Charlotte?" "No," faintly answered the queen, "but I connived at it!" We pledge ourselves to the truth of this statement, however incredible it may appear to those who have considered Queen Charlotte as "a pattern to her sex." When the general servility of the press to royalty is taken into consideration, it is hardly to be wondered at that people are misinformed as to the real characters of kings and queens. Take the following false and most inconsistent eulogium, copied from the "Atlas" newspaper, as an example of this time-serving violation of truth:

> "Queen Charlotte's *constant attendance on the king*, and her GRIEF FOR THE LOSS OF HER GRAND-DAUGHTER, gained ground on her constitution; and her majesty expired at Kew, on the 17th of November, 1818. *In all the relations of a wife and mother*, the conduct of the queen had been EXEMPLARY. Pious, without bigotry; virtuous, but not austere; serious, yet capable of the most perfect enjoyment of innocent pleasure; unostentatious, economical, adorned with all domestic virtues, and not without the charities of human nature, the queen had lived respected, and she died full of years and honour, regretted by her subjects, and most by those who knew her best. If her talents were not shining, nor her virtues extraordinary, she never employed the first in faction, nor bartered the second for power. She was occasionally accused of political interference, by contemporary jealousy; but history will acquit her of the charge. She was a strict moralist, though her conduct to one part of her family (the heroic Caroline, we suppose) was perhaps more RIGOROUS than JUST. Her proudest drawing-room was the hearth of her home. Her brightest gems were her children, (heaven save the mark!) *and her greatest ambition to set an example of* MATRONLY VIRTUE *and feminine dignity to the ladies of her adopted country*!"

We should absolutely blush for the writer of this paragraph, did we think that he really *meant* his panegyric to be taken *literally*. For the sake of *common honesty*, however, we will not suppose he so intended it; he must be some severe critic who adopted this style as the *keenest kind of wit*, for

"Praise undeserved is satire in disguise!"

The *august* remains of this royal lady were, on the 2nd of December, deposited in the vault prepared for their reception, with all the parade usual on such expensive occasions. We will not detain our readers by describing the funeral pomp, though we cannot avoid noticing that the body was not opened, but immediately enclosed in prepared wrappers, and very speedily deposited in the first coffin, which was a leaden one. Indeed, her majesty was not in a fit state to undergo the usual formalities of embalming, &c. Her body was literally a moving mass of corruption.

Let us now sum up the mortal train of evils which were so *generously* nourished "by the departed," for virtues she had none. The power of royalty may intimidate the irresolute, astonish the uninformed, or bribe the villain; but, as we do not claim affinity with either of these characters, we honestly avow, that her majesty did not deserve the title "of blessed memory." At the commencement of her alliance with the much-to-be-pitied George the Third, she took every advantage of his weakness, and actually directed the helm of government *alone*, which untoward circumstance England has abundant cause to remember!

The next brother to the king, (Edward) whom we have before mentioned, was most unexpectedly and unaccountably sent abroad, notwithstanding his being next in succession. His royal highness' marriage with a descendant of the Stuarts, though strictly legal, was never acknowledged by Queen Charlotte, and his only child, soon after its birth, was thrown upon the compassionate attention of strangers. As there is something so horrible relative to the death of this amiable duke and duchess, and something so heartless and cruel in the treatment to which their only son has been subjected, we are induced, for the sake of truth and justice, to lay a brief statement of the matter before our readers.

Historians have either been treacherous or ignorant of the circumstances connected with the case of this Duke of York, who was the second son of Frederick, Prince of Wales, and next brother of George the Third. Most writers have represented "that he died in consequence of a malignant fever," as we have before mentioned; but one historian ventured to assert that "Edward, Duke of York, was ASSASSINATED in September, 1767, near Monaco, in Italy!" This statement, we are sorry to say, is but too true, which caused the book containing it to be bought up at an immense expense. The unhappy widow of his royal highness was then far advanced in pregnancy, and very shortly after this melancholy, and (to her) irreparable loss, she came over to England, and took up her residence at Haverford West, in South Wales. At this place, her royal highness gave birth to a son, whose baptism was duly entered in the register of St. Thomas' parish. What afterwards became of this illustrious lady, however, is not known; but her infant was, shortly after its birth, conveyed to London, and placed, by George the Third, under the immediate care and protection of a tradesman and his wife, by whom he was represented to be their own son. This tradesman, although only twenty-seven years of age, enjoyed the particular confidence of his majesty, and has been known to walk with the king by the hour, in the gardens adjoining Buckingham House, conversing with all the familiarity of an old acquaintance or an especial friend, and who at all times could command an interview with his majesty, or with the ministers. When about twelve years old, this ill-fated offspring of the duke was placed at Eton, upon which occasion his majesty took especial notice of the youth, and was in the habit of conversing very freely with him. He had not been long at Eton when his majesty allowed him to go with his *reputed* father to see the hounds throw off at Taplow Heath; a chaise was ordered for this purpose, and they arrived just before the deer were let out. Upon their alighting, the king rode up to them, and expressed his very great satisfaction at the appearance of the youth; and, after asking many questions relative to the arrangements made for him at school, said, "Well, my little fellow, do you be a good boy, and you shall never want friends. Good bye, good bye; the deer will soon be out!" His majesty then rode back to his attendants. Whenever George the Third passed through Eton, it was his invariable practice either to speak to, or inquire after, this youth, in whose welfare he ever appeared deeply interested. From Eton, he was removed to college; and after this period, vexations of an unpleasant nature were experienced by this orphan: his income was too limited, and unkindness and illiberality were too frequently his portion; even during severe indisposition, he was permitted to languish without being supplied with sufficient means to procure the needful restoratives. His life now became little else than one continued scene of unhappiness; his associates at the university were well acquainted with these facts, and appeared deeply interested in his welfare, regretting that the mind and talent of such an amiable and promising youth should be enervated by the severity or inattention of his connexions. But as he had been severely rebuked for making a complaint, and offering a remonstrance, he resolved to suffer in "silent sorrow," much to the injury of his mental enjoyments. During a vacation, and previous to his removal from college, a dispute arose amongst the members of his reputed father's family upon the subject of religion. The debate at length assumed a formidable appearance, and bigotry plainly supplied the place of sound reasoning. The family separated in the evening, each displeased with the other, and all, except one individual, at issue with the royal protégé. Early in the ensuing morning, this dissentient member of the family requested the favour of an interview with the illustrious youth, and remarked, that the occurrence was not a matter of surprise, as the very peculiar circumstances connected with the reputed father of the young gentleman were of a most serious description. "To what do you allude?" said the youth. "You ought to know," answered this honourable friend, "that you have no right to submit to insult here. You are the highest person in this house, and are, by your rank, entitled to the greatest respect from every one. Your *pretended* father forgets his duty and his engagements, when he permits you to be treated with disrespect; and if his majesty knew these circumstances, your abode would soon be changed; and your profession would be abandoned. The king never would allow an indignity to be offered to you in any way, much less by the person into whose care he has so confidingly entrusted you." "What!" said the young prince, "am I not the son of Mr. ******? but, if I am, why should his majesty take so much interest in my case?" "No," answered his informant, "you are not the son of Mr. ******. But ask no more; my life might probably pay for my explanation!" From this period, the subject of our memoir was treated with the greatest unkindness and personal indignity by almost every member of his reputed father's family. Indeed, the imperious behaviour of the elder branches was such as could not be passed over in silence; in consequence of which, the high-spirited and noble victim was sent back to college for the remainder of the vacation, with little more in his purse than would defray the expenses of the journey; but the command was peremptory! After remaining some time in utter destitution, the royal protégé wrote to request an early supply of cash, naming for what purposes. This appeal was considered as the effect of extravagance and profligacy, and, instead of being properly complied with, was answered with acrimony, everything the reverse of parental feeling. Under these heart-rending circumstances, did this ill-fated son of Prince Edward labour for nearly four years at the university,—not daring to make any further appeals to the austere, impatient, and arbitrary person, to whose care the king had so fully, though *secretly*, entrusted him. At length, however, a severe illness was the consequence; and censure, in no very measured terms, was heaped upon the unfeeling character who had so cruelly immolated a promising and worthy young gentleman, and who, he well knew, was of the most illustrious descent. Those who were acquainted with the particulars of the case were most incensed against such heartless conduct. Mr. ****** had undertaken the important charge of seeing this protégé able to realize the ardent wish of his majesty, either as a legal or clerical character, and thereby, in some degree, provided for. But, while his majesty's nephew was refused means to live respectably, and excluded from all youthful amusements, the real sons of his reputed father were allowed all the pleasures and enjoyments of life. At his final removal from college, this ill-treated prince represented to his unfeeling guardian that he should take greater pleasure in pursuing legal to clerical engagements; but his wishes in this, as in most other matters, were totally disregarded, and the church was destined, by arbitrary will, to be his profession. He, therefore, at the proper age, was compelled to take orders, and enter upon a profession he had not chosen. As the home of his reputed father was scarcely to be endured, a curacy was eagerly accepted, and the son of the Duke of York, the nephew of George the Third, was transformed into "a clergyman of the church of England!!!" Here he toiled in an obscure village, scarcely receiving sufficient means to discharge the small demands required for his maintenance!

Shortly after this, the principal of the living died insolvent, and the little remuneration due to the curate could not be obtained. In this distressing state of affairs, the persecuted prince could obtain no settlement from his guardian; yet from comparative nothingness, this man was raised to affluence, and was then living in much style, keeping his carriage and horses, inhabiting a mansion of very superior description, and the whole of his family enjoying every superfluity of life. *He*, however, on whose sole account this sumptuous appearance was bestowed, was "eating the bread of Carefulness, and reposing upon the couch of Sorrow!" We need not enter more fully into the case of this unfortunate, but worthy, descendant of Prince Edward, than say, that, from the commencement of his studies to a very recent period, he has been the victim of Power! His sufferings and his sorrows have been too great for language to describe; and, but for the blessings of a fine constitution, he must have fallen under them. But, if he be called upon in a suitable manner, we doubt not that he has yet preserved to him sufficient of his natural courage, though in his 65th year, to make "False Accusation blush, and Tyranny tremble at Patience!"

We claim the attention of our readers while we offer PROOF that our assertions are founded upon the glorious principle of TRUTH. We have ourselves, to elucidate this matter, examined all the registers of the various parishes in Caernarvonshire and Carmarthenshire, and found every register complete from 1760, until we came to that of St. Thomas, Haverford West, at which place we could not find a single register before the year 1776. To substantiate this fact, we subjoin the following certificate of the parish clerk:

"Haverford West,
"Parish of St. Thomas.
"There are no registers in the possession of the present rector of the above parish, prior to the year 1776.
(Signed) "Joseph Lloyd Morgan,
"Parish Clerk."
"13th Sept., 1831."

Here, then, is a BLANK for which no apology can be received,—no obsequious profession of sorrow or regret can compensate. We presume to declare that if the parish registers throughout the whole of the United Kingdoms be investigated, a similar defect will not be found. We are, therefore, justified in supposing that this defect arose *solely* and *entirely* from concerted measures, to keep the subject of our memoir from ever having it in his power to bring *legal* proof of his noble descent.

The time will probably arrive when we may be permitted to enter more fully into this atrocious business, and then we shall not spare the "Oppressors of Innocence," for truth is bold, and not always to be defied! It would have been better for such oppressors to have never seen the light than to have gained their wicked purposes by such an unmanly sacrifice of the rights of nature. Every individual ought to feel interested in the full and fair explanation of this chicanery; for if such misdeeds are suffered to remain unpunished, a safeguard is offered to future tyrants! Startling facts like these speak volumes, and any honest and upright member of the community will not need more than their simple avowal to rouse his indignation. Such encroachments on the rights of individuals call aloud for retributive justice, and we trust the call will not long be made in vain. Surely there is yet sufficient virtue left amongst us to prevent this once great nation from being sacrificed to the fluctuating interests or wayward prejudices of ministers, or even of a monarch! It is high time to shake off all lethargy! This, as well as many other subjects, which we have exposed,—*deserve*,—nay, DEMAND,—*parliamentary investigation*. Hitherto, some dreadful infatuation seems to have presided over the councils of this country. Insatiable ambition has caused all the horrors imposed upon the United Kingdoms, and has plunged a professedly free and great people into debt and disgrace. Indolence now, therefore, is only comparable with the conduct of a prodigal, who has wasted his estate without reflection, and then has not the courage to examine his accounts; far be this from Britons!

From this digression, we return to the consideration of Queen Charlotte's character. The open and virtuous conduct of the Earl of Chatham, and his rebuffs from the queen in consequence thereof affords another proof of the domination which her majesty endeavoured to exercise over all advisers of the crown. The imbecility of the king, owing to circumstances formerly noticed by us, as well as the horrors of a ruinous war, must also be ascribed to the dictatorial conduct of Queen Charlotte. The unjustifiable hatred her majesty imbibed against the Princess of Wales, and the consequent unfeeling demeanour she exhibited to that victim, would of itself be sufficient to refute the praises of her minions, and stamp her name with everlasting infamy. But many other convincing proofs are upon record. Her majesty well knew that the country was bending under an enormous load of debt, which encumbered its inhabitants; she knew of their sufferings and complaints; but the appealing voices of reason and supplication were never deemed worthy of her attention. What traits of "matronly" goodness or natural affection did she exhibit for the Princess Charlotte, when advancing to the hour of her peril? And what proofs have we of "her grief for the loss of her grand-daughter" so satirically ascribed, by the writer quoted a few pages back, to be one of the causes of her majesty's last illness? Alas! her majesty's abject, though horrible, confession on her death-bed, relative to this unfortunate princess, too fatally corroborated the infamy of her general conduct! We need not proceed farther with her majesty's character; this, this unnatural act is enough to chill the blood in the veins of every human being!

At this time, very little was said of the afflicted king; indeed the bulletins assumed such a sameness of expression, that the country thought there was not satisfactory evidence to prove the sovereign was *really alive*. His majesty's disorder did not require that close and solitary confinement so arbitrarily imposed upon him. If he had been a private gentleman, associated with an affectionate wife and dutiful children, would he not have frequently been persuaded to take an airing in an open carriage? But how infinitely superior were the facilities attendant upon the situation of the king than could possibly be possessed by any private gentleman! His majesty had long been languishing, and was, at the commencement of

1819,

insensible to all around him. Death was evidently making rapid strides, and yet the bulletins continued of the same general expression.

At this time, we had the honour of being personally acquainted with one of the king's sons, whose integrity has ever been considered unimpeachable, both in his public and private character. The information we received relative to the KING'S DEATH came directly from his royal highness.

It will be remembered, that much doubt prevailed upon the reality of the king's existence, and numerous bets were entered into upon the subject by persons in the higher circles. Notwithstanding this, on the 25th of January, the Earl of Liverpool introduced a motion to the House of Lords for the purpose of nominating the Duke of York to the office of "guardian to the king," as, in consequence of the demise of her majesty, that trust had become vacant. Much altercation ensued. The duke's former delinquencies had not been forgotten, and the country was tired with the subjection they then endured from the IMPOSING privileges of royalty. But, in despite of all opposition and remonstrance, the care of the king's person was committed to the Duke of York, for which his royal highness had the unblushing effrontery to receive TEN THOUSAND POUNDS A YEAR FOR VISITING HIS DYING FATHER TWICE A WEEK!!! What an unprecedented example of avarice and undutifulness was here manifested by a son to his parent, who would have travelled the same distance any time to have gratified his passions! Oh, Shame! where is thy blush? Oh, Infamy, art thou not now detected? A few weeks after this motion had received the approbation of the agents of corruption, the long-afflicted and disappointed George the Third DIED! but the event was carefully concealed from the public. Prayers were still read in churches for his recovery, though the bishops knew they were *mocking heaven*, by praying for the life of one who was *already dead*! Ye sticklers for upholding the present impious system of church government, what say ye to this? Could Infamy and Blasphemy go any farther? And yet those at the head of this system are still allowed to insult the country by proposing general fasts to people already starving, as well as impiously accusing the Almighty with spreading distress and pestilence over the land which they themselves have laid waste by their rapacity and worldly-mindedness! While the clergy were praying for the life of the *deceased* king to be preserved, the apartments formerly in the occupation of his majesty were kept in the same state as when the monarch was alive, and the royal body, after being embalmed, was placed in a leaden coffin of needful substance. Our royal informant went on to state, that these impositions were practised upon the public to give time for selecting proper persons to be despatched to Milan, or elsewhere, to gain intelligence what the Princess of Wales intended upon the demise of the king, as, in that event occurring, her royal highness would become queen consort.

Notwithstanding all this cunning and trickery, her royal highness was informed of the death of her father-in-law many months before it became publicly known. A junior branch of the royal family wrote to her, "The king is now dead, but this event will not be made known to the nation till certain arrangements are made, on behalf of the prince regent, *to degrade you*; and either keep you abroad for the remainder of your life, void of your title as Queen of England, and with other restrictions, or to obtain witnesses, and, giving you the *form* of a trial, insult and destroy you!" Her royal highness, however, was precluded from *acting* upon this information by her correspondent, who enjoined her to the strictest secrecy till the event should be made known to her by the ministers of the crown.

In the meantime, every opportunity to suppress unpleasant inquiries or investigations upon subjects connected with royalty and the time-serving ministry were carefully embraced. That unparalleled junto, Liverpool, Castlereagh, Sidmouth, and others of

The death of George III after a long period of illness, as depicted in *Cassell's History of England* (1865).

the same profession, not forgetting our dear venerable Lord Eldon and the *pious* bishops, were well aware of George the Third's death, at the time it happened. They had, indeed, been expecting it for some time; yet these were the persons who assisted to deceive the public mind, and prevent the straightforward acknowledgment of TRUTH! The evidence we have adduced of this fact is so palpable and strong, that he who can resist its force must be strangely void of perception, or else have made a previous resolve not to suffer himself to be the subject of conviction.

In the early part of May, several persons were introduced at court, and received the royal smile, on being appointed to investigate the private conduct of the Princess of Wales. Their *purses* were also amply supplied by the royal command, and if further sums were found needful, they received letters of credit upon the principal banking houses named in the route they had to take. If any person in the common ranks of life gives away that which is not his to give, he renders himself liable to transportation; but it is said, a "king can do no wrong!" The most disreputable of society were solicited to give information against the Princess of Wales, either with regard to any public or private intelligence they might have received; the most liberal offers were also made to remunerate the persons so inquired of. After an immense expense, information, though of a doubtful character, against the princess was obtained, ONLY BY PURCHASE; and various were the despatches sent over to this country, and answered by the ministerial plotters, who exerted all their energies to bring the business to a consummation.

During such disreputable transactions, the princess knew the *real* cause of all the attempts to insult and degrade her character; and she, therefore, without delay, advised with her legal friends what steps were most proper to take. Alas! the princess was doomed only to receive fresh insults; delay followed delay; excuses of the most palliative description were used, instead of sound advice and positive opinion, and it appeared as if every hand were raised against her! Indeed, the perplexed and mortifying situation of the princess was attended with such dangerous consequences, that, had she not been a most *courageous* woman, and supported by her *innocence*, she must have sank under her fears. Driven into exile, abandoned by the ministry, deserted by her friends, through the bribery of her enemies, attacked by her *nearest relations*, the only resource she had left was in committing her person, her sceptre, her crown, and her honour, to the care of the representatives of the British people. For our own parts, we cannot forget that when she was accused before parliament on a former occasion, the whole nation was melted into tears, or inflamed with rage; and, except those princes and their minions, who should have felt for her the most, there was found but one heart, one will, and one voice, on the subject throughout the kingdoms! Nor can it have escaped the observation of our countrymen, that all those persons, originally employed in bringing to trial this illustrious and virtuous woman, have been munificently rewarded; while those who advocated her cause, and stood between her and the axe uplifted for her destruction, have experienced nothing but the blackest calumny and detraction.

Lord Moira, the author of the first investigation, was made Marquis of Hastings, and Governor-General of India. This individual, however, desired his *right hand might be amputated immediately after his decease, as an expiatory judgment against himself, in having signed dishonourable deeds to injure the happiness of the princess.* Conant, the poor Marlborough-street magistrate, who procured the attested evidence for impeachment, was created Sir Nathaniel, with an increase of a *thousand pounds* a year, as chief of all the police offices. The Douglases were all either elevated to wealth, office, or rank. The Jerseys stood in the sunshine of the court; and the Rev. Mr. Bates, then editor of the "Herald," and her bitterest enemy, was created a baronet, and promoted high in the church! Such was the fortune of her accusers; but how different was that of her supporters!

In June, the Chancellor of the Exchequer submitted his plan of finance. It proved that the revenue was reduced eighteen millions, to meet which, extra loans were proposed to be raised and new taxes enforced. In doing this, the Speaker of the House of Commons, in the address to the regent, said, "In adopting this course, his majesty's faithful Commons do not conceal from themselves that they are calling upon the nation for a *great exertion*; but, well knowing that honour, character, and independence have at all times been the first and dearest objects of the hearts of Englishmen, we feel assured that there is no difficulty that the country would not encounter, and no pressure to which it would not *cheerfully* submit, to enable us to maintain pure and unimpaired that which has never yet been shaken or sullied,— our public credit, and our national good faith." Now let us ask the reason why an extra immense burden of taxation was to be levied upon the people. The queen was *acknowledged* to be dead, and certainly could not be chargeable to the nation by her personal expenditure or allowance. The king was also *dead*, though *his income was received as usual*! as well as the Duke of York's *ten thousand pounds for attending him*!!! Royal and ministerial extravagance likewise caused the useless outlay of twenty thousand, five hundred pounds, for SNUFF-BOXES, besides twelve hundred guineas as presents to three German barons. The gift of *an axe* or *a halter* would have better accorded with the financial state of the empire!

The prince regent closed the session in person on the 13th of July; and, at the conclusion of his speech, adverted to the *seditious spirit* (what sensible man could feel surprised at it?) which was evident in the manufacturing districts, and avowed a firm determination to employ the powers provided by law for its suppression, instead of promising the people redress of grievances!

In Glasgow, Leeds, Manchester, and Stockport, the meetings of the inhabitants now became very numerous, while all means were taken by the local authorities to provoke general confusion.

On the 16th of August, the MEMORABLE MEETING at Manchester took place, for the purpose of petitioning for a reform in the representation. The assembly consisted of from sixty to one hundred thousand persons, who conducted themselves in the most peaceable manner. The assembled multitude, however, were suddenly surprised by the arrival of the Manchester yeomanry cavalry; to which were afterwards added a regiment of the Cheshire yeomanry, and a regiment of huzzars,—the outlets being occupied by other military detachments. The *unarmed* thousands were now driven one upon another, and many were killed and wounded,

Engraving titled *The Massacre of Peterloo; or, Britons Strike Home* (1819) as reproduced in *Social England* (1904).

while others were ridden over by the horses. The number ascertained to have been killed were eight men, two women, and one child; but the wounded were about six hundred! How well the words of a celebrated author apply to this diabolical proceeding: "A kingdom for a stage, princes to act, and to behold the grand effect; but at their heels, leashed in like hounds, may not sword, famine, fire, crouch for employment?" Numerous imprisonments followed, and many poor families were consequently deprived of support.

Historians are at issue whether or not the riot act was read before the scene of carnage commenced, as it is unconstitutional to send a military force *to act* before so doing. We, however, confidently assert IT WAS NOT READ in the hearing of any of the populace, neither was it at all likely that the soldiers could have come so suddenly and unexpectedly upon the multitudes, unless by previous order and arrangement. Further than this, an hour ought to have transpired after such reading before a soldier or civil officer could be authorised to interfere in dispersing the meeting. As a proof of the corresponding features of this unexampled and murderous business, a letter was written by the *pious* Lord Sidmouth, *in the name of the regent*, to the Earl of Derby, presenting thanks for the vigorous and able conduct of the magistracy and military of Manchester on the 16th. Thus were the lives and liberties of the open-hearted population of these kingdoms allowed to be at the controul of an impotent and heartless statesman; for it appeared that the regent was not at hand to have given his assent to this unparalleled piece of barefaced audacity. Lord Sidmouth should have been more careful of dates, as the "royal dandy" was at that time taking a little pleasure near the Isle of Wight. But the following particulars will explain the *systematic* plan of this cold-blooded massacre:

Mr. H. N. Bell, before this period, was confidentially employed at the office of the secretary of state, in the capacity of genealogist, under the immediate controul of Lord Sidmouth. Some considerable period before the melancholy butchery, he was engaged to proceed to Manchester, in company with two other persons, for the avowed purpose of inflaming the public mind against the ministry. He went, and the result was as his patron and employer, Lord Sidmouth, desired it. Mr. Bell and his associates expressed to the people of Manchester, that they need not remain in their then starving condition, if, in an orderly and peaceable manner, they were to assemble on some convenient spot, and unanimously resolve to petition for a reform, so much needed, in the representation. These tools of the secretary of state told the famishing multitudes, that if they pleased to enjoy happiness and plenty, together with civil liberty, they had now an opportunity of accomplishing their most earnest wishes. Under their influence, clubs and unions were soon formed, and public notices were ultimately given, that a general meeting would take place on the 16th of August.

These preliminary arrangements being completed, the *soldiery* had instructions to be ready. The result was as before stated; and Mr. Bell and his accomplices returned to London as soon as their object was attained. The Duke of York acted a prominent part in this plot, from his military facilities; but the besotted prince was persuaded to get out of the way until the affair should be concluded.

Mr. Bell proved very useful in the office of the secretary, and as he had once forfeited his own good opinion, by lending himself to the diabolical plot just mentioned, he made no further scruple, but became a passive engine, directed in his actions by the command of ministers and state empirics. Lord Sidmouth was dissatisfied with the Manchester business; he had hoped that many more might have been brought to suffer the extreme penalty of the law, thereby affording an awful example to deter others from daring to question the excellency of the government under which they lived, and the generous disposition of the governors. We are aware that some people attributed this affair to the magistracy; but they would not have dared to interfere in such a manner as they did, unless sanctioned and supported by the higher powers. The cause of a selfish, cruel, and despotic ministry, required the assistance of corresponding heartless servants, and they obtained it. Lord Castlereagh, however, threw out many insinuations that the Manchester plot was a very bold and desperate undertaking; but the *pious doctor* "laid the flattering unction to his soul of its *expediency*," believing some such infamous procedure needful to rivet the iron sceptre of despotism. How well does the repentant language of a certain wicked king apply here!

> "My fault is past. But, O, what form of prayer
> Can serve my turn? Forgive me my foul murder!—
> That cannot be, since I am still possess'd
> Of those effects for which I did the murder!

*   *   *   *   *

> In the corrupted currents of this world,
> Offence's gilded hand may shove by justice;
> And oft 'tis seen, the wicked prize itself
> Buys out the law!"

This has proved but too true, as well in the Manchester affair as in many other diabolical state proceedings. The little value, indeed, which the ministers of this period entertained for human life ought never to be pardoned. Property, if seized or lost, may be restored; or if not, man may enjoy a thousand delightful pleasures of existence without riches. The sun shines as warmly on the poor as on the rich; the gale of health breathes its balsam into the cottage casement on the heath no less sweetly and salubriously than in the portals of the palace. But can the lords of this world, who think so little of the lives of their inferiors in wealth, with all their boasted power, relume the light of the eye once dimmed by the shades of death? "Accursed despots!" as a talented author well observes, "shew the world your authority for taking away that which ye never gave, and cannot give; for undoing the work of God, and extinguishing the lamp of life which was illuminated with a ray from heaven! Where is your CHARTER TO PRIVILEGE MURDER?" All the gold of Ophir, all the gems of Golconda, cannot buy a single life, nor pay for its loss,—it is above all price. Yet when we take a view of the proceedings of Lord Sidmouth's junto, we are led to believe any thing of more value than human life. Crimes which had very little moral evil, if any, and which, therefore, could not incur the vengeance of a just and merciful God, were unceremoniously punished with death by this minister. Men, for instance, were liable to be shot for meeting peaceably together and making speeches, though proceeding from the purest and most virtuous principles, from the most enlarged benevolence, from wisdom and unaffected patriotism; or for such speeches as might proceed from mere warmth of temper, neither intending nor accomplishing any mischief. Was not such the case in that horrible affair which we have just related? But despots are ever frightened at their own shadows; they tremble and become offended at the least alarm, and nothing but the blood of the accused can expiate the offence. It is, however, from such savage acts of barbarity that the Goddess of Liberty is aroused; it is from the tyranny of her jailors that she eventually makes a progress irresistible, and carries with her fires destined to consume the throne of every despot that cannot bear the light! Various motions have been made since that accursed day to bring the *surviving* actors in the Manchester tragedy to condign punishment. Amongst the foremost in this laudable endeavour stands Mr. Hunt; but his efforts have hitherto proved unavailing. Although we disapprove of the general conduct of the member for Preston, the meed of praise ought not to be withheld from him for the admirable speech he delivered, relative to this subject, in March, 1832, as follows:

> "Mr. Hunt said the grossest misrepresentations had been made in parliament respecting that occurrence; and he felt that it was a matter deeply to be regretted, that there was not in the House of Commons, at the time, some person who had witnessed the transaction, and who could put the House in

possession of the real facts. There was a hope, however, that the present government would grant an inquiry for which he was about to apply, in conformity with the prayer of the petitions which he had just presented, and with the desire of his constituents. He proceeded to detail the circumstances under which the meeting of the Manchester reformers, at which he presided, took place. He described the horrible scene which ensued upon the dispersion of the meeting by an unprovoked and unresisted charge of the yeomanry cavalry. The House would have some notion of the violence and cruelty of the military from this fact, that when a number of men, women, and children had crowded into a small court, from which there was no thoroughfare, one of the yeomanry drove them out, whilst another struck at each of them with his sabre, as they came out. The number of persons killed on that day amounted to fifteen, while the maimed and wounded were no fewer than four hundred and twenty-four. It was true that it might be said that some of these did not suffer from the sabres of the yeomanry, but a very large proportion, he would take on himself to say, were wounded in that manner; and, at all events, it was quite certain, that no accident whatever would have occurred but for the outrageous attack that had been made on the peaceable multitude. Nor was it men alone that suffered. Women were cut down also. And were these men to be called soldiers? Was this their way of showing their high courage and their honour by cutting down *inoffensive females*? He would ask any man of humanity in that House, whether such disgraceful acts ought to be passed by unnoticed and unpunished, merely because it could be said that twelve years had elapsed since the transaction had taken place? But another excuse that perhaps might be made was, that the meeting was an illegal one. In answer to that, however, he would take on himself to say, that in his opinion, and in the opinion of those who constituted the meeting, they were as legally, aye, and as meritoriously assembled, as that House was assembled; and for as useful a purpose. No one was insulted—no tumult took place—no symptoms of riot were evinced; and yet was it for a moment to be said, that in such a country as this, where there was a continual boast of the *omnipotence of justice*, such things were to be passed over *without notice and without censure*? He could assure the House, that if this inquiry was not granted, there would be thousands of hearts rankling dissatisfied and discontented, and which could never be set at ease till *justice was awarded*. The petitioners, in whose name he was speaking, recollected that *Earl Grey*, and many of his *colleagues*, expressed, *at the time of this outrage*, a desire for an investigation into the matter. And how was that inquiry then resisted? First, by the production of official documents, emanating from the guilty party themselves; and next, by allusion to the trial at York; and the cry that the courts of justice were open to those who had any complaint to make. But the courts of justice were *not* open; for the relations of those that were killed had gone to those courts of justice, and even there *all retribution had been denied them in the most cruel and indifferent manner*! Nor was this all. All sorts of calumnious statements were allowed to be made in the House of Commons as to the conduct of the mob, by paid spies of the government. The general presumption was, that it was the intention of the Manchester meeting, had it not been interrupted, to pass resolutions similar to those passed at Smithfield, declaratory that without a reform in parliament, taxes ought not to be paid; and he believed that that presumption was the main reason why he had been found guilty. But now, what an alteration had taken place! It was only the other day that 150,000 persons had met at Birmingham, and actually made a declaration to the same effect; and yet they were not cut down—the yeomanry had not been called out to act against them. This motion for a select committee had, in a manner, become absolutely necessary; for when he had moved for the correspondence that had taken place between Lord Sidmouth (then the secretary of state) and the lord lieutenant of the county, that correspondence had been refused; and, therefore, he had no other course to pursue than to ask for a committee for general inquiry into the whole question. Some part of Lord Sidmouth's correspondence, however, was before the public; for he had in his hand that letter of his lordship's in which he, in the name of the prince regent, thanked the magistracy for the way in which they had acted—yes, actually thanked them for having directed the execution of these COLD-BLOODED MURDERS,—by which name he must call those deeds, and by which name they were ever designated in that part of the country where they had been committed. The consequence of this letter was, that the parties, so far from shrinking abashed as they ought, actually gloried in the share they had taken in the transaction; and, in particular, he might mention that an Irishman of the name of Meagher, who was the trumpeter on that occasion, had boasted, when he returned to Ireland, that he had in one day spilled more Saxon blood than had ever been spilled by any one of his countrymen before! The real truth of the matter was, in spite of the false colouring that interested parties had endeavoured to put on it, that the meeting at Manchester was neither more nor less than a reform meeting, that every thing was going on peaceably, that not even so much as a pane of glass was broken, and though the government took the trouble to send Messrs. Oliver and Castles among the people to corrupt them, they were not able to succeed in their virtuous endeavours. As to his own personal feeling on the subject, he was quite willing to remember that twelve years had elapsed, and in that recollection to drown the memory of all he had himself suffered in consequence of the transactions of that day. It was enough for him, when he recollected the object of that meeting, to see the noble lord introduce such a measure of reform as he had never expected to see any government in this country introduce; and which, though it did not go the length that he could have desired, fully admitted the allegation, that the present House of Commons was not chosen by the people,—the allegation on which he had all along built his own proposition of reform. This, he repeated, was quite enough to wipe away any personal resentment that he might ever have felt. But if not—if he still were vindictive—

what revenge might he not find in the events that had since taken place! Who was the prime minister of that day? The Earl of Liverpool! And where was the Earl of Liverpool? Who were the principal officers of state of that day? Lord Sidmouth, Mr. Canning, and Lord Castlereagh! Of these, Lord Sidmouth alone remained; and where was Mr. Canning? Where Lord Castlereagh, and how did he go out of the world? A remarkable fact it was, that two years afterwards, on the very anniversary of that fatal 16th of August, while he was lying in prison, the very first letter that he opened detailed to him the end of that minister. Who was the reigning prince of that day?— George the Fourth—where was he? They had all gone to answer for their deeds at a tribunal where no jury could be packed, where no evidence could be stifled, and where unerring justice would be meted out to them! To carry this further, if it needed it, he might mention that two of those very yeomanry committed suicide on the very anniversary of the 16th of August, and many were now to be seen walking about the streets of Manchester, objects of a horrid pity. He would not say that all this was a just judgment on these participators in the murders of Manchester: but one might almost fancy, that though a House of Commons could not be found to deal out impartial justice, there was still a wise Providence over all, which, by its interference, had taken care not to let the guilty escape; and, as a climax to the whole, he hoped to live to see the day when the noble lord who yet lived should be brought to the bar of justice for having sent Castles, and Edwards, and Oliver, as spies, for the purpose of instigating the peaceful people to revolt. Nor was this all. Other retribution had taken place; the government of that day and its friends had not only countenanced this destruction of the people for the sake of shewing their enmity to reform, but had actually undertaken a continental war with the same objects in view; and yet now those very persons saw a reform taking place in spite of themselves, and had even been condemned unsuccessfully to battle its progress night after night in that House. He would say this too, that if this committee of inquiry should be refused, and if he should live a few years longer, he did not doubt that he should see the day arrive when a much heavier retaliation, in another way, would take place. He himself desired no such thing; but was it in the character of human nature that persons who had been so deeply injured should sit down quiet and satisfied, when every thing in the shape of redress was denied them? But he trusted that the government would not refuse this motion for inquiry; should, however, such a refusal be given, he should feel it to be his duty to bring the question again and again before the country, as often as the forms of the House would allow. In making his proposition to the House, he had not provided himself with a seconder; but, after what had taken place, he would call on the noble Chancellor of the Exchequer to second the motion. The noble lord had, twelve years ago, pretty freely expressed his opinion as to the transaction; and, he presumed, that that opinion had not been altered by the lapse of time. The laws of England and of every country had always been unanimous in expressing their abhorrence of the crime of murder; and it was because he charged those parties with being guilty of a deliberate and cold-blooded murder that he demanded an inquiry, in the name of justice and retribution."

We offer no apology for introducing this eloquent and manly appeal in behalf of long-delayed justice. The popularity or unpopularity of Mr. Hunt forms no consideration in our minds; nay, even if the Duke of Cumberland himself (much as we loathe his character!) had been its author, it should still have found a place in our volume. How the ministers could reconcile it with their duty, both to God and man, to *refuse* the inquiry, we are at a loss to determine, particularly as each of them formerly expressed a desire for it! It is really astonishing with what different eyes men see things when in office and when toiling to get in!

In the October of this year, the Princess of Wales removed to Marseilles, weary of the attempts to traduce and insult her character by hirelings from the English court. A friend of our's had the pleasure of enjoying her royal highness' confidence at this period, and, after her removal to Marseilles, the persecuted Caroline made the following observations: "What could I do, when I found such base attempts made to destroy my reputation by the most disreputable characters? I left Milan, and I have carefully preserved a journal of each day's history, which, upon perusal, will do much more than *merely satisfy* the nation, to which my heart so fondly clings." "I wished," added the princess, "very ardently to have gone to England in the early part of this year, and I had resolved to do so; but my legal advisers prevented me, expressing their opinion that they should see me first." It is a fact that the interview with Mr. Brougham, so much desired in April, 1819, was not granted until a later period in 1820! Might not an earlier arrangement than this very probably have put the enemy to flight? The princess was not ignorant of the demise of the king, as we have before stated; and the source from which her royal highness received that information was too worthy of reliance to be doubted. Yet, being bound in honour to conceal the information and informant, both were kept in profound silence. It was generally

Henry Hunt campaigning for the universal suffrage, as depicted in *Cassell's History of England* (1865).

supposed, however, that this event had taken place, because no man, afflicted as his majesty was said to be, could possibly exist for any lengthened period. But in the then art of governing, there were frequently many circumstances which were highly necessary to be concealed from the knowledge of the people. That precious trio, Sidmouth, Castlereagh, and Canning, environed the throne, and their dictatorial will was soon converted into law. Under their auspices, the already enormous standing army was still increased; while, like the tyrannical son of Philip, when he reprimanded Aristotle for publishing his discoveries, they whispered to their myrmidons, "Let us diffuse darkness round the land. Let the people be kept in a brutal state. Let their conduct, when assembled, be riotous and irrational as ignorance and *our spies* can make it, that they may be brought into discredit, and deemed unfit for the management of their own affairs. Let power be rendered dangerous in their hands, that it may continue unmolested in our own. Let them not taste the fruit of the tree of knowledge, lest they become as wise as ourselves!" Such were the political sentiments of those at the head of affairs at this period;—how successfully they acted upon them is too well known.

The session opened in November, and never did ministers commit themselves more than by the speech then put into the mouth of the regent. It contained little else than vindictive sentiments, breathing vengeance on all who dared oppose the "powers that be," but seemed utterly forgetful of this good advice, "It is the sovereign's duty to ease with mercy's oil the sufferer's heart."

The infamous and notorious "Six Acts" were introduced this session by "the Oppressors," the principal object of which was to impose further restrictions on the freedom of the press. This plan was considered likely to be the most successful, as well as the most insidious, mode of abolishing the few liberties remaining to Englishmen. Ministers thus thought to leave the FORM of our dearest safeguard untouched, and so gradually annihilate its ESSENCE. The voracious worm eats out the kernel completely, while the husk continues fair to the eye, and apparently entire. The husbandman would crush the insect, if it commenced the attack on the external tegument; but it carries on the work of destruction with efficacy and safety, while it corrodes the unseen fruit, and spares the outside shell. At this despotic period, the press was erected as a battery by the people to defend the almost vanquished citadel of their liberty; but, by these acts, Castlereagh, instead of attacking this citadel, opened the dams, locks, and flood-gates, so that the waters might secretly undermine its foundation, when he hoped to see it fall ingloriously into the hands of its enemies. While these base deeds were being accomplished, no thoughts were bestowed upon the people's wretchedness, which stood in dread array against ministerial imbecility. Indeed, the servile papers in the pay of government not only stoutly denied that such distress existed, but made the grossest attempts to impose on the public credulity. Let any one read such papers of the period we are speaking, if the employment be not too nauseous, and they will there see KNOWN FACTS, if they militated against the credit of the voluptuous regent, or his government, either DOUBTED or DENIED; uncertain victories extolled beyond all resemblance to truth; and defeats, in the highest degree disgraceful and injurious, artfully extenuated. Notwithstanding all this effrontery and falsehood, the "Six Acts" were still thought necessary to gag that which corruption and bribery could not render quite inefficient in the cause of truth. While contemplating such acts of tyranny, we are led to exclaim with Cato, when seeking out the little barren spot of Utica, "Wherever there is a regard for LIBERTY, JUSTICE, and HUMANITY, there will we gladly take up our abode; for there we shall find a country and a home!"

The extraordinary events that occurred in the year

1820

are so closely interwoven with the weal and wo of the British people, that it may be considered as one of the most serious periods in English history.

On the 15th of January, the Duke of Kent became indisposed with a severe cold. On the 17th of the same month, it was reported, "that his royal highness' illness had assumed most alarming symptoms;" and Sir David Dundas went off expressly to Sidmouth to attend his royal highness. The duke's disorder increased, and at half-past one, P. M., January 23rd, this prince was deprived of his mortal existence, in the fifty-third year of his age. But a few days before, his royal highness was in good health, and in the prime of life! The public will one day be made acquainted with the particulars of the REAL CAUSE of his death. At present, we shall only observe, that his royal highness was too virtuous to be allowed to live long in a vicious court!

The public journals dwelt with much force upon the kind attentions and tender offices performed by the duchess, which, if true, were only what every good wife ought to have done. Who can be nearer to a wife than her husband? and what lady of feeling and integrity would not blush to be negligent in the best services and the most unwearied attentions to the ordained partner of her life? Royalty, however, has so many and such peculiar privileges, that what is considered *wonderous grace* with them is merely thought *common decency* in the vulgar part of Adam's offspring.

About this time, the king's health was stated to be "very much on the decline," (hypocrisy!) and the journals announced "that George the Third expired without a struggle, on the 29th of January, in the eighty-second year of his age, and the sixtieth of his reign." But we have the gratification of setting history right in this particular. Of course, the letters and notices of this intelligence were immediately forwarded by the appointed messengers to the several foreign courts. It would be unnecessary for us here to offer any remark upon the character of George the Third, as we have previously noticed the origin of that unhappy disease which so lamentably afflicted him during the latter years of his truly unfortunate life. His majesty bequeathed a sum of money to each of his sons; but George the Fourth thought proper to withhold the Duke of Sussex's portion. This unjust act was the primary cause of the quarrel between these royal brothers, which lasted till the death of George the Fourth. But, as "kings can do no wrong," little was thought of his majesty's dishonesty. Monarchs are aware of their privileges, and have, therefore, in many instances, not scrupled to commit the most heinous crimes. His late majesty was one of this kind, and

The arrest of the Cato Street Conspirators from a contemporary print published in 1820.
(*Licensed under Wikimedia Commons*)

yet he was called "His most gracious, religious, and benevolent majesty!" What a profanation of terms were these!

As a necessary preliminary to a new reign, George the Fourth was proclaimed in London on the 31st of the same month.

In February, a *pretended* mysterious political plot was publicly adverted to, by the name of "The Cato-street Conspiracy." It was said that information having been received at Bow-street, that a meeting of armed persons was to be held at a house in Cato-street, Mary-la-bonne, and, as the magistrates feared something serious would be the result, they forwarded a formidable body of their officers to the place. On the arrival of these persons, they found the number of men amounted to thirty, armed with guns, swords, daggers, and other weapons, and appeared ready to leave the place, which was a hayloft at the top of the house. The officers demanded an entrance, which was refused. Captain Fitzclarence then arrived, with a party of the guards, and a scene of much violence ensued. Some of the party were taken to Bow-street, which was lined with soldiers. The result proved serious to a police officer, named Smythers, who was stabbed in the affray, which produced his death; and it was sworn, that Arthur Thistlewood inflicted the wound.

This heart-rending tragedy was generally thought to have been produced by *government spies*; indeed, several newspapers stated as much at the time. We, however, KNOW such to have been the case, and that the characters of "blood-hounds" were but too well performed. Our bosoms swell with indignation at the recollection of such monstrous plots against the lives and liberties of our countrymen, and we regret that the plotters did not fall into their own snares.

On the morning after this lamentable occurrence, a "Gazette Extraordinary" was issued, signed "Sidmouth," offering one thousand pounds for the detection of Arthur Thistlewood, who stood charged with the crime of high treason. The reward had the desired effect, as he was soon apprehended. Three of his companions were afterwards taken, and FIVE MARTYRS, in all, suffered as traitors on the 1st of May.

Let us not, in common with hirelings, talk of the "wisdom of ministers," and the "bravery of the guards," combined with the several loathsome execrations on artificers and agriculturists; but let us inquire, is there no resemblance to be observed between this conspiracy and the Manchester massacre? The intelligent reader will not find the similarity difficult to trace.

The queen's return to England being now expected, Mr. Canning resigned his place in the cabinet as president of the Board of Controul, and retired to the Continent. One of his biographers says, "His conduct on this occasion, according to universal consent, was marked by the most perfect correctness and delicacy of feeling." Perhaps it might be so considered by some people; but to us it does appear that a man of sound public principles, of high and honourable private feelings, had no middle course to take at this juncture. Either the Queen of England was GUILTY, or she was the MOST PERSECUTED AND AGGRIEVED OF WOMEN. Will any one say that, in the *first* instance, it was the duty of a minister of high station to desert the painful, but responsible, situation in which he stood, from any feeling of esteem or attachment to an individual so unworthy? In the other case, if Queen Caroline, as almost everybody believed, and as Mr. Brougham *solemnly swore he believed*, was INNOCENT, was there any circumstance or consideration upon earth,—the wreck of ambition, the loss of fortune, or the fear of even death itself,—which should have induced an English gentleman, a man of honour, a man who had the *feelings of a man*, to leave a FEMALE, whom he called "FRIEND," beneath the weight of so awful an oppression? To us, we must confess, Mr. Canning's conduct on this occasion appears one of the greatest blots we are acquainted with upon his public and private character, the almost unequivocal proof of a mind unused to the habit of taking sound and elevated views of the human action. Mr. Canning had, during a long career,—a career continued through nearly thirty years,—been the forward and unflinching opponent of popular principles and concessions. He had never once shrunk from abridging the liberties of the subject; he had never once shown trepidation at any extraordinary powers demanded by the crown. With his arms folded, and his looks erect, he had sanctioned, without scruple, the severest laws against the press; he had advocated the arbitrary imprisonment of the free citizen; he had eulogized the forcible repression of public meetings; and he had constantly declared himself the determined enemy of parliamentary reform. The only subject on which he professed liberal opinions (the Catholic question) was precisely that subject to which the great bulk of the community was indisposed. Such had been the career, such was the character, of Mr. Canning up to the time of his cowardly desertion of the injured Caroline, Queen of England!

Her majesty was now daily expected to land upon our shores; and powerful as was the arm of tyranny, her arrival was much feared by her husband and his ministers.

We have before mentioned that the queen desired several times, *most particularly*, to see Mr. Brougham. It is true that various places for meeting had been appointed; but some apology or other was invariably made by the learned gentleman. Her majesty finally wrote that she should be at St. Omers on a certain day, on her way to England, in the metropolis of which she was resolved to arrive as soon as possible. Her majesty had previously appointed Mr. Brougham her attorney-general, desiring he would choose a solicitor to act with him, and he named Mr. Denman. One excuse for not attending to his appointment with the queen, Mr. Brougham ascribed to his electioneering business in Westmoreland; and another was, Mrs. Brougham's being in a situation too delicate for him to leave her. Such excuses ought not to have prevented Mr. Brougham's giving his attention to the important business of the queen; indeed, he was once within four leagues of her majesty's abode, with a CERTAIN LETTER in his pocket from the *highest authorities*; but Mr. Brougham did not venture to lay it before the queen, nor did he seek for an interview. The commission thus entrusted to this learned gentleman was the same which Lord Hutchinson undertook some time afterwards.

The queen felt very indignant at Mr. Brougham's so repeatedly declining his engagements, and wrote to Lord Liverpool to request his lordship would send a frigate to convey her to England. Fearing, however, that this might be against the state projects then in contemplation, the queen, by the same post, wrote to her former friend and lady in waiting, Lady Anne Hamilton, to repair to her immediately at St. Omers, and attend her in her former capacity; and also, to Alderman Wood, that if Lord Liverpool refused or delayed to send a frigate, the Alderman would hire a vessel for the purpose of bringing her to this country immediately.

Little time was lost in obeying these commands of the Queen of England. In the mean time, Mr. Brougham wrote to her majesty, requesting leave to meet her at Calais; to which the queen replied, she should choose to see him at the inn at St. Omers. Shortly after the arrival of her majesty's lady in waiting and the alderman, Mr. Brougham was

Henry, Lord Brougham, photographed in later life. (*Smithsonian Institute*)

announced, and informed her majesty that he was accompanied by Lord Hutchinson, (now Lord Donoughmore) the KING'S PARTICULAR FRIEND, who was the bearer of a message to her majesty from the king, and asked leave when he might have the honour of introducing him to her majesty. "No, no, Mr. Brougham, (said the queen) no conversations for me; he must put it in writing, if you please; we are at war at present." "But, madam, it is impossible that so many scraps of different conversations can be properly arranged." "Then, I don't see Lord Hutchinson," said the queen. "Madam, if you insist upon it, it shall be done; and when will your majesty be pleased to receive it?" "To-morrow morning you may bring it me; and so good evening to you, as I suppose you are fatigued with your journey."

The next morning, Mr. Brougham arrived with Lord Hutchinson's letter, which the queen opened and read in Mr. Brougham's presence; in the conclusion of that letter, her majesty was earnestly entreated to wait the return of a courier from Paris. "Paris! Paris!" said the queen, "what have I to do with Paris?" Mr. Brougham, in *much confusion*, said, "Your majesty MUST HAVE MISTAKEN; it must mean *Calais*; my friend is too honourable to mean anything of that kind, or to do anything wrong." "No, no, Mr. Brougham; Paris, Paris! Look there!" pointing the sentence out to him. Then added the queen, "You will come and dine with me to-day." "May not I bring Lord Hutchinson with me, please your majesty?" "Certainly not. But I hope you will see Lord Hutchinson?" "Yes; let him come directly." The queen then assembled her whole household, and received his lordship in the midst of a *formal circle*, talked upon indifferent subjects for about a quarter of an hour; then rose, and, gracefully courtesying, left the room. Most of the household followed; and Mr. Brougham, with his friend, Lord Hutchinson, did not remain long behind. Mr. Brougham afterwards returned; but appeared exceedingly disconcerted. Lady Hamilton was present, and tried to draw him into conversation upon various subjects; but he answered, rather abruptly, "You and the alderman are leading the queen to her destruction." The lady replied, that was a mistake; she did not interfere in political affairs. Mr. Brougham begged pardon, and the subject was ended by the queen entering the room to dinner. The dinner passed off very well; her majesty appeared in good spirits, as did Mr. Brougham. It was the queen's general practice not to sit long after dinner; she, therefore, soon retired with her lady; and the gentlemen adjourned to the drawing-room to await the serving of coffee. By her majesty's orders, her maids were waiting with her travelling dress, with the carriages all ready in the court-yard, in the first of which her majesty immediately seated herself, as also Lady Hamilton and Alderman Wood. The moment before her majesty drove out of the yard, she desired her *maître d'hôtel* to inform Mr. Brougham "that the queen would drink coffee with him *in London*;" yet five minutes had not elapsed from leaving the dinner-table to her driving out from the inn, as fast as four post-horses could convey her. This was the only time her majesty was ever known to show fear; but, at the appearance of any horseman, she became very much agitated from the supposition that she should be detained in France, under a PRETENCE of not having a correct passport, the want of horses, or some such trivial excuse. The queen was aware that the King of England had, not long before, placed Louis the Eighteenth upon the throne of France; therefore he could not object to *any* proposition her husband thought proper to require. Her majesty also KNEW that a courier had been despatched to Paris, and that that courier was one of *Mr. Brougham's brothers*! Mr. Brougham himself actually joined with Lord Hutchinson in trying to persuade her majesty to remain in France till the return of the courier. The queen's active and intelligent mind saw everything at a glance, and she *acted* with the promptitude of her character. Alderman Wood proposed that her majesty should rest that night at D'Estaing's fine hotel at Calais, instead of sleeping on board a common packet, which would not sail till the morning. "No, no," said the queen, "drive straight to the shore;" and out she got like a girl of fifteen, and was in the packet before anyone else. "There," said her majesty, "now I can breathe freely—now I am protected by English laws." The queen was hardly seated, when Alderman Wood presented her with a note from Mr. Brougham, entreating her majesty to return, if only for the night, to D'Estaing's, and promising that no harm should happen to her. "No, no," replied the queen, "I am safe here, and I WILL NOT TRUST HIM;" and then threw a mattress in the middle of her cabin, with some blankets, and slept there all night. In the morning, when her majesty was about to land at Dover, she seemed a little intimidated, in consequence of the dense multitude through which she had to pass. Her majesty's fears, however, were entirely groundless, as she soon found the hearts of Britons were friendly to her cause, though they exemplified it rather roughly; for her feet were never permitted to touch the ground from the time her majesty left the vessel till her arrival at the inn, which she availed herself of with feelings of the most gratifying description, at the sympathy manifested in the cause of persecuted virtue.

As soon as her majesty could procure horses, she set forward to Canterbury, where she was received with similar acclamations. The populace insisted upon drawing her majesty out of the town, and then would not suffer the horses to be put to without her personal entreaties. Thousands of blessings were poured on her head, without one dissenting voice; and in this manner did her majesty proceed all the way to London.

The queen took up her abode at 77, South Audley-street, until another more suitable residence could be provided for her. The family of Alderman Wood, who previously inhabited this house, left it immediately after receiving intelligence that her majesty would make a temporary use of it, and they occupied apartments at Flagdon's hotel.

On the ensuing day, several of the nobility and members of the House of Commons called to inquire after her majesty's health. On the ninth of this month, her majesty removed from South Audley-street to 32, Portman-square, the residence of the Right Honourable Lady Anne Hamilton, by whom the queen was attended. Her ladyship's servants were continued, and her majesty was much pleased with the respectful and generous attentions rendered.

On the 16th, the queen received an address from the common council of the city of London, to which she returned an answer, so feelingly expressed, as to excite the sympathy and admiration of all present.

On the afternoon of the sixth day of the queen's entry into London, a message was delivered from the king to both houses of parliament, communicating certain reports and papers respecting the queen's misconduct while abroad. On the following Thursday, a committee was appointed in the House of Lords; but the queen transmitted a communication to the House of Commons, protesting against the reference of her accusations to a SECRET TRIBUNAL, and soliciting an open investigation of her conduct.

Thus was commenced a prosecution in principle and object every way calculated to rouse the generous and constitutional feelings of the nation; and the effects were without a parallel in the history of all countries! Could a more outrageous insult possibly have been offered to her dignity, to the honour of her husband the king, or to the morality and decency of the community at large?

Up to this time, Prince Leopold had not tendered his respects to her majesty; yet he was the widowed husband of the queen's only and dearly-beloved daughter! His serene highness had been raised from a state of comparative poverty and obscurity to be honoured with the hand of England's favourite princess, from whose future reign was expected a revival of commerce and an addition of glory. Though this prince was enjoying an annual income of FIFTY THOUSAND POUNDS from the country; though he had town and country residences, of great extent and magnificent appearance; though he abounded with horses and carriages; yet not one offer did he make of any of these superfluous matters to the mother of his departed wife, by whose means he had become possessed of them all! Gratitude, however, is generally esteemed a *virtue*, and therefore a German prince could not be supposed to know anything about it.

About this period, her majesty received numerous communications, tending to prove the infamous proceedings against her to have been adopted without reference to honour or principle, and to warn her from falling into the snares of her mercenary and vindictive enemies. We lay before our readers the following, as sufficient to establish this fact.

> "An officer of the frigate which took her majesty (when Princess of Wales) to the Continent averred, in the presence of three *unimpeachable* witnesses, that a very few days before her majesty's embarkation, Captain King, while sitting at breakfast in his cabin with the surgeon of the frigate, received a letter from a *brother of the prince regent*, which he read aloud, in the presence of the said surgeon, as follows:

> "Dear King,
> "You are going to be ordered to take the Princess of Wales to the Continent. If you don't commit adultery with her, you are a damned fool! You have *my* consent for it, and I can assure you that you have that of *MY BROTHER, THE REGENT.*
> "Your's,
> (Signed) ********.

"The officer who made the above statement and declaration is a most CREDITABLE PERSON, and the witnesses are all in this country."

"*London, May 7th, 1820.*

"Furnished to supply the queen with PROOF that the *royal duke* in question is leagued against her, in accordance with the WISHES OF THE KING!"

"Private Document.

"Captain King's agent is Mr. Stillwell, 22, Arundel-street, Strand, London; and the surgeon, [350] who was present during the period the royal duke's letter was read, is James Hall. The witnesses were—Mr. Freshfield, 3, Tokenhouse-yard; Mr. Holmes, 3, Lyon's-inn; and Mr. Stokoe, 2, Lancaster-court; as also before Barry O'Meara.

(Signed) "Barry E. O'Meara."

On the 24th of June, a deputation of the House of Commons was appointed to wait upon her majesty with the resolutions adopted by the House on Thursday, the 22nd. They arrived at a quarter past one o'clock. Mr. Wilberforce and Mr. S. Wortley occupied the first carriage. At their appearance, strong symptoms of displeasure were indicated. They were then introduced to the queen, Mr. Brougham standing at her majesty's right hand, and Mr. Denman at her left. They severally knelt and kissed her majesty's hand. Mr. Wilberforce then read the resolutions, and her majesty replied to them. On their departure, Mr. Brougham accompanied the deputation to the door; and, after they had taken their seats in the carriages, Mr. Brougham returned to shake hands with them, although the multitudes assembled outside hissed them exceedingly.

Her majesty's answer to the before-mentioned resolutions was superior to the tricks of her enemies. In it the queen refused terms of conciliation, unless they accorded with her duty to her own character, to the king, and to the nation! "A sense of what is due to my character and sex," said the queen, "forbids me to refer minutely to the REAL CAUSE of our domestic differences!" Indeed, her majesty's reply was an appeal to those principles of public justice, which should be alike the safeguard of the highest and the humblest individuals. Mr. Wilberforce exposed himself to much censure upon the part he had taken in the House; and, as he so unhesitatingly hinted at the awful contents of the "Green Bag," he said, "by suppressing her own feelings, the queen would endear herself to the country." We suppose Mr. Wilberforce meant, that, by suppressing her own feelings of honour, she would gratify the honour of the country; and, by again quitting it, demonstrate her gratitude for its unshaken loyalty; but the queen was firm in her resolve to *claim justice*, whether it was given or withheld.

In considering these base endeavours to injure innocence, in order to raise the *noble* character of a voluptuous prince, we cannot help remarking that Power was the *only* weapon of the vitiated monarch, while Right and Justice formed the shield of the oppressed Queen of England! Indeed, every man, glowing with the sincere love of his country, and actuated by that honourable affection for its welfare, which takes a lively and zealous interest in passing events, must have considered such proceedings against her majesty fraught with inevitable evil. If her innocence, according to the prayers of millions of her subjects, should be made manifest, the public indignation would be sure to be roused, and probably prove resentful. The evidence was known to be of a description on which no magistrate would convict a common pickpocket, and therefore if the legislature should even be induced to consider her majesty guilty of the charges preferred against her, public opinion would certainly refuse to ratify the sentence, and turn with disgust from those promulgating it. In either case, those venerable tribunals, consecrated by our forefathers, must lose that beautiful, that honourable, that unbought, homage which a free people have ever been proud to pay them. No Englishman, we say, accustomed to reverence, with a prejudice almost sacred, the constitution of a parliament, *majestic even in its errors and infirmities*, could contemplate, without pain, the possibility,—nay, the almost certainty,— that the hour was not far distant when the whole nation would look with cold indifference, or gloomy distrust, on the acts of a senate, their generous obedience to which (though it had been accompanied with suffering, and followed by privation) had been "the admiration of the whole world."

On the 6th of July, Sir Thomas Tyrwhitt, usher, of the black rod, waited upon her majesty with a copy of the "Bill of Pains and Penalties" against her, presented the previous day to the House of Lords, and which was forwarded by order of their lordships. Her majesty went into the room where the deputation were waiting, and received a copy of this bill with great calmness. Upon an examination of the abominable instrument, her majesty said, "Yes, the queen who had a sufficient sense of honour and goodness to refuse the base offer of fifty thousand pounds a-year of the public money, to spend it *when, where, how, and with whom she pleased*, in banquetings, feastings, and excesses, providing it were in a foreign country, and *not at home*, has sufficient resolution to await the result of every investigation power can suggest." Like another Cleopatra, our insulted queen might have played "the wanton" with impunity; her imperial bark might have displayed its purple streamers, swelled with the softest Cyprian breezes. It might have sailed triumphantly down the Adriatic, to meet some highly-favoured lover! Yes, by desire of the king, her husband, the queen was requested to accept any terms beside those of a legitimate character. But her majesty preserved her usual firmness and serenity of mind during the unequalled proceedings instituted against her, and frequently repeated the unequivocal expression, "Time will furnish sufficient proof of my innocence."

On the 5th of August, the queen took possession of Brandenburgh House, formerly the residence of the Margravine of Anspatch, situated near the Thames, and in the parish of Hammersmith. Her majesty left Lady Hamilton's house at four o'clock, attended by her ladyship, and accompanied by Dr. Lushington, in an entirely new and elegant open carriage, drawn by four beautiful bay horses. They drove off amidst united shouts of applause from the assembled people.

Will future generations believe the historian's tale, that a queen,—yes, a brave and virtuous Queen of England too!—was refused a house and a home by the sovereign, her husband? That she, who was lured from her princely home, arrived in the centre of England, and was denied a resting place by the king and his ministers! In consequence of which, she was necessitated to take up her abode in the mansion of a late lord mayor for the space of three days, and then to accept the use of the house of her lady in waiting for nearly two months; while there were palaces totally unoccupied, and even mouldering into decay for want of being inhabited! This statement will, doubtless, appear overdrawn to future generations; but there are thousands now living who can testify to its accuracy. Ministers, indeed, entered into compact with Deception, and so glaringly committed their sentiments and characters, that, to preserve their own pretended *consistency*, they would have even uncrowned the king himself! A feverish sensation now pervaded the whole public mind, and from the highest to the lowest, the case of the queen was one universal theme of conversation.

On the 6th of August, her royal highness the Duchess of York died. Up to a very late hour of the day on which this occurred, no official communication had been made to the queen; but, in consequence of the event, her majesty requested to postpone several addresses which she had previously appointed to receive.

On the 7th, the queen sent a letter to the king, but it was returned from Windsor unopened, with a communication that "Such a letter addressed to the king cannot be received by his majesty, unless it passes through the hands of his minister." Why, after the refusal to receive this letter, should the princess be blamed for permitting its contents to be published? If the king were under obligations of such a description as to incapacitate him from exercising his own judgment, and giving his own opinion, was he fit to administer the laws, or ought he to have sanctioned the appeal of miscreants who sought their own, and not their country's, good? Let us consider the delays attending this letter. It was sent to Windsor, directed *expressly for the king*, accompanied with a note, written by the queen, to Sir B. Bloomfield, desiring it might be immediately delivered into the king's hand. Sir B. Bloomfield was absent, and Sir W. Keppell, as the next in command, received it, and forwarded the same to Sir B. Bloomfield, at Carlton House, immediately, who returned the letter on the 8th to her majesty, saying, "I have received the king's commands and general instructions, that any communications which may be made should pass through the hands of his majesty's government." The queen immediately despatched a letter to Lord Liverpool, enclosing the one she had addressed to the king, by the hands of a messenger, in which her majesty desired the earl to present it. Lord Liverpool was then at Coombe Wood, and wrote in reply, that he would "lose no time in laying it before his majesty." Up to the 11th, no reply had been received; and the queen wrote to Lord Liverpool again, to know if further communication were needful. Lord Liverpool replied, that he had not received the king's commands upon the subject, and therefore could not give any positive answer relative to it. How does this strange and incomprehensible conduct appear to any unbiassed Englishman? Was the king, who ought to be the dispenser of the laws, to be free from imputation, when he thus exposed his unrelenting temper and unbending determination, wherever his private inclinations were concerned? We dare avow, if that letter could have been answered, it would; but its contents were unanswerable! "Aye," said the hireling Castlereagh, "it is no matter what the conduct of the Princess of Wales has been; it is the king's desire that he may no more be obliged to recognise her in her former character of Princess of Wales." Oh! most sapient speech of a most sapient lord; truly this was a bold doctrine to broach, that kings have a right divine to subdue, injure, oppress, and govern wrong!

We pass by the number of addresses presented to her majesty at this period, and also the not-to-be-mistaken expression of public opinion against the projector of her injuries. Were they not concocted by the authority of the monarch, her husband? Was it not by his *divine* decree that his consort's name was erased from the liturgy? Did he not send down to parliament that message which denounced his queen a criminal? Yet, after all this, Lord Liverpool said, "The king has no *personal* feeling upon the subject." Very true, his majesty could not have any *personal* feeling towards the queen; his royal feelings had always been confined to the libidinous and the most obnoxious of society! Had he been a worthy and upright plaintiff against the most unfortunate of defendants, would he have scrupled to have shewn himself in his regal chair upon the continued debates arising from this most important question; and would not a sense of greatness and virtue, *had he possessed either*, after hearing the infamous statements of *false witnesses*, have influenced him to *decline further proceedings*, though his pride might have withheld an acknowledgment of error? This line of honest conduct was not followed, and we are therefore obliged to brand him as one of the most despicable and mean of the human race!

During the disgraceful proceedings against the queen, such was the public feeling in her favour, that the peers actually feared for their personal safety in going to and returning from the House. This threatened danger was, as might be expected, properly guarded against by the *military*, who poured into London and its environs in vast numbers. The agitated state of the public mind probably was never more decidedly expressed than on the 19th of August, the day on which the trial commenced. At a very early hour in the morning, workmen were employed in forming double rows of strong timber from St. Margaret's church to the King's Bench office on the one side, and from the upper extremity of Abingdon-street on the other, so as to enclose the whole area in front of the House of Lords. This was done to form a passage to the House, which was devoted exclusively for the carriages of the peers, to and from the principal entrance. Within this extensive area, a large body of constables were stationed, under the controul of the high bailiff and high constable, who were in attendance before seven o'clock. A very strong body of foot-guards were also posted in the King's Bench office, the Record office, and in the other apartments, near or fronting the street. Westminster Hall was likewise appropriated to the accommodation of the military. All the leading passages from St. Margaret's church into Parliament-street were closed securely by strong partitions of timber. The police-hulk and the gun-boats defended the river side of Westminster, and the civil and military arrangements presented an effectual barrier on the opposite side. At nine o'clock, a troop of life-guards rode into the palace yard, and formed in line in front of the principal gate of Westminster Hall; they were shortly afterwards followed by a detachment of the foot-guards, who were formed under the piazzas of the House of Lords, where they piled their arms. Patrols of life-guards were then thrown forward, in the direction of Abingdon-street, who occasionally formed near the king's entrance, and at intervals paraded.

At half-past nine, a body of the Surrey horse-patrol rode over Westminster-bridge, and for a short time paraded Parliament-street, Whitehall, and Charing-cross; they afterwards drew up near the barrier at St. Margaret's church. The peers began to arrive shortly afterwards; the lord chancellor was in the House *before eight o'clock*. The other ministers were equally early in their attendance.

At a quarter before ten, an universal cheering from a countless multitude, in the direction of Charing-cross, announced to the anxious spectators that the queen was approaching. Her majesty, attended by Lady Anne Hamilton, had come early from Brandenburgh-house to the residence of Lady Francis, St. James' Square, and from thence they departed for the House of Lords, in a new state carriage, drawn by six bay horses. As they passed Carlton Palace, the Admiralty, and other such places, the sentinels presented arms; but, at the Treasury, this mark of honour was omitted.

When the queen arrived at the House, the military stationed in the front immediately presented arms. Her majesty was received at the door by Sir T. Tyrwhitt and Mr. Brougham; and the queen, with her lady in waiting, proceeded to an apartment prepared for their reception. Shortly afterwards, her majesty, accompanied as before, entered the House by the passage leading from the robing-room, which is situated on the right of the throne.

During this initiatory part of the trial, and until nearly four o'clock, her majesty was attended by Lord Archibald Hamilton and his sister Lady Anne, who stood close to the queen all the time.

Upon returning from the House in the same state in which her majesty arrived, she was greeted by the most enthusiastic acclamations and shouts of applause from every class of society, who were apparently desirous to outvie each other in testimonies of homage to their ill-fated and insulted queen.

Each succeeding day of the pretended trial, her majesty met with a similar reception; and, during the whole period, addresses were lavishly poured in upon her, signed by so many persons, and testifying such ardent regard and devotion, that every moment of time was necessarily occupied with their reception and acknowledgment. Thus, though the queen was insulted by the king and the majority of the peers, it must have afforded great consolation to her wounded feelings, while witnessing the enthusiasm and devotion manifested in her cause by all the really honourable of the community. We say *really honourable*, because her persecutors were either actuated by "filthy lucre," or by a desire to recommend themselves, in some way or another, to the favour of the king and his ministers.

To justify these remarks, we here present our readers with a list of those time-serving creatures who voted against the queen, with the annual amounts they were then draining from the country:

The Duke of York, with immense patronage,[4] nearly 100,000*l.*; and the Duke of Clarence, 38,500*l.*; but we must not suppose her majesty's BROTHERS voted through *interest*; their *virtuous minds could not tolerate her iniquities*!!!

Dukes.—Wellington, 65,741*l*., including the interest of 700,000*l*., which he received to purchase estates; Northumberland, possessing immense patronage and family interest; Newcastle, 19,700*l*.; Rutland, 3,500*l*.; Beaufort, 48,600*l*.; and Manchester, 16,380*l*.

Marquises.—Conyngham (!) 3,600*l*., but the exact sum his wife received, we have not been able to ascertain; Thomond, 13,400*l*.; Headfort, 4,200*l*.; Anglesea, 11,000*l*.; Northampton, 1,000*l*.; Camden, 4,150*l*.; Exeter, 6,900*l*.; Cornwallis, 15,813*l*.; Buckingham, 5,816*l*.; Lothian, 4,900*l*.; Queensberry, great family interest; and Winchester, 3,200*l*.

Earls.—Limerick, 2,500*l*.; Ross, governor of an Irish county; Donoughmore, 4,377*l*.; Belmore, 1,660*l*.; Mayo, 15,200*l*.; Longford, 7,369*l*.; Mount Cashel, 1,000*l*.; Kingston, 6,400*l*.; St. Germains, brother-in-law to Lord Hardwicke, who received 7,700*l*.; Brownlow, 4,400*l*.; Whitworth, 6,000*l*.; Verulam, 2,700*l*.; Cathcart, 27,600*l*.; Mulgrave, 11,051*l*.; Lonsdale, 14,352*l*.; Orford, 6,700*l*.; Manvers, 4,759*l*.; Nelson, 15,025*l*.; Powis, 700*l*.; Liverpool, 33,450*l*.; Digby, 6,700*l*.; Mount Edgecumbe, 400*l*.; Strange, 13,988*l*.; Abergavenny, 3,072*l*.; Aylesbury, 6,300*l*.; Bathurst, 15,423*l*.; Chatham, 13,550*l*.; Harcourt, 4,200*l*.; Warwick, 6,519*l*.; Portsmouth, *non compos mentis*; Macclesfield, 3,000*l*.; Aylesford, 6,450*l*.; Coventry, 700*l*.; Abingdon, 2,000*l*.; Shaftesbury, 6,421*l*.; Cardigan, 1,282*l*.; Balcarras, 46,050*l*.; Winchelsea, 6,000*l*.; Stamford, 4,500*l*.; Bridgewater, 13,700*l*.; Home, 2,800*l*.; and Huntingdon, 200*l*. We must not here omit Lord Eldon, whose vote would have been against her majesty if it had been required; his income amounted to 50,400*l*., with immense patronage.

Viscounts.—Exmouth, 10,450*l*.; Lake, 7,300*l*.; Sidmouth, 17,025*l*.; Melville, 18,776*l*.; Curzon, 2,400*l*.; Sydney, 11,426*l*.; Falmouth, 3,578*l*.; and Hereford, 1,200*l*.

Archbishops.—Canterbury, 41,800*l*.; Tuam, 28,000*l*.; both with immense patronage.

Bishops.—Cork, 6,400*l*., besides patronage; Llandaff, 1,540*l*., with twenty-six livings in his gift; Peterborough, 4,140*l*., with an archdeaconry, six prebends, and thirteen livings in his gift; he had also a pension granted him by the king's sign manual, in 1804, of 514*l*.-4,654*l*.; Gloucester, 3,200*l*., twenty-four livings, besides other patronage, in his gift; Chester, 4,700*l*., with six prebends and thirty livings in his gift; he has also a son in the *secret* department in India, 2,000*l*., and another a collector in India, 2,500*l*., as well as sons in the church with benefices to the amount of 2,750*l*.-11,950*l*.; Ely, 21,340*l*., and the patronage of one hundred and eight livings; St. Asaph, 6,000*l*., his son has two livings in the church, 1000*l*., and he has ninety livings in his gift,—7,000*l*.; St. David's, 6,260*l*., besides one hundred livings, prebends, and precentorships in his gift; he has also a relation in the church, with two livings, 1,000*l*.-7,260*l*.; Worcester, 9,590*l*., besides the patronage of one archdeaconry and twenty-one livings; London, 10,200*l*., with ninety-five livings, twenty-eight prebends, and precentorships in his gift.

Lords.—Prudhoe, 700*l.*; Harris, 3,800*l.*; Meldrum, of the Gordon family, who annually devour about 30,000*l.*; Hill, 9,800*l.*; Combermere, 13,500*l.*; Hopetoun, 15,600*l.*; Gambier, 6,800*l.*; Manners, 21,500*l.*; Ailsa, *expectant*; Lauderdale, 36,600*l.*; Sheffield, 3,000*l.*; Redesdale, 5,500*l.*; St. Helens, 1,000*l.*; Northwick, 1,500*l.*; Bolton, 4,000*l.*; Bayning, 1,000*l.*; Carrington, 1,900*l.*; Dunstanville, 1,500*l.*; Rous, *motive unknown*; Courtown, 9,800*l.*; Galloway, 9,845*l.*; Stuart, 15,000; Douglas, 2,500*l.*; Grenville, 4,000*l.*; Suffield, brother-in-law to the *notorious Castlereagh*,—need we say more to point out *his* motive for voting against the queen? Montagu, 3,500*l.*; Gordon, 20,990*l.*; Somers, 2,000*l.*; Rodney, 6,123*l.*; Middleton, 700*l.*; Napier, 4,572*l.*; Gray, 200*l.*, with great family interest; Colville, 4,600*l.*; Saltoun, 3,644*l.*; Forbes, 8,400*l.*; Lord Privy Seal, 3,000*l.*; and Lord President, 4,000.

Notwithstanding this phalanx of corruption being arrayed against one virtuous female, after an unexampled multiplication of abuse and perjury, on the fifty-first day of the proceedings, the infamous bill was LOST, and, with it, the pretensions to uprightness and manly feeling of every one who had voted for it! What was the dreadful, the overwhelming, responsibility of those who had ventured to prosecute, of all others, a great, a noble, a glorious woman, (we speak unhesitatingly, for we speak from the EVIDENCE OF HER OWN PUBLIC ACTS) by a "Bill of Pains and Penalties," which was so far from being a part of our common law, that that was necessarily sacrificed in order to give effect to this? The mock trial was supported by the evidence of witnesses who, day after day, perjured themselves for the sake of wealth, and by the ingratitude of *discarded* servants, treacherous domestics, and cowardly calumniators; evidence, not only stained with the infamy of their own perfidy to their generous benefactress, but polluted with the licentious and gross obscenity of their own debased instincts, for we cannot call their cunning by any other name. This, Englishmen! was the poison, this the vast and sweeping flood of iniquity, which was permitted by the government to disseminate itself into the minds of the young, and to inundate the morals of the whole country! A great moral evil was thus done; but the antidote luckily went with it. The same press, upon which the absurd, foolish, and dangerous imbecility of incompetent and unmanly ministers imposed the reluctant office of becoming the channel for the deluge of Italian evidence, also conducted the refreshing streams of national sympathy and public opinion! The public sustained their own honour in upholding that of Caroline, Queen of England! When that public beheld her intelligent eyes, beaming with mind and heroism; when they heard of her pure beneficence, holy in its principle, as it was unbounded in its sphere; when they felt her glowing affection for a devoted people; when they observed her, scorning alike the weakness of her sex and the luxury of her station,—actuated solely by the mighty energies of her own masculine sense and powerful understanding,—braving fatigue and danger, traversing the plains and mountains of Asia, the sands and deserts of Africa; and contemplating the living tomb of ancient liberty in modern Greece; when they heard of this dauntless woman sailing over foreign seas with a soul of courage as buoyant and as mighty as the waves that bore her; but, above all, when they knew of her refusing the glittering trappings and the splendid price of infamous security, to face inveterate, persecuting, and inflexible enemies, even on their own ground, and surrounded by their own strength and power, they felt confident that such a woman must be at once a favourite of heaven, a great queen, and a blessing to the people, who fervently offered up their prayers for her safety and her triumph! It will readily be supposed, then, with what joy the result of this important and unprecedented investigation filled the hearts of thousands, which manifested itself by shouts of exultation from the centre of the metropolis, and was re-echoed from the remotest corners of the land, by the unbought voices of a brave and generous people, who considered the unjust proceedings alike "derogatory to the dignity of the crown and the best interests of the nation."

From the very commencement of the queen's persecution, her majesty's counsellors appeared more in the capacity of MEDIATORS in the cause of *guilt* than as *stern, unbending, and uncompromising champions of honour and truth*! In one of Mr. Brougham's speeches, he declared the queen had no intention to *recriminate*; but Mr. Brougham cannot, even at this distance of time, have forgotten that, when her majesty had an interview with him after this public assertion on his part, she declared herself INSULTED by such a remark, as her case demanded all the assistance it could possibly obtain from every legal quarter. Another peculiar trait of defection was conspicuously displayed during this extraordinary trial. The letter we gave a few pages back, written by an illustrious personage to the captain of the vessel in which the princess went in the memorable year 1814, offering him a reward to procure any evidence of improper conduct on the part of her royal highness, was submitted to Mr. Brougham, and shortly afterwards, at the supper table of the queen, he said aloud, that he HAD SHEWN THAT LETTER TO THE OPPOSITE SIDE OF THE COURT; and when remonstrated with for such extraordinary conduct, his only reply was, "Oh, it will do very well;" and soon after left the room. This and many other singular acts of the learned gentleman will seem surprising to his admirers. Such suspicious conduct, indeed, is hardly to be accounted for; but we could not dispute the evidence of our own senses!

At this period, a lady of her majesty's household received a note from a young person, stating the writer to be in possession of some papers of GREAT CONSEQUENCE TO THE QUEEN, which she wished to deliver to her majesty. A gentleman was sent to the writer of the note, and her information to him was, in substance, as follows:

That certain property, of a large amount, had been bequeathed to her; but that for many years she had been deprived of all interest arising from it. That Dr. Sir Richard Croft, *accoucheur* to her late royal highness, the Princess Charlotte, was an attendant witness to the will of her mother, by whom the property had been willed,—her father having engaged, upon his return from abroad, to put his daughter in possession of her rightful claims, proving her descent, &c. That, during her unprotected state, her guardian had caused her to sign bonds to an enormous amount; and, in consequence, she had been deprived of her liberty for nearly twelve months. As Dr. Sir Richard

Croft was her principal witness and friend, she frequently consulted him on different points of her affairs, and also gave him several private letters for his inspection; but these letters not being returned to her when she applied for them, she reproached the doctor with his inattention to her interests. In consequence of this, Dr. Croft called upon her, and promised to send the letters back the next day. The doctor accordingly sent her a packet; but, upon examination, she found them to be, *not the letters alluded to*, but letters of VAST IMPORTANCE, from the HIGHEST PERSONAGES in the kingdom, and elucidating the most momentous subjects. Sometime after, she sealed them up, and sent a servant back with them, giving him strict injunctions to deliver them ONLY into Sir Richard's hand. While the servant was gone, the doctor called upon her, and, IN GREAT AGITATION, inquired if she had received any other letters back besides her own. She replied she had, and said, "Doctor, what have you done?" He walked about the room for some time, and then said, abruptly, "I suppose you have read the letters?" She replied, "I have read enough to make me very uncomfortable." After some further remarks, he observed, "I am the most wretched man alive!" He then said he would communicate to her all the circumstances. Sir Richard commenced his observations by stating, that he was not the perpetrator of the deed, but had been made the instrument of others, which the letters proved. He then alluded, by name, to a NOBLEMAN; and said the circumstance was first discovered by the NURSE'S observing that a sediment was left at the bottom of the cup in which the Princess Charlotte took her last beverage, and that Mrs. Griffiths directly charged the doctor with being privy to the act. He examined the contents of the cup, and was struck with horror at finding that it was the SAME DESCRIPTION OF MEDICINE WHICH HAD BEEN OBTAINED FROM HIS HOUSE, A FEW DAYS PREVIOUS, BY THE NOBLEMAN BEFORE ALLUDED TO!!! However, he endeavoured to persuade the nurse that she was mistaken; "but," said the doctor, "the more I endeavoured to persuade her, the more culpable, no doubt *I* appeared to her."

Sir Richard said he was farther strengthened in his suspicions of the said nobleman by a conversation he had had a few days before with his lordship, who said, "If anything should happen to the princess,—IF SHE WERE TO DIE,—it would be a melancholy event; yet I consider it would, in some considerable degree, be productive of good to the nation at large." Dr. Croft asked him how he could say so. "Because," said the nobleman, "everybody knows her disposition sufficiently to be convinced, that she will ever be blind to her mother's most unequalled conduct; and I think any man, burdened with such a wife, would be *justified* in using ANY MEANS in seeking to get rid of her! Were it my case, the friend who would be the means of, or assist in, releasing me from her shackles, I should consider would do no more than one man ought to do for another so circumstanced." Dr. Croft then said, he went to this nobleman directly after the death of the princess, and charged him with committing the crime. He at first denied it; but at length said, "It was better for one to suffer than that the whole country should be put into a state of confusion, which would have been the case if the princess had lived," and then alluded to the Princess of Wales coming into this country. The nobleman exonerated himself from the deed; but said "It was managed by persons immediately about the doctor's person." At this part of the narrative, the doctor became very much agitated, and the lady said, "Good God! who did do it?" To which question he replied, "*The hand that wrote that letter without a name, in conjunction with one of the attendants on the nurse!*" The lady further stated, that the doctor said, "Certain ladies are depending upon me for my services as accoucheur, and I will not extend life beyond my attendance upon them." This conversation took place just after the death of the Princess Charlotte.

Before Dr. Croft left the lady, she informed him of her anxiety to return the letters as soon as she discovered their importance, and mentioned that the servant was then gone with them. Sir Richard quickly exclaimed, "You bid him not leave them?" and inquired what directions had been given to the servant. Having been informed, he said, "Don't send them again; keep them until I come and fetch them, and that will be to-morrow, if possible." But the lady never saw him afterwards, and consequently retained the letters.

The gentleman then received exact copies of all the letters before alluded to. We here present our readers with three of the most important, which will substantiate some of our former statements.

COPY OF A LETTER FROM SIR B. BLOOMFIELD TO DR. SIR RICHARD CROFT.

"My dear Croft,

"I am commanded by his royal highness to convey to you his solicitude for your health and happiness; and I am to inform you, that the aid of so faithful a friend as yourself is indispensable. *It is by her majesty's command I write this to you.*

"We have intelligence by the 20th ult. that the Princess of Wales is to take a road favourable to the accomplishment of our long-desired wishes; that we may keep pace with her, there is no one upon whose fidelity we can more fully rely than you yourself.

"A few months relaxation from the duties of your profession will banish all gloomy ideas, and secure the favour of her majesty.

"Come, my boy, throw physic to the dogs, and be the bearer of the happy intelligence of a divorce, to render ourselves still more deserving the confidence of our beloved master, whose peace and happiness we are bound in duty to secure by every means in our power.

"Remember this: the road to fortune is short; and let me see you to-day at three o'clock, without fail, in my bureau.

"Yours faithfully,"
****

"Carlton House, Monday, 9th November, 1817."

COPY OF A LETTER FROM DR. CROFT TO HIS ROYAL HIGHNESS THE PRINCE REGENT.

"The gracious assurance of his royal highness for my happiness was this day conveyed to me, by *the desire of her most gracious majesty.*

"The many former favours and kindnesses bestowed by my royal benefactor is retained in my mind with the deepest sense of gratitude.

"That I regret, with heartfelt grief, the invisible power that determined my inevitable misery, and marks the hand that gave the blow to my eternal peace. Could no other arm inflict the wound than he who, in happier moments, indulged me with the most apparent unfeigned friendship? That I shall not, to my latest breath, cease to complain of such injustice, heaped upon me in the eyes of the world, and before the nation, who at my hands have lost their dearest hopes.

"My conscious innocence is the only right I plead to a just and Almighty God! That I consider this deed of so foul a nature as to stamp with ignominy, not only its perpetrators, but the throne itself, now to be obtained by the death of its own offspring, *and that death enforced by the Queen of England,* whose inveterate hatred is fully exemplified, by heaping wrongs upon the unfortunate partner of your once happy choice, who now only impedes your union to another.

"To remove now this only remaining obstacle, I am called upon by the ministers. With a view of tranquillizing my mind, every restitution is offered me. But, no doubt, many will be found amongst them, who can, without a pang, enjoy the reward of such services—*as her majesty will most liberally recompense.*

"It has ever been my highest ambition to fulfil the arduous duty of my situation; to be rewarded by upright encomiums; and to merit, as a subject and a servant, the approbation of my most gracious benefactor, as conveyed to me on the 9th of this month by Sir B. Bloomfield, would have been a sufficient recompense to me under any circumstances of life.

"I can, therefore, only assure his royal highness, with unfeigned sincerity, that I should feel happy upon any occasion to forfeit my life for his peace and happiness; nor can I more fully evince the same than by assuring his royal highness, that this melancholy circumstance shall be eternally buried in my mind.

(Signed) "Richard Croft."
"November 10th, 1817."

COPY OF A LETTER FROM QUEEN CHARLOTTE TO DR. CROFT.

"We are sensible how much it were to be desired that the obligations provided for could have been traced without the necessity of our writing. But we are yet more sensible how much it is our duty to promote the happiness of our most dear and most beloved son, who so justly deserves the efforts which we make for him. Whatever price will cost our tender love, we shall at least have the comfort, in the melancholy circumstance of this juncture, which our kingdom most justly laments with us, to give to our subjects a successor more worthy of the possession of our crown, either partly or wholly, than the detested daughter of our dearest brother, who, by her conduct, has brought disgrace upon our royal house, and whom now we will, for us, and our descendants, without difference of the substance of blood and quality, that she shall at all events be estranged from us and our line for ever. To this end, we believe the method concerted by our faithful friends at Trieste is the most effectual to ensure it, not by divorce; be it by whatever means which may seem effectual to our friends, to whom we grant full power in every thing, as if we ourselves were present, to obtain the conclusion we so much desire; and whosoever shall accomplish the same shall be placed in the immediate degree with any peer of our kingdom, with fifty thousand pounds, which we guarantee to our worthy friend, Sir Richard Croft, on whom we can rely in every thing,—his services being considered unavoidable on this occasion. And for the better security of all, we promise the bearer hereof, being in every part furnished with sufficient power to write, sign, and secure, by letter or any other obligation, in our name, and which is to be delivered to Sir Richard Croft before his departure from London,—reminding him of his own engagements to the secrecy of this also,—whereunto we put our name, this 12th day of November, 1817.

"Let him be faithful unto death.

(Signed) "C. R."

Who can peruse these letters, and the particulars with which they are accompanied, without being shocked at the dark and horrible crime proved to have been committed, as well as those deep-laid plans of persecution against an innocent woman, which they unblushingly state to have had their origin in the basest of motives,—to gratify the vindictive feelings of her heartless and abandoned husband! It must appear surprising to honourable minds that these atrocities did not find some one acquainted with them of sufficient virtue and nerve to drag their abettors to justice. But, alas! those who possessed the greatest facilities for this purpose were too fond of place, pension, or profit, to discharge such a duty. Queen Caroline, at this period, resolved to ask for a public investigation of the causes and attendant circumstances of the death of her daughter, and expressed her determination to do so in the presence of several noblemen. Her majesty considered these and other important letters to be amply sufficient to prove that the Princess Charlotte's death was premeditated, and procured unfairly. Her majesty also knew that, in 1817, a most respectable resident of Claremont publicly declared that the regent had said, *"No heir of the Princess Charlotte shall ever sit upon the throne of England!"* The queen was likewise *personally* assured of the truths contained in the letter signed "C. R." dated 12th of November; for the infamous Baron Ompteda, in conjunction with another similar character, had been watching all her movements for a length of time, and they were actually waiting her arrival at Trieste, at the time before named, while everyone knew they had a coadjutor in England, in the person of Souza Count Funshall!!!

Her majesty was also well acquainted with the scheme of the king or his ministers, that the former or the latter, or both conjointly, had caused a work to be published in Paris, the object of which was "to set aside the succession of the Princess Charlotte and her heirs, (under the plea of the illegality of her father's marriage) and to supply the defect by the Duke of York!" Lord Moira offered very handsome terms to an author, of some celebrity, to write "Comments in favour of this book;" but he declined, and wrote explanatory of the crimes of the queen and her family. This work, however, was bought up by the English court for seven thousand pounds! In this book of comments was given a fair and impartial statement of the murder of Sellis, and, upon its appearance, a *certain duke* thought it "wisest and best" to go out of this country! *Why* the duke resolved to seek safety in flight is best known to himself and those in his immediate confidence; but to uninterested and impartial observers, such a step was not calculated to exonerate the duke's character. This took place at a very early period after the murder had been committed in the palace of St. James, and all the witnesses were then ready again to depose upon the subject, as well as those persons who had not been permitted to give their evidence at the inquest. Another examination of the body of Sellis might have been demanded, though doubtless in a more public manner than before, as it was not supposed to be past exhumation! The people reasoned sensibly, when they said, "The duke certainly knows something of this awful affair, or else he would cause the strictest inquiry, rather than suffer such a stain upon his royal name and character, which are materially injured in public opinion by the royal duke's refusal to do so, and his sudden determination to go abroad." The duke, however, *did* go abroad, and did not return until inquiry had, apparently, ceased.

Such were the remarks of Caroline, Queen of England, upon these serious subjects, of which she felt herself competent to say more than any other subject in the realm. The secret conduct of the government was not unknown to her majesty, and her sufferings, she was well aware, had their origin in STATE TRICK; while fawning courtiers, to keep their places, had sacrificed *truth*, *justice*, and *honour*. "Then," said the queen, "can I wonder at any plan or plans they may invent to accomplish the wish of my husband? No; I am aware of many, very many, foul attempts to insult, degrade, and destroy me! I cannot forget the embassy of Lord Stewart, the base conduct of that most unprincipled man, Colonel Brown, and other unworthy characters, who, to obtain the favour of the reigning prince, my husband, condescended to say and do any and every thing prejudicial to my character, and injurious to my dignity, as the legitimate princess of the British nation; and for what purpose is this extraordinary conduct pursued? Only to gratify revengeful inclinations, and prevent my full exposures of those odious crimes, by which the honour of the family is and will ever be attainted! But," added her majesty,

> "The untimely, unaccountable death of my Charlotte is, indeed, heavy upon my heart! I remember, as if it were only yesterday, her infant smile when first I pressed her to my bosom; and I must always feel unutterable anguish, when I reflect upon the hardships she was obliged to endure at our cruel separation! Was it not more than human nature was able to endure, first to

be insulted and deceived by a husband, then to be deprived of an only and lovely child, whose fondness equalled her royal father's cruelty? Well may I say, my Charlotte's death ought to be explained, and the bloodthirsty aiders in the scheme punished as they really merit. Who are these proud, yet base, tyrants,—who, after destroying the child, still continue their plans to destroy her mother also? Are they not the sycophants of a voluptuous monarch, whose despotic influence has for a long period destroyed the liberties and subverted the rights of the people, over whom he has exercised such uncontrouled and unconstitutional power? And what is the MORAL character of these state hirelings, (continued the queen) who neither act with judgment, or speak with ability, but who go to court to bow, and cringe, and fawn? Alas! is it not disgraceful in the extreme?—are they not found debasing themselves in the most infamous and unnatural manner? From youth, have not even some of the late queen's sons been immoral and profane? Was not one of them invited to dinner, by a gentleman of the first rank, during his stay in the West Indies, and did he not so conduct himself before one of the gentleman's daughters, that his royal highness was under the necessity of making a precipitate retreat? Yet this outrage upon decency was only noticed by one fearless historian! And amongst the courtiers, where is morality to be found? Yet these individuals are the judges, as well as the jury, and are even empowered to assault, insult, and reproach the consort of the first magistrate, their sovereign the king! But he is in their power; guilt has deprived my lord and husband of all ability to set the perfidious parasites at defiance! If this were not the case, would his proud heart have allowed him to be insulted by my Lord Bloomfield, or Sir W. Knighton? No; the answer must be obvious. Yet such was actually the fact, as all the *private* friends of his majesty can testify. My honour is indeed insulted, and yet I am denied redress. I suspected what my fate would be when so much equivocation was resorted to during my journey to this country. I was not treated as any English subject, however poor and defenceless, ought to expect; far otherwise, indeed. I waited some months to see Mr. Brougham, and was disappointed from time to time, until I determined to return to England in despite of all obstacles. I reached St. Omers on the 1st of June; Mr. Brougham did not arrive until the evening of the 3rd; he was accompanied by his brother and Lord Hutchinson; and I judged from their conversation, that my only safety was to be found in the English capital. Propositions were made me, of the most infamous description; and, afterwards, Lord Hutchinson and Mr. Brougham said, 'they understood the outline of those propositions originated with myself.' How those gentlemen could indulge such an opinion for one moment, I leave the world to judge. If it had been my intention to receive fifty thousand pounds per annum to remain abroad, UNQUEENED, I should have reserved my several establishments and suite. I was requested to delay my journey until despatches could be received; but my impatience to set my foot once more on British ground prevented my acquiescence. I had been in England a very short time, when I was most credibly informed the cause for soliciting that delay; namely, that this government had required the French authorities to station the military in Calais, at the command of the English consul, for the express purpose of seizing my person, previous to my embarkation! What would not have been my fate, if I once had been in the grasp of the Holy Alliance!! This fact will satisfy the English people, that the most wicked plans were organized for my destruction. The inhabitants of Carlton House were all petrified upon my arrival, having been assured that I never should again see England, and that my legal adviser had supported the plan of my remaining abroad, and had expressed his opinion that I should accept the offer. It is also a solemn fact that, at that period, a PROCESS OF DIVORCE, in the Consistory Court in Hanover, was rapidly advancing, under the direction of Count Munster; and, as the king is there an arbitrary sovereign, the regal will would not have found any obstacle. When the day of retribution shall arrive, may God have mercy upon Lords Liverpool, Castlereagh, and their vile associates,—even as they wished to have compassion upon their insulted and basely-treated queen! Had I followed my first opinion after these unhandsome transactions, I should have changed my counsel; but I did not know where to apply for others, as I too soon found I was intended to be sacrificed, either privately or publicly. Devotion in public characters is seldom found to be unequivocally sincere in times of great trouble and disappointment! What is a defenceless woman, though a queen, opposed to a despotic and powerful king? Alas! but subject to the rude ebullition of pampered greatness, and a mark at which the finger of scorn may point. Well may I say—

"Would I had never trod the English earth,Or felt the flatteries that grow upon it!Ye have angels' faces; but heaven knows your hearts.What will become of me now, wretched lady?I am the most unhappy woman living.No friend, no hope, no kindred, weep for me;*Almost no grave allowed me*! Like the lily,That once was mistress of the field, and flourished,I'll hang my head, and perish!"

A very few weeks after making these remarks, her majesty, in correspondence with a friend, wrote as follows:

"I grow weary of my existence. I am annoyed upon every occasion. I am actually kept without means to discharge my honourable engagements. Lord Liverpool returns the most sarcastic replies (if such they may be called) to my notes of interrogation upon these unhandsome and unfair delays, as if I were an object of inferior grade to himself. I think I have sufficient perception to convince me what the point is to which the ministers are now lending their ready aid, which is nothing less than to FORCE ME TO RETURN ABROAD! This they never shall accomplish, so long as my life is at all safe; and in vain does Mr. Wilde press upon my notice the propriety of such a step."

Illuminations and other rejoicings were manifested by the people at the queen's acquittal; but the state of her majesty's affairs, as explained in the above extract, were such as to preclude her receiving that pleasure which her majesty had otherwise experienced at such testimonies of the affectionate loyalty of the British people.

We must now proceed to the year

1821,

in which pains and penalties supplied the place of kindness, and the sword upheld the law! while men who opposed every liberal opinion hovered around the throne of this mighty empire. In the hardness of their hearts, they justified inhumanity, and delighted to hear the clank of the chains of slavery. They flattered but to deceive, and hid from their master the miseries of his subjects! This was base grovelling submission to the royal will, and not *REAL LOYALTY*; for loyalty does not consist in a slavish obedience to the will of a tyrannical chief magistrate, but in a firm and faithful adherence to the law and constitution of the community of which we are members. The disingenuity of Lord Liverpool and his coadjutors, however, who were impelled by high church and high tory principles, wished to limit this comprehensive principle, which takes in the whole of the constitution, and therefore tends to the conservation of it all in its full integrity, to the *person* of the king, because they knew he would favour their own purposes as well as the extension of power and prerogative,—the largesses of which they hoped to share in reward for their sycophantic zeal, and their mean, selfish, perfidious adulation. With such views, the king's ministers represented every spirited effort in favour of the people's rights as originating in *disloyalty*. The best friends to the English constitution, in its purity, were held up to the detestation of his majesty, as being disaffected to his person. Every stratagem was used to delude the unthinking part of the people into a belief that their only way of displaying loyalty was to display a most servile obsequiousness to the caprices of the reigning prince, and to oppose every popular measure. The ministers themselves approached him in the most unmanly language of submission, worthier to have been received by the Great Mogul or the Chinese emperor than the chief magistrate of a professedly free people. In short, George the Fourth only wished to be feared, not loved. The servile ministry fed this passion, though they would have done the same for a Stuart, had one been in power. It was not the man they worshipped, but the *power* he possessed to add to their *own dignity and wealth*! Let us not here be misunderstood. We are willing to award honour to the person of a man invested with kingly power, provided his deeds are in accordance with his duty, though not otherwise. A good king should be regarded with true and sincere affection; but we ought not to pay any man, reigning over a free country, so ill a compliment as to treat him like a despot, ruling over a land of slaves. We must, therefore, reprobate that false, selfish, adulatory loyalty, which, seeking nothing but its own base ends, and feeling no real attachment either to the person or the office of the king, contributes nevertheless, by its example, to diffuse a servile, abject temper, highly injurious to the spirit of freedom.

Though "the bill" was now ingloriously abandoned by Lord Liverpool, the queen received but little benefit. Her majesty was even refused means to discharge debts unavoidably contracted for the bare support of her table and her household. As a proof of the economical style of her living, we witnessed one evening a party of friends sitting down to supper with her majesty, when a chicken at the top and another at the bottom of the table were the *only dishes* set before the company. What a contrast this would have presented to the loaded tables, groaning under the luxurious display of provisions for gluttony, in the king's several residences, where variety succeeded variety, and where even the veriest menial lived more sumptuously than his master's consort!

On the 5th of May, the Emperor Napoleon Buonaparte expired at St. Helena, having endured captivity, under the most unfavourable circumstances, and with a constitutional disease, more than six years and a half. As we

Napoleon in exile on St. Helena, from an engraving in John C. Abbott's *Napoleon at St. Helena* (1855).

shall have occasion, in our second volume, to speak of this illustrious man and his cruel treatment by our government, it would be unnecessary to say more in this place than merely give an outline of his extraordinary career. Napoleon was born at Ajaccio, the capital of Corsica, August 15, 1769; and was, consequently, fifty-two years of age, wanting three months, when he died. He was the eldest son of a lawyer, of Italian descent, and his family had pretensions to ancestry of high birth and station in Italy. He was educated in the *royal* military school; and first attracted notice when, as an officer of engineers, he assisted in the bombardment of Toulon in 1793; next signalized himself by repressing an infuriated mob of Parisians in 1795, which caused his promotion to the command of the army of Italy; was made first consul in 1799; elected emperor in 1804; "exchanged" the sceptre of France and Italy for that of Elba (so it was expressed in the treaty of Fontainbleau) on the 11th of April, 1814; landed at Cannes, in Provence, on the 1st of March, 1815; entered Paris triumphantly, at the head of the French army, a few days afterwards; fought the last fatal battle of Waterloo on the 18th of June in the same year; abdicated in favour of his son; threw himself upon the generosity of the English, through promises made to him by Lord Castlereagh; was landed at St. Helena on the 18th of October, 1815; and died as before stated, a victim to the arbitrary treatment of our government, which we shall presently prove.

Leopold now (in July) called upon her majesty, for the first time since her return to this country. His serene highness was announced and ushered into the presence of the mother of his late consort. The queen appeared exceedingly agitated, though her majesty did not urge one word of complaint or inquiry at the delay of the prince's visit. Previous to the departure of Leopold, the queen appeared much embarrassed and affected, and, addressing the prince, said, "Do you not think that the death of my Charlotte was too sudden to be naturally accounted for? and do you think it not very likely that she died unfairly?" The prince replied, "I also have my fears; but I do not possess any PROOF of it." He then said, "My suspicions were further excited by the *EXCESSIVE JOY* the royal family shewed at her death; for the Regent and the Duke of York got DRUNK upon the occasion." These, we pledge ourselves, were his highness' OWN WORDS, *verbatim et literatim.*

About this time, when the coronation was expected to take place in a few days, her majesty, in writing to one of her firmest friends, said,

"I do not foresee any happy result likely to ensue from my attempting to get into the Abbey; for my own part, I do not think it a prudent step. My enemies hold the reins of power, and *most* of my professed friends appear rather shy; so I fear the advice I have received upon the subject. Alderman Wood intends to go in his civic capacity, which, to me, is very unaccountable indeed; for certainly, if I ever required the assistance and presence of my *real* friends, it is most probable I shall need both at such a period. I can unbosom myself to you, for *I know you to be my real friend*; believe me, I do not assure myself that I have another in the whole world! To *you alone* can I speak freely upon the death of my child and her infant, and I dare tell *you*, I yet hope to see the guilty murderers brought to condign punishment. I say, with Shakespeare,

"'Blood will have blood! Stones have been known to move, and trees to speak, To bring forth the secret man of blood.'

"Such is my earnest hope; may it yet prove true in the case of my lovely departed daughter. While her remains are dwelling in the gloomy vault of death, her father and his associates are revelling in the most abominable debauchery, endeavouring to wash that,—THE FOUL STAIN, THE ETERNAL STAIN,—from their remembrance. Still I live in expectation that the dark deed will be avenged, and the perpetrators meet with their just reward.

"The deep-rolling tide of my enemies' success against me will find a mighty barrier, when all shall be explained, in the simple and unaffected language of truth. Weak and presumptuous as my Lord Liverpool is, I did not believe he would dare to promise one thing, and act the reverse before the world. I did think he was too anxious to retain A NAME for honour, if he merited it not; but I am deceived, and very probably not for the last time. You will sympathize with me; I labour under the pressure of many heavy misfortunes, and also under the provocation of great and accumulated injustice. Yes, and though so unfortunate, I am scarcely at liberty to lament my cruel destiny. These things frequently hang heavy, very heavy, upon my heart; and I sometimes reflect, with inexpressible astonishment, upon the nerve with which I still bear up under the trying burden. For more than fourteen years I have been a victim to perjury and conspiracy; my enemies were in ambush in the shade, but they aimed at me poisoned arrows; they watched, most eagerly watched, for the moment in which they might destroy me, without its being known who drew the bow, or who shot the shaft. You, my friend, know that I delight in disseminating happiness. My bliss is to diffuse bliss around me; I do not wish misery to be known within the circle of my influence. I covet not the glory arising from the carnage of battle, which fills the grave with untimely dead, or covers the earth with mutilated forms. I wish you distinctly to understand me upon these several subjects. I have not any personal feelings against the king, in my own case. I do assuredly pity his majesty, that he should allow himself to be a tool in the hands of a wicked ministry; but my cause for sorrow is, that he should leave this world without exposing the base schemes formed against the SUCCESSION and LIFE of his royal daughter. If his majesty will make restitution upon this point, my anxieties would be in some degree relieved, although nothing on this side the grave will ever make any atonement for the loss of such an amiable and well-formed mind. Well indeed may his majesty be afraid to be left alone; well may he discharge all persons from naming the departed child he ought to have protected; at this I do not wonder, for guilt produces terror and dismay.

"I cannot conclude this without adverting again to the pecuniary difficulties I have to endure. For nearly eight years, I have given up fifteen thousand pounds per annum out of the annuity allowed me by parliament. This amounts now to above one hundred thousand pounds; yet, notwithstanding this, I am refused means to live in a respectable style, to say nothing of regal state. All the royal family have had their debts paid, and the Duke of Clarence received his *arrears*. The Chancellor of the Exchequer promised I should receive an outfit, if the prosecution against me failed. It did fail; but I have received no outfit at all,—not even the value of one shilling,—so that, of necessity, I am involved in debt to the amount of thirty thousand pounds. How differently was the late Queen Charlotte situated; and, since her demise, more than twenty thousand pounds per annum have been paid in pensions to her numerous and already wealthy household! while I am incapable to acknowledge my real sentiments to those who have been generous to me, even at the expense of being unjust to themselves, unless I do it from borrowed resources.

You will not feel surprised at these remarks. Alas! I wish it were not in my power to make more serious ones; but I will await, with firmness, the coronation.

"Believe me ever,
"Your faithful and grateful friend,
"C. R."

Nearly at the same time, the following letter was forwarded to the same friend of the queen, by a professional gentleman, who had for some time been employed to arrange some of her majesty's affairs:

"You may indeed rest assured that no consideration shall induce me to give up 'The Documents' I hold, relative to the queen and her lost, though lamented, daughter, unless you require me to return them to her majesty, or to entrust them into your own care. For, as I obtained them from no other motive than to serve the queen, so I will certainly retain them and use them in this noble cause, without regard to any personal consideration, or convenience, until that object be fully accomplished; and feeling (as you do) the very great importance of such proofs, I will defy all the power of the enemy to dispute the matter with me. Yet, at the same time, I am very candid to acknowledge, that it is my confident opinion every effort will be used to suppress all testimony which may have a tendency to bring THE FAMILY into disgrace. With whom to trust this business, I am at a loss to determine, as it would no doubt be considered rather a ticklish affair. I have thought of Dr. Lushington; but, as you are better acquainted with this learned gentleman's sentiments and opinions upon her majesty's case than I am, I beg to submit the suggestion for your serious deliberation. No time ought to be lost; every thing that CAN be done OUGHT to be done, without delay. The queen is placed in the most serious situation. You ought not to forget, for one moment, that her enemy is her sovereign; and such is the utter absence of principle manifested to this illustrious lady since her left-handed marriage with the son of George the Third, that every person must fear for her safety, unless their hearts are hard as adamant, and themselves actors in the villanous tragedy.

"I give my opinion thus boldly, because I know your fidelity to the queen to be unshaken, even amidst all the rude and unmanly clamours raised against her friends by the agents of her tyrannical husband. This is, and ought to be, your satisfactory reflection,—that you have been faithful to this innocent and persecuted queen, from *principle* [393]*alone*. 'Honourable minds will yield honourable meed,' and to such you are justly entitled. To-morrow evening, I intend to give you further intelligence, as I am now going out for the purpose of meeting an especial enemy of her majesty, by whose rancour I may judge the course intended.

"I have the honour to be,"
&c. &c. &c. ******

Continuation from the same to the same, two days after the foregoing.

"I am sorry to say my fears were not groundless, as I learn, from the first authority, that the king has changed his opinion, and the queen will not be allowed to enter the Abbey. The seat provided is otherwise disposed of. If her majesty's attorney and solicitor generals would *now*, without any loss of time, press 'The Documents' upon the notice of the ministers, either by petition or remonstrance, I think the ceremony would be postponed, and justice be finally administered to the queen. But if they delay this, they may assure themselves the cause of their royal mistress will be lost for ever. Her majesty's proofs are too astounding to be passed over in silence; they would forcibly arouse the guilty, and SUCH FACTS at SUCH A TIME ought to be instantly published. I should not express myself with such ardour upon these solemn points, if I had not made myself most minutely acquainted with every bearing of the subject; and I give you my decisive *legal opinion*, that 'The Documents' in question contain a simple statement of facts, which no judge, however instructed, and no jury, however selected, or packed, could refute. If, however, fear should get the better of duty, I do not doubt sooner or later the country will have cause to repent the apathy of those individuals who were most competent to do, or cause justice to be done to this shamefully injured queen.

"I have not entered upon these opinions from interested views, and I am well convinced your motives do not savour of such baseness; but as disinterestedness is a scarce virtue, and so little cultivated in this boasted land of liberty, I warn you to avoid the ensnaring inquiries of those by whom you may most probably be assailed.

"I also must remind you that, at the present moment, her majesty is watched in all directions. Major Williams is employed by the government to be a spy upon all occasions, and drove his carriage with four grey horses to Epsom last races, and remained upon the ground until the queen drove away. At this time, he occupied an elegantly furnished house in Sackville-street. P. Macqueen, M. P., a protégé of Lord Liverpool's, was doubtless the person who arranged the business with the premier. If this be considered dubious information, I will forward you PROOFS which will set the matter at rest.

"I scarcely need tell you that the case of her majesty is one unprecedented in history, and unheard of in the world. The king and his ministers have resolved upon her destruction, and if the royal sufferer be not destroyed by the first plans of attempt, I indeed fear she will fall a victim to similar plans, which, I doubt not, are in a forward stage of preparation against her; and how can the queen escape from the grasp of such powerful and dishonourable assailants? All their former arrangements and stratagems, to which they subscribed, failed, decidedly failed; but the malignity which instigated those plans will, without any question, furnish materials for new charges, and supply the needful reserve to complete the destruction of a lady, whose talents are envied, whose knowledge of affairs in general is deemed too great, and whose information upon FAMILY SECRETS render her an enemy to be feared.

"I see in this mysterious persecution against the queen, the intended annihilation of the rights and privileges of the nation at large; and I, therefore, protest against the innovation. I argue, that which was unconstitutional and unprincipled in William the Third is equally dangerous and unconstitutional in George the Fourth! If such unprecedented injustice be allowed in the case of her majesty, where must we look for an impartial administration of justice? and how may we reasonably expect that violence will not be offered, if other means fail, to accomplish the intended mischief? In case of indisposition, what may not occur! May not the life of her majesty be in the greatest jeopardy, and may not a few hours terminate her mortal existence? These are questions of vital importance; they do not only materially affect the queen, but, through the same medium, they most seriously relate to every individual of the community; and, if the constitution is not to be entirely destroyed, the queen must be honourably saved from the overpowering grasp of her relentless oppressors. Her majesty reminds me of the words of Seneca: 'She is struggling with the storms of Adversity, and rising superior to the frowns of Persecution; this is a spectacle that even the gods themselves may look down upon with envy.'

"I verily believe that bold and energetic measures might set this question at rest for ever, but time lost is lost for ever; and, in my opinion, retribution can only slumber for a short period. I beg and entreat you not to be subdued or deterred by the arrogance of inconsistent power. The nation is insulted, the independence of the country is insulted; its morality and patience have been outraged!

"What could I not add to this page of sorrow, this blot upon our land? But I have acted openly and honourably to you in this unparalleled case, and have, in so acting, only done my duty.

"Excuse haste, and allow me the honour to remain

"Your most obedient and respectful servant,

******

"July 12th."

Such are the recorded sentiments of a professional gentleman, who volunteered his services to the queen at this period of anxious expectation. He hailed, or affected to hail, the appearance of the star of liberty, whose genial rays should dispel the gloom of the desolating power of her enemies. But, alas! how soon were such opinions changed by the *gilded* wand of ministerial power! *Pension* reconciled too many to silence upon these all-important subjects; even he, who wrote thus boldly in defence of an injured queen and her murdered daughter, shortly afterwards acted the very reverse of his duty for the sake of paltry gain! But, independent of the lavish means which ministers then possessed of bribing those who felt inclined to bring these criminal matters before a public tribunal, an unmanly fear of punishment, as well as an obsequiousness to the king and some of his *particular* friends, operated on the dastardly minds of pretended patriots and lovers of justice. There is also an habitual indolence which prevents many from concerning themselves with anything but that which immediately affects their pecuniary interest. Such persons would not dare to inquire into the actions of a sovereign, however infamous they might be, for fear of suffering a fine or imprisonment for their temerity. The legal punishments attending the expression of discontent against the king are so severe, and the ill-grounded terrors of them so artfully disseminated, that, rather than incur the least danger, they would submit to the most unjust and tyrannical government. They would even be content to live under the Grand Seignior, so long as they might eat, drink, and sleep in peace! Had the lamented Princess Charlotte been the daughter of a cottager, the mysterious circumstances attending her death would have demanded the most public investigation. But, because a powerful prince had expressed his SATISFACTION at the treatment she received, it was deemed impertinent, if not treasonable, for any other individual to express a wish for further inquiry! Yet such is the effect of political artifice, under the management of court sycophants, that the middle ranks of people are taught to believe, that they ought not to trouble themselves with matters that occur in palaces; that a certain set of men come into the world like demigods, possessed of right, power, and intellectual abilities, to rule the earth without controul; and that free inquiry and manly remonstrance are the sin of sedition! Thus many people are actually terrified, through fear of losing their wealth, their liberty, or their life, into silence upon subjects which they ought, in duty to their God, under the principles of justice, fearlessly to expose. "Better pay our taxes patiently, and remain quiet about state crimes," say they, "than, by daring to investigate public measures, or the conduct of great men, risk a prison or a gibbet!" But let us hope that such disgraceful sentiments are not *now* to be found in the breast of any Englishman, however humble his condition. Our noble ancestors were famed for seeing justice administered, as well to the poor as to the rich. If, therefore, we suffer *personal* fear to conquer duty, we are traitors to posterity, as well as cowardly deserting a trust which they who confided it are prevented by death from guarding or withdrawing. We know that this justice has been lamentably neglected, though we do not yet despair of seeing it overtake the guilty, however lofty their station may be in society.

Volume Two

The coronation of George the Fourth, which had been postponed from time to time, at length took place on the 19th of July. We think, situated as her majesty then was, she ought to have been attended to the Abbey by all the noblemen and gentlemen whose courage and honour had permitted them to espouse and support her cause; and, with such a phalanx, could she have been refused admittance? Instead of such arrangement, however, her majesty went at an early hour, accompanied by two ladies and one gentleman!—was refused admittance at the first door, and sought for entrance at another, with the same ill success. It was true, her majesty had not an imperative right to be *crowned*, though she had an undoubted title to be present at the ceremony of her husband's coronation. Nay, claiming her right of admission in the character of cousin to his majesty, ought to have entitled her to very different treatment. Her majesty would not have encroached upon another's privileges, by entering Westminster Hall, because that might be considered the king's dining room; and the queen was too well informed to pass the boundary of privilege.

On the evening of the 18th of July, Lord and Lady Hood slept at Cambridge House, and, after retiring for the night, they were disturbed by the announcement that a messenger waited from Mr. Brougham to see Lord Hood. His lordship saw the messenger, whose business was to say, "If Lord Hood wanted any tickets for the coronation, he might have as many as he pleased." Lord Hood said, "I have *my own*, and that is quite enough; I need no more." It becomes a wise general to provide against the inroad of an enemy, and Lord Hood *ought*, and was in duty bound, to have accepted Mr. Brougham's offer of tickets, though that offer was made so SECRETLY, and at *such a late hour*. Lord Hood was either not sufficiently *firm* in the interest of her majesty, or else some previous understanding had existed upon the subject of these tendered tickets; for all well-dressed ladies were admitted upon the presentation of a ticket, and the name never required. There cannot be a doubt that the king had positive fears of the arrival of her majesty, because his carriage was kept in waiting to convey him to Carlton House, should the queen be announced. Well might he say to the bearers of his train, "Hold it wider." Yes, indeed, he required room to breathe, for CONSCIENCE is an obtrusive monitor, as well as a privileged guest, in all companies.

In addition to the negligence of the *professed friends* of the queen, we are sorry to say, that the ministers had prepared means, very demeaning, as well as perfectly *unconstitutional*. A covered boat was in waiting at the back of the hall, on the Thames, to convey the queen (if deemed needful) to the Tower; but, some persons

Print showing George IV of the United Kingdom with his train borne by eight sons of Peers and the Master of the Robes at his Coronation in 1821. The painting, commissioned by the king, was started by Francis and James Stephanoff and finished by Edward Scriven. From a reproduction in Sir George Nayler's *The Coronation of His Most Sacred Majesty King George IV* (1839).

of principle and property being aware of this abuse of power, many boats were upon the river, to render assistance, if required, to an insulted queen. Eight regiments of soldiers were in and near London, FIVE of which were THE DETERMINED FRIENDS OF THE QUEEN! Was it not rather a peculiar circumstance that Alderman Wood (who was in the procession of the lord mayor) was the loudest in his applause to the king? But, before we conclude this work, our readers will have no reason to be surprised at this conduct of the inconsistent and interested alderman. It was likewise very strange, that Lord Liverpool, the then first lord of the Treasury, was NOT PRESENT AT THE CORONATION! From whence was this unusual non-attendance upon the monarch to be attributed? Because Lord Liverpool, seeing the danger likely to result from the refusal of her majesty to the coronation, had advised the king to receive his consort. At first, his majesty consented, but shortly afterwards retracted his promise. Lord Liverpool, however, had caused this permission of his majesty for the queen's presence at the coronation to be made known to her, and a plan of the interior of the Abbey was enclosed at the same time, in which a seat was expressly ordered to be prepared for her majesty. We can positively assure our readers of the truth of this; for, two evenings previous to the coronation, we were sitting with one of her majesty's private friends, when the servant brought in a note, which that friend read with the greatest vivacity. It contained an assurance, that the king had consented to her majesty's being received at the banquet, and a plan was produced, exhibiting a seat, in which the queen and her attendants were to sit. Her majesty's impression was, we can confidently say, "That the Earl of Liverpool had advised the king to permit her to be received, in order to prevent ill consequences; for that, in case any riot should take place during the procession, the king *might have been smothered in the crowd*!" The Earl of Liverpool, however, had disobliged his majesty in the November previous, by abandoning the Bill of Pains and Penalties; but what else could he have done? If sentence had been passed against her, the mighty rush of public opinion would have probably overwhelmed the whole regal circle. Doubtless, Earl Lauderdale had given his royal master another version of the matter, as, from *his representation*, the king *again refused* to see his consort; in consequence of which, the most arbitrary measures were taken to prevent the appearance of the queen at the coronation. We must also place upon record that, on the 24th of the same month, Lord Lauderdale's honours (*extra* knight of the thistle, &c.) appeared in the Gazette, which were, no doubt, bestowed upon him for his avowed enmity to the queen.

We are sorry that Lord Hood, her majesty's only *male* attendant to the coronation, did not act a little more as became his duty to his royal mistress on this trying occasion. His lordship offered neither resistance nor remonstrance to the insult of refusing her majesty an admittance to the Abbey; but tamely, not to say *cowardly*, submitted to it, as he immediately led the queen to her carriage! Yet Lord Hood was a peer! but, gentle reader, he was also a—PENSIONER! We put the question to every honest-hearted Englishman, what force would have dared to oppose the queen's entry into the Abbey, if she had been properly surrounded and attended by her legal advisers and friends? Had such been the case, the "accomplished gentleman" would have met his injured, basely-treated wife, whose gaze must have brought a blush upon his guilty cheek. Such an unexpected visit had been contrary to his royally-fixed determination, as he then *would* have "met her in public."

The English character has ever been proverbial for morality, gallantry, justice, and humanity; though we cannot help thinking it suffered a little degradation when the queen was refused admittance to the scene of her husband's coronation. This, indeed, is a blot upon the annals of our country, which the stream of time will never be able to wash away. History cannot forget the conduct of the sovereign in this instance, who, when about to enter into a solemn compact with his people, and while calling the Omnipotent God to witness his faith and sincerity, "that he will most truly deal out justice, and love mercy, in his kingly station," at the same moment *refused* BOTH to his own wife! Let not such vindictive and disgraceful conduct be forgotten, when the *taste* and *elegant manners* of George the Fourth are extolled!

Amongst the gay throng of fawning courtiers that attended this ceremony was the Marquis of Londonderry, whose glittering appendages and costly array were of an unusual quality. Yet, gorgeous as was the sight, the absence of the queen rendered the coronation pomp an uninteresting scene of solemn mockery in its character, and an insulting imposition to the nation, who, while hearing the royal engagements made to them, nationally and individually, saw the first law of nature inverted by the very personage for whom this "mighty show" was designed. But are we not justified in supposing that George the Fourth possessed but a weak understanding, a frail heart, and strong prejudices, and that his judgment was perverted by bad counsel? Had his majesty been a sensible man, he would have perceived that all the advantages of his rank and station were conferred upon him by his fellow-men, and would not have squandered the national wealth upon unworthy characters. The title of king carries no such charm with it as to exempt its possessor from any of those infirmities which are incidental to his species; but he is doomed to drag about with him a frail tenement of clay, sometimes well and sometimes ill shaped, and liable every moment to be dissolved, and reduced to a state of putrefaction, in common with all those who contribute, by their labour, to its support. But how differently did George the Fourth consider his title and power at this period of his vanity! He concealed, as much as possible, the defects of his nature from "vulgar eyes," by exhibiting himself on a public stage, in borrowed plumes, like the jackdaw in the fable, who astonished his fellow-daws by assuming the gaudy plumage of the peacock. Thousands of weak mortals flocked about the royal actor, and expressed such extreme delight at the pageant scene, that we could hardly wonder to find him and his created nobles so inflated with pride as to consider themselves of a superior nature to the rest of mankind, and to believe that those who so much admired their external appendages were born to be their slaves. We deprecate such grovelling servility in the people as much as we pity the pride of the nobles. As well might a worm or a grub, when decorated with the ephemeral wings of a butterfly, look contemptuously on the crawling snail!

But a few years before the insult was offered to the queen at the coronation, her brother, the Duke of Brunswick, had fallen in the field of battle, while bravely fighting against Napoleon at Waterloo. Her majesty was now, therefore, bereft of every natural connexion, save her vindictive and cruel husband; and history hardly presents a more trying situation than that in which the persecuted and shamefully-treated Queen of England was placed.

The Duke of Newcastle, who *distinguished* himself upon the queen's trial, by pronouncing judgment against her majesty without hearing the evidence in her favour, was the boroughmonger selected to bear the "sword of mercy" before the king at the coronation! We ought not, probably, to find fault with the choice of George the Fourth in this instance; as the duke's subsequent acts have proved him so *worthy* of being the bearer of such an emblem,—to which the people of *Newark* can fully testify!

Upon her majesty's arrival at Brandenburgh House, after being refused admittance to the coronation, she took a cup of tea, and then retired to her room for nearly four hours. In this interval, the queen resolved to visit Scotland; she wrote to Lord Liverpool upon the subject, and requested his lordship to apprize the king of her intention. This letter was received by his lordship, and answered in the usual strain, "that he (Lord Liverpool) had laid her majesty's letter before the king, but had not received his majesty's commands thereon." In the intermediate time, it was announced, the king would visit Ireland; and his majesty left Carlton House at half-past eleven o'clock, on the 31st of July, on his way to Portsmouth for Dublin.

The Trial of Queen Caroline in the House of Lords, as depicted in The Life, Trial, and Defence of Queen Caroline (1821).

On the 30th of July, the evening previous to the king's departure, her majesty visited the theatre, and was much indisposed, but would not be persuaded to retire before the performance was concluded; indeed, it was the queen's usual line of conduct not to disturb any public assembly by retiring earlier than was positively needful. Before her majesty went to the theatre, she felt indisposed, but declined remaining at home, for fear of disappointing the people. When her majesty returned from the theatre, she was very sick, and had much pain in her bowels the next day. In the afternoon of this day, Dr. Holland called, apparently by chance, and, on feeling her pulse, said she must have further advice. She objected, as having most confidence in him, who had travelled with her; but to satisfy his mind, her majesty said he might bring whom he liked. Next day (Wednesday) he brought Dr. Ainslie, who desired to have more assistance called in; and on Thursday morning, Dr. Warren accompanied the other two, both *king's physicians*, according to *etiquette*, we believe. *Previous to this*, she seemed much surprised herself at her illness, and said to Dr. Holland, "DO YOU THINK I AM POISONED?" This day she was told, they hoped things would end well; but if she had any papers of consequence, she had better dispose of them, as, in the event of her decease, every thing must go to the king, or the ministers,—we forget which. At this, she astonished them all by her greatness of mind; for her majesty did not betray the slightest agitation, but immediately and coolly answered—"O yes, I understand you; it shall be done." She sat up almost the whole of that night with her maid Brunette only, burning letters, papers, and MS. books. She then called Hyronemus (her *maitre d'hôtel*) and made him swear to burn every thing she gave, him in the kitchen fire. More letters, papers, and MS. books were then given him, besides a large folio book, full, or nearly so, of her own writing. It was about two feet long, and five or six inches thick, and bound. This book she always said contained the whole history of her life ever since she came to this country, together with the characters of the different persons she had been intimate with. Besides papers, she sorted all her little trinkets, wrapped them in separate papers, and wrote herself the names of all her different friends who were to have them, charging Brunette to dispose of them after her death according to the directions; but these presents *never reached their destination*.

From Thursday, her majesty seemed regularly to get worse, and the inquiries after her health by the people at large were equal to the interest she had raised in the country. It was pretty generally said that her majesty's danger arose from a stoppage in the bowels. Various were the remedies prescribed; and, among innumerable others, a bottle of *Croton Oil*, with the following kind letter, was sent to an individual of her majesty's household:

"Sir,
"I am aware that nothing but the great, the very great, danger her majesty is in would excuse this unauthorised intrusion; but, learning from the papers the nature of her majesty's complaint, I have taken the liberty to forward to you, with the view of having it handed to Doctor Maton, or Dr. Warren, a medicine of strong aperient properties, called *Croton Oil*, one drop of which is a dose. There is no doubt but it is known to some of her majesty's medical advisers. It is but lately known in this country. It may be proper to observe that Doctor Pemberton has *himself* taken it. I have given it to more than one person; its operation is quick and safe. Two drops, when made into pills with bread, usually produce alvine evacuations in half or three quarters of an hour. It has struck me that this medicine may be administered with success to her majesty. At all events, I can have done no harm in taking the liberty to suggest it. Fearful of appearing anxious to make myself obtrusive, I have declined giving my name.
"Yours respectfully,
"A CHEMIST."
"Some suspicion may, perhaps, be attached to the circumstance of this letter being anonymous. I can only answer, that Dr. Warren or Dr. Maton will know the medicine to be what it is represented; if not, the chemist at Hammersmith may be referred to.
"God save the Queen!"

Both the medicine and the letter were referred to Dr. Pemberton, of Great George-street, Hanover-square, who used to attend her majesty, but had been obliged to give up practice from suffering with the "tic douloureux." The poor old man came, though bent double with pain, saw the remedy, and gave it as his decided opinion, "that, if a passage cannot be obtained in any other way, I certainly would try this, which is *sure* to have EFFECT, as without it her majesty must die; I have, indeed, taken two drops of it myself, therefore the queen might very safely take one."

When the king's physicians were told Dr. Pemberton's opinion, they still persisted that *they could not take it upon themselves to give her majesty the medicine*!

No one was suffered to approach the queen but the king's physicians, *except in their presence*, though her majesty most anxiously asked for William Austin, saying, "How odd it is that he never comes near me;" in the meanwhile, he was weeping bitterly outside the door, but was always told, either "the queen is asleep," or else, "too ill to see him." Her majesty's sufferings must have been dreadful, and they seemed to come on periodically, when her cries could be heard in all the adjacent rooms, and then it appeared that the doctors *dosed* her with laudanum, which, of course, added to the CONSTIPATION of her bowels, as well as rendered her quite insensible when her friends did see her. Her majesty seemed most partial to Dr. Holland, who sat up with her every night, till Saturday, when she was a little better; but, being called to town, he left her majesty under the care of Dr. Ainslie, we think. Next morning, being Sunday, her majesty got up and dressed herself, and sat in her chair. Either in the night or in the morning, Dr. Ainslie brought her majesty a draught to take, which the queen dashed out of his hand, in a very marked manner, spilt it, and said, "I am well; do you not see I am well, Sir? I want no physic." At which, Dr. Ainslie felt somewhat offended, as well he might.

On the Sunday before her death, her majesty said, "I should much like to take the sacrament; and I desire that the clergyman who does the duty at Hammersmith may be sent for to administer it." Application was immediately made; but the gentleman said, "I cannot administer it, without leave from the rector, who is now at Richmond." A messenger went to Richmond, and found that the rector had gone to dine in London, and that the clergyman must either go there to him, or solicit permission from the king's ministers! Notwithstanding this unfeeling piece of tyranny, her majesty said, "I do not doubt but my intentions will be accepted by God, the same as if I had been permitted to receive it." The queen was truly an example of patience and resignation, for she never repined, not even in her most agonizing moments. Her majesty, alas! too well knew she must eventually be the VICTIM OF TYRANNY.

Let every thinking being contrast the profession of Christianity with the contemptible procedure set forth in the anecdote just related. At the time her majesty requested to receive the sacrament, she believed herself near death; and, in accordance with the sentiments and doctrines of the Church of England, she very naturally desired to express her reliance on the Saviour by receiving this ordinance; yet even this gratification was denied her, until she was sinking into the embrace of death! This disgraceful circumstance is almost without a parallel in the annals of persecution. A virtuous and noble-minded queen, lying on the bed of death, which had been prepared for her by the hand of cruel and ill-judged Malignity, was refused this last comfort of religion; while a felon, who may have imbued his hands in the blood of his fellow-creature, is allowed to receive this emblem of salvation previous to his transition from time to eternity! Here, then, is sufficient to inform "The Many" of the policy of the "Established Church." May we not ask how far the English clergy are removed from Popery? as it is evident that the attentions of a rector or a bishop (under the crown) are equally difficult to be obtained as the Catholics believe those of St. Peter to be!

In contemplating the above exposure of malice, many questions naturally suggest themselves; for instance, What could prevent the curate's *immediate attention* to the wish of the dying queen? for had even the meanest parishioner desired it, HE MUST have attended to the request. What was meant by asking leave of "the rector, or the king's ministers," who were at some distance from the abode of sorrow? Was it not intended to add fresh insults to injuries already too deep? Did the ministry think thereby to prevent an *encroachment* upon his majesty's comforts in the world to come, (as he had declared, that he never again would meet the queen) and, by refusing the outward rites of the church, shut the door of hope in the sufferer's face?

Her majesty, in her agony, frequently exclaimed, "I know I am dying,—THEY HAVE KILLED ME AT LAST! but I forgive all my enemies, even Dumont," her maid Brunette's sister, who had done her majesty the greatest injury,—"I charge you (turning to her maid Brunette) to tell her so." Brunette and her majesty's *maître d'hôtel*, Hyronemus, wished to marry. Her majesty called them to her, and joined their hands over her body, (one standing on each side of the couch) and charged Hyronemus to be kind to Brunette. Her majesty then told them, she had left them all her linen (by right, belonging to her lady in waiting) and two of her carriages. On Tuesday, her majesty became much worse, and moaned terribly with pain, from four o'clock till ten at night, when she rapidly grew weaker, till Dr. Holland, with the awful watch in his hand, feeling her pulse, at last closed her majesty's eyelids, and declared "All is over!"

Malice and Crime had now done their worst; the fatal blow had been struck, and Caroline, the injured and innocent Queen of England was for ever relieved from her despicable and heartless persecutors!

"O, what a noble mind was here o'erthrown!"

Every person now left the room, except Dr. Lushington (one of the executors) and Lady Hamilton. Dr. Lushington said, "You, my lady, or Lady Hood, must not quit the body." Lady Hamilton replied, "Then, sir, let it be me." Shortly afterwards, the alderman and Mrs. Wood went into the chamber of death, the alderman offering the services of his wife to assist in the last sad duties to the lamented queen. In the interval, Brunette, the queen's maid, said that her majesty had desired no one might go near her body except herself; and Dr. Lushington complied with the request. Lady Hamilton observed, Brunette was not strong enough to move the body; Brunette, therefore, chose the *housemaid* to assist her. Shortly afterwards, Dr. Lushington requested Lady Hamilton's presence again; and, upon her appearance in the gloomy chamber, said, "Now, you must remain here; and promise me not to lift up the sheet which covers the body, or permit anyone else to do so." Lady Hamilton promised; when very soon afterwards Mrs. Wood went into the room, as she said, "to have a peep." Lady Hamilton prevented it, saying, she had given her word, and Mrs. Wood must therefore desist. The body, very speedily after life was extinct, became much discoloured, and, though it was washed and prepared for the grave-clothes in less than two hours after the decease, it exhibited a very great change, as well as being much swollen. The housemaid who assisted Brunette to prepare her majesty for the grave-clothes, said, the body turned quite BLACK before their task was finished, and swelled exceedingly, and on the following Thursday became quite offensive, when the leaden coffin arrived. On the Monday after, the rooms were lighted up, and hung with black, for her majesty *to lie in state*! Oh! sad mockery to her persecuted remains!

The housemaid, who helped Brunette to lay her majesty out, was quite disgusted at the unfeeling manner in which Brunette performed this sad duty; for she tossed the body about most indecently; and, when remonstrated with for such behaviour, said, "La! I mind her no more than an old hen!!!" The morning after her majesty's death, Lady Anne Hamilton's own maid went creeping into Brunette's room, expecting to find some show of grief, at least, for the loss of so good a mistress. What, then, was her astonishment to find her up, dressed, and in the highest spirits! "I never was so happy," said she, "in all my life. I can now get up when I like, go to bed when I like, and do every thing as I like!"

Previous to the funeral, some difficulty arose from an uncertainty *where* the deceased queen had kept her cash; and, without any ceremony, Mr. Wilde took up her majesty's watch, (the one presented by the inhabitants of Coventry, and which was very valuable) and said, "I will advance forty pounds, and return the watch when the money is paid!!!" Yet, at the time of her majesty's death, she must have been in possession of fourteen or fifteen hundred pounds! because Mr. Obequina had advanced the queen, but a few days before her death, the sum of two thousand pounds; and it was an indisputable fact, that not more than four or five hundred pounds had been expended out of this sum. The queen deposited this money where she always kept her trinkets, in a small blue box. In this box also her majesty frequently kept the Coventry watch, (which she seldom wore) as well as two miniature pictures of herself. This identical box, the executors gave into the care of Lord Hood; but he very properly refused to receive it, until they locked it and took the key. Dr. Lushington promised one of the miniatures to Lady Hamilton, and the other to William Austin, the protégé of the ill-fated queen; but, up to this period, such promise has not been fulfilled in either case.

It is well known that the queen, in her jocular moments, used to say, "They did not like my young bones, so they shall not have my old ones;" and, in her last illness, her majesty unfortunately added, "and that as soon as possible." This formed an excuse for the tools of George the Fourth to hurry her funeral beyond all decorum; as, in one single week after her majesty's death, did Lord Liverpool order that all the cavalcade should be ready. The route was chalked out, and strict orders given that, on no account, was the procession to go through the city; but every avenue was so choked up and barricaded by overturned coaches, carts, and rubbish, that they were *obliged*, at Piccadilly, to turn through Hyde Park; and, at Cumberland Gate, the scene of bloodshed commenced. We observed a pool of blood in the gateway, and a woman with her face all over blood, and two men lying dead. The people had pulled down the wall and railing for a hundred yards opposite Connaught-place; and the horse-soldiers (the Blues, we think) were pursuing the unarmed multitude down the park. A spent ball had fallen *very near the hearse*, and a gentleman in the retinue got off his horse, picked it up, and said, "This will be proof against them." At last Sir Robert Wilson, being a military man, rode up to the soldiers, and contrived to end the combat. The procession was then suffered to pass quietly along Edgeware and the New Roads till it came opposite to Portland-road, when the same obstructions of overturned carts, waggons, &c., prevented the cavalcade from continuing along the City-road, or turning into *any street* eastward, until it arrived at Temple Bar, when it turned into the city, to the great joy and acclamations of the millions of people who had followed, and who had lined the streets, windows, and tops of houses, although it rained in torrents, and the well-dressed women who attended were ancle deep in mud; nor did the people gradually drop away till the procession had entirely left the suburbs of London.

Sir George Naylor, king at arms, had his instructions where they should rest each night. The delays in London had been so many, that they were obliged (to fulfil orders) to travel at *full trot* to Ilford, where the procession arrived a little after six o'clock in the evening, having been more than twelve hours in performing this first stage of the journey. We pass over the insulting orders of Lord Liverpool, in their *minute detail*, and only advert to that part of them wherein he states to Mr. Bailey, the undertaker, that the body was to reach Harwich the second night. Various disgraceful altercations took place during the several stoppages on the road; and the mourners were treated similarly to their departed mistress. At length the sea opened upon their view; and the most prominent object upon it was the "Glasgow" frigate, stationed at some distance from Languard Fort. The procession arrived at Harwich, on Thursday, at half-past eleven, at which place, not even a single hour was allowed for retirement or repose; for the order was almost immediately given, that the coffin should be taken to the quay, and from thence lowered by a crane into a small barge. This was not accomplished without great difficulty, the coffin being extremely heavy. Four men rowed the boat to the side of the "Glasgow," which was waiting to receive the remains of England's injured queen. Sir G. Naylor and his secretary, with Mr. Bailey, accompanied it, and added the sad mockery of laying a paltry crown upon the coffin. The ladies and the rest of the suite followed in boats. At this moment, the first gun was fired from the fort. Such was the indelicate hurry and rude touch of the persons engaged in the removal of the royal coffin, that before it was received on board the "Glasgow," the crimson velvet was torn in many places, and hung in slips. When the boat reached the "Pioneer" schooner, the coffin was hoisted on board, the crown and cushion were laid upon it, and the pall was thrown out of the boat to a sailor on deck, by one of the three gentlemen who had it in charge, with no more ceremony than if it had been his cloak. Before it could possibly be announced that the corpse was safe on deck, the sailors were busily employed in unfurling the sails, and in less then ten minutes the "Pioneer" was under sail, to join the "Glasgow" frigate. The body and the mourners were at length received on board the "Glasgow," and here followed perplexity upon perplexity. The captain had not been informed of the probable number in this melancholy procession, and was incompetent to set before them sufficient food, or furnish them with suitable accommodation. Corn beef was therefore their daily fare; and hammocks, slung under the guns, were the beds assigned to the gentlemen, while the ladies were very little better provided for in the confined cabins. The coffin was placed in a separate cabin, guarded by soldiers, and with lights continually burning. On the 19th of August, the "Glasgow" appeared before the port at Cuxhaven; and, as she drew too much water to get up the Stade, she resigned her charge to the "Wye," commanded by Captain Fisher.

On Monday evening, the 20th, the remains of the Queen of England were landed at Stade. The coffin, *without pall*, or *covering of any kind*, was brought up the creek, a distance of three miles, the mourners following in boats. On their arrival at the quay, no preparation had been made for receiving the body on shore, and had it not been for the sympathy of the inhabitants of the place, the coffin must have been laid upon the *earth*; but they were so impressed with the necessity of paying regard to decency, and so incensed against the heartless and abominable conduct manifested towards the queen, that they, as if by one consent, brought out their tables and chairs, to afford an elevation for the coffin from the ground; and thus a kind of platform was raised, on which it was protected from further injury. After a short delay, arising from want of due notice having been given of the arrival of the procession, the citizens of the town, headed by the magistrates and priests, proceeded to meet it. The coffin was then taken up, and carried into the church, which was lighted, and partially hung with black. A solemn anthem was sung, accompanied by the deep-toned organ; after which the numberless crowd retired, leaving the royal corpse to the care of those who were appointed to watch over it. Early the next day the procession departed for Buxtehude. About a quarter of a mile from this town, it was met by the citizens and magistrates, who attended it, bareheaded, to the church, where the royal remains were deposited for the night. On the ensuing day, the 22nd, the procession was met on its entrance into Saltan, by the authorities, in the same manner as before named. On the 23d, it reached Celle, where the coffin was carried into the great church of the city, and placed upon the tomb of the unfortunate sister of George the Third, Matilda, Queen of Denmark. On the 24th, the procession was met at Offau, by Count Aldenslaben, the grand chamberlain of the court, and arrangements were made, that the funeral should take place at midnight. The mourners were immediately to proceed to Brunswick, and the funeral procession to follow, so as to arrive by ten the same night at the gates of the city, there to be met by the mourners; but further delay of interment than this was strictly forbidden. At the appointed hour, the last stage of the cavalcade commenced. On a near approach to the church, whose vaults were to receive the remains of this royal victim, the children of a school (founded and supported by a lady of truly patriotic principles) walked before the hearse, strewing flowers on the road. Arriving at the church, the Brunswick soldiers demanded the privilege to bear the remains of their beloved princess through the church to the vault, in which were deposited those of her illustrious ancestors. This being granted, the corpse was borne by as many of them as could stand under the coffin into the abode of death. It was then placed upon an elevation in the centre of the vault, which had previously been prepared for its reception, and where it will remain until another occupy its place; her majesty's coffin will then be removed to the space appointed for it. After an oration had been delivered in German, the curtain was drawn over our persecuted and destroyed queen. The mourners retired, and the assembled crowds dispersed, shortly after two o'clock.

It may possibly be asked, "Did not the nephew of the queen (the son of her brother, the late duke) meet the funeral, and follow it to the last abode of royalty?" To the eternal disgrace of George the Fourth, this youth was not permitted to do so. The kingdom of Brunswick was governed by two commissioners, under the controul of the King of England, and the young prince had been commanded to leave Brunswick previous to the ceremony of the interment of his aunt! The inhabitants of Brunswick had also been ordered to keep within their houses, to shut their windows, and not to appear upon the occasion. This imperious order was generally attended to. One gentleman, however, was independent and noble-minded enough to furnish flambeaux to be carried before and on each side of the procession, until it had reached the church. Every expression of the inhabitants indicated how much they were attached to the Princess of Brunswick, and the more superior and well-informed part of the community mourned that her days had been blighted by the delusive prospects held out to her family, in her alliance to the heir-apparent of England. The Brunswickers were afraid to express their sentiments in public companies; but, privately, they could not suppress their opinions, that "it was very strange not the least notice of the funeral had been communicated to them until the evening previous to the ceremony."

These unconstitutional and vindictive arrangements for the queen's funeral will ever be considered an indelible stain on the characters of those who concocted them. The law enacts that the dead shall be carried the nearest way to the place of interment; but the "notorious government" laid all possible restrictions in this case, and, in short, offered every indignity to the departed. If the English people had been resolute, and the lord mayor but consented, the body might have been taken into the Mansion-House, and the corpse EXAMINED, previous to its being taken from London, as considerable suspicion was caused by the unusual privacy and secrecy required immediately after her majesty's demise. The lord mayor (Thorpe) was the acknowledged friend of the queen, and ought not to have demurred to the generally-expressed opinion upon this subject.

It was rather a peculiar circumstance that George the Fourth should have *contrived* so well to be out of the way of death, both in his daughter's and his consort's case! But the prerogatives of royalty are numerous as well as *unnatural*, particularly when exercised by DESPOTIC PRINCES, who live only for their own gratification, and with whom the good of the people is an unimportant consideration. When the tidings of her majesty's death were communicated to her heartless husband by Lord Londonderry, the royal yacht was lying in Holyhead roads. Etiquette prevented the landing of the king while the unburied remains of his consort were upon English ground; therefore, despatches were forwarded to cause the first lord of the Treasury to press for an early removal of the body of the queen, in order that facility might be given to the landing of the king in Ireland.

After paying this *formal* attention to the awful intelligence he had received, his majesty landed at Howth, and, as soon as he had reached the viceregal lodge, addressed the gaping multitude in the following *eloquent* speech:

"*My Lords and Gentlemen, and my good Yeomanry*,

"I cannot express to you the gratification at the kind and warm reception I have met with on this day of my landing amongst my Irish subjects. I am obliged to you, *very much* obliged to you; I am *particularly* obliged by your escorting me to my *very* door. I may not be able to express my feelings as I wish. I have travelled far; *that is*, I have made a long *sea voyage*; I have sailed down the English Channel, and sailed up the Irish Channel; and I have *landed* from a *steam boat*; besides which, *particular circumstances* have occurred, known to you all, of which it is BETTER, at present, *not to speak* (alluding to the queen's sudden death) upon these subjects. I leave it to your DELICATE and *generous hearts* to APPRECIATE MY FEELINGS! However, I can assure you that THIS IS THE HAPPIEST DAY OF MY LIFE! I have long wished to visit you; my heart has always been IRISH!! From the day it first beat, I have loved Ireland. This day has shewn me, that I am beloved by my Irish subjects. *Rank, station, honours, are nothing*; but to *feel* that I *live* in the hearts of my *Irish subjects* is, to me, the most *exalted happiness*!

"I must now, once more, thank you for your kindness, and bid you farewell. Go and do by me as I shall do by you; drink my health in a *bumper*; and I shall drink all your's in a bumper of good *Irish whiskey*!!!"

Who that reads this address will not acknowledge his majesty's genius for speaking was equal to his talents for ruling? Shades of Fox, Grattan, and Sheridan, what a display of eloquence was here, delivered, too, by the "most polished man in Europe!" We may easily account for the rapturous admiration which the Irish people evinced for their monarch! Naturally eloquent themselves, they knew how to appreciate the energy and beauty of what a *king* addressed to their taste and understanding. When he assured them, in the *most elegant* and *lofty* language, that "his heart was *entirely Irish*," and that, in proof of the sincerity of his royal professions, he would "drink all their healths in a bumper of good Irish whiskey," they felt, with its superiority, the exhilirating stimulant of kingly declamation, and yielded to all the ecstacy that forms so prominent a characteristic of their sensations. The declaration of a *British* king, that his heart was *wholly Irish* was a kindness as highly strained, with respect to them, as disheartening to the feelings of all his other subjects. Great as was our *admiration* of the *nobleness*, both in matter and style, of this oratorical display, we scarcely were able, for a time, to reconcile our startled judgment to the perfect equity of this *sudden* partiality for a people who had never before experienced any mighty favours from the same quarter. But our error, we frankly confess, was the child of our stupidity: we understood his majesty to the simple letter, rather than in the *royal* meaning, of what he addressed to his long-forsaken children, and were too dull to understand his language till some time afterwards, when he visited his German dominions. But when, after assuring his Hibernian subjects that his heart was *wholly Irish*, he, in the same *exquisite* style, protested that his heart was *entirely Hanoverian*, we were wise enough to comprehend his majesty. There is a kind of ductility in this sort of affection that soars as much above the ordinary course of human feeling as the language in which the sentiment is conveyed surpasses the general powers of lingual eloquence. *Such goodness* and *such eloquence* may be ADMIRED, but we hope they will never be COPIED!

However gaily and flatteringly his majesty was received by his Irish subjects, all unbiassed people were shocked at the unbecoming incongruity of a king lost in the intoxication of mirth and wine, while his persecuted consort's passing hearse was calling forth the tears of his pitying people. Even under circumstances the most proper and respectful towards her late majesty, in regard to the conveyance of her remains to their destined place of rest, the appalling knowledge that, while her obsequies were performing, her husband's heart and soul were wrapped in the transports of convivial enjoyment, would have deepened the gloom of the dismal occasion, and excited exclamations of anguish and astonishment; but, witnessing the sordid neglect and studied insult with which the government conducted the melancholy preparation and procession, they combined with the sad spectacle the idea of her husband's simultaneous joy and merriment, and felt disgusted at such indecent and unmanly conduct. Of the qualities of the Irish character, generally viewed, there is much to admire; they are liberal and kind-hearted, and, in some few instances, have shewn a public spirit and a manly sense of their political wrongs and oppressions. We cannot, however, compliment either their delicacy, as men, in not feeling for the *cruel death* of an amiable woman, or their loyalty, as subjects, in slighting the memory of their sacrificed queen. At the cold indifference manifested by the Hibernian *ladies*, at this period, we were perfectly amazed. Over and above the tenderness natural to their hearts, their sex had an interest in her case, which ought to have awakened their concern, and commanded their tears. But the whole drama of life abounds with discordant scenes; and, without *female* inconsistency, the piece would be incomplete.

> "All the world's a stage,
> "And men and women are the players!"

A tyrant drops his head upon the scaffold, and they weep!—an innocent queen is poisoned, and they "show no sign of sorrow!"—a cruel, cowardly yeomanry, and a brutal, sanguinary soldiery, massacre an unarmed populace, and thanks and a subscription acknowledge and reward their heroism!—*here* a people are stripped of their rights and privileges, and content themselves with complaining!—*there* a country is overwhelmed in penury and wretchedness, and finds a cure for all its distresses in the casual visit of its despotic ruler, and his unmeaning and stupid speeches!

The despicable figure which the king made at this period, and the fulsome flatteries bestowed upon him by the Irish people, did not escape the keen penetration of the illustrious and patriotic Lord Byron. We had the pleasure of his lordship's acquaintance for some years before his lamented death; and he was in the habit of sending us many brilliant effusions of his muse, which he probably never intended for publication. But the following verses, on the subject of which we have just been speaking, possess so much poetical beauty and justness of expression, that we cannot refrain from gratifying our readers by inserting them in this place.

The Irish Avater.[1]

Ere the daughter of Brunswick is cold in her grave,
And her ashes still float to their home o'er the tide;
Lo! George the triumphant speeds over the waveT
o the long-cherish'd isle, which he lov'd like his—bride.

True, the great of her bright and brief era are gone,—
The rainbow-like epoch, where freedom would pause
For the few little years out of centuries won,
Which betray'd not, or crush'd not, or wept not her cause.

True, the chains of the Catholic clank o'er his rags;
The castle still stands, and the senate's no more;
And the famine, which dwelt on her freedomless crags,
Is extending its steps to her desolate shore.

To her desolate shore,—where the emigrant stands
For a moment to gaze, ere he flies from his hearth;
Tears fall on his chain, though it drops from his hands,
For the dungeon he quits is—the place of his birth!

But he comes! the Messiah of royalty comes!
Like a goodly leviathan roll'd from his waves;
Then receive him, as best such an advent becomes,
With a legion of cooks and an army of slaves!

He comes, in the promise and bloom of three-score,
To perform in the pageant the sovereign's part;
And long live the shamrock which shadows him o'er,—
Could the green on his *hat* be transferred to his *heart*.

Could that long-withered spot but be verdant again,
And a new spring of noble affections arise,
Then might freedom forgive thee this dance in thy chain,
And the shout of thy slavery which saddens the skies.

Is it madness or meanness which clings to thee now?
Were he God,—as he is but the commonest clay,
With scarce fewer wrinkles than sins on his brow,—
Such servile devotion might shame him away.

Age roar in his train, let thine orators lash
Their fanciful spirits to pamper his pride;
Not thus did thy Grattan indignantly flash
His soul o'er the freedom improved and denied.

Ever glorious Grattan! the best of the good!
So simple in heart, so sublime in the rest,
With all that Demosthenes wanted endued,
And his rival, or victor, in all he possess'd.

When Tully arose, in the zenith of Rome,
Tho' unequalled preceded, the task was begun;
But Grattan sprung up like a god from the tomb!
Of ages, the first, last, the saviour, the one.

With the skill of an Orpheus to soften the brute,
With the fire of Prometheus to kindle mankind,
Even Tyranny, listening, sat melted, or mute,
And Corruption shrunk, scorch'd, from the glance of his mind.

But back to my theme; back to despots and slaves!
Feasts furnished by Famine, rejoicings by Pain;
True Freedom but welcomes, while Slavery still raves,
When a week's Saternalia has loosened her chain.

Let the poor squalid splendour thy wreck can afford
(As the bankrupt's profusion his ruin would hide)
Gild over the palace. Lo, Erin, thy lord!
Kiss his foot with thy blessing for blessings denied.

Or if freedom, past hope, be extorted at last;
If the idol of brass find his feet are of clay;
Must what terror, or policy, wring forth be class'd
With what monarchs ne'er give but as wolves yield their prey?

Each brute hath its nature,—a king's is to reign;
To reign!—in that word see, ye ages, comprised
The cause of the curses all annals contain,
From Cæsar the dreaded to George the despised!

Wear, Fingal, thy trappings! O'Connell proclaim
His accomplishments!—His!!!—and thy country convince
Half an age's contempt was an error of fame,
And that *"Hal is the rascaliest, sweetest young prince!"*

Will thy yard of blue ribbon, poor Fingal, recall
The fetters from millions of Catholic limbs?
Or will it not bind thee the fastest of all
The slaves, who now hail their betrayer with hymns?

Aye, build him a dwelling; let each give his mite,
Till, like Babel, the new royal dome has arisen;
Let thy beggars and helots their pittance unite,
And a palace bestow for a poor-house and prison.

Spread, spread for Vitellius the royal repast,
Till the gluttonous despot is stuff'd to the gorge,
And the roar of his drunkards proclaim him at last
The FOURTH of the fools and oppressors,—called George!

Let the tables be loaded with feasts till they groan,—
Till they groan like thy people through ages of woe;
Let the wine flow around the old Bachanal's throne,
Like the blood which has flow'd, and which yet has to flow.

But let not his name be thine idol alone;
On his right hand, behold a Sejanus appears!
Thine own Castlereagh!—let him still be thine own!
A wretch never nam'd but with curses and jeers!

Till now, when the isle, which should blush at his birth,
Deep, deep as the gore which he shed on her soil,
Seems proud of the reptile which crawl'd from her earth,
And for *murder* repays him with *shouts and a smile*!

Without one single ray of her genius, without
The fancy, the manhood, the fire of her race,
The miscreant, who well might plunge Erin in doubt
If she ever gave birth to a being so base.

If she did, let her long-boasted proverb be hush'd,
Which proclaims that from Erin no reptile can spring;
See, the cold-blooded serpent, with venom full flush'd,
Still warming its folds in the breast of a king!

Shout, drink, feast, and flatter! Oh, Erin, how low
Wert thou sunk by misfortune and tyranny, till
Thy welcome of tyrants hath plunged thee below
The depth of thy deep to a deeper gulph still.

My voice, though but humble, was rais'd for thy right;
My vote, as a freeman's, still voted thee free;
This hand, tho' but feeble, would arm in thy fight,
And this heart, tho' outworn, had a throb still for thee!

Yes, I love thee and thine, tho' thou art not my land;
I have known noble hearts and great souls in thy sons,
And I wept with the world o'er the patriot band
Who are gone,—but I weep them no longer as once.

For happy are they now reposing afar,
Thy Grattan, thy Curran, thy Sheridan,—all
Who for years were the chiefs in the eloquent war,
And redeem'd, if they have not retarded, thy fall.

Yes, happy are they in their cold English graves;
Their shades cannot start to thy shouts of to-day,
Nor the steps of enslavers and chain-kissing slaves
Be stamp'd in the turf o'er their fetterless clay.

Till now I had envied thy sons and thy shore;
Tho' their virtues were hunted, their liberties fled,
There was something so warm and sublime in the core
Of an Irishman's heart, that I envy their dead!

Or if aught in my bosom can quench for an hour
My contempt for a nation so *servile*, tho' sore,
Which, tho' trod like the worm, will not turn upon power,
'Tis the glory of Grattan, the genius of Moore!

Speedily after the queen's death, Lord Sidmouth retired from office, and was succeeded by Mr. Robert Peel. Several other changes also took place in the ministry.

There was only *one* occurrence that could have been more gratifying to the people of England than the secession of Lord Sidmouth from office, and that was—his being rendered amenable to the laws for his share in the frequent outrages of the constitution, and his almost numberless violations of the liberties of the subject. We had hoped that he would have remained in office until he had received his FULL REWARD, in the return of the days of ministerial responsibility, in spite of bills of indemnity and venal majorities. But, for the honour of justice, we hope yet to see the day when he shall be subject to an honest tribunal for his political misdeeds. His name will ever awaken the liveliest indignation in the bosoms of

Robert Peel, the Home Secretary who founded the Metropolitan Police in 1829 and later became Prime Minister.

Englishmen; not, indeed, that his *talents* made him formidable against the liberties of his country, but because he so readily lent himself to the dangerous views of his *superiors*. Personally, he was of no importance. The son of a provincial medicine-vender, he had neither rank nor birth to command respect. The tool of Mr. Pitt in early life, Mr. Addington had cunning enough to stipulate for a peerage just at the time he was found unfit for a minister. The failure of his attempt to abridge the liberties of the dissenters covered him with disgrace. Such a design should have been entrusted to abler hands; but it was not his lordship's fault that the dissenters escaped religious persecution. His next exploit, however, proved more successful; he declared eternal hatred of reform and reformers in 1816. The seizure, the imprisonments, the tortures, and the outrages, occasioned by the employment of his *moral friend* Oliver have, in the language of Pope, occasioned him to be

"Damned to everlasting fame!"

The liberation of his victims, after long confinements, ruined in circumstances, wounded in mind, and some of them destined to premature death, through their unwholesome confinement, complete the picture of this nobleman's LEGISLATION! To prevent an investigation into such cruel acts, a bill of indemnity screened his lordship, his agents, and minions, from the tribunals of that day; but if *earthly* justice should never be vindicated, there is a tribunal before which he must one day meet his victims! The part which Lord Sidmouth had in the *reward of the Manchester massacre* is well known, and will not be likely to add to the quiet of his repose. This lamentable portion of his history involves the double charge of misadvising his prince, and patronising a violation of the laws, in the most wanton and cruel manner! No man, indeed, has been more instrumental in the ruin of his country, and he may probably live to reap some of the bitter fruits himself!

During this year, the *affable* king made his pompous entrance into Hanover, where he threw gold and silver amongst the crowd, with as much confidence as if it had been his own!! If he had allowed some of this said "gold and silver" to have remained in the pockets of its real owners, it would have redounded much more to his credit.

In one single week this year, eleven persons were hung for forging Bank of England notes. Such a sanguinary penal code of laws as ours would really disgrace a nation of savages! Even our common laws, which ought to be intelligible to the meanest understanding, are an unfathomable abyss, and frequently exceed the utmost penetration of even the "gentlemen of the long robe." Indeed, our laws appear designed to perplex rather than to elucidate, to breed contentions rather than to prevent them. The principal MERIT of the English jurisprudence seems to consist in its *intricacy*, and the learned professors of it may almost be said *to live upon the vitals of their clients*. It not unfrequently happens that, for trivial omissions upon some useless observance of forms, the victim is incarcerated in a prison, and, after enduring all the horrors of these dens of thieves, expires in want, disease, and apparent infamy!

The year

1822

was one of great interest and importance, both abroad and at home; but to the latter we shall chiefly confine ourselves.

On the 18th of January, a cabinet council was held, at which Lord Sidmouth was present, notwithstanding his previous resignation of the seals of office. From this, it is evident that, though out of OFFICE in reality, this *noble* **lord was in place** *specially.*

Ireland, at this time, presented a sad appearance; outrages of every kind were of daily occurrence, and famine, with its appalling front, stared the lower classes in the face. Much blood was shed, and yet no efficient means were taken to subdue the cause of these fatal insurrections. The King of England, though he had professed so much *love* for his dear Irish subjects in his late *eloquent* speech, screened himself, under his assumed popularity, from blame on such serious charges, while his incompetent and mean advisers, believing their persons safe under the protection of their PUISSANT PRINCE, gave themselves no trouble about so *insignificant* a matter. Disgrace and infamy, however, will ever be attached to their names for so flagrant a dereliction of duty to the Irish people!

In April, Thomas Denman, esq., the late queen's solicitor-general, was elected to serve the office of common-sergeant for the city of London; and, on the 27th of May, he commenced his career with trying the unnamed servant of a bookseller for selling an irreligious and seditious book. Mr. Denman sentenced him to eighteen months' imprisonment in the House of Correction and, at the end of that time, to find sureties for five years, himself in one hundred pounds, and two others in forty pounds each!

In narrating this circumstance, we cannot forbear expressing our detestation of all prosecutions in matters of RELIGION. They neither redound to the honour of Christianity, nor effect the slightest benefit to morality. Everyone has an undoubted right to entertain what religious opinions may best accord with the dictates of that all-powerful monitor—Conscience; and all endeavours to *force* different opinions are only so many attempts to make men *hypocrites.* "But," say our religious prosecutors, "the Bible must not be attacked, or the true religion will fall into contempt." As an answer to this argument, we say, that if the said true religion will not bear the test of examination and argument, the sooner it falls into contempt the better! The glorious truths of the New Testament, however, are sufficiently manifest, and do not require the puny and adventitious advocacy of Cant. The strong arm of the law is not requisite to uphold Christianity, for it possesses within its own pure doctrines sufficient to recommend it to the admiration and gratitude of mankind. When these doctrines are attacked, let Christians endeavour, by fair and mild reasoning, to support their beneficence and purity, and they will be sure to make converts. But, if they once attempt to FORCE CONVICTION, their defeat is inevitable! It is, therefore, contrary to common sense, as well as being unjust and deplorable, that a man should be punished for disbelieving any particular sentiment. What proof did Mr. Denman give of the mild and forgiving doctrines of Christianity in his severe sentence against this man?[2] Was it from motives of Christian charity that he traduced him before a public tribunal? Were the proceedings of the court at all calculated to impress the man's mind with the true spirit of Christianity? The contrary might well be said. For neither was the accusation distinguished by that moderation which ought to be observed even against the worst of criminals, nor was it very humane to imprison him eighteen months, and afterwards keep the arm of justice suspended by binding him in sureties for five years not to so offend again. It will be but fair to ask, whether, if the *religious* welfare of this man had been deemed by his prosecutors worthy of the slightest consideration, they would not have proceeded directly contrary to what they did? But, as Dr. Watts has justly observed, when speaking of religious prosecutors, "They are too apt to denounce damnation upon their neighbours without either justice or mercy; and, while pronouncing sentences of divine wrath against supposed heretics, they *add their own human fire and indignation!*" Such prosecutions, therefore, only tend to excite the contempt of those very persons who are expected to be made better by them. With respect to the other count of the foregoing indictment, "that the publication was calculated to bring the king and his ministers into contempt," we think such an attempt of the publisher was totally unnecessary; for both the king and his ministers were then in the full zenith of their *fame*, and had the sincere prayers of the greater part of the community for their speedy deliverance from—this world!

In the early part of this month, an elegant service of plate was presented to Alderman Wood, as an acknowledgement for his *disinterested* services in the cause of the late queen; while, strange to say, the large service of plate subscribed for the queen by the country, at only one shilling each, never reached its destination! The funds for this purpose were entrusted to the care of Messrs. Wood, Hume, and others; the amount collected was more than three thousand pounds during the first few months of the subscription, which regularly increased till the queen's death. The cause of the opening of this subscription was owing to the fact of her majesty being refused all suitable conveniences for the dinner table, as she could only have a dinner served upon blue-and-white earthenware! To this fact, the noblemen and gentlemen who dined at her majesty's table can fully attest. We are inclined to think, however, that the alderman's services to the queen have been a little overrated. That Mr. Wood was her majesty's best and most disinterested friend, thousands were led to believe; but that he was not so, we shall endeavour to PROVE.

When a subscription was proposed for a service of plate for her majesty, a Scotch lady forwarded one hundred guineas towards it. Alderman Wood had the chief management of this subscription, as of almost everything else that related to the queen. The alderman employed one Pearson to collect the money. This Pearson was the fellow that cut such a figure in the Manchester massacre; and, therefore, he was thought, we suppose, a *very capable person* for such an undertaking. After collecting a considerable sum of money, Pearson was about taking his leave of this country for America; but, intimation having been given of his perfidy, he was stopped.

Alderman Wood said his friends also wished *him* to have a service of plate, but his subscription was to be raised by *half-crowns*; indeed it was expected that four or eight friends would join, and not present the alderman with less than a GOLDEN PIECE. Unfortunately, the poor queen died before the money the people intended to raise for her plate was completed. At first, her friends wished to have a monument erected to her memory in Hammersmith; but no ground could be obtained for this purpose, and it was feared that her enemies would treat any pillar to her honor with the same indignity that they had treated herself. Alms-houses were then proposed to be built, but *NOTHING HAS YET BEEN DONE WITH THE MONEY*, (amounting to about three thousand pounds) either principal or interest. Mr. Wood has been frequently applied to, through the public papers, concerning this money, but no answer has ever been given. The alderman managed the subscription for his own plate much better; for he took good care to receive it as soon as possible! The alderman is known now to be very *rich* from his Cornwall mines; he has, besides, two distant relations in Gloucester, brothers, worth a million between them, which he may probably share, they having no relations. When, however, he went for the queen, his mines were unprofitable, and himself embarrassed. Be that as it may, the queen certainly, by his urgent entreaties, employed *his* coach-maker in South Audley-street, and most of *his* other tradespeople.

The ill-natured world will talk; and some people went so far as to accuse the *disinterested* and *patriotic* alderman with sinister motives in these recommendations, and that he had actually "a feeling in everything that came into her majesty's house!" Whether or not this was the case, the alderman most assuredly spoke to the queen, very animatedly, to purchase Cambridge House, opposite to his own, in South Audley-street, though her majesty said she would never sleep in it, nor did she. The enormous sum which Mr. Wood persuaded the queen to give for this house was sixteen thousand pounds! but, notwithstanding her majesty made several improvements in it, it only sold at the queen's death for six thousand pounds!! This fact will speak volumes. Are no interested motives to be traced here?

We do not wish to deprive Alderman Wood of any merit that may justly be his due; but, though he accompanied her majesty to England, he certainly did not persuade her to come over, as some people have imagined. He, nor any one else, had any hand in that; it was the spontaneous determination of the queen herself! That the alderman REFUSED the house, 22, Portman-street, which was offered for the queen's accommodation till a better could be provided cannot be denied; he preferred receiving her majesty into his own house. It is also well known that the alderman, by his officious and ungentlemanly, nay, we may say, IMPUDENT conduct, lost her majesty many friends in the higher circles, who would not act with *him*. Nor can this be wondered at when his vulgar manners to his superiors are taken into consideration. That we may not be supposed to assert this without reason, we will here relate a few instances, which came immediately under our own observation.

The queen gave a dinner to the Duke of Bedford, Earl Grey, Lord Tankerville, and other noblemen and gentlemen. His grace of Bedford handed her majesty down the room, and sat on her right, and Earl Grey on her left. Instead of the vice-chamberlain (according to etiquette) sitting at the top of the table to carve,

Mr. Wood seated himself *there, above every one*, and, *grinning*, ordered her vice-chamberlain to go to the other end opposite him, thus publicly proclaiming his ignorance and impudence! Earl Grey is reckoned the proudest man in England, and it was said, he observed, "It is the first, and shall be the last, time that the alderman shall sit above me."

When the queen came from Dover to town, accompanied by this alderman and Lady Anne Hamilton, he presumptuously seated himself by her majesty's side, thus forcing her lady to take the seat opposite, with her back to the horses! We need hardly offer a remark upon so great a breach of good manners; for any individual, possessing the spirit of an Englishman, would always give precedence to a lady.

When her majesty went to St. Paul's cathedral, Mr. Wood placed himself at the coach door to attend her out, and kept laughing and talking to her till they arrived near the statue of Queen Elizabeth, where the lord mayor and his retinue met her, after coming from the church for that purpose; but when his lordship (Thorpe, naturally a modest man) perceived that the queen was so engaged that she never lifted up her eyes, he and his procession were turning back in confusion to re-enter the church, when one of the queen's followers caught firmly hold of the officious alderman's gown, stopped them, and said, "Mr. Wood, Mr. Wood, don't you see the lord mayor come to hand the queen?—you would not affront the city so as not to let him?" Sir Robert Wilson, who was near, said, "Do run and call the lord mayor back, thousands of eyes are upon us!" His lordship turned round, and the procession proceeded into the church, as it ought to have done from the carriage door; but Mr. Wood was exceedingly angry, and would follow next to her majesty, though repeatedly told that it was Lady Anne Hamilton's place, as her majesty's lady in waiting.

At the city concert, also, Alderman Wood displayed his indecorous conduct. The orchestra was elevated about a foot, and at the right of the orchestra two chairs were placed, one for the queen, and the other for her lady in waiting, who sat next the people. Alderman Wood stood behind her majesty the whole time, laughing and whispering, in the most intimate style, in her ear; and though her lady kept her face towards them, wishing it to appear *to the public* that at least she had a *share* in the conversation, alas! too many saw she was never spoken to by either!

From such impudent and vulgar conduct as this, we heard a certain royal duke observe, "I wish to serve the queen, but I will not be Mr. Wood's cat's-paw, nor play second fiddle to him!" Similar observations were made by noblemen of the very first rank in this country. It may be asked, "Why did the queen allow herself to be guided so much by this alderman?" Because her majesty thought him *honest*, and was not aware that he kept any other persons away. "Could no one tell her majesty the real state of things?" No! for Mr. Wood actually set her against every one, except himself and his own creatures, in order to preserve entire influence over her majesty. Indeed, her legal advisers could hardly speak to the queen, without this very officious gentleman being present. He began by prejudicing her majesty against them all; for he said, "No lawyers are good for anything; I esteem *myself* above them all." *We ourselves heard him say so.* **When he had thus persuaded her** majesty of his own superiority, and introduced himself into all the consultations of her law advisers, (unless they demanded a *private* audience) he began to attack the *Whigs*, and amused himself by constantly abusing them. He has frequently been heard to say, "The Whigs are worse enemies of your majesty than the ministers; they would sacrifice you if they could." But, for himself, he led her to believe that he could do anything with the people! In the city, he conceitedly told her majesty, at the head of her own table, (where he *usually sat*, till Lord Hood took his place) in November, when his friend Thorp was elected mayor, that "they wanted to elect me mayor a third time, but I would not accept the office;" while, at this very election, there was but ONE SINGLE VOTE for him, and that was the new lord mayor's, who could not vote for himself!

It is very lamentable to consider that her majesty was so much guided by this one man in most of her actions, even to the fatal day of the coronation, upon which occasion, however, he took particular care not to attend her. There is every reason to believe, notwithstanding, that her going at all was owing to his *secret* advice, though he pretended to the contrary. Those who heard him at the *king's dinner* were disgusted at his being the *loudest* to applaud his majesty! Most certainly, the coronation day did not end to her majesty as she had been led to expect; and she discovered, or fancied so, that she had no friend or adviser in England on whom she could rely; and, therefore, determined to visit Scotland. It was remarked to the queen, by a *true* friend, who sought only her honour and happiness, that Scotland was a proud nation, and that it would not be there thought that Alderman Wood was of sufficient rank to attend her majesty. The queen quickly and *indignantly* replied, "Alderman Wood! I should never think of taking *him*! No, no; I shall only take Lord and Lady Hood, and Lady Hamilton!" All the world knows her majesty never named the alderman in her will; but all the world does not know that, a short time before her death, she said, "I owe Wood nothing!"

The alderman also seized every opportunity he could to persuade the queen to go *abroad again*. On one of these occasions, a friend of her majesty overheard the hypocritical adviser, and immediately said, "How can you, Mr. Wood, pretend to be her majesty's best friend, and yet want her to do that which would ruin her in the eyes of the whole country?" "I do not *want* her to go," replied he, "but if she *will* go, I wish to point out to her the best way of doing it." "Sir, there is *no good way* for the queen to quit the country, and if you should unfortunately succeed in persuading her to do it, you will be her ruin!"

Thus it will be seen, that "all is not gold that glitters;" but Mr. Wood ought hardly to find fault with us for stripping him of his borrowed plumes, considering the length of time he has been allowed to wear them! If the public had known these particulars at the time they occurred, it is doubtful whether the alderman would have ever received *his plate*; therefore, he owes us a little gratitude for not mentioning them before that (to him) *golden* opportunity!

Alderman Wood, however, we are sorry to say, was not the only false friend her majesty had to lament. Many others "held with the hare in one house, and ran with the hounds in another." Some of these even attended public meetings in the quality of friends, and then wrote as enemies in the public journals. Some inveighed against her in public, and wrote, spoke, and acted for her cause in private. One of her judges, to our positive knowledge, spoke admirably for her in parliament, and yet privately, in more places than one, impugned the character of her majesty! Even while the queen was abroad, her *presumed* friends were extremely negligent at home. They permitted insidious paragraphs to appear in the newspapers, day after day, month after month, and year after year, without either contradiction or explanation; by which shameful neglect, the public mind became so impregnated with falsehood and insinuation, that, had not the queen returned to this country as she did, her name would have been recorded in history as infamous! Sure never woman was so shamefully treated, both by friends and foes; indeed, her majesty might well have exclaimed, with Gay,

> "An open foe may prove a curse,
> But a *pretended* friend is worse!"

On the 12th of August, while his majesty was absent on a visit to Scotland, an extraordinary excitement prevailed by the reported "sudden death" of the Marquis of Londonderry. It is hardly necessary to enter into the various causes assigned for so unexpected an event; it is sufficient to know, that his lordship committed suicide, by cutting his throat with a small knife, at his seat, Foot's Cray, and that a coroner's inquest (either from conviction, or in kindness to his surviving friends) returned a verdict, that his lordship inflicted the wound while "delirious and of insane mind."

It is an obligation imposed upon every independent historian to lend his assistance to a just and honest estimate of the character of public men. It leads to useful, though not always to gratifying, reflections, to examine the causes which pointed them out as objects worthy of being entrusted with political command. By what strange union of circumstances, then, or by what unlucky direction of power, did the Marquis of Londonderry attain to the high and important offices which he successively held for so long a period?—a period the most momentous and ominous, the most fertile in change, the most wicked in court intrigue, and the most fraught with terror, of any in our annals! We have heard his lordship described as having been amiable in private life; but who has denied the manifest mediocrity of his genius for the situations he was allowed to fill? Some of his public proceedings, however, prove him not to have possessed much of "the milk of human kindness," as we shall presently shew. He was, indeed, only qualified to act as a mere associate, to be put forward in the face of Europe, not as himself a high and original power, but as a passive organ for the expression of sentiments, or for the execution of measures, hereafter traceable only as the opinions and actions of the "united cabinet" of a wicked chief magistrate. The panegyrists of his lordship have also trumpetted forth eulogiums on his "personal bravery." And if bravery consists in fighting duels, proposing the most unconstitutional acts, fearlessly oppressing the innocent, and in defying the power of a justly-enraged people, Lord Londonderry assuredly possessed "personal bravery" in an eminent degree!

His lordship was born on the 18th of June, 1769, and consequently died in the 53rd year of his age. He commenced his career, like his patron, Mr. Pitt, as the advocate of parliamentary reform; and, also like that apostate minister, Lord Londonderry abandoned his early patriotic pledges and principles for the emoluments of office, which he first entered in 1797, as keeper of the privy seal, and, shortly after, one of the lords of the treasury, of Ireland. In the following year, he became secretary to the lord lieutenant. Honours and places were now lavishly heaped upon him. In 1802, his lordship received the appointment of the Board of Controul, and, in 1805, was raised to the high and responsible office of minister of war! On the death of Mr. Pitt in 1806, his lordship was obliged to resign, with all the other "clerks in office," as the *débris* of Mr. Pitt's cabinet were called. On the resignation of the Grey and Grenville administration, in 1807,

George Cruikshank's illustration of the suicide of Lord Londonderry (also known as Lord Castlereagh).

he resumed his former situation of minister of war, in which he continued till the ill-starred Walcheren expedition and his duel with Mr. Canning drove him from office, scorned and ridiculed by the whole of Europe. The year 1809 gave his lordship an opportunity of shewing how much he admired the existing abuses in church and state; for, on an investigation taking place into the Duke of York's shameful neglect of duty, as commander-in-chief, this year, the noble marquis was peculiarly active in his defence, and circulated a considerable sum of money in bribing those who were likely to appear as witnesses against the royal libertine. On the assassination of Mr. Perceval, in 1811, his lordship was made foreign minister, in which situation he continued till his death. Holding so high an office at a time when our foreign exertions were the most extensive and important, and acting as our negotiator when Europe might have been composed and re-adjusted by our councils, he had opportunities, which few ministers have enjoyed, of benefitting his country and the whole human race. But how did he employ these rare opportunities? Alas! his name is only to be found in treaties and conventions for clipping the boundaries, impairing the rights, or annihilating the existence of independent states; and he gloried in the opportunity of stifling liberty in all the lesser states of Europe. Even the colonial and commercial interests of Great Britain herself were bartered away for snuff boxes and the smiles of Continental despots! If, however, there is one action more than another calculated to brand the name of Castlereagh with immortal infamy, it is the mean, tyrannical, and inglorious conduct which he exercised towards the greatest man that ever reigned over a free and enlightened people—the Emperor Napoleon! To view the career of this truly illustrious man is to look back upon the course of a blazing star, that, drawing its fiery arch over the concave of heaven, fixes the admiring attention of the sublunary world, and dazzles, while it arrests, the wondering eye! What language can do justice to the mental powers and noble daring of the man who subdued the blood-thirsty enemies of his country, and laid Europe at his feet? In Napoleon, we saw the triumphant opposer of all despots, and the restorer of order to his own disorganized and distracted subjects. See him from his bold and judicious exertions at Toulon to his assumption of the imperial title, and the dread-inspiring attitude he presented to terrified and retiring Russia,— then judge his gigantic energy and valour! As first consul, he pacified Europe; and, as emperor and king, revenged her breach of the peace. Russia, Sweden, Denmark, Holland, Prussia, the Netherlands, Germany, Sardinia, Spain, Portugal, Italy, and Naples, were all in arms against his power; yet—all fell before it!

The termination of the great war in Europe was not the peculiar triumph of that cabinet of which Lord Londonderry was the most prominent tool. The campaigns of 1813 and 1814 were guided by the skill and spirit of Russian and German officers,—aided, to be sure, by British soldiers,—and with the whole civilized world for their allies. The English ministers, or rather, the MONIED INTEREST of England, were bankers to the "Grand Alliance," and furnished the sinews of the war. But, even with such mighty odds against him, the towering and gigantic genius of Napoleon would have defied them all, if English money had not BRIBED some of his generals. It was this, and this only, that completed his downfall. To talk of the Duke of Wellington as the conqueror of Napoleon is an insult to the understanding of any intelligent man, and for Lord Castlereagh to have boasted of having subdued him, as his lordship was wont to do, "was pitiful, was wonderous pitiful!" The English cabinet, at this period, was the same "incapable" cabinet. The men were the same satellites to Mr. Pitt, subordinates to Mr. Perceval,—nay, even to Lord Sidmouth, of Manchester notoriety,—whom the independent members of parliament had long known and despised. Circumstances ruled these ministers, whose position was chosen for them, and improved by others. They could not have resisted that universal impulse which they had not created, but which Bonaparte himself had provoked; for he defied the whole "Grand Alliance," and, so far, was the author of his own reverses, which, however, he would not so soon have experienced if Fouché, Duke of Otranto, had not suffered his avarice to get the better of his duty. It was this wicked duke, who, dreading the detection of his treachery, devised a plan for assassinating the Emperor Napoleon on his road to Waterloo. But, though this diabolical intention proved a failure, he succeeded too well in putting his illustrious master in the power of the British government. Not content, however, with betraying his king, Fouché, though he capitulated for Paris, gave up the rest of France to the discretion of her enemies and the tender mercies of the Russian cossacks! This most consummate of traitors likewise exposed those who had assisted him to execute his diabolical plans, and actually signed lists for their proscription! Even the treaty for the capitulation of Paris proved a mere juggle; for none of its provisions were properly adhered to by Lord Castlereagh. The Parisians were here most shamefully deceived. It could never have been contemplated by them, for instance, that the capital was to be rifled of all the monuments of art and antiquity, whereof she had become possessed by right of conquest. A reclamation of the great mortar in St. James' Park, or of the throne of the King of Ceylon, would have just as much appearance of fairness as that of Apollo by the Pope, and Venus by

Lord Grenville, from a print published in 1839. (*Wikimedia Commons*)

the Grand Duke of Tuscany. What a preposterous affectation of justice did our foreign secretary evince in employing *British* engineers to take down the brazen horses of Alexander the Great, that they might be re-erected in St. Mark's Place at Venice,—a city to which the Austrian emperor has no more equitable a claim than we have to Vienna! Lord Castlereagh's authority for emptying the Louvre was not only an act of unfairness to the French, but one of the greatest impolicy as concerned our own countrymen, since, by so doing, he removed beyond the reach of the great majority of British artists and students the finest models of sculpture and of painting the world has produced. Although England was made to bear the trouble and expense of these removals, the complacent Castlereagh gave all the spoil to foreign potentates, whose smiles and a few trifling presents compensated *him* for their loss! But what will posterity think of a British minister's violating a treaty for such paltry gratifications?

We come now to speak of the conduct of the departed minister to the betrayed Emperor of the French. Napoleon always declared that he gave himself up to England, in the confidence of promises, sacredly made to him by Lord Castlereagh, that he should be allowed to remain in this country. "My having given myself up to you," were Napoleon's words, "is not so simple a matter as you imagine. Before I went to Elba, Lord Castlereagh offered me an asylum in England, and said that I should be very well treated there, and much better off than at Elba." But how did his lordship fulfil these promises? This will be best explained in the language of Napoleon himself, in a protest which he wrote on board the Bellerophon, August 4th, 1815, of which the following is a translation:

> "I hereby solemnly protest, in the face of heaven and of man, against the violence done me, and against the violation of my most sacred rights, in forcibly disposing of my person and my liberty. I came voluntarily on board

of the Bellerophon; I am not a prisoner, I am the guest of England. I came on board even at the instigation of the captain, who told me he had orders from the government to receive me and my suite, and conduct me to England, if agreeable to me. I presented myself with good faith, to put myself under the protection of the English laws. As soon as I was on board the Bellerophon, I was under shelter of the British people.

"If the government, in giving orders to the captain of the Bellerophon to receive me, as well as my suite, only intended to LAY A SNARE FOR ME, it has forfeited its honour and disgraced its flag.

"If this act be consummated, the English will in vain boast to Europe of their integrity, their laws, and their liberty. British good faith will be lost in the hospitality of the Bellerophon.

"I appeal to history; it will say that an enemy, who for twenty years waged war against the English people, came voluntarily, in his misfortunes, to seek an asylum under their laws. What more brilliant proof could he give of his esteem and his confidence? But what return did England make for so much magnanimity? They feigned to stretch forth a friendly hand to that enemy; and when he delivered himself up in good faith, they sacrificed him.

(Signed) "Napoleon."

Napoleon, however, acquitted the English PEOPLE of any participation in this crime, and said, "We must not judge of the character of a people by the conduct of their government."

Europe should understand how little the English people are implicated in the crimes of their king or his ministers. The PEOPLE did not vote millions after millions for a crusade against French and American liberty. *They* did not commission a Wellington to interfere in the re-enthronement of a Bourbon; *they* did not depute a Castlereagh to dictate the slavery of Saxony and Genoa; nor should *they* be charged with the gross injustice, dastardly inurbanity, and forcible imprisonment of the greatest man and the most magnificent monarch of modern or ancient times,—of a man whose mental superiority was honourable to human nature, and which threw into utter darkness the abilities of every other sovereign!

British annals have, indeed, been stained by many a dark and unsightly spot; our volumes will exhibit divers foul and desperate deeds in the domestic history of the last two kings: but never was an act more *nationally* disgraceful than the banishment of Napoleon to St. Helena! He was never accountable to England, much less to the English boroughmongers, for his political conduct. He had been the general, the first consul, and the emperor of the French. He arose amidst the storms of the revolution; he was (as he himself felt and said) the "sword-arm of the republic," with which it chastised and humbled to the dust the accursed confederacy of despots who had endeavoured to rivet an old, worn-out, oppressive, and rejected dynasty on thirty millions of Frenchmen. He conquered at first by the help of that flame of liberty which raged with a fierceness proportioned to its long suppression; and, latterly, having raised himself above his contemporaries by his powerful genius, he was made emperor by his countrymen and fellow-soldiers, partly because a large portion of the people, weary of the violent fluctuations of an ill-constituted democracy, desired the repose even of absolute government, and partly because he was looked upon as the fittest instrument for foreign conquest, which had become a favourite habit, though originating in an absolute necessity. Never let it be forgotten, that he was chosen first consul for life (a distinction used only for the sake of republican appearances, and known to mean king all over Europe) by the votes of the French people at large! The question was submitted to them in the separate departments; all voted that took interest in the affirmative or the negative; and the result was, his election by more than 3,500,000 voices against 374! Can the House of Hanover say as much for their succession to the throne of the Stuarts? Napoleon was not only the elected sovereign of the French people, but he was acknowledged in that capacity by all his enemies. As first consul, the allies, including England, made the treaty of Amiens with him. As emperor, the Continental sovereigns not only often acknowledged, but *flattered*, and bowed to the earth before him; and this country, at the least, negotiated with him for peace. Whence, then, arose Lord Castlereagh's right to treat him as an offender amenable to England? When, by a marvellous succession of ill-fortune, he fell from his towering height, and left for ever his post at the head of the French government, he became a private individual; and this country had no more business to interfere with his personal freedom than with that of Marshal Soult, or any other of the military men who had equally sought to crush us. Some canting and arrogant people talked of his *crimes*—his tyranny—his unjust aggressions in Spain and elsewhere. But we deny that Napoleon was a tyrant. After his return from Elba, he wished to be at peace with all mankind, and to devote the remainder of his days to increase the happiness and prosperity of his people. Which of his enemies could say as much? We quote the following letter in justification of what we here advance, which the emperor addressed to all the sovereigns of Europe:

"Paris, April 4, 1815.

"Sires, my Brothers,—You have no doubt learnt in the course of the last month my return to France, my entrance into Paris, and the departure of the family of the Bourbons. The true nature of those events must now be made known to your majesties. They are the results of an irresistible power,—the results of the unanimous wish of a great nation, which knows its duties and its rights. The dynasty which force had given to the French people was not fitted for it; the Bourbons neither associated with the national sentiments nor manners; France has therefore separated herself from them; her voice called for a liberator. The hopes which induced me to make the greatest sacrifice for her have been deceived; I came, and, from the spot where I first set my foot, the love of my people has borne me into the heart of my capital. The first wish of my heart is to repay so much affection by the maintenance of an honourable peace. The restoration of the imperial throne was necessary for the happiness of the French people. It is my sincere desire to render it at the same time subservient to the maintenance of the repose of Europe.

Enough of glory has shone by turns on the colours of the various nations. The vicissitudes of fortune have often enough occasioned great reverse, followed by great success; a more brilliant *arena* is now open to sovereigns, and I am the first to descend into it. After having presented to the world the spectacles of great battles, it will now be more delightful to know no other rivalship in future but that resulting from the advantages of peace, and no other struggle but the sacred one of felicity for our people. France has been pleased to proclaim with candour this noble object of her unanimous wish. Jealous of her independence, the invariable principle of her policy will be the most rigid respect for the independence of other nations. If such then (as I trust they are) are the personal sentiments of your majesties, general tranquillity is secured for a long time to come, and Justice, seated on the confines of the various states, will of herself be sufficient to guard the frontiers.

"I am, &c.

"Napoleon."

If further proof be needed against his being a tyrant, it may be found in the following extracts from the Additional Act to the Constitution of the Empire of France, 1815:

"Rights of Citizens.—All Frenchmen are equal in the eye of the law, whether as contributors to the public taxes and imposts, or as to admission to civil and military employments. No one can be prosecuted, arrested, imprisoned, or exiled, except according to the forms prescribed by the law.

"Liberty of worship is granted to all.

"Every citizen has the right of printing and publishing his thoughts (signing his name) without any previous censorship, and subject only to legal responsibility after the publication, by the verdict of juries, even where there should be no occasion but for a correctional penalty. The right of petitioning is secured to all citizens. Every petition is individual.

"The French people declare moreover that, in the delegation which they have made, and which they shall make, of their powers, they have not intended to give, nor do they give, the right of proposing the re-establishment of the Bourbons, or any prince of that family, upon the throne, even in case of the extinction of the imperial dynasty; nor the right of re-establishing either the ancient feudal nobility, or the feudal and signorial privileges or titles, or any privileged and dominant worship; nor the power of making any attempt upon the irrevocability of the sale of the national domains: they formally interdict to the government, the chambers, and the citizens all propositions to that effect.

"Done at Paris the 20th of April, 1815.

(Signed) "Napoleon.

"The Duke of Bassano."[3]

Nothing but their own love of tyranny, therefore, could induce these sovereigns to wage war against a happy people, like the people of France. But Napoleon's virtues were too luminous for their dim eyes to look upon. The abolition of the slave-trade ought to be held in everlasting remembrance by all the friends of justice and humanity.

"IMPERIAL DECREE.

"Napoleon, Emperor of the French. We have decreed, and do decree, as follows:

"Art. 1.—From the date of the publication of the present decree, the trade in negroes is abolished. No expedition shall be allowed for this commerce, neither in the ports of France nor in those of our colonies.

"Art. 2.—There shall not be introduced to be sold in our colonies any negro, the produce of this trade, whether French or foreign.

"Art. 3.—Any infraction of this decree shall be punished with the confiscation of the ship and cargo, which shall be pronounced by our courts and tribunals.

"Art. 4.—However, the ship-owners who, before the publication of the present decree, shall have fitted out expeditions for the trade may sell the produce in our colonies.

"Our ministers are charged with the execution of the present decree.

(Signed) "Napoleon.

"The Duke of Bassano."

Beside these noble examples of good government, many other advantages were bestowed on the French people by their emperor. Their "Code Napoleon," their "Legion of Honour," their "Central Schools," their *new roads*, *bridges*, and *canals*, will be lasting evidences of the gigantic powers of his mind, and of his sincere desire to serve his country, and render himself worthy of the exalted station to which he had been called by her gratitude for his pre-eminent military services. Had Napoleon bounded his ambition to the glory of ruling France upon free and liberal principles, it had been happy for himself, his relations, and his country; but to talk of his foreign despotism, and his *carrying* tyranny to where, in fact, he *found* tyranny,—tyranny the most rank and inveterate,—is to use the language of folly or of knavery, and to merit the contempt of every thinking mind.

But if it be even allowed that Napoleon was all that his enemies would make him, where did our ministers get the unheard-of privilege of setting themselves up as cosmopolite censors? By what right did the British government constitute itself a tribunal to judge and punish, in the last resort, delinquent monarchs? Could it by any reasoning have made out a claim to that office, was it just or decent to make a victim of *one*,—a man of unquestioned talent and greatness of soul,—and at the same moment to compliment and make alliances with all the worse tyrants, the maudlin hypocrites, and base violaters of their word? Or did these moral Quixotes and immaculate judges only profess to "do *justice*" upon *one* sinner "against the spirit of the age,"—and that one a *fallen* enemy?

The only plausible pretence for the treatment of the abdicated emperor was—that his surpassing genius, and his great hold on the military part of the French character, rendered him a necessary exception to the rule regarding prisoners of war, and made it indispensable to the safety and repose of the world, that he should be prevented from appearing again on the grand stage of European politics. This is confessedly on the dangerous plan of doing positive injustice for the sake of what the doers think safe and necessary. But we deny the necessity. We say the argument is built on utter ignorance of human nature, and a wilful blindness to all history and experience. Napoleon was grand in his views, because he admired and loved greatness for its own sake. He never sullied his conquests by partitioning and dividing the conquered. He could afford not to weaken his enemies by petty violations of national integrity. He encouraged everything liberal and noble,

An early printed version of the Code Napoleon.

which did not at the same time interfere with his personal authority. He cherished literature, art, and science; and they, in return, reflected true glory upon him. He never insulted and mocked mankind by pretending an eternal right in himself and his successors to trample them under his feet, because he was an emperor. He had always a respect for liberty, though he so often forgot it in his greater eagerness for power. He never laid claim to *holiness*, but acknowledged himself, in his proudest moments, sovereign, "*by the constitutions of the empire.*" He was not vindictive; his long military rule was never sullied by any act which could be compared in infamy with the imprisonment of the unfortunate Trenck by that Prussian Frederick, whom the legitimate abusers of Napoleon call "the *Great*." The prominent fault of his career as a leader of a new and revolutionary period, was that, instead of looking forward, he looked backward, and became an imitator instead of an original. He evidently had the glories of former ages strongly in his view; and was to be a great conqueror, not because the times wanted *him*, but because there are medals and statues in the world, and dynasties were founded by Cæsar. In the height of his prosperity, he was a Charlemagne—another "Emperor of the West;" and, in his adversity, he forgot the Prince Regent of England so far as to talk to him of Themistocles.[4] And yet there was a romance even in this, which set him above all ordinary conquerors. He had the poetry, as well as the prose, of the military art about him. *He* would never have sunk into a mere lounger and man of pleasure, or stood behind any commonplace man with a gold stick in his hand.

As a soldier, his military career has never been surpassed in brilliancy. Quick, active, decisive, he never paused in the vigorous and persevering execution of the plans which his genius prompted him to undertake. He introduced a new, high, and successful mode of conquest, by striking immediately at the centre of armies and countries; and he was finally overthrown, both as general and sovereign, not because his individual antagonists were greater, but because the very physical remains of old English liberty were greater, and because public opinion was greater than all. He possessed, in an eminent degree, the great art of estimating and working upon the characters of his adversaries, and the still greater art of gaining the affections of his soldiers, who were always passionately fond of him, and who at this day adore his memory.

As a prince and a conqueror, his master-passion was a restless ambition, the impetuous tide of which bore him onward to his ends through many signal acts of injustice and violence. We shall not dwell upon them: there has been plenty of "envy, hatred, and all uncharitableness," to ring the changes on his worst deeds, and an abundance of those feelings, we find, survive the object that particularly roused them. Neither shall we indulge in uselessly regretting the good he *failed* to do, or in reproaching him with the want of moderation and wisdom. Our business is with the illustrious soldier as he was, not as he might have been without his defects:

> "His warlike mind, his soul devoid of fear;
> His high-designing thoughts were figured there."

His character was spoilt, or at least not adapted to the purposes of freedom, by a military education. The Bourbons brought him up at one of their military schools, where his head was filled with Cæsar and Alexander, and then complained of him for his ambition: that is to say, the legitimate monarchs will let you be as ambitious and warlike as you please, provided you assist *their* ambition and wars; but if not, you are a blood-thirsty conqueror and a tyrant. Some writers have attempted to confound, on *this* occasion, ambition with mere ordinary selfishness. This is paltry and ridiculous. Napoleon was never so cool as when contemplating eminent success. Those who have carried him the news of victory have frequently supposed that he had learnt it before, or that he did not credit them. It warmed no feature of his countenance; it lit up no additional lustre in his eye. Yet this was not indifference; he had acquired a habit of subduing the ordinary emotions of mankind. Defeat and error certainly enraged him towards those who contributed to such mortifications; but they never had power to hurry him into any efforts to repair disaster. His intemperance never extended itself to his plans or resources, as a general. Let us look to the course of his feelings when the thunderbolt of his fortune was expended at Moscow. He had recourse to no dribbling efforts on which to hang the flame of military hope. He negotiated the plan of his retreat with all the precision of an attorney, who leaves nothing unprovided for. Trifles alone disturbed Napoleon. The offence of an inattention on the part of an attendant would make him angry; but if the world had burst asunder, and only left him a place to stand upon, he would have regarded it through his eye-glass as an experiment in natural philosophy!

Had Napoleon lived in times of less turbulence, he would have been a still greater statesman than a warrior. It is a fact not to be disputed, that it was this great man who definitively freed the entire Continent of Europe from that democratic mania, of all other tyrannies the most cruel, savage, and unrelenting, and which was in full, though less rapid, progress when he, by accepting the diadem of France, restored the *principles* of monarchy to its vigour, and, at one blow, overturned the many-headed monster of revolution. To attain this beneficial end, HE SPILT NO BLOOD! The decapitation of Louis, in which he could have had no concern, completely overwhelmed the Bourbon dynasty; but Napoleon, in one single day, re-established that monarchial form of government which the imbecile ministers of England had, with so much expense of human life and treasure, been for many years unsuccessfully attempting to restore!

One of Napoleon's greatest admirers was Mr. Fox, who, speaking of him one day, said, "If we even shut our eyes on the martial deeds of this great man, we must allow that his *eloquence alone* has elevated the French people to a higher degree of civilization than any other nation in Europe,—they have advanced a century during the last five years. Bonaparte combines the declamation of a Cicero with the soul-stirring philippicks of a Demosthenes; he appeals *to the head and the heart*, to honour and to self-interest, at the same time. Had this wonderful man turned his attention to poetry, instead of war, he would have beaten Homer out of the field! Whatever his manner of delivery may be, and I understand it is impressive, he is certainly the greatest orator that the world ever produced. The soaring grandeur of his conceptions is admirable, and his adaptation of the deeds and sayings of the heroes and statesmen of ancient times to present circumstances, not only shows the extent of his reading and the correctness of his taste in their application, but also serves to assure the French people that he is as capable of governing as he has proved himself to be in leading them forth to conquest. But it is in his power of simplification that he shines most; although as romantic as Ossian, he disdains all rodomontade and circumlocution; and, by stripping his subject of all extraneous matter, he reduces the most complex proposition down to the laconic simplicity of a self-evident axiom."

What, then, are we to think of a British minister, who could violate his most sacred pledges of protection to a man of this exalted description? But Lord Castlereagh's mind was not capable of estimating the worth and talents of Napoleon, and the mean expedient to which his lordship resorted to gain possession of the emperor's person will ever reflect the greatest possible disgrace upon his character, both as a man and a minister. The petty, vexatious, and unjustifiable conduct, to which the Emperor Napoleon was afterwards subjected at St. Helena, was equal in meanness to his capture. When the emperor quitted the *Bellerophon*, on the 8th of August, the officers and ship's company were in consternation; they felt implicated in the shame and the injustice of such a procedure. Napoleon traversed the deck to descend into the sloop, with calmness and a smile upon his lips, having at his side Admiral

Keith. He stopped before Captain Maitland, charged him to testify his satisfaction to the officers and crew of the Bellerophon, and, seeing him extremely grieved, said to him, by way of consolation, *"Posterity cannot, in any way, accuse you for what is taking place; you have been deceived as well as myself."* Napoleon enjoyed, during twenty-four days, the protection of the British flag; he sojourned in the inner roads of Torbay and Plymouth; and it was not until after that lapse of time, on the 8th of August, when passing on board the Northumberland, that Admiral Keith disarmed the French,—the delivering up of arms being one of the characteristics of prisoners of war. The arms of the emperor, however, were not demanded.

It would be unnecessary to give a copy of the "official" regulations, which Lord Castlereagh ordered to be observed towards the illustrious Napoleon; their tyrannical operation will be made manifest in the following correspondence:

LETTER FROM COUNT MONTHOLON TO THE GOVERNOR, SIR HUDSON LOWE.

"Longwood, 23rd August, 1816.

"General,

"I have received the treaty of the 2nd August, 1815, concluded between his Britannic Majesty, the Emperor of Austria, the Emperor of Russia, and the King of Prussia, which was annexed to your letter of the 23rd July.

"The Emperor Napoleon protests against the contents of that treaty. He is not the prisoner of England: after having abdicated, into the hands of the representatives of the nation, for the advantage of the constitution adopted by the French people, and in favour of his son, he repaired voluntarily and freely to England, to live there as a private individual, in retirement, under the protection of the British laws. The violation of all laws cannot constitute a right; in point of fact, the person of the Emperor Napoleon is in the power of England; but in fact, and of right, he has not been and is not in the power of Austria, Russia, and Prussia, even according to the laws and customs of England, who never admitted into the balance, in the exchange of prisoners, the Russians, the Austrians, the Prussians, the Spaniards, the Portuguese, although she was united to those powers by treaties of alliance, and made war conjointly with them. The convention of the 2nd August, made fifteen days after the Emperor Napoleon was in England, cannot, of right, have any effect; it exhibits only a spectacle of a coalition of the four great powers of Europe for the oppression of a SINGLE MAN!—a coalition disclaimed by the opinion of all people, and at variance with all the principles of sound morality. The Emperors of Austria and of Russia, and the King of Prussia, not having, either in fact or of right, any controul over the person of the Emperor Napoleon, they have had no power to decree anything concerning him. If the Emperor Napoleon had been in the power of the Emperor of Austria, that prince would have recollected the relations which religion and nature have placed between a father and a son,—relations which are never violated with impunity. He would have recollected, that Napoleon has four times restored him to his throne:

at Leoben, in 1797, and at Luneville, in 1801, when his armies were under the walls of Vienna; at Presburg, in 1806, and at Vienna, in 1809, when his armies were masters of the capital, and of three-fourths of the monarchy. That prince would have recollected the protestations which he made to him at the bivouac of Moravia, in 1806, and at the interviews at Dresden, in 1812. If the person of the Emperor Napoleon had been in the power of the Emperor Alexander, he would have called to mind the bonds of friendship contracted at Tilsit, at Erfurt, and during twelve years of daily intercourse. He would have remembered the conduct of the Emperor Napoleon on the day after the battle of Austerlitz, when, having it in his power to make him prisoner with the wreck of his army, he contented himself with his parole, and suffered him to operate his retreat. He would have called to mind the dangers which the Emperor Napoleon personally braved to extinguish the conflagration of Moscow, and preserve to him that capital. Certainly, that prince would not have violated the duties of friendship and gratitude towards a friend in misfortune. If the person of the Emperor Napoleon had even been in the power of the King of Prussia, that sovereign would not have forgotten, that it depended on the emperor, after the day of Friedland, to place another prince on the throne of Berlin; he would not have forgotten, in the presence of a disarmed enemy, the protestations of devotedness and the sentiments which he expressed to him in 1812, at the interviews of Dresden. Accordingly, it is obvious in the Articles 2 and 9 of the said treaty of the 2nd August, that, being unable in any way to influence the fate of the Emperor Napoleon's person, which is not in their power, those same persons agree to what shall be done thereon by the King of Great Britain, who undertakes to fulfil all obligations. These princes have reproached the Emperor Napoleon with having preferred the protection of the English laws to their protection. The false notions which the Emperor Napoleon had of the English laws, and of the influence which the opinion of a great, generous, and free people had on their government, induced him to prefer the protection of their laws to that of his father-in-law, or his old friend. The Emperor Napoleon was ever competent to ensure what concerned him personally, by a diplomatic treaty, either by replacing himself at the head of the army of the Loire, or by placing himself at the head of the army of the Gironde, which General Claus commanded. But, seeking thenceforward only retirement, and the protection of the laws of a free nation, either English or American, all stipulations appeared to him unnecessary. He thought the English would be more bound by his frank, noble, and confident procedure, than they would have been by the most solemn treaties. He was mistaken. But this error will always make true Britons blush; and, both in the present and in future generations, it will be a proof of the faithlessness of the English administration. An Austrian and a Russian commissioner have arrived at St. Helena. If the object of their mission be the fulfilment of the duties which the Emperors of Austria and Russia contracted by the treaty of the 2nd of August, and to see that the English agents, in a small colony, in the midst of the ocean, do not fail in the attentions due to a prince, bound to them by the ties of kindred and by so many other relations, there may be recognised in this procedure some characteristics of those sovereigns. But you, sir, have affirmed that those commissioners had neither the right nor the power to form any opinion as to whatever takes place on this rock.

"The English ministry have caused the Emperor Napoleon to be transported to St. Helena, 2000 leagues from Europe. This rock is situated in the tropic, 900 leagues from any continent; it is subject to the consuming heats of this latitude; it is covered with clouds and fogs during three quarters of the year; it is at once the driest and the most humid country in the world; such a climate is most adverse to the emperor's health. It was hatred that dictated the choice of this abode, as well as the instructions given by the English ministry to the officers commanding at this place. They have been ordered to call the Emperor Napoleon, 'General,' wishing to oblige him to acknowledge that he has never reigned in France; and this has determined him not to assume a name of incognito, as he had resolved to do on quitting France. As first magistrate, for life, of the republic, he concluded the preliminaries of London and the treaty of Amiens with the King of Great Britain; he received, as ambassadors, Lord Cornwallis, Mr. Merry, and Lord Whitworth, who sojourned in this quality at his court. He accredited to the King of England Count Otto and General Andreossy, who resided as ambassadors at the court of Windsor. When, after an interchange of letters between the two administrations of foreign affairs, Lord Lauderdale came to Paris, invested with full powers from the King of England, he treated with plenipotentiaries invested with full powers from the Emperor Napoleon, and sojourned several months at the court of the Thuilleries. When, subsequently, at Chatillon, Lord Castlereagh signed the ultimatum which the allied powers presented to the plenipotentiaries of the Emperor Napoleon, he thereby recognised the fourth dynasty. That ultimatum was more advantageous than the treaty of Paris; but it was demanded that France should renounce Belgium and the left bank of the Rhine, which was contrary to the propositions of Frankfort, and to the proclamations of the allied powers, which was contrary also to the oath by which at his coronation the emperor had sworn to the integrity of the empire. The emperor then thought that the natural limits were necessary to the guarantee of France, and to the equilibrium of Europe. He thought that the French nation, in their then existing circumstances, ought rather to incur all the chances of war than to depart from them. France would have obtained that integrity, and with it preserved her honour, if TREASON had not come to the aid of the allies.

"The treaty of the 2nd August and the British bill in parliament call the emperor, 'Napoleon Bonaparte,' and do not give him the title of general. The title of General Bonaparte is doubtless eminently glorious; the emperor bore it at Lodi, at Castiglione, at Rivoli, at Arcola, at Leoben, at the Pyramids, at Aboukir; but for seventeen years he has borne that of first consul and of emperor. It would be to allow that he has not been either first magistrate of the republic, or sovereign of the fourth dynasty. Those who think that nations are mere flocks, which belong, *by divine right*, to certain families, are not in the spirit of the age, nor even in that of the English legislature, which several times changed the order of its dynasty, because great changes that had taken place in opinions, in which the reigning princes did not participate, had rendered them inimical to the welfare and to a great majority of that nation. For kings are only hereditary magistrates, who exist but for the welfare of nations, and not nations for the satisfaction of kings. It was the same spirit of hatred which ordained that 'the Emperor Napoleon should not write or receive any letter, unless it was opened and read by the English ministers and the officers of St. Helena.' He has thus been denied the possibility of receiving news from his mother, his wife, his son, his brothers; and when, desirous of avoiding the inconvenience of seeing his letters read by subaltern officers, he wished to send letters sealed to the Prince Regent, the answer was, that they could only undertake to let open letters pass; that 'such were the instructions of the ministry.' This measure needs not be reflected on; it will give strange ideas of the spirit of the administration which dictated it; *it would even be disclaimed at Algiers*! Letters have arrived for general officers of the emperor's suite; they were unsealed, and were remitted to you; you did not communicate them, because they had not passed through the channel of the English ministry. It was necessary to make them travel over again 4000 leagues, and those officers had the pain of knowing that there existed on this rock, news from a wife, a mother, children, which they were not to know for six months. The heart rises at this!! We were not allowed to subscribe for the Morning Chronicle, the Morning Post, and some French journals. Some odd numbers of the Times were now and then sent to Longwood. Upon the demand made on board the Northumberland, some books were sent, but all those relative to transactions of late years were carefully withheld. It was afterwards wished to correspond with a London bookseller, in order to have direct means of obtaining some books that were wanted, and those which related to the events of the day: this was prevented. An English author having performed a voyage in France, and having printed it in London, took the trouble to send it you, that it might be offered to the emperor; but you did not think yourself empowered to transmit it to him, because it had not come to you by the channel of your government. It is also said that other books sent by their authors could not be transmitted, because on the title page of some were the words 'To the Emperor Napoleon,' and on others 'To Napoleon the Great.' The English ministry are not authorized to order any of these vexations; the law of the British parliament, though iniquitous, considers the Emperor Napoleon as a prisoner of war; and prisoners of war have never been forbidden to subscribe for journals, or to receive books which are printed. Such a prohibition is made only in the dungeons of the inquisition.

"The isle of St. Helena is ten leagues in circumference; it is inaccessible on all sides; the coast is surrounded by some brigs, and there are posts placed on its verge within sight of each other, which render all communication with the sea impracticable. There is only one small village, James Town, where vessels arrive and depart. To prevent an individual from quitting the island, it is sufficient to guard the coast by sea and land. In interdicting the interior of the island, therefore, there can only be one object, that of excluding an easy ride of eight or ten miles, which exclusion, in the opinion of professional men, is shortening the life of the emperor.

"The emperor has been established at Longwood, a site exposed to all winds, a sterile tract, uninhabited, destitute of water, unsusceptible of any culture. There is a precinct of about 1200 toises uncultivated; at the distance of 300 or 400 toises, upon a peak, they have established a camp; another has just been placed about the same distance, in the opposite direction; so that, amidst the tropic heats, on whatever side we turn, we behold nothing but camps. Admiral Malcolm, having conceived how useful a tent would be to the emperor in such a situation, has caused one to be pitched by his sailors, twenty paces in front of the house; this is the only place where any shade can be found. However, the emperor has no reason but to be satisfied with the spirit which animates the officers and soldiers of the brave 53rd., as he also was with the crew of the Northumberland. Longwood House was built to serve as a barn for the Company's farm; subsequently, the lieutenant-governor of the island had some rooms fitted up there; it served him as a country-house, but it had none of the conveniencies of a dwelling. For a year past, men have been constantly at work there, and the emperor has been continually exposed to the inconvenience and insalubrity of inhabiting a house in a state of building. The room in which he sleeps is too small to contain a bed of ordinary dimensions: but every addition to Longwood House would prolong the annoyance of the workmen's attendance. Yet in this miserable island there are beautiful spots, presenting fine trees, gardens, and pretty good houses, Plantation House among others; but the positive instructions of the ministry prohibit you from giving that house, which might have spared much expense from your treasure, expense employed in building at Longwood some cottages covered with pitched paper, which are already out of repair. You have forbidden all correspondence between us and the inhabitants of the isle; you have in fact placed the house of Longwood in a state of exclusion; you have even fettered the communications of the officers of the garrison. It seems to have been a study to deprive us of the few resources which this miserable country affords, and we are here as we should be on the uncultivated and uninhabited rock of Ascension. During the four months that you, Sir, have been at St. Helena, you have deteriorated the situation of the emperor. Count Bertrand observed to you, that you were violating even the law of your legislature; that you were trampling under foot the rights of general officers, prisoners of war: you answered, that you recognised only the letter of your instructions, that they were worse even than your conduct appeared to us.

"I have the honour to be, General,

"Your very humble and obedient Servant,

(Signed) "The General Cte. De Montholon."

"P.S. I had signed this letter, Sir, when I received your's of the 17th. You annex to it an estimate of an annual sum of twenty thousand pounds sterling, which you deem indispensable to meet the expenditure of the establishment at Longwood, after all the reductions have been made which you have judged practicable. The discussion of this statement cannot in any manner concern us. The emperor's table is scarcely what is strictly necessary; all the provisions are of bad quality, and four times dearer than at Paris. You ask of the emperor a fund of twelve thousand pounds sterling, your government allowing you only eight thousand pounds sterling, for all these expenses. I have had the honour to tell you that the emperor had no funds; that for a year past he had not received or written any letter; and that he was in complete ignorance as to what is passing or may have been passing in Europe. Transported by violence to this rock, 2000 leagues distant, without the power of receiving or writing any letter, he now remains entirely at the discretion of the English agents. The emperor has always desired, and does desire, to defray all expenses whatever himself; and he will do so as soon as you will make it possible for him, by removing the prohibition imposed on the merchants of the island, of forwarding his correspondence, and by consenting that it shall not be subject to any inquisition by you or any of your agents. As soon as the wants of the emperor shall be known in Europe, the persons who are interested concerning him will send the necessary funds for supplying them.

"The letter of Lord Bathurst, which you have communicated to me, gives rise to some strange ideas. Were your ministers then ignorant that the spectacle of a great man struggling with adversity is the sublimest of spectacles? Were they ignorant that Napoleon at St. Helena, amidst persecutions of all kinds, which he confronts only with serenity, is greater, more sacred, more venerable, than on the first throne in the world, where he was so long the arbiter of kings? Those who in this position are wanting in what is due to Napoleon, vilify only their own character, and the nation which they represent.

(Signed) "The Gen. Cte. De Montholon."

FROM THE SAME TO THE SAME.

"Longwood, 9th September, 1816.

"General,

"I have received your two letters of the 30th August; there is one of them which I have not communicated. Count Bertrand and myself have had the honour of telling you several times, that we could not take charge of anything which would be contrary to the august character of the emperor. You know better than anyone, Sir, how many letters have been sent from the post-office to Plantation House; you have forgotten that, upon the representations which we have made to you repeatedly, you answered, that your instructions obliged you to let nothing go to Longwood, either letter, book, or pamphlet, unless those articles had passed the scrutiny of your government. The lieutenant of the Newcastle having been the bearer of a letter to Count Lascases, you kept that letter, but the officer deeming his delicacy compromised, you transmitted it thirty days after it had reached this island, &c. We are sure that our families and our friends write to us often; hitherto we have received very few of their letters. But it is by virtue of the same principle, that you this day disavow that you have retained the books and pamphlets that have been addressed to you, and yet you keep them.

"Your second letter of the 30th August, Sir, is no answer to that which I had the honour to write to you, to remonstrate against the changes effected by you in the course of that month, and which demolish all the basis of our establishment in this country.

"1. 'There is no part of my written instructions more definite, or to which my attention is more pointedly called, than that no person whatever should hold any communication with (the emperor) except through my agency.' You give a Judaical interpretation to your instructions; there is nothing in them which justifies or authorizes your conduct. Those instructions your predecessor had; you had them for three months previous to the changes which you effected a month ago. In short, it was not difficult for you to reconcile your different duties.

"2. 'I have already acquainted (the emperor) personally of this.'

"3. 'In addressing all strangers and other persons, except those whose duty might lead them to Longwood, in the first instance to Count Bertrand, (or asking myself) to ascertain whether (the emperor) would receive their visit, and in not giving passes, except to such persons as had ascertained this point, or were directed to do it, I conceive,' &c.

"4. 'It is not, Sir, in my power to extend such privilege, as you require, to Count Bertrand,' &c.

"I am obliged to declare to you, Sir, 1st, That you have communicated nothing to the emperor. 2nd. For more than two months you have had no communication with Count Bertrand. 3rd. We require of you no privilege for Count Bertrand, since I only ask a continuation of that state of things which existed for nine months.

"5. 'I regret to learn that (the emperor) has been incommoded with the visits,' &c. This is bitter irony.

"Instead of endeavouring to reconcile your different duties, Sir, you seemed determined to persist in a system of continual vexations. Will this do honour to your character? Will it merit the approbation of your government and your nation? Permit me to doubt it.

"Several general officers, who arrived in the Cornwallis, desired to be presented at Longwood. If you had referred them to Count Bertrand, as you had hitherto referred all strangers presenting themselves in the island, they would have been received. You have doubtless your reasons for preventing persons of some distinction from coming to Longwood; allege, if you choose, as you commonly do, the tenour of your instructions; but do not misrepresent the intentions of the emperor.

"The younger Lascases and Capt. Pionkowski were yesterday in the town. An English lieutenant accompanied them thither, and then, conformably to orders existing until that day, left them at liberty to go and see what persons they wished. Whilst young Lascases was talking with some young ladies, the officer came, and, with extreme pain at being charged with so disagreeable a commission, declared that your orders were not to lose sight of him. This is contrary to what has taken place heretofore. It would, I think, be proper that you should make known to us the changes you are effecting. This is forbidding us every visit to town, and thus violating your instructions.[5] Yet you know that scarcely one of the persons at Longwood goes to the town once a month, and there is no circumstance which can authorize you to change the established order. This is carrying persecution very far! I cannot conceive what has occasioned your letter of the 8th of September; I refer, Sir, to the postscript of my letter of the 23rd August. The emperor is ill, in consequence of the bad climate and privations of all kinds, and I have not made known to him all the fastidious details that have been made to me on your part. All this has been going on for two months, and should have been terminated long ago, as the postscript of my letter of the 23rd August is explicit. It is now high time that the thing should be ended; but it appears to be a text from which to insult us.

"I have the honour to be, General,
"Your very humble and obedient servant,
(Signed) "The Gen. Cte. De Montholon."

Count Lascases also felt so indignant at the treatment which his noble master experienced, that he reproached the governor, in no very measured terms, with his want of common humanity, and boldly asked him, "Do you or do you not wish to kill the emperor?" For this, and writing complaints to his friends, all his private papers were seized, and himself dismissed the island. The following farewell letter was written to him, on this occasion, by the emperor:

"My dear Count Lascases
"My heart sensibly feels what you endure; torn away fifteen days ago from my presence, you were shut up during that period in secret, without my being able to receive, or give you, any news, without your having communicated with any one, French or English; deprived even of the servant of your choice.

"Your conduct at St. Helena has been, like your life, honourable, and without reproach: I love to tell you so.

"Your letter to one of your friends, a lady in London, has nothing in it that is reprehensible; you there pour forth your whole heart into the bosom of friendship. That letter is like eight or ten others, which you have written to the same person, and which you have sent unsealed. The commandant of this place, having had the delicacy to sift out the expressions which you confide to friendship, has reproached you with them. Latterly he threatened to send you away from the island, if your letters contained any more complaints against him. He has, by so doing, violated the first duty of his place, the first article of his instructions, and the first sentiment of honour. He has thus authorized you to seek the means of conveying the effusions of your feelings to the bosom of your friends, and of acquainting them with the culpable conduct of the commandant. But you have been very artless: it has been very easy to take your confidence by surprise.

"They were waiting for a pretext to seize your papers; but your letter to your London friend could not authorize a police visit to you; for it contains no plot, no mystery; it is simply the expression of a noble and frank heart. The illegal and precipitate conduct pursued on this occasion bears the stamp of a very base personal hatred.

"In countries the least civilized, exiles, prisoners, and even criminals, are under the protection of the laws, and of the magistrates. The persons appointed to guard them have chiefs, either in the administrative or judicial order, who superintend them. Upon this rock, the man who makes the most absurd regulations executes them with violence, transgresses all laws, and there is no one to restrain the excesses of his temper.

"They envelop Longwood with a mystery, which they would wish to render impenetrable, in order to conceal a criminal conduct; and this leaves room for suspecting the most criminal intentions!!

"By some rumours artfully spread, it was wished to mislead the officers, strangers, inhabitants, and even the agents who are said to be maintained by Austria and Russia in this place; doubtless, the English government is deceived in the same way by adroit and fallacious statements.

"Your papers, among which it was known that there were some belonging to me, have been seized without any formality, near my apartment, with a marked and ferocious exultation. I was apprized of this a few moments afterwards: I looked through the window, and saw that they were taking you away. A numerous staff was parading round the house; I could fancy I saw so many South Sea islanders dancing round the prisoners whom they were going to devour.

"Your society was necessary to me; you alone read, spoke, and understood English. How many nights have you sat up, during my fits of sickness! Yet I enjoin you, and, if need be, I order you, to request the commandant of this place to send you back to the Continent. He cannot refuse that, since he has no controul over you, but by the voluntary act which you have signed. It will be a great consolation to me to know, that you are on your way to more fortunate countries.

"On arriving in Europe, whether you go to England, or return home, dismiss the remembrance of the ills which they have made you suffer; boast of the fidelity which you have shewn me, and of the great affection which I bear you.

"If you should one day see my wife and my son, embrace them. For two years, I have not heard from them, directly or indirectly. There has been for six months in this place a German botanist who saw them in the garden of Schoenbrunn, some months before his departure; the barbarians have carefully prevented him from giving me any news from them.

"My body is in the power of the hatred of my enemies; they forget nothing which can glut their vengeance. They are killing me by inches. But the insalubrity of this devouring climate, the want of every thing that sustains life, will, I feel, put a speedy end to this existence, the last moments of which will be an opprobrium on the English character; and Europe will one day signalize with horror that crafty and wicked man,[6] whom true Englishmen will disown as a Briton.

"As there is every reason to think, that you will not be permitted to come to see me before your departure, receive my embraces, the assurance of my esteem, and my friendship. Be happy.

(Signed) "Napoleon."

"11th December, 1816."

We might add many other proofs of the inhumanity exercised towards Napoleon, were it necessary to our purpose. Let our readers look over the writings of O'Meara, Lascases,[7] and numerous other persons now living, both French and English, who bear the most heart-rending testimony to all that was done to torture and to put an end to the life of this great man.

The inhuman conduct pursued towards the captive emperor at length became the subject of parliamentary inquiry. A motion to this effect was introduced to the House of Peers by Lord Holland, in the month of March, 1817. Of the motives by which this noble lord was actuated, it is difficult to award sufficient praise. He declared, "My chief motive in bringing forward this motion is to rescue parliament and the country from the stain that will attach to them, if any harsh or ungenerous treatment has been used towards Napoleon." Such an anxiety for the character of his country was, doubtless, a patriotic and proper motive; but it never ought to claim precedence of the great, permanent, and universal feelings of pity for the unfortunate, which are among the noblest characteristics of our nature. His lordship, therefore, might have insisted more upon the merit of a motive to which, on all occasions, he has shewn himself to be eminently entitled. That the praiseworthy object of Lord Holland's motion was not attained must be matter of deep regret to every man who wishes to maintain the reputation of his country. But the ministers shuffled over the charge by reading partial extracts from those documents which his lordship wished to have produced, while they refused an examination of the entire papers. This, to say the least of it, had a very suspicious appearance. Such a mode of proceeding was contrary to the long-established usages of the House, to the laws of evidence, and to the common course of practice in all investigation; and, however it might answer Lord Castlereagh's purpose, was little calculated to dispel the doubts of impartial inquirers, or to make a satisfactory case to the world and to posterity.

What judgment would a foreigner form of this matter, who might have heard the blessings of our happy administration of justice extolled to the skies? A captive, the most illustrious ever classed under that head, complained of the unnecessary rigour of his treatment. A British peer made a motion in parliament to inquire into the truth of these allegations, and for the production of papers connected with and tending to elucidate the subject. The secretary of state contended, that the assertions of the complainant were groundless, read partial extracts from the papers in question, but refused their entire production, and negatived the motion for them, without assigning any sufficient reason. If Lord Castlereagh thought the inference to be drawn from such a garbled statement would be favourable to his cause, he must have built his logic, not upon the REASON of the matter, but upon the VOTES OF HIS PENSIONED ADHERENTS,—a mode of conclusion not at all uncommon or unnatural to this minister. His lordship, indeed, considered his conduct to Napoleon as meritorious, on account of that great man having been the enemy of England! But does it follow that, because the uncertain events of war had placed the French emperor in a situation to claim the protection of our laws as a private individual, that his lordship was justified in betraying his misplaced confidence, or in treating him with the same spirit of hostility when he was a helpless captive, as when he was a powerful general arrayed in arms against the whole of Europe? A doctrine, more repugnant to humanity, more dangerous in its consequences to society, cannot be conceived. From what code of morality, or from what system of religion, did his lordship borrow such a principle? Much has been said of Lord Castlereagh's kindness of heart; but what a dark scroll of evidence does the treatment of Napoleon at St. Helena exhibit against such an assertion! To commiserate a fallen foe, to be moved by the sad spectacle of his fortunes, is the natural propensity and inseparable concomitant of every man possessing "PERSONAL COURAGE," or "KINDNESS OF HEART:"

> "The truly brave
> Will valorous actions prize,
> Respect a great and noble mind,
> Albeit in enemies;

while to oppress an adversary in your power, whether among nations or individuals, is not only considered *cowardly*, but abject, ungenerous, and savage. There is no circumstance which reflects so much disgrace on the national character of the Romans as their behaviour to Hannibal. The treatment which he received has been stigmatized as an act of complicated meanness, cruelty, and injustice. In modern times, the case of Napoleon seems most closely to resemble that of Hannibal, both in the splendour of his achievements while he was victorious, and in the sad similitude of fortune after his being defeated and betrayed into the hands of his enemies. It is true that Napoleon did not "play the Roman" and kill himself, as Hannibal did;[8] but a portion of the words which the Carthaginian general used on that occasion might have been aptly repeated by Napoleon, with merely an alteration of names: "The victory which Flamininus gains over a man, disarmed and betrayed, will not do him much honour. This single day will be a lasting testimony of the great degeneracy of the Romans. They have deputed a person of consular dignity to spirit up Prusias impiously to murder one who is his guest!" It is curious to reflect that, in the annals of the world, the same action, according to circumstances, at one time is a crime,— at another, an act of heroism! The same man is at one time a Claudius,—at another, a Marcus Aurelius. Cataline is but a vile conspirator. If, however, he had been able to found an empire, like Cæsar, he would have been esteemed a benefactor. Our Oliver Cromwell was acknowledged till his last hour, and his protection sought by all sovereigns; but after his death, his body was suspended on a gibbet: he only wanted a son like himself to enable him to form a new dynasty. So long as Napoleon was fortunate, Europe bowed at his footstool, while the first princes thought it an honour to ally themselves with his family, and to obtain his smile was esteemed a favour. As soon, however, as he fell a prey to treachery, it was pretended that he was nothing more than a miserable adventurer, an usurper, without talent and without courage!

But, even allowing that any sufficient argument could have been urged for the detention of Napoleon, surely all restraint beyond what was strictly necessary for the security of his person was unjustifiable, and every species of mortification, not only ungenerous, but absolutely criminal. Lord Castlereagh ought, at least, in giving directions for his custody, to have been particularly circumspect that no real or seeming unkindnesses were exercised against the captive emperor. If the coercive measures adopted were thought necessary, they should have been introduced in a more conciliatory manner, and with every allowance for the irritation and impatience which exile and imprisonment will be sure to produce upon the most apathetic being in creation. But, when we take into consideration the ungentlemanly and ignoble proceedings pursued against Napoleon at St. Helena, can we feel surprised at the bursts of indignation which now and then escaped him at the cowardly conduct of his jailer? That he should have viewed Sir Hudson Lowe as the meanest creature in existence, is not at all to be wondered at; for it appeared as if

> "Some demon said, 'Sir Hudson Lowe,
> Although we've got the dreaded foe,
> Yet here the question pinches:
> How shall we crush this mighty man?
> 'Sir Hudson cried, 'I know the plan;
> We'll make him DIE BY INCHES!'"

Neither could Napoleon help considering Lord Castlereagh as the "demon" here alluded to. His lordship had induced him on board a British ship, under the most sacred promises of bringing him over to this country, that he might pass the remainder of his days under the blessings of our so-much-boasted constitution, as being "the envy and admiration of the whole world!" What milder appellation than "demon," therefore, did his lordship deserve, when, violating every principle of hospitality, he took advantage of Napoleon's faith in such promises, and seized upon the opportunity it afforded him of arresting the emperor as a prisoner of war, and of sending him to a barren rock, far from his wife, child, and friends, to be a prey to an unwholesome climate, and the rude insults of a mean and pitiful man like Sir Hudson Lowe!

> "Great God of war, and was it so
>   That Britons crush'd a fallen foe!
>   Had Wellington been taken,
>   (And there were chances on that day)
>   Would Bonaparte have used his sway,
>   And left him thus forsaken?"

Indeed, there was once a time when this same Lord Castlereagh might have been taken prisoner by Napoleon, which would most probably have been done, if the French emperor had possessed no loftier ideas of justice and honour than his lordship exhibited. This circumstance is related by Mr. O'Meara, in Bonaparte's own words, as follows:

> "When Castlereagh was at Chatillon with the ambassadors of the allied powers, after some successes of mine, and when I had, in a manner, invested the town, *he was greatly alarmed lest I might seize him* **and make him** *prisoner*. Not being accredited as an ambassador, nor invested with any diplomatic character to France, I might have taken him as an enemy. He went to Caulincourt, to whom he mentioned that *he laboured under considerable apprehensions that I should cause violent hands to be laid upon him*, as he acknowledged I had a right to do. It was impossible for him to get away without falling in with my troops. Caulincourt replied, that as far as his opinion went, he would say that I should not meddle with him; but that he could not answer for what I might do. Immediately after, he (Caulincourt) wrote to me what Castlereagh had said, and his answer. I signified to him in reply, that he was to tell Castlereagh to make his mind easy, and stay where he was: that I would consider him as an ambassador. At Chatillon, (continued Bonaparte) when speaking about the liberty enjoyed in England, Castlereagh observed, in a contemptuous manner, that it was not the thing most to be esteemed in England; that it was an USAGE they were obliged to put up with; but that it had become an abuse, and would not answer for other countries."

It will thus be seen that GRATITUDE, at least, ought to have prompted different conduct in Lord Castlereagh towards Napoleon; instead of which, the charges brought against Sir Hudson Lowe by Mr. O'Meara were not only deemed unworthy of inquiry, but his lordship actually dismissed the accuser from the British service. Thus a deserving and generous-minded officer was ruined, without even a hearing, for merely attempting to do an act of justice to the exiled Emperor of France! The charges against Sir Hudson Lowe, however, remained the same, and this summary mode of revenge inflicted on Mr. O'Meara was not at all calculated to acquit Lord Castlereagh from sharing in the accusation of wantonly oppressing Napoleon. Could anything tend more to criminate his lordship than the sudden

242 The Secret History of the Royal Court of England

punishment of the accuser, while in the act of preferring his complaint? Grant that Mr. O'Meara had misconducted himself, and that he had thus given his employer a right to dismiss him, surely he ought not, in common honesty, to have done so till he had first given him every opportunity of making good his charges. His lordship's readiness to stigmatize, and even silence him, in this manner, wore any appearance but that of an honourable anxiety to meet and to defy his adversary. We cannot devote space sufficient to bring forward the charges of Mr. O'Meara; but the inquirer will find himself amply repaid for his trouble by their perusal. As Sir Hudson Lowe can only be looked upon as a cowardly ruffian, who scrupled not to *execute* the orders of his superiors in office, however unjust they might be, the real odium of Napoleon's treatment and death must rest upon the government, of which Lord Castlereagh was the most active member. Mr. O'Meara was appointed medical attendant upon the emperor by this government, and his professional ability and private worth have never been questioned. If Lord Castlereagh, therefore, willed not the death of Napoleon, it was his duty to have removed those causes of complaint which Mr. O'Meara emphatically pointed out "would render Bonaparte's PREMATURE DEATH as inevitable as if it were to take place under the hands of the EXECUTIONER!" The public are aware how fatally this prediction was fulfilled; but the whole evidence of Mr. O'Meara would carry conviction to the mind of any man who had not previously determined to disbelieve truth. Indeed, he has been confirmed in many essential points of his statements by the admissions of either the governor's advocates or the governor himself. One of these advocates stated that Mr. O'Meara was discharged for disobeying orders; but of what nature were those orders? The governor wanted him to act as a spy upon the emperor, and to sign false reports of the state of his health! Consequently, Mr. O'Meara did indignantly refuse to perform such a base and cruel service; and what man of honour and principle would not have done the same? A refusal of this kind reflects no disgrace upon Mr. O'Meara, but will rather hand his name down to posterity as one deserving better treatment than he unfortunately experienced.

In contemplating the manifold deprivations to which Napoleon ultimately fell a victim, we cannot help remarking upon one peculiar trait of the human mind,— that of being more moved by fiction than reality; for a tale of imaginary woe will excite more exquisite feeling, more real sympathy, than the severest reverses of fortune which may have occurred in our time, or which may be even present to our view! If Napoleon, for instance, had been an ideal personage, and the history of his life had been made the subject of romance or poetry, what mind so dull but would have moralized upon the vicissitude of human affairs?—what heart so cold but would have felt some commiseration for the captive? But when all that a poet's fancy could have formed and blended of surprising extremes, to raise the interest of the reader in the hero of the tragedy, had actually occurred and been signally manifested in this extraordinary man,—when he, who at one time was raised to an elevation and possessed a power never enjoyed by any other individual, was hurled headlong from his height to the abyss of humiliation, was imprisoned, exiled, captive, and forlorn,—how happened it that the feelings of our nature were not to take their accustomed course, that the sources of sympathy were to be dried up, and compassion, which had hitherto been considered amongst the most amiable of virtues, was all at once to lose its very essence and property, and not only not to be numbered amongst our weaknesses, but catalogued amongst our crimes? For the prevalence of this disposition,—which, alas! was too observable even among those classes in whom education and the intercourse of enlightened society would have naturally led to an expectation of better feelings and sounder conclusions on the subject,—it is difficult to account; unless it be true in morals, as in mechanics, that the motion may be continued when the impulse has ceased, and that to this we must refer the state of national feeling at the time Napoleon was suffering an accumulation of indignities at St. Helena. Since his death, however, the injustice and inhumanity of his treatment have been freely acknowledged and severely commented on; and there is every reason to believe that his great name will be finally rescued from that misrepresentation which interested writers have endeavoured to surround all his actions.

From the affinity between fear and hatred, there is no wonder that when Napoleon was arrayed as our enemy, we joined hatred with hostility. But, at the time of his seizure on board the Bellerophon, he was no longer formidable; he was then in our hands. Upon what principle, then, did active hatred continue when both hostility and apprehension had ceased? Did a consciousness of inclemency (to use the mildest term that the occasion will admit) towards the object of it sufficiently account for the continuance of this hatred? It had been better, indeed, if Lord Castlereagh, as well as his coadjutors at that period, who cherished this inextinguishable species of enmity, had considered whether the world and posterity might not be apt to ascribe the meanest and most wicked of motives to such conduct. And let all the detractors of Napoleon recollect, that the illiberal invectives in which they have so freely indulged against him will, instead of making any lasting impression upon his fame, only serve to perpetuate their own disgrace and that of his ignoble persecutors. While his figure will stand conspicuous through history, the crowd of monarchs and ministers, who have alternately crouched to and calumniated, truckled to or trampled upon him, can only escape oblivion as they make the group which shade the back ground of the picture, and give a force, *by forming a contrast*, to the grandeur of the leading figure. Lord Castlereagh will assuredly form one of this back-ground group; but we envy him not in *such fame*. The conduct of his lordship to Napoleon, instead of displaying that dignified sentiment and enlightened understanding which should adorn the character of a nobleman, and which we should naturally be led to expect from a "secretary of state for foreign affairs," has degraded his name to the level of the meanest of the mean. We will not say that we had rather been a chimney-sweeper than have been guilty of his lordship's treachery to Napoleon; but, considering it as a deliberate exposition of the wickedness of his heart and his abandonment of every honourable feeling, which will be put on record, and handed down to posterity, we certainly will say, that all the wealth and titles of Lord Londonderry, together with his immense political power and the smiles bestowed on him by his despotic patrons, should never have induced us to have done the like.

Would that it were in our power here to close the catalogue of crimes, which are written in characters of blood, against the Marquis of Londonderry. The death of Napoleon was followed by the persecutions of an innocent and noble-minded WOMAN,—"the injured Queen of England!" But this self-important man had been so hardened in iniquity, that it was by no means a difficult task to persuade him to assist in her ruin. Her majesty was too well acquainted with the SECRETS OF STATE to be allowed the free exercise of her rights; and as his lordship had lent his assistance to prevent many of these disreputable secrets from being made public,[9] self-preservation might have operated as a further inducement for him to enter the lists of her most bitter enemies. How fatally the Marquis of Londonderry and his colleagues succeeded in their diabolical plans have been already explained. But the inglorious triumph added not to his lordship's peace of mind; for, from that period, he was observed to exhibit "a conscience ill at ease." And it was a very remarkable fact, that the marquis should have selected the precise time of the year, only twelve months after, for his own destruction as that in which his royal mistress met her fate! A circumstance of this singular nature should operate as a great moral lesson for the consideration of mankind generally, though Providence might have designed it as a warning to the "titled wickedness" of our land. Such is the condition of our nature, that we cannot mortgage either our moral or our physical energies so as always to repel the accusations of our own hearts, which are sure, eventually, to reprove us for evils committed.

> "O then beware;
> Those wounds heal ill that men do give themselves:
> Omission to do what is necessary
> Seals a commission to a blank of danger;
> And danger, like an ague, subtly taints
> Even then when we sit idly in the sun!!"

On what a slender thread hangs human life, and how worthless are titles and wealth, if all is not at peace within! On what a "beetling ledge" the favourite of royalty tracks his uncertain way! By what a fragile tenure the courtier holds the rewards of his servility, on which he is so accustomed to pride himself! The suicide of the gay and puissant Marquis of Londonderry was, indeed, a memento full of lessons of humility to the fawning parasites of power.

In the October of this year, Mr. Henry Nugent Bell, of whom we have before had occasion to speak, died at his house, Whitehall Place, in the 30th year of his age. This individual merits a little commiseration, notwithstanding the disgraceful part he took in the Manchester murders, and other similar missions of Lord Sidmouth; because, though the tool of despotic ministers, he made some amends to the public by *betraying* his base employers. The newspapers generally reported his death to have proceeded from a *natural cause*; but this was not the case. We can POSITIVELY state that he died UNFAIRLY; but whether from his own hand, or from the design of an enemy, we are not able to determine. Mr. Bell appears never to have forgiven himself for his dereliction from the path of virtue, and only urged, in extenuation of his conduct, the *cruel necessity* he was under to oblige his patron. Once enlisted under the banners of Sidmouth, the unfortunate man soon found out the necessity of not being over-scrupulous in his actions. One crime succeeded another; and thus a man of education and talent was made the victim of unjust and diabolical proceedings.

After a great deal of ministerial manœuvring, Mr. Canning succeeded in his suit for the foreign secretaryship. The situation of the Marquis of Londonderry had long been the darling, though for many years the unattainable, object of this gentleman's intrigues or importunities. The country, however, had no cause to rejoice in the appointment of Mr. Canning to an office of such conspicuous importance, and many people felt considerable surprise at so unexpected a promotion, as the right honourable gentleman had been previously selected as the new governor-general of India. It was a well-known fact, that Mr. Canning had fallen into personal disgrace with his majesty, and all his vacillating conduct with respect to our ill-treated queen had not been able to restore him to royal favour. There have, however, been instances where a minister has been forced upon the king by public opinion, as was the case with the *first* Mr. Pitt, in the reign of George the Second. This Mr. Pitt was in high favour with the PEOPLE of England, acquired through his known attachment to freedom, and through the irresistible ascendency of his upright and unbending character. George the Second, notwithstanding, showed great opposition to the appointment of this worthy man, who was hated by his king *only* because he feared his politics; yet Mr. Pitt was finally made secretary of state, and proved himself worthy of the popularity with which the PEOPLE had invested him. But the case of Mr. Canning was of a widely different nature. In him, the PEOPLE took no interest, except that which leads all men to watch their enemy's motions. He had not the *honour* of being disliked at court for his politics,—they were of the most accommodating character; he had given a *personal* offence to the "first gentleman of the land." By the country, on the other hand, it was his political principles, history, and character, that were held in the most disrepute. Placed in such circumstances, the public must have been aware that this political adventurer would not be *very patriotic* in his endeavours to obtain pardon for his crime against the "puissant prince;" and how far, therefore, such a man could be entrusted with power was a question not difficult to solve. As for the nation generally, they regarded Mr. Canning but in the nature of an HIRED ADVOCATE, retained for the mean purpose of palliating the weaknesses or transgressions of a cabinet, the great majority of whose members he excelled in making witty or fallacious speeches. His countrymen recollected his conduct through life too well to imagine that he was made foreign secretary to introduce any real improvement into the policy or councils of the nation. They felt convinced of his being chosen as the apologist of bad measures, not the author of good ones; and that he held the language of one of Shakespeare's heroes to be good sentiment: "A plague of opinion!—a man may wear it on both sides, like a leather jerkin!"

Mr. Canning was, indeed, known to be a fit agent for the "Holy Alliance;" he was the sworn antagonist of every reform in church and state; and wheresoever a grievance or an abuse appeared, there stood he, arrogantly to charge as public enemies all who testified to the existence of either. Even the unfortunate country gentlemen, reduced as they now were, by their blind support of Mr. Canning's system, to a state bordering on pauperism, could hardly have hoped, from such a rooted foe to liberty, for any shadow of relief or of assistance. "Be quiet, gentlemen," was the self-important style of his addresses, "see what an example the poor have set you; be patient, as they are, and you will soon be prosperous, like me!" From a minister of this description, no consolatory expectations could possibly be formed by any class or party. We might certainly look for a few better speeches than Lord Londonderry made; for his were, indeed, but poor maudlin affairs. The new acts would only have a better chance of being varnished over, while we might expect them to be much worse in their nature than they had been; because, as ministers had no intention to reform the system, it must, of necessity, become more vicious every day. The only measure on which Mr. Canning had ever taken any particularly active part, was the emancipation of the Catholics; and our readers will form some opinion of his SINCERITY on this subject, and of the IMPORTANCE which Mr. Canning attached to it, when we inform them that the *honourable* gentleman actually promised the Earl of Liverpool not to discuss the matter if he might only be allowed to retain the foreign secretaryship! The conduct of the Earl of Liverpool, also, leads to an observation which reflects any thing but honour on the character of his lordship. We know that the power of this premier over the king was omnipotent, owing to his being in possession of SECRETS, of the most vital importance to his majesty and the royal family. By his lordship threatening to be no longer prime minister, he could, at almost any time, have forced his own schemes of policy upon the vitiated court. By the admission of Mr. Canning to office, he had driven his royal master to the wall, and compelled him to do that which all the world had before supposed would have been more unpalatable to his proud feelings than the admission of even the Whigs to office. If Lord Liverpool could, therefore, bring in a minister so personally disliked as Mr. Canning notoriously was by his majesty, could he not also have prevented that odious and atrocious measure, commonly called the "Queen's TRIAL,"—Mr. Canning's declared disapprobation of which created the very difficulty which had just been overcome? That disgraceful proceeding against an injured woman, with all its horrid consequences, it now became indisputably evident, might have been avoided, had Lord Liverpool but only have shown as much pertinacity in the CAUSE OF INNOCENCE as he had now done in that of PARTY. His personal power in the cabinet was, however, much increased by the nomination of Mr. Canning. There was a tacit, though well-understood, separation of interests during the life of Lord Londonderry, who usually headed one division of the ministers, with the Duke of Wellington in the number of the subalterns of his party, while Lord Liverpool led the other wing of Tory pensioners. There was nothing now, therefore, to stand against the first lord of the Treasury, unless Mr. Canning's inveterate spirit of intrigue should possess him (a thing by no means unlikely) to see a rival in his benefactor, and to undermine Lord Liverpool, as he had done one of his former colleagues.

The Battle of Waterloo. (*British Library*)

What an enviable opportunity to enter office did this period afford to any man having the real welfare of his country at heart; for all the blessings that had been promised from the "glorious battle of Waterloo,"—that wind-up of a war against the liberties of Europe,—were yet to come: taxation remained undiminished; the liberties of the subject were gradually declining; the commerce of England was almost at an end; and her people poor and unhappy. Here, then, was a wide field for a patriotic minister to display his abilities, by restoring the country to its wonted prosperity! But, while Mr. Canning and his colleagues were indulging in luxury at the expense of the nation, the just complaints of the public were designated "the cries of a faction," and the miserable victims of their misrule said to betray an "ignorant impatience" when they prayed for relief. After years of peace, the expenditure of government exceeded the income of the Treasury, and our visionary and delusive system of finance required to be bolstered up by additions to our already overwhelming debt; strength of council was superseded by strength of army; all public discussion, however peaceably conducted, was opposed; acts of coercion were encouraged and abetted; and England, once the pride of nations, became desolated by the worst complication of ignorance and obstinacy that ever disgraced a cabinet! To whatever department of the state we turned our eyes, the same indifference to its prosperity seemed manifest. The ARMY, preponderating beyond all precedent in time of peace, had become an overgrown source of profligacy and barter; commissions and promotions, instead of being rewards for service and merit, were sold to the best bidder, and the produce applied to pamper the vitiated appetite of royalty. In the NAVY, once our bulwark and our boast, the services of effeminate lordlings seemed more courted than those of bluff and able seamen, commissioners more important than shipwrights, and large expensive establishments kept up on shore, while our fleets were rotting in the docks. Our TRADE was neglected, while pirates infested the seas, and destroyed our merchantmen. In our FOREIGN POLICY, all was danger and uncertainty; the calm of peace was only prolonged by our unexampled apathy and puerile forbearance. Foreign powers owed us money that we dare not demand; nations were struggling for liberty and independence that we must not assist; and outrages committed that we could not avenge. In the past, a long and sanguinary war, in which were sacrificed an incalculable number of lives and immense treasure; while in the future was exhibited the most dreary prospect of our declining power. At home, our decay was still more apparent: the sacred flame of liberty, to which we were indebted for our preference over other nations, was attacked on all sides by every means that treachery could devise; the malignity of the ministers visited faithful servants with dismissal without inquiry or hearing; the sovereign was recommended and advised to treat his subjects with contumely and neglect; while the constitution itself was assailed by spies and informers, who first created and abetted the commission of the crimes which they afterwards denounced! This was, indeed, a fearful state of affairs; but history will justify us in the picture we have drawn. Though these and ten thousand other evils were evidently the results of imbecility, folly, and knavery, which had mainly been assisted by bribery, lavishly bestowed on those who had possessed themselves of those secrets of state recorded in our volumes, yet he who dared to hint at such an unpleasant truth, or even to doubt the honesty of ministers, was sure to be denounced a traitor. But, thank heaven! the power of the Tories now received a check. The manly stand made by a few members of the House of Commons, during the previous session of parliament, had opened the eyes of the long-blinded public, and the late acts of oppression, with which the Londonderry cabinet had disgraced itself,[10] furnished fresh cause for censure and new inducements for perseverance. The ministry, therefore, which Mr. Canning joined were humbled and degraded before he became one of its members; but, instead of raising it from the disgrace into which it had fallen, his underhanded conduct only aggravated matters, and rendered him a greater object of suspicion to patriotic men than even their avowed enemies.

Various royal diversions and exhibitions were displayed throughout this year, and the "first gentleman in the world" was too often made to appear the "first knave on the stage of life." George the Fourth's means had been bestowed so bounteously, that he had become arrogant, and considered THE PEOPLE merely in the light of SLAVES, created only to administer to his passions and caprices. He could hardly be said to know the nation, except by the representation of his hirelings. Neither did he care to know the subjects from whom his strength was derived, because they sometimes exhibited more independence than suited his princely ideas of decorum. Indeed, he not unfrequently found the popular voice rather formidable against the attainment of some of his wishes; and it would have been well if parliament had taken a lesson from former and better times in this particular. In the works of our oldest honest historians, we find very plain language used by parliaments to their kings, and the latter generally receiving the sharpest rebukes for their vanity and partiality,—not as designed affronts, but as wholesome chastisements. Matthew Paris tells us, when Henry the Third asked for money to defray the expenses of a foreign expedition, "which his people thought did not at all concern England," that his parliament told him, "It was very imprudent in him to ask money for any such purposes, and thereby impoverishing his subjects at home, by his squandering it in idle expeditions, and that they flatly refused supplying him on any such account." Upon thus remonstrating, "that he had engaged his royal word to go abroad in person that year, and that he must have a supply," they asked him, "What has become of all the money your majesty has had already, and how it comes to be lavished without this kingdom being one shilling the better?" But the freedom with which the people treated their sovereigns in those days was not confined to remonstrances. One of the greatest and most victorious of our princes, Edward the First, had an inordinate desire of making, in person, a campaign in Flanders, that he might support a confederacy he had entered into, to reduce the power of France, and had demanded an extraordinary supply for that purpose. The people, conceiving the quarrel to be very indifferent to England, strongly opposed his leaving the kingdom upon any such idle expedition. "The people of England," said the parliament, "do not think it proper for you to go to Flanders, unless you can secure out of that country some equivalent, which may indemnify us for the expense." We have a like instance in the reign of that great and powerful king, Henry the Second. This prince being strongly tempted to make an expedition abroad, in person, became so fond of the proposal that he laid it before his parliament, with a most earnest request for their consent, "it being the sole and darling purpose of his heart!" But his parliament, honest to the people, thought that he had no business abroad, and "that it was much better for him to keep the money at home." Accordingly, the question was put and carried, for "An address to the king to keep within his own dominions, according to his duty." Edward the Third likewise received several mortifications of the like kind; and it appears from the whole tenor of history, that the great care of our ancestors was to root from the breast of their kings every principle of vain glory, which, the more ridiculous it is, becomes generally the more expensive to the nation. What an amazing contrast, then, does all this offer to the proceedings of the parliament of George the Fourth, who generally addressed him

Nicholas Vansittart, 1st Baron Bexley.
(*National Library of Wales*)

in the most adulatory language, and gave him money to gratify all his inordinate vanity. But the House of Commons, during his reign, spoke not the sentiments of the PEOPLE.

At the commencement of the year

1823,

some friends of the late ill-fated queen addressed Mr. Canning upon the subject of certain letters and papers, preserved from the period of her majesty leaving this country in 1814. Mr. Canning, however, did not think proper to reply to this communication. At the expiration of two months, another respectful inquiry was submitted, but it also shared the fate of its predecessor. A third expostulatory epistle was forwarded, and a certain individual received an anonymous reply, saying, "Things were changed; times were altered; and it was impossible that Mr. Canning could serve the king and the cause of the person so much disliked by his majesty!" This circumstance affords indubitable proof, that a man in office can never prove himself free from the trammels of party, or unwarped by elevation to power. Humanity and generosity were, however, alike forgotten in this case for *interested* motives,—a meanness which no man of integrity would have committed. But, to any one acquainted with the truckling arts of Mr. Canning, such conduct was no more than might have been expected.

Early in this year, Mr. Vansittart was released from the *fatigues* of the financial department, and raised to the chancellorship of the duchy of Lancaster, at the same time sinking his humble name for the more agreeable title of Lord Bexley. Mr. Robinson succeeded him in the Exchequer, and Mr. Huskisson was appointed president of the Board of Trade. The latter changes gave the public much pleasure, as those individuals were supposed to possess a manly sense of propriety, as well as liberal opinions, from which the country hoped to reap some benefit in financial and commercial administration.

Very soon after these political arrangements were completed, the royal family were much annoyed by applications on behalf of the *protégé* of her late majesty, William Austin, as the trifling income he received was not sufficient to support him in comfort and respectability. But, although he had been left her majesty's residuary legatee, his claims were totally disregarded.

Notwithstanding the bold language used in memorials and private addresses to the king at this time, the interest and happiness of the population of this mighty empire were treated as subjects of no consequence. The besotted "Prince of Dandies" was rioting in luxury and adulterous embraces, and neither felt nor cared for public distress. He was too great, *in his own estimation*, to condescend to men of low estate; he was too mighty to listen to the cry of the destitute; and too noble to heed the incessant petitions of the rabble, as all those who complained of existing grievances were denominated by him and his ministers. But the "accomplished gentleman" was not above receiving half the peasant's loaf; and, like the locust, he made the increase of the land his prey. It was *acknowledged* in the House of Commons that the coronation expenses amounted to two hundred and thirty-eight thousand pounds! and that even the DRESS of the monarch, for whom such a mighty show was made, cost twenty-four thousand pounds!!! This abominable expenditure, too, was for the *honour* of George the Fourth, whose excesses and debaucheries would have disgraced the most debased of his subjects,—the man who had dishonestly permitted the most valuable jewel to be extracted from the crown of England, to bestow upon the *lusty person* of his mistress. A beautiful jewel, that formerly belonged to his deceased daughter Charlotte, was also given to this same *kind* lady. The jewel belonging to the crown was, upon compulsion only, afterwards restored, but the other is still retained! Some celebrated jewellers, not ten miles from Ludgate Hill, could bear testimony, that the choicest trinkets in their possession were culled, by this "Prince of Abominations," for presents to his mistresses and confidants. Such, however, was the easy character of the English nation, that they submitted to the absolute command of a tinselled despot, and became dupes to custom.

The misrule of the year

1824

opened with the unfortunate ratification of the "movements" in Italy and Spain, which tended to consolidate arbitrary power throughout Europe, so that the Continent might be considered as one federal despotism, each state possessing its peculiar coercive government, under the controul of the "Holy Alliance," improperly so called.

The public now lost an uncompromising friend in Thomas, Lord Erskine, who died on the 17th of January, in the 74th year of his age. His lordship was not a favourite with the king; his sentiments were of too liberal a cast for George the Fourth's ideas of subjection and tyranny. Neither did Lord Erskine ever become a welcome visiter at the palace, because the court-minions knew that he despised intrigue and villany. The poison of the court was of too malignant a character for his lordship. There, all direct terms were disused in discourse, and distant insinuations supplied their place. Every shining reputation was sure to be sullied, and the ministers, as well as the officers of the army, and clergymen of the "Established" church, were perpetually left to the discretion of that sort of people, who, as they could not be useful to the state themselves, suffered none to serve it with reputation and glory. The king himself had no informations but what were conveyed to him by the canal of a few favourites, who acted always in concert together, and even when they seemed to disagree in their opinions, they were only in the province of a single person to their sovereign. A tainted atmosphere like this was, therefore, ill-suited to the enlightened and patriotic mind of Lord Erskine, who proved himself to be a talented and equitable judge, an admirable statesman, and a most accomplished and kind-hearted gentleman. The native sweetness of his disposition inclined him to universal humanity; his unbiassed judgment and his keen penetration well fitted him for the important situation of Lord Chancellor; and his unclouded understanding guided him to support beneficial measures for the people, while his indignant and noble soul poured forth its majestic language on the oppressors of his long-enslaved country. His lordship was ever actuated by the best of motives, while his conduct was free from all party extremes. On the memorable proceedings against Queen Caroline, his lordship freely delivered his sentiments upon their unjustness and wickedness, and we shall never forget the energy with which he closed his eloquent remarks: "All the powers of Europe," said he, "are in array against one deserted, betrayed, and unprotected woman! I am an old man, and have had more experience than most of your lordships in proceedings of this kind; I could not have interest or object in attempting to deceive or mislead you; and, therefore, I shall ever defend myself

Thomas, Lord Erskine. (*National Library of Wales*)

against any imputation which may be directed against the purity of my motives, in doing what I thank my God I have done, and which, under similar circumstances, if unhappily they occurred, I should repeat." The freshness and vigour of youth glistened in his lordship's eye as these words burst from his lips, which proclaimed him deserving of being numbered among the venerated champions of our injured and oppressed queen.

We have also to record the death of another determined enemy of tyranny, in the person of Lord Byron, who expired at Missolonghi, on the 19th of April, after an illness of ten days. His lordship had rendered himself highly popular among the Greeks by his pecuniary and personal services in their good cause, and, to show their great respect for his worth, and sorrow for his loss, they would not permit the celebration of their usual festivities at Easter. His lordship's genius as a poet is freely acknowledged; but, though he possessed many public and private virtues, they have been but little estimated, while the tongue of Slander has enlarged upon his frailties with much greater severity than they really deserved. As we were personally intimate with his lordship, we may be allowed to know something of his private sentiments and opinions, and we willingly testify to the exalted ideas he entertained in the cause of universal freedom and equitable government, as well as to his general benevolence and kindness of heart. In religion, his lordship avowed himself a free thinker, a determined enemy to pious fraud and cant, and a despiser of all prosecutions, having for their object the stifling of conscientious opinion. These liberal sentiments called forth the pious rage of many ignorant and intolerant ministers of the gospel, who attempted to darken his bright fame by their bigotted tirades against his pretended infidelity, as well from the PULPIT as in their numerous vituperating pamphlets. Such a system of enforcing the mild and benevolent doctrines of Christianity, however, will work no conversions but on those whose minds are clouded by the baneful effects of ignorance. The gigantic power of Lord Byron's genius could not tamely endure the thraldom of being confined to certain modes of narrow-minded faith. He felt that he had a right to examine and to judge for himself in matters of such vital importance to his eternal peace, and for which no one should have condemned him. If his lordship occasionally expressed his indignation at religious prosecutors and Pharisees, ought it, therefore, to be inferred that he was an infidel? No real Christian, we are convinced, would so demean himself; and from the intolerant portion of religious professors, his lordship's fame has little to fear. Posterity will be the best judge of such matters, as it will be sure to discard all private acrimony and party feeling; to its award, therefore, we shall confidently look for a removal of the stigma of "INFIDEL" from the character of the illustrious author of "Childe Harold."

Would that it were in our power, before closing the account of this year, to record the passing of some beneficial act for relieving the oppressed people of England; but we cannot. Our ministers seemed as resolutely determined as ever to plunge and flounder onward in the track that had already procured them the detestation of the British public, and effected the ruin and misery of our once-flourishing and happy country. Looking backward upon their conduct, nothing could be seen but political turpitude; the present was pregnant with wretchedness; but, in contemplating the future, the patriot was animated to exertion by the cheering star of Hope. The baneful influence of the cabinet over our legislative assemblies, the time-serving

Reproduction of Theodoros Vryzakis's painting of Lord Byron's arrival at Missolonghi completed in 1861. The original is held in the National Gallery of Athens. (*Wikimedia Commons*)

politics of our church dignitaries and their dependants, and the sycophantic spirit of all those who came within the vortex of the court, formed in themselves a combination of evils, to remove which would indeed require the united moral energies of the people.

The king, as usual, was hunting after the most frivolous pleasures, and gave himself no manner of concern about the grievances of his people. How applicable is the language of Cowper to this vitiated monarch:

> "King though he be,
> And king of England, too, he may be weak,—
> May exercise amiss his proper powers,
> Or covet more than freemen choose to grant;
> Beyond that mark is TREASON!"[11]

That derogatory doctrine, however, which proclaims "the king can do no wrong," has proved the evil genius of liberty, and the very soul of despotism. George the Fourth ever made it his shield, and was content to let the odium of his actions fall upon his ministers. But his majesty should have recollected that a king of England is not king by hereditary right. The nation is not a patrimony. He was not king by his own power, but by the power of the LAW. All the authority he possessed was given him by the law, under whose protection alone he reigned. It may, therefore, seem surprising that this monarch so frequently dared to outrage the very power to which he owed his existence as a king; but it is still more surprising that the people permitted him to do it with impunity: for no king ought to have been allowed

> "To smother Justice, property devour,
> And trample Law beneath the feet of Power;
> Scorn the restraint of oaths and promis'd right,
> And ravel compacts in the people's sight;
> For he's a TYRANT!—and the PEOPLE FOOLS,
> Who basely bend to be that tyrant's tools!"

This is, indeed, powerful language; the importance of the subject was deeply felt by the poet; but its truth will plead the best justification of the censure. George the Fourth unhappily considered himself of a different species to the rest of mankind, and lost all the natural feelings of our nature for his subjects. Blinded with prejudices, the truth stung him like a scorpion; his wounded pride instantly took the alarm, and the rash intruder upon his dignity and his pleasures was sure to be dismissed with hauteur, if not ever after denied the royal presence. This was, indeed, a lamentable state of things; but which, however, had one consolation: it was impossible that it could continue much longer; for if nothing else happened, its own iniquity would be sure to produce its destruction.

We now enter upon the year

1825,

the eleventh of peace, though not of plenty. It is true that public opinion now began to gain considerable ascendency, though every possible advantage was taken to undermine the *liberty of the press*, and heavy fines were imposed upon various persons for publishing facts disreputable to the lordlings in power.

In the January of this year, several most respectable individuals expressed an earnest desire to press for a public inquiry into the mysterious and hitherto-unaccounted-for death of her royal highness the Princess Charlotte. Among the rest was Lord Tullamore, who obtained an audience of the Earl of Liverpool for this purpose on the 18th. The premier, at first, treated his lordship with much coolness and reserve; but when Lord Tullamore mentioned the letter of Queen Charlotte to Dr. Sir Richard Croft, the noble earl exhibited signs of the most acute pain, and became dreadfully agitated. His lordship eagerly inquired if that letter was forthcoming; and admitted, that the subject had been mentioned to him before, but that the party was not so respectable as the present. Lord Tullamore then repeated those words from the other letter to the doctor—"Come, my boy, throw physic to the dogs,"—when the earl became so confused and embarrassed, that it was quite evident he was well acquainted with the contents of both those letters. Previous to Lord Tullamore's retiring from this audience, the premier requested to know if he had Queen Charlotte's letter in his possession, to which Lord Tullamore replied, that his instructions went no further. Though suffering exceedingly from the gout in his feet, the Earl of Liverpool politely rose from his seat, pressed his lordship's hand, called him his dear lord, and hoped to see him again.

When detailing the particulars of this interview on the ensuing day, Lord Tullamore said, that the noble earl had certainly admitted the fact of THE MANNER OF THE DEATH OF THE PRINCESS!

Shortly afterwards, a second interview took place with the same noblemen, when Lord Liverpool was more composed, and said the business did not rest with him, but that it must be investigated in the office of the secretary, by Mr. Peel. His lordship then, saying he was in haste, took leave of Lord Tullamore in the kindest manner, very different from the cool and reserved demeanour and address so conspicuous upon his *first reception*. Immediate application was made at Mr. Peel's office, but *that* secretary was not in the administration when the melancholy event occurred, and therefore could not be responsible for any circumstance attending it!!

Let the unprejudiced reader duly weigh this simple statement of facts, and judge dispassionately. Lord Liverpool was first lord of the Treasury at this time, as well as at the period of the princess' death; he was, therefore, of necessity the principal actor in all state business; he well knew that a secretary of state was answerable only for circumstances and transactions in his department during his secretaryship; no one could be amenable for that which occurred at the period his predecessor held office. Yet this premier, by the most unmanly and guilty-looking subterfuge, put off all inquiry upon such an important subject, pretending that it did not belong to his department, and then referring it to a secretary, by whom Lord Liverpool well knew the matter could not be investigated, for the reasons before mentioned. In consequence of these shuffling contrivances against justice, this most serious inquiry was negatived, while every principle of right was set at open defiance, and the most honourable of the community privately insulted. One fact, however, may clearly be deduced from this circumstance: that Lord Liverpool was TOO WELL INFORMED upon all this most heart-rending tragedy, and he therefore, for his own sake, put off the inquiry, hoping the subject would be either forgotten, or adverted to in a more agreeable manner.

While these unsuccessful attempts were making to obtain a public inquiry into the cause of the Princess Charlotte's death, the well-paid court-minions were busily employed in calumniating the characters of every person engaged in so laudable an undertaking. The most unfounded reports were industriously circulated to wound their good names, while reasons, the farthest from the truth, were injuriously assigned to blacken their motives. Yet, if we take into account the wickedness and voluptuousness of the court at this period, as well as the imbecility and arrogancy of the king's ministers, Surprise will naturally give way to Disgust, and Anger wonder at Toleration. The Junius that exposed and animadverted upon the ministerial delinquencies of a Bedford and a Grafton, a Sandwich and a Barrington, neither knew, nor could possibly imagine, the incomparably bolder task of doing justice to the public and private turpitude of a Liverpool and a Sidmouth, a Bathurst and a Canning, a Wellington and a Bexley, an Eldon and a Melville! To paint the characters of these men in their true colours would, indeed, be a difficult task. Our darkest tints and our deepest shades would give but a faint outline of the blackness of the originals. When we look back upon the accumulated burthens, the ills upon property and patience which they inflicted, what an ocean of insults and what a wild waste of oppressions do we behold! The three grand pillars of the state *in its purity*, and the people *in their freedom*, were nearly demolished. Magna Charta, the Bill of Rights, and the Family Compact, were scrolls mouldering on the shelves of these ministers, and ready to be swept out of their several departments, together with the copies of their oaths "to advise their royal master according to the dictates of their consciences,"—consciences, the only proof of the existence of which was given in their constant violation. If it be urged, that Lord Sidmouth, who was the home-secretary at the death of the Princess Charlotte, was not in office at the time of Lord Tullamore's interview with the premier, we can only say, his power to do harm was as great as if he had been, if not greater, and that he took especial care to exert himself strenuously, that no "inquiry" about the Princess Charlotte should be instituted.

The premier, at this eventful period, was eager to engage the assistance of all his Tory friends, whether in or out of office, to enable him to bolster up his own misrule. The ancient author who correctly observed, that "there are vices of MEN and vices of TIMES," would have improved, as well as have enlarged, his maxim by adding, that "bad times are made by bad men." Of the truth, that "bad rulers too often make a mean people," the ministerial subjugation of nations has afforded innumerable evidences. But, with science and the manual arts, the knowledge of the best means of banishing liberty and liberal sentiments had now wonderfully advanced. The proficiency in despotism to which the Earl of Liverpool and his junto had attained certainly entitled them to take precedence of any anterior ministry. These men, throughout their whole conduct, from the highest down to the humblest of their misdeeds,—whether they betrayed the king who received their services, or the people who paid their salaries,—whether they dishonoured the crown by insulting a virtuous queen, or injured the country by screening public plunderers and private murderers,—whether they outraged justice by acquitting the guilty and convicting the innocent,—were ever true to themselves. With all their arts, however, they could not destroy the SPIRIT of our free constitution; for that will ever remain immovably fixed in the British bosom. The flame whose rays shot hence across the Atlantic can never be wholly extinguished. The sparks with which England herself animated the hearts of her regenerated colonists, warmly cherished by every American, will never cease to feed the parent fire. Lord Liverpool might have assisted to re-burthen France with the hated Bourbons, and other parts of the Continent with their legitimate despots; but this could only last for a time. The fire of liberty was but smothered for a season, as after events have sufficiently attested.

It will assuredly be matter of great surprise to posterity, how men of such circumscribed talents as were to be found in the cabinet of the Earl of Liverpool should find it possible to effect so much mischief. But Fortune delights in maintaining a sort of rivalship with Wisdom, and piques herself on her power to favour fools as well as knaves. These beings, however, were indebted to various aids for their long and too successful career; yet their principal dependance rested on the supineness of the people. The generous forbearance of Englishmen unhappily cherished the power which their patriotic vengeance should have destroyed. They were looking for gratuitous justice and liberality, instead of deserving relief by the ardour and nobleness of their own exertions. Had Britons but borne in mind that "zeal, without *action*, is nothing worth," their condition had been very different to what it was at the period of Lord Tullamore's praiseworthy attempts to obtain an inquiry into one of the blackest crimes recorded in our annals; for Thought is the projector, and Faith the encourager, of all our views and wishes; though it is only Action that can render them effectual and profitable.

At the period of Lord Tullamore's interviews with the premier, the Marchioness of Conyngham held an entire and very injurious sway over the actions of our voluptuous monarch; her will soon became an absolute law, and, to supply means for this lady's insatiable wishes, the nation was burthened beyond all honourable limits. Yet, strange to say, one of her ladyship's sons, Lord Mountcharles, professed himself most anxious to be entrusted with the previously-named "INQUIRY." His lordship was, consequently, allowed to undertake that the matter should be investigated; but no sooner had the marchioness' son obtained an interview with George the Fourth, than he hypocritically said, "The inquiry into the death of the Princess Charlotte is all useless. You may rely upon it, the idea has originated in some ungenerous feeling towards his majesty." But, in this particular, my Lord Mountcharles acted dishonourably to the trust reposed in him. From undoubted authority, WE KNOW that George the Fourth received Lord Mountcharles into his friendship *to prevent the further elucidation of this matter*,—at least, as far as his lordship was concerned. Another of the *professed* friends of justice, also, who was known to have been a witness upon this business, was speedily afterwards enlisted under the "royal banner," and, though previously *poor* and in "holy orders," soon found abundant means to play for no trivial sums in St. James. But his principles may be more correctly ascertained by the fact that, after receiving the most generous services from his friends, he was mean enough to abscond from his bail, when fifty pounds was offered for his apprehension. Such was the Reverend Joseph B——, whose apostacy in this common cause fixes upon his name eternal discredit. Yet, notwithstanding his dissolute habits, this clergyman has very frequently occupied a seat at the table of Lord Teynham, and was in the habit of receiving considerable attentions from many of the lordlings in power. If his word might be deemed worthy of credit, he was no stranger to the friendship of his royal highness the Duke of Sussex, and other branches of the royal family. But of one point, we are well assured, that he who was mean enough to desert a post of duty, though it might be a post of danger, to revel in ease and luxury, was, at least, undeserving the notice of any honourable man. However strange it may appear, this divine (so called) was most unceasing in his endeavours to rouse the country to a due sense of the impositions forced upon it, declaring all consequent sufferings would be "light as dust in the balance," compared to the tortures of a guilty and harassed conscience. Thus, under the mask of religion and patriotism, did this faithless character hide his real sentiments and intentions, and while professing to serve the cause of liberty, he was in reality the aider and abettor of tyrants,—dishonourable in his engagements, and a disgrace to his order. We may pity and even forgive his want of honour to his friends; but the subject from which he shrunk was of such vast national importance, that his desertion of the cause of justice and his dereliction from the path of duty in this matter must always be considered as unpardonable offences.

Such vacillating conduct, however, we are sorry to record, was not confined to the two gentlemen just mentioned. Many, whose prospects of aggrandizement appeared upon the wane, exhibited an anxiety to ascertain the probable result of this inquiry. Amongst this number, was a fashionable fortune-hunter, who boasted of being the illegitimate son of a royal duke,—the sudden and unexpected death of whom, it was currently reported, had left this unfortunate offspring totally unprovided for. Added to a tolerably honest appearance and pleasant address, this gentleman possessed considerable talent, which he could exemplify in farce, comedy, or tragedy, as the circumstances might require. In the words of Lord Byron, "he had ten thousand names, and twice as many attributes." He also professed himself the uncompromising enemy of oppressors, and as being ever ready to hazard his life in bringing the murderers of the Princess Charlotte to their merited punishment. But exteriors are too frequently deceptive, and this self-styled patriot was ultimately proved unworthy of the notice of any respectable person. Under false pretences, he found means to reach "the board of hospitality," fed upon the ample provision, and then, like the reptile of eastern climes, stung the benevolent hand that had furnished the sources for his enjoyment, by an attempt to defame one of the proudest and most noble characters our country can boast!

Would that we had no more instances of treachery to offer; but too many others might be given of persons, calling themselves *professional* gentlemen,—particularly one residing in Duke-street, St. James',—who, after volunteering their services to bring this "hidden thing of darkness to light," forsook their friends, and accepted a BRIBE as a reward for their silence. We could also extend our record of mean expedients adopted by men in power to suppress this disgraceful business,—such, indeed, as would almost stagger the faith of those who had not been eye-witnesses of their depravity. Indignation rises in our breasts while contemplating such a picture of human wickedness! Our readers, we feel assured, do not desire more proofs than we have already given of the principal fact,—that the Princess Charlotte was poisoned, through the instrumentality of those who ought to have been the first to protect so amiable and virtuous a woman! It is, therefore, only a matter of minor importance to expose those who have failed in their loud professions of seeing justice enforced on her murderers. No history, perhaps, is richer in recorded crime than that of our own country; but neither the annals of this or any other empire can furnish a more striking instance of unmanly barbarity, of greater wickedness, or of more horrid depravity, than that of which we are now speaking. Let us hope the people of 1832 will seriously reflect on the enormity of this revolting act, and be no longer lost in an apathy that has already proved so disastrous to their liberties. Let them not suffer their good sense to be lulled and amused by the "raree-shows" of royalty, or by the glitter of any grandeur supplied by the produce of their own labour. Nothing confers, either on a king or his ministers, any real dignity or glory, except their virtue and their good deeds; and the people ought, therefore, not to suffer their courage to be deterred, or their judgment to be imposed upon, by the pomp and glare of state ostentation. The people, we say, ought now to make amends for their long neglect, and exhibit a stronger and more determinate resolution than ever for that "inquiry" which Lord Liverpool so often refused; for, so long as the death of the Princess Charlotte remains unavenged, so long will cowardice and ignominy be attached to the name of Englishman!

In the month of April, Mr. Brougham visited his native country, for the purpose of being invested with the title of "Lord Rector of the University of Glasgow." We should not have noticed a circumstance of such trivial importance to the public, did it not afford us an opportunity of introducing a most admirable speech, which that learned gentleman had an opportunity of delivering on the occasion by reason of some allusion being made to the trial of the late Queen Caroline. To explain the impropriety of calling such persecuting proceedings a "trial," Mr. Brougham said,

> "If he could bring himself, on such a day as this, to those habits of contentious discussion to which he was sometimes accustomed, he should have to analyze his friend's splendid speech, and object to the whole of his eulogy. But there was one part of that speech which had caused him considerable pain: his friend had talked of 'the trial' of the late queen. Never had he (Mr. Brougham) either

in public or private, before heard so great a profanation of the attributes of those judicial proceedings, which by profession and habit he had been taught to revere, than to use the name of 'trial' when speaking of such an event. It was no trial, he said, and so did the world. The subject was gone by, and not introduced by him; but still the phrase, when dropped, must be corrected; for 'trial' it was none. Was that a trial where the accused had to plead before those who were interested in her destruction?—where those who sat on the bench of justice, aye, and pretended to be her judges, had pre-ordained her fate? Trial!" continued Mr. Brougham, "I repeat there was, there could be, none, where every channel of defamation was allowed to empty itself upon the accused, borne down by the strong arm of power, overwhelmed by the alliance of the powers and the princedoms of the state, and defended only by that *innocence* and that law which those powers and those princedoms, united with the powers of darkness, had combined to destroy. Trial it was none, where every form of justice was obliged to be broken through on the very surface before the accusers could get at the imputed grounds of their accusations. This, forsooth, a trial!—call it not so, for the sake of truth and law. While that event deformed the page of their history, let them be silent about eastern submissiveness; let them talk not of Agas, the Pachas, and the Beys,—all judges, too, at least so they call themselves,—while they were doomed to remember they had had in their own times ministers of their own crown, who, under the absolute authority of their own master, consented to violate their own pledge, to compromise and stifle their own avowed feelings, and to act as slaves, crouching before the foot-stool of power, to administer to its caprice. Let them call that a trial which was so conducted, and then he would say the queen had been tried at the time when he stood for fifty-six days witnessing the sacrilegious proceeding. Did he now, for the first time, utter this description of its character? No, no; day after day did he repeat it in the presence of all the parties, and dared them to deny the imputation; he dared them then, but not now, lest he should be forced to see the same faces in the same place again, professing to exercise the same functions. If it were in his power to repeat in their hearing now what he had said in their presence before, they might, indeed, call that a trial in his case which they had called it in the other; but to whom it looked not like a chamber of justice, but rather the gloominess of the den; not indeed of judgment, for he could not liken it to such, but rather to others—(here Mr. Brougham paused)—But no, he could not sustain the allusion, lest, perchance, for the very saying of it, (for he could not be prevented from thinking of it so) he should again have to submit to the test of power,—an alternative which his veneration for the constitution of his country and its honours forbade him to precipitate.

"How many long years," said Mr. Brougham, "had they not seen, when to be an Englishman on the Continent was a painful, if not a degrading, condition? He meant, during that dark and murky night of power, when the machinations of the family of the tyrants of Europe were at work, and when they could reckon upon the minister of England as silently suffering, nay, permitting their deadly march against the liberties of mankind. England then had her fair name degraded by being considered as the ABETTOR of every tyrant's plan for the subjugation of his subjects. Then was the time when no despot could open his glaring eye, flashing with vengeance for his prey, without catching the glistening eye of the supplicant British minister. Then was the time when no tyrant could hold out his hand, after shaking in it the chains he had forged to bind and excoriate his people, without its meeting the cordial grasp of friendship of the British minister. Then was the time when the oppressor stalked abroad with the countenance of the rulers of that land, which was called the champion and the protectress of the free. Then did horrid tyranny, more grim in its blasted actions than even in the vices of its original debasement, disfigure the fair face of Europe, while linked and leagued (O, shame upon the pen of history!) with the freest government upon earth,—to which, nevertheless, the tyrant never turned his glance, or stretched his hand in vain, during such disastrous times. That black and disgraceful night of intellect and freedom had now gone down, the sky was clear, and the view was changed into a brighter prospect. Now," continued Mr. Brougham, "we can *speak out*, and look abroad with clear vision. What man is there now, I ask, in half-represented England, in unrepresented Scotland,—aye, where and which of you, in either country, or even in tortured, insulted, and persecuted Ireland,—where, I say, can the man be found, who dared to look forth in the broad face of day, who dared to raise his voice before his fellow-men, and say, '*I befriend the Holy Alliance?*' Not only, I repeat, is there no such man, I will not say so wicked, but so childish,—I will not say so stricken with hostility to free principles, or so bent upon the destruction of his own individual character,—in the whole walk of society, as to avow such sentiments. O, no; not out of Bedlam could we find him!—hardly there, save in the precipitation of a maniac's rage, could we behold a being in the shape of a man to stand up and say, '*I am the friend of the Holy Alliance.*' If there be the man where freedom shines, who could look with complaisance on the accomplished despot who fills the Calmuc throne, who can behold with meekness that specious and ungrateful imbecility which promised first, and then refused, free institutions to the Germans who had bled and died in thousands to restore his throne; if there be any man who can approve the scourge of fair Italy, and the tyrant of Austria; if there be, I repeat, any such man, so reckless of himself as to admire or approve, (for that is out of the maddest rage of speculation) but even to *tolerate* the mere mention of the name of that cruel tyrant of his people at home,—the baffled despot, thank God! of South America,—but whose sway it pleased Providence still to permit at home, and to suspend for a short season the doom of that nameless despot. If there be a man, I say, so monstrous and unnatural as to approve of these royal minions, then it was a consolation to know that he had the grace to confine his thoughts to the regions best adapted for their culture, to lock them up in the innermost recesses of the offices of state, or to confine his silent migrations to the merest purlieus of the court, or perchance to lurk 'behind the arras,' to live there among the vermin which were its natural tenants, and there to gloat upon the merits of Alexander, Frederick, Francis, or Ferdinand,—have I named him?—among the spiders, the vipers, the toads, and those who hated the toads, the lizards. To such an association and contact were these lovers of despots confined; not a word of approbation from any member of the government could be extorted for them. He had often seen much ability and ingenuity devised and exercised to endeavour to get out even a smooth word in favour of the Holy Alliance in parliament; but no, the attempt was fruitless,—all cheered the sentiments which were breathed against these tyrants. So that whoever loved them 'behind the arras,' had at least, if not the better principle, the better taste,— was, if not better in demeanour, at least more ashamed in practice to avow himself as their champion, and rather to prefer to hide himself from that sun of day, which would almost feel disgraced by being compelled to shine upon him in common with the better part of mankind."

The facts and well-merited castigations contained in this most eloquent address were not very creditable to the character of the voluptuous king and his servile ministers. Mr. Brougham here uttered some startling TRUTHS, and accompanied their recital with that keenness of remark for which he is so famous. We need hardly say how heartily we agree with him in the detestation he expressed against the queen's persecutors. Would that he had performed HIS OWN PART more consistently with her majesty's wishes and interests!

On the 6th of March, Science mourned the death of her favourite son, in the Reverend Doctor Samuel Parr, a celebrated philologist, erudite classical scholar, and a profound mathematician, in the 79th year of his age. The weekly, monthly, and annual registers, did not forget to name the transcendent merits of the deceased in *literary pursuits*; but they either forgot or declined to mention the interest this worthy gentleman had taken in the cause of the Princess of Wales, and also after she became Queen of England. The memorials and testimonies of Doctor Parr in her cause were not chimerical opinions, as some have imagined, but the real sentiments of his honest and manly heart.

The close of this eventful year was marked with unprecedented calamity. The "panic," as it was briefly termed, which prevailed in the city of London, seemed to have overtaken the most wealthy of its inhabitants, and poverty and consternation appeared in all their terrors. The political horizon was also of the most foreboding and gloomy character. The "House of Incurables," however, still arrogantly boasted of the "freedom and prosperity of the nation," and shut their eyes against all the proofs of a contrary nature.

There was a time when some atonement for unjust acts would have been instantly demanded from the sovereign by the people; for we read in "Rapin," that Edward the Second, when conquered and made prisoner by his wife, was tried by the parliament, which decreed, "that (though kings are supposed *incapable* of doing wrong) he had done all possible wrong, and thereby must forfeit his right to the crown." Again, for the sake of illustration, we may mention, that the parliament tried and *convicted* Richard the Second; thirty-one articles were alleged against him, in the form of an impeachment, two of which were very remarkable, though perhaps not uncommon; the first was, "that he had BORROWED MONEY WITHOUT INTENDING TO PAY IT AGAIN!!!" the other, "that he had declared, before witnesses, he was master of the lives and property of his subjects." What a lesson, also, does the wretched death of our first Charles offer of the imbecility of kings, and of their blind contempt for the people, from whom their crowns and their wealth must always be derived. But, with some men, example is disregarded, and advice neglected, if not despised. George the Fourth, for instance, reckless of all consequences, appears to have held it as a maxim, "I am determined to make every body as miserable as I can; and, so long as all my wants are supplied, no matter from what source they are derived!"

At an early part of

1826,

the Duke of Devonshire attended the coronation of the despotic Nicholas, since the murderer of the brave Poles, as the representative of George the Fourth, King of England; and his splendid retinues and sumptuous fêtes created no little astonishment in the Russian capital at John Bull's extravagance.

In January, his majesty *returned* one thousand pounds of the public money, to relieve the distressed Spitalfields weavers, who were suffering every possible hardship from the want of employment. We feel great pleasure in recording every instance of the *charitable* intentions of this king, entertaining no fear of being wearied with their detail. We should be equally happy, were it in our power, to record the payment of those loans and promissory notes, to which this personage had subscribed while Prince of Wales. It is a good old maxim, "Be *just* before you are *generous*;" and we cannot help thinking, that if the "first gentleman in the world" had given his accommodating ladies a little less, and satisfied the demands of the holders of those bonds, he would have acted more "as became a man." But no; his kingly dignity kept him aloof from the civil proceedings of his foreign creditors, and, being a stranger to honour, the documents were left undischarged!

The king at this period being reported unwell, the parliament was opened by commission. His majesty's indisposition could hardly be wondered at, when the gay life he had led was taken into consideration. Besides, as he was now getting into the "sear and yellow leaf," it might naturally be supposed that the prickings of Conscience sometimes annoyed him into bodily pain. Indeed, though the fact was only known to a few persons at court, his majesty had long been getting into a very low and desponding state, and frequently appeared lost in abstraction, from which he was but seldom relieved by shedding tears! He knew that there were blemishes upon his escutcheon, which, though he had long been able to conceal them by bribery and trickery, might some day or another be exposed to the rude gaze of the multitude. He had long unsheathed the sword of oppression against his suffering people, and he could not possibly tell at what period it might be lifted against his royal self.

The Tory government of persecuted England still appeared to think that the persons composing their *Sanhedrim* were the only interested individuals in giving and opposing laws. But had not every Englishman a direct interest in the affairs of government? If government should act a part that might endanger the safety of the community, surely every man's property would be equally at stake. All national affairs, therefore, ought to be conducted with a view to the *general* good, and not for the mere aggrandizement of a privileged and self-elected set of hirelings. When *secret missions* were the order of the day, as was the case at this period, the public might be assured that "something was rotten in the state of Denmark!" for state secrecy is always the forerunner of evil to the people. But no men of upright principles were to be found in George the Fourth's cabinet. We do not mean to say that England did not possess such characters, but then they had taken the advice of the poet,

> "When evil men bear sway,
> The post of honour is a private station!"

When the Chancellor of the Exchequer brought forward his budget this year, the galleries and lobbies of the House of Commons were actually converted into a "Stock Exchange." We need not offer a remark upon this circumstance,—the intelligent reader will draw his own inferences from such an exhibition. Shortly after this, the House proposed "that five thousand pounds per annum be added to the salary of Mr. Huskisson." Repeated discussion ensued, but the proposition was finally abandoned, and two thousand pounds only agreed to. Mr. Huskisson was undoubtedly a man of great talent; yet he was already in the receipt of a sufficient remuneration for the exercise of that talent, as he then enjoyed *two* incomes from the people: as treasurer to the navy, three thousand pounds, and as president of the Board of Controul, five thousand pounds, making together the *annual* amount of eight thousand pounds! Some people, however, are not to be satisfied, as Mr. Huskisson said, that he felt considerable anxiety and *hardship* arising from the union of the two offices or situations, and that, from the great pecuniary responsibility attached to the treasurer of the navy, the two offices were more than he could possibly attend to! "Then," *modestly* added the president, "the pay-master is an officer fully acquainted with the details of business, and perfectly familiar with all the operations necessary for the proper and effective management of the department." We do not doubt the verity of this remark, or dispute the qualifications of Mr. Huskisson for *one* of the offices; yet we cannot help thinking it was a *little* slip of the tongue, when this gentleman said, "I cannot say from *my own knowledge* whether, at this moment, matters are going on *right or wrong* in my office, but I have entire confidence in the *pay-master*." This curious confession of Mr. Huskisson proved that he enjoyed the emoluments arising from a situation, to the business of which he paid little or no attention! Would an unprejudiced and honest administration have exercised the imposing means here set forth? or would any real representatives of the people have sanctioned such mal-practices by their vote?

The manufacturing districts unfortunately continued in a most melancholy and alarming situation. Riots, disorder, and distress, universally prevailed. To relieve the people's grievances, however, the king returned eight thousand pounds more of the public money to the distressed weavers of Spitalfields. But we cannot help thinking, that such an inadequate sort of relief very much resembled a bankrupt's paying one farthing in the pound, and then claiming the gratitude of his ruined creditors!

Let not our readers suppose that the *worthy* parliament were idle this year. The matter printed for the House during its short sitting, from February to May, occupied twenty-nine bulky folio volumes, independent of the journals, votes, private acts, and other matters of equal importance to the nation! In this brief session, also, no less than seventy-nine new acts of parliament were added to the already ponderous and indigestible statute-book. Here was industry indeed! But, good reader, in all this mass of business, not a single act was passed for the amelioration of the distressed condition of the people.

The health of the Duke of York now began to decline; and, although he had been in the receipt of such enormous sums from the people, he was actually destitute of a home,—at least of one he could call his own. Here was a disgraceful circumstance!— the heir presumptive to the throne of England, through his abominable and reckless extravagance, obliged to accept the hospitality of an acquaintance! An accumulation of diseases, arising from excesses of every kind, soon became manifest, and the duke was at length declared to be seriously indisposed. On the 14th December, he was pronounced, by his medical attendants, to be in the most imminent danger.

The revenue was deficient in its returns from the former year, two hundred and thirty-three thousand, nine hundred, and forty pounds! which arose from the very general stagnation of trade and the paralization of commerce. This enormous deficiency in the country's income, however, had no effect upon the men in power; for the most wanton expenditure was still kept up, both at home and abroad. Our ambassadors appeared the very type of their sight-loving and spendthrift master, and thousands were swallowed up in glittering baubles and unmeaning pageantry. At the time the "Dandy of Sixty," (as the ingenious and patriotic Mr. Hone usually termed him) was meditating on the most expeditious way of squandering the hard-earnings of the poor, his wicked and unmanly ministers pampered the royal appetite in all its childish wishes and unconstitutional desires, verifying the words of Pope,

"Fools grant whate'er Ambition craves."

The internal state of the country at the opening of

1827

exhibited the most lowering prospects; for when the people are suffering from oppressive enactments and injurious policy, the country cannot possibly wear a smiling countenance. Some of the milk-sop daily journals, notwithstanding, were very profuse in their complimentary language to royalty, and announced, as a matter of wonderful importance, the kindness and brotherly affection manifested by the king to the Duke of York, as his majesty had spent nearly two hours with his brother at the residence of his Grace of Rutland! What astonishing kindness! what inexpressible condescension that a man should visit his own brother who was at the point of death! But the king's condescension did not put aside the visit of the general conqueror, Death! for the Duke of York expired, at the mansion of the before-named nobleman, on the 5th of January, being then in the sixty-fourth year of his age.

If we were to form our judgment by the eulogiums bestowed on the character of the deceased duke, by the greater portion of the press, he was one of the brightest and most illustrious ornaments of society. But such disgraceful truckling to royalty and the "powers that be" could only tend to degrade the national character in the consideration of all well-informed men, who would observe in such unmerited compliments a convincing proof that Truth was a creditor, whose claims were "more honoured in the breach than in the observance." To prove that our complaints on this head are well-founded, let our readers look over the following outline of the royal duke's virtues, which we copy from "Baldwin's Annual Register for the year 1827:"

"Never was the death of a prince accompanied by more sincere and universal regret; and seldom have the public services of one so near the throne BEQUEATHED TO THE COUNTRY SO MUCH SOLID AND LASTING GOOD, as resulted from his long administration of the British army. His private character, frank, HONOURABLE, and SINCERE, was formed to conciliate personal attachments; a personal enemy he had never made, and a friend once gained, he had never lost. Failings there were: he was improvident in pecuniary matters; his love of pleasure, though it observed the decencies, did not always respect the moralities, of private life; and his errors in that respect had been paraded in the public view by the labours of unwearying malice, and shameless unblushing profligacy. But in the failings of the Duke of York, there was nothing that was un-English, nothing that was un-princely.

"Never was man more easy of access, *more fair and upright in his dealings*, more affable, and even simple, in his manners. Everyone who had intercourse with him was impressed with the openness, sincerity, and kindness, which appeared in all his actions; and it was truly said of him, that *he never broke a promise, and never deserted a friend.* Beloved by those who enjoyed the honour of his private intercourse, his administration of a high public office had excited one universal sentiment of respect and esteem. In his youth, he had been tried as a general in the field. The campaigns in Flanders terminated in a retreat; but the duke,—unexperienced as he was, at the head of an army which, abounding in valour, had yet much to learn in tactics, and compelled to act in concert with allies who were not always either unanimous or decided,—

displayed many of the qualities of an able general, and nobly supported that high character for daring and dauntless courage which is the patrimony of his house. He was subsequently raised to the office of commander-in-chief of all his majesty's forces; that office he held for upwards of thirty-two years, and his administration of it did not merely improve, it literally created, an army. During his campaigns, he had felt keenly the abuses which disgraced its internal organization, and rendered its bravery ineffectual; he applied himself, with a soldier's devotion, to the task of removing them; he identified himself with the welfare and the fame of the service; he possessed great readiness and clearness of comprehension in discovering means, and great steadiness and honesty of purpose in applying them. By unceasing diligence, he gave to the common soldier comfort and respectability; the army ceased to be considered as a sort of pest-house for the reception of moral lepers; discipline and regularity were exacted with unyielding strictness; THE OFFICERS WERE RAISED BY A GRADUAL AND WELL-ORDERED SYSTEM OF PROMOTION, which gave merit a chance of not being pushed aside to make way for mere ignorant rank and wealth. The head as well as the heart of the soldier took a higher pitch; the best man in the field was the most welcome at the Horse Guards; *there was no longer even a suspicion that unjust partiality disposed of commissions*, or that *peculation was allowed to fatten upon the spoils of the men*; the officer knew that one path was open to all, and the private felt that his recompense was secure."

In a similar strain, the writer continues at a far greater length than our patience will allow us to quote. What man of understanding but must have felt disgusted at such a fulsome panegyric, which has not so much as a word of truth to recommend it! We despise the historian who sacrifices his integrity by an attempt to mislead posterity in this manner. It will, however, prove but an attempt; for will posterity overlook the general iniquitous and abandoned conduct of the royal libertine, both abroad and at home?—his cowardice and want of skill in the field?—his tergiversation to his creditors?—his infamous conduct with regard to certain foreign bondholders?—his notorious practices as a seducer?—his gross and unpardonable dereliction of duty at the Horse Guards?—his refusal to inquire into the conduct of the soldiers at the Manchester massacre?—his shameful acceptance of ten thousand pounds a year of the public money, for only calling upon his dying father twice a week, which Earl Grey pronounced to be "an insult to the people to ask it?"—his receiving this sum, and his going down to Windsor with a bible in his carriage, on *pretence* of visiting his royal father after he had ceased to exist?—or his bigotted, ridiculous, and futile opposition to the claims of the Catholics? Will posterity, we repeat, forget to canvass all this, and much more, of which the Duke of York was notoriously guilty?

If we pass over the meanness of the royal duke in accepting payment for visiting his own father, we are naturally led to inquire why this money was paid from the public purse, when the king was allowed sixty thousand pounds per annum for his private demands? Could this fund have been better applied than for the use of him for whom it was voted? If, therefore, it was considered necessary to pay a son for visiting his father, surely such money ought to have been applied for the purpose. Was it justifiable, in times of universal suffering and distress, to raise from an over-taxed and over-burthened people such a sum unnecessarily, when there were funds from which it might have been taken,—funds which must else be diverted from the purpose of their creation, and pass into hands for whom they were not intended? Was it not an insult to the sense of the nation to debate about what might be the feelings of the sovereign, if he should recover from the gloomy condition into which he was plunged by the afflicting hand of providence, and find his money had been so appropriated? Would not his majesty's feelings have been more hurt, in such an event, by his knowing that a reward was necessary to induce a son to take care of his father? Was there no delight in filial affection? Was not the sense of duty powerful enough? Was there no beauty in the common charities of our nature? No loveliness in gratitude? Were the claims of veneration cold?—the warmth of regard frozen? With respect to the country, it presented a serious aspect. Admitting that his royal highness, in the discharge of his office, must attend twenty times a-year at Windsor, then he would be paid five hundred pounds a time for such attendance: a single journey would discharge the wages of a thousand labourers for a week, and the annual salary satisfy twenty thousand for the same period. Would it not have been more beneficial to the state, more conducive to the happiness of society, to have expended the ten thousand pounds in some honourable employment, in the erection of some work of art, that would have called hundreds into action, who were steeped up to the neck in penury, and worn down to the earth by wretchedness, than in forming a salary for the royal duke for doing that which it was his bounden duty to perform? But even this view does not put the question in its broadest light. The sixty thousand pounds set apart as the annual privy purse of the king was now useless to his majesty, for he could no longer recognize his property, direct its disposal, or enjoy it. In fact, during the greater part of the Duke of York's guardianship, his father was a corpse! On what ground, on what pretence, then, could this wicked grant be continued, as well as the accumulation of the sixty thousand pounds a year, for the service of one who no longer needed either? Why, only for the purpose of feeding the inordinate profligacy of the Duke of York, and for the gratification of the regent's malice against his innocent, though calumniated, wife! What, also, will posterity think of Lord Castlereagh's conduct on this occasion, who proposed the disgusting grant to parliament? He stigmatized as infamous the refusal to grant from the *public* purse that which the public *ought not to pay*; thus boldly classing *virtue* with *crime*,—pourtraying *prodigality* to be right,—disguising *corruption* under the mask of honour,—and attempting to cast the dark shade of *infamy* over those few who were honest enough to oppose measures, which justice disapproved, and good policy condemned. By reducing such cases down to the level of common life, we the better discover their injustice and unfold their rapacity. If the constable of a village possessed of a rental, arising from a parochial allowance for his services more than adequate to supply his wants, were deprived of reason, and rendered unfit for his office, and if one of his sons were to declare that he would not superintend the care of his infirm and aged father, unless he was allowed a salary for performing his duty, what would be thought of such a son? But if this son averred that he would not take this salary from his father's allowance, but would demand *it from the parish*, how severe would be the censure that would follow his footsteps, and imprint itself on his name! However difficult it may be found to believe, it is nevertheless a fact, that the Duke of York would only receive the said ten thousand pounds a year from the PUBLIC, and refused to take it from the privy purse of his father. But this privy purse being already drained by his royal elder brother, he had not the opportunity of taking it from that source! Ought the country to have been thus trifled with and plundered, when it was writhing under general distress and an immense load of taxation,—taxation produced by bestowing unmerited pensions and unnecessary salaries? But ministers imagined, that when their countrymen became impoverished, their spirits would get depressed, and their liberties fall an easier prey to their pecuniary plunderers. But why were not bolder exertions made to defeat this grant by those members of the House of Commons who were in the habit of talking loudly of their patriotism? Why was not the unblushing audacity of ministers and their time-serving tools put to the test? Why were they not told that, among all the distressing periods of our history, not one could be mentioned in which the people were less able to sustain any additional burthens,—not one in which it would have been more indecorous, disgraceful, and unfeeling than at that juncture? Why did they not represent how much better it were that a son should pay to his father the attentions dictated by nature, without fee or reward, than that, oppressed as the community already was with the failure of trade and the expenses of government, another shilling of taxation should be added to their burthens? Why did they not ask the Treasury Bench with what face it could talk of retrenchment and economy, while it augmented the weight by which the country was borne down? When we reflect on the scandalous meanness that turned so many poor clerks adrift, while it kept safely floating in the harbour of ease and plenty, men who were doing so little for the public service,—when we consider this, and add to it the circumstance of the Duke of York's unconscionable grant,—when we place together the wretchedness of the ministry's savings, and the enormity of their waste,—our indignation rises at the injustice. We feel that we are Britons; for we feel that we detest such oppression and oppressors. Our hearts are held to the patriotic *minority* by a spontaneous and involuntary attachment, as sure and lasting as our hatred and disdain of that portion of parliament, whose only object in obtaining their seats, and only business in exercising their privileges, was to serve the interest of the ministry at the expense of the people, and to promote and help to perpetuate the mystery and the humiliation, the impoverishment and the slavery, it was their especial duty to prevent or diminish.

Of his royal highness' profligacy and neglect of duty, enough was proved in the exposures of Mrs. Clarke to satisfy the most scrupulous of their enormity. Of his utter recklessness of every honourable principle and disregard of virtue, many families, whose peace he was the cause of ruining, yet live to bear their afflicting testimony. Of his imbecility and cowardness in the field of battle, we need only mention his disastrous and disgraceful campaign in Holland, to call forth the indignation and contempt of every honest man, who must also feel shocked at the number of lives sacrificed to his royal highness' headstrong obstinacy. Of his achievements, particularly after his return from Germany, we believe they were chiefly confined to the parade in St. James' park, and to the Tennis Court in James-street, with pretty frequent relaxation amongst the nymphs of Berkeley-row. Nevertheless, his royal parents early pronounced him the "Hope of the Family;" and once, in an hour of festivity, when this prince was so intoxicated as to fall senseless under the table, his *elegant* and *accomplished* elder brother, with his glass in hand, standing over the fallen soldier, performed the ceremony of baptism, triumphantly and sarcastically exclaiming,

"HERE LIES THE HOPE OF THE FAMILY!"

Of his ridiculous and futile opposition to the Catholics, after times have given abundant proof. And of his getting into debt without the means of paying is a deplorable fact, to which his ruined creditors are even now (in 1832) freely testifying! Would it not have been thought treason had they suspected that the king's son,— the prince who, according to the writer in the "Annual Register," "never broke a promise," "whose failings had nothing in them un-English or un-princely," and "who was fair and upright in his dealings,"—would have treated them as a common swindler, by getting their forbearance during his life, and dying without discharging his obligations? It is true that the duke left some property, which he consigned to his brother, the king, for the purpose of discharging his debts. We also know that the king promised to do so, and to supply any deficiency that might arise; but with what fidelity it was kept, the world is pretty well aware. The extortionate demands of a mercenary mistress were stronger in the eyes of George the Fourth than a solemn engagement made to a brother on his death-bed!

Though the executors of the late duke declared that his freehold and leasehold estates were mortgaged beyond their intrinsic value, nothing satisfactory was said about the jewels of his royal highness, which were valued a very few days after his death, and were calculated as being worth one hundred and fifty thousand pounds. These jewels, we are aware, were carried down to Windsor by desire of his majesty, but how they were disposed of remains to be explained. It was known that a large portion of these valuables had belonged to the Duchess of York in her lifetime, and as some legacies bequeathed by her royal highness at her demise have been paid since the death of her husband, it is inferred that the jewels have been, in some way or other, made available for that purpose. The legality of the application of any part of the personal property of the duke to purposes in which the interests of the creditors at large have not been consulted is, however, very questionable. Some part of the duke's property was bequeathed to his sister Sophia; but how far such a bequest was consistent in a man overwhelmed in debt, or how any honourable woman could accept from a brother that which was not his to give, is a matter totally irreconcilable with our notions of justice and fair dealing. One of these said jewels was also bestowed on the king's mistress, which, whenever and wherever it is recognized, cannot possibly add any lustre to her corpulent charms.

The Duke of York was *elected* Bishop of Osnaburgh when only *eleven months old*; but we leave the reader to judge how *capable* a child of this age was to perform the duties of a bishop! Here, indeed, was a wanton disgrace inflicted on religion and the Established Church of England! If money had been wanted to purchase toys for this baby prince, could it not have been supplied from some more creditable source? We are here naturally led to inquire, who was the *former* Bishop of Osnaburgh? If this question should lead to inquiry among the friends of Truth and Justice, it may possibly be productive of much good to a CERTAIN INJURED AND PERSECUTED INDIVIDUAL.

Among the high church and high tory characters, his royal highness was held in much esteem for his PIETY! They boasted of his always travelling with a bible in one pocket of his carriage and a prayer-book in the other, but we know that the last journey he took, thus equipped, was on a Sunday, in order to make some bets on a race-course for the ensuing day!

In contemplating the enormous means possessed by his royal highness, we are at a loss to account for his dying so deeply in debt. We find him enjoying out of the taxes an annuity of twenty-six thousand pounds, a pension of seven thousand pounds, and an annuity of twelve thousand pounds sponged from the poor people of Hanover. Notwithstanding this income of forty-five thousand pounds a-year, and his immense receipts as commander-in-chief, colonel of regiments, &c. &c., such an embarrassed, pauper-like state of existence has seldom been exposed,— head and ears in debt, and himself dying in another man's house, without a roof of his own to cover his shame! At his principal banker's, he had but a balance of forty-four pounds, fifteen shillings, and a penny, at his death. Like the old story of the many items of sack to one item of bread, we find that his royal highness' horses were more valuable than his books. But one of his disgraceful transactions more deeply concerns the public:—the scandalous grant of public land for a rent never paid, and an advance of forty-seven thousand pounds of the public money, by way of accommodation, upon a mortgage of land which already belonged to the people. Common honesty required that the late Tory ministers, in leasing public land to the duke, should exact its fair value; but, so far from it, the duke obtained an immediate advance of thirty thousand pounds, and eventually of forty-seven thousand pounds, upon his lease. Never was there a more flagrant exposure of the insolent impunity with which Tory ministers betrayed the public interests. It was the duty, *the sworn duty*, of the Tory commissioners of woods and forests, to let the public land upon the best terms. Instead of which, they not only granted a lease to a notorious insolvent, a man who for very many years had never paid his way,—a man so involved that sheriff's officers followed his carriage and seized it directly he got out of it,—but they granted this man a lease so much under its value that he immediately got thirty thousand pounds advanced upon it. In other terms, the public were defrauded of thirty thousand pounds; but this is purity compared to what follows. These Tory ministers advance forty-seven thousand pounds of the public money to the duke, knowing that he is insolvent and cannot pay the interest. Their mode of securing the principal is still more nefarious. Instead of pursuing the usual course of business, when ground landlords advance money to tenants covering their estates on building leases, they paid the money, not to those who built on the land, or not by instalments exactly as the land was covered, but to the duke, *who* got people to build for him on credit, and never paid them. The crown, of course, seized for its claims of rent and loan, and, possessing itself of the property of the duke's creditors, the builders, left them the victims of their misplaced confidence in the royal honour,—of a man who once thought that his mere word "on the honour of a prince" was sufficient to paralyze the House of Commons in their inquiries into his malversation of office. Such a playing into the hands of the duke, whilst he was defrauding the confiding tradesmen and workmen, is monstrous. We ask a question, Were not sums of money clandestinely paid to the duke, and smuggled into the accounts of the Army Pay-office, and did not, on one occasion, one of the sworn commissioners, in examining and passing the accounts of the paymaster-general, publicly declare, that the ministers who had signed the warrant for this illegal payment to the duke,—a payment without any vote of parliament,—deserved to be IMPEACHED?

From the above statement, it will be seen why the late Tory administration so resolutely resisted all attempts made in the House of Commons to obtain an annual statement of the land-revenue department. The grant to the duke of a lease for sixty years of valuable mines in Nova Scotia, also appears to be a job infamous beyond any recent precedent. The public ought to have nothing to do with the private debts of this weak, bad man; and it should rest with the royal family whether they suffer the duke to go to his account, with all his imperfections on his head, as an insolvent, defrauding his creditors.

When the disreputable life of the duke is taken into consideration, what an insult was offered to the understandings of an informed people, at the command issued for all persons to robe themselves in garments of decent mourning, upon the demise of this son of Mars and Venus! The country, indeed, had more cause for rejoicing than mourning; as they had lost an enemy to everything liberal and beneficial. "What!" said the inquiring citizen, "am I to put on the garb of sorrow when I have no cause to mourn? What was the Duke of York to me, or to my family? Nothing less than an intruder upon our scanty means, and yet we are commanded, as good citizens and loyal subjects, to put ourselves and families into decent mourning?" But such was the order issued from the office of the Lord Chamberlain, and it was certainly

Sir Walter Scott, one of the most popular poets and novelists of the nineteenth century. (*Stephen Basdeo Personal Collection*)

complied with by all those who depended upon the favour of the court, and by persons who wished to be thought—*fashionable*! Happy, however, are we to know, that the sensible and independent portion of the nation viewed such an absurd order with the contempt it merited. Had the duke been a private gentleman, he would have had the exact portion of tears shed to his memory as he deserved,—would have been buried and forgotten, except by his creditors, who would scarcely have waited till the turf had covered him, before his house and effects would have been sold, his family turned into the street, and every one paid as much in the pound as his property would have allowed. But the adored of Mrs. Clarke, being the son of a king, no such insult was offered to his manes. His disappointed creditors were left nothing but promises for the articles with which he had been so lavishly supplied; and some of these broken-hearted men, we can attest from personal knowledge, were afterwards reduced to the greatest possible distress, while others have closed their miserable days in a parish work-house,—martyrs to the broken faith of his royal highness the Duke of York, of whom Sir Walter Scott impiously said, in the language of Scripture "There has fallen this day in our Israel, a prince, and a great man!" How forcibly the language of Shakespeare applies here:

> "The devil can cite Scripture for his purpose.
> An evil soul, producing holy witness,
> Is like a villain with a smiling cheek,—
> A goodly apple rotten at the heart;
> O, what a goodly outside falsehood hath!"

Indeed, the whole panegyric which follows the quotation from Scripture is of that description which is sure to raise for its author a monument, whereon will be engraved, "Grovelling servility to royalty, and a mean sacrifice of public duty at the altar of private friendship." The following brief extract will be sufficient to establish the justness of our censure:

> "The RELIGION of the Duke of York was SINCERE. His family affections were strong, and the public cannot have forgotten the *pious* tenderness with which he discharged the duty of watching the last days of his royal father. No pleasure, no business, was ever known to interrupt his regular visits to Windsor, where his unhappy parent could neither be *grateful* for, nor even be sensible of, his unremitted attentions. (!!!) His royal highness prepared the most splendid victories our annals boast, by an unceasing attention to the character and talents of the officers, and the comforts and health of the men. Terms of service were fixed for every rank, and neither influence nor *money* was permitted to FORCE any individual forward. (!!!) It has never been disputed (?) that, *in the field*, his royal highness displayed INTELLIGENCE,(!) MILITARY SKILL,(!!) and his family attribute, the most UNALTERABLE COURAGE.(!!!) If a tradesman, whose bill was unpaid by an officer, thought proper to apply to the Horse Guards, the debtor received a letter from HEADQUARTERS, requiring to know if there

existed any objections to the account, and failing in rendering a satisfactory answer, he was put on stoppages until the creditor's demand was satisfied. Repeated applications of this kind might endanger the officer's commission, *which was then sold for the payment of his creditors.*"

While Sir Walter enlarges upon the duke's VIRTUES, (virtues, indeed!) in a similar strain to the above, he uses the most palliative language to gloss over his notorious vices. Not a syllable does he say about his royal highness' OWN CREDITORS BEING LEFT UNPAID, nor does he advocate the propriety, that the commander-in-chief ought to have been "put on stoppages until HIS numerous creditors were satisfied," or that the several commissions he held in the British army should have been "sold for the payment of HIS creditors!" In eulogizing the "military skill, intelligence, and unalterable courage of his royal highness," all allusion to the duke's *precipitate flight from Lisle* is carefully omitted, and that Houchard, the governor of that fortress, lost his head for not driving him into the sea, which it was proved he might easily have done, through the duke's obstinacy and WANT of *military skill*!!! Are the very clear statements and unshaken evidence of Mrs. Clarke also to be set at nought, because a small majority of the most venal House of Commons of any in our history thought proper to acquit his royal highness from her charges? Was not every honourable man in England convinced of their verity? And did not universal execration COMPEL the commander-in-chief TO RESIGN, in defiance of that contemptible and loathed majority? Yet all these well-known FACTS are so smoothed down by misrepresentation and shuffling excuses, that his royal highness is actually made to appear a MARTYR TO POPULAR OPINION!!! When speaking of the duke's *"pious* attentions" to his royal father, the "celebrated novel-writer" says not a syllable about the infamy of receiving ten thousand pounds a-year for such unnecessary services,—unnecessary, because, at their commencement, they were only formally bestowed for the sake of gain, and not through a sense of filial duty; and, for a greater part of the period, they were less necessary, for *forms* could be of no use to a *dead monarch*!

We entertain the highest possible opinion of Sir Walter Scott's literary talents, which makes us the more regret that so fair a fame should be clouded by this incontestable proof of his want of principle and his total disregard of historical verity. We do not wish to quarrel with the talented knight's POLITICS or his *gratitude* to George the Fourth for bestowing on him a title, which adds little to the character of any man of sterling worth, and nothing to him who was before a stranger to virtuous principles; but we do not like to see the historian's glorious shield—TRUTH—broken in pieces by bespattering a public defaulter with praises, when such a man deserved nothing but the contempt and detestation of all who regard upright dealings. Let not Sir Walter Scott, then, thus attempt to mislead the people of England in the character of their princes, by palliating their public abuses, and varnishing their private misconduct; nor let him disseminate doctrines unnatural, nonsensical, and injurious to the rights of human nature. History is materially injured when the waters of truth are corrupted by infusing into their channel the flatterer's poison.

Such a vile cause cannot be maintained without having recourse to falsehood, and the cowardly concealment of conscious malversation. Honest purposes love the light of truth; and the friends of liberty and man become justly alarmed whenever they see the press disgraced by its perversion. We are well aware that the Tories were lavish in their rewards to obsequious political writers, and that needy, unprincipled, and aspiring persons, to receive the infection, were always at hand. But can any man be really great and honourable, can he be a patriot or a philanthropist, can he be a zealous and sincere friend to law, order, and religion, who thus hesitates not to break down all the fences of honour, truth, and integrity? Did Sir Walter Scott, when he penned the character of the late Duke of York, mean to proclaim to the world that vice is virtue, guilt is innocence, cowardice is bravery, swindling is correct dealing?—or that conscience is but a name, and honour a phantom? Since the art of printing was invented,—since the era when Ignorance and Superstition were first driven before the light of Reason, exhibited in the circulation of a free press,— we unhesitatingly affirm there has never been published an eulogium so totally at variance with fact as that written by the author of "Waverley" on his royal highness of York. In sober reason and in the language of common sense, we would calmly appeal to the dispassionate reflection of every thinking Englishman, whether such a prostitution of truth and genius is becoming the proud fame of Sir Walter Scott? The power of such a celebrated writer over general opinion is too considerable not to deeply deplore the certainty of his misguiding some portion of the public by the apparent sincerity of his mis-placed eulogium, and by his neglecting to lead his readers to a path of just thinking. Scorning alike the meanness of flattery and the crime of delusion, we have not hesitated to deliver our unbiassed sentiments on the character of the Duke of York, (which are certainly more in accordance with facts) with that freedom to which we deem the historian to be justly entitled. We have not allowed the example of Sir Walter Scott to interfere with our fixed purpose,—that of "AWARDING HONOUR ONLY WHERE HONOUR IS DUE!"

It is a melancholy reflection that so little protection or encouragement should have been afforded to writers of strict independence and integrity, more particularly about the period of the Duke of York's death, when Toryism was flourishing in the plenitude of its glory and its power. The former patriotic spirit of literary men had almost disappeared before ministerial bribery; and to write with that honesty and boldness of purpose which Junius wrote was a matter of rare occurrence; and when any author did venture to imitate that great benefactor of mankind, his temerity was sure to call down the vengeance of the powerful, and, too frequently, without awakening the sympathy of the public. Had those noble authors, who once defended the cause of freedom and truth, been living at this period, how would they have despised such instances of the degradation of talent as those we have quoted! Could they, for a moment, have risen from their graves, what would have been their astonishment at such a perversion of the blessings of the press? In a country professing to be free, and boasting of its rights and privileges, it was surely natural to expect, that he who advocated its best and dearest interests would be certain of its ardent support; that whoever devoted his time and talent to the exposition of public abuses would be an object of general esteem, and enjoy the protection of the PEOPLE, at least, if not of the government. But such was seldom the case; and hence but too many writers resigned their probity, and betrayed the public, by making ministerial delinquencies appear as good government, and royal vices as elegant pastimes and gentlemanly exploits! Most of the daily and other periodical publications were in the pay of government, and they scrupled not to deny the most glaring truths, if, by so doing, they could please their patrons.

We deeply regret that so many could be found to wage war against the sound principles of the English constitution, and so few that invariably adhered to the cause of liberty and justice. That writer, who is prompted by the pure love of his country's weal, and acknowledging no party, seeks no adherents but those who are friends to her sacred cause, will look back upon such a debased state of the press with mingled feelings of indignation and pity. Be it ever remembered, that the general corruption of that powerful engine is always first aimed at by a minister who intends the slavery of the people. Had public writers but maintained one grand universal adherence to the broad and general light of TRUTH, the people of England would never have been burthened by such men as Liverpool, Londonderry, and Sidmouth; nor would they have had to endure their present immense load of taxation. Whenever the people are properly united, and headed by an honest press, not all the standing armies of their enemies will prevent them from obtaining their constitutional rights. But when the people stand apart from each other, and when ministers can obtain the services of venal writers, the star of liberty grows dim, and patriotism becomes dangerous and obsolete.

The Earl of Liverpool was prevented from taking his seat at the head of the government at this period, by a sudden attack of paralysis. His cabinet were consequently thrown into great disorder and contention. The united influence of Lord Eldon, the Duke of Wellington, and Mr. Peel, however, proved inefficient to prevent the choice of prime minister falling on Mr. Canning. Many discussions arose upon this change of administration, and the frequent quarrels in the cabinet were of a nature not very reputable to the members composing it. Within forty-eight hours after Mr. Canning had received his majesty's commands to form a ministry, no less than seven of the former leading members resigned office, through vexation and jealousy at his appointment. The inconsistent Lord Bexley, however, considered that *second* thoughts were best, and retracted his resignation. Sir John Copley was created Baron Lyndhurst, and appointed Lord High Chancellor, upon the resignation of the Tory veteran Lord Eldon, who, though he had for so many years been amassing enormous wealth, was now *mean* enough to be an idle pauper upon the resources of our impoverished country for the annual income of four thousand pounds! His lordship had been for more than twenty years Speaker of the House of Peers, at a salary of three thousand pounds, and Lord Chancellor at fifteen thousand pounds per annum; while the salaries of the offices in his gift, in the legal department alone, amounted to more than forty-two thousand pounds per annum. The legal and ecclesiastical patronage at his disposal was also immense; yet this pretended *poor* man would not retire without an ex-chancellor's salary! While "this keeper of the king's conscience" took especial care of his own purse, he did not forget to look after that of his family; and places, pensions, and church preferments were most bountifully heaped upon them.

In contemplating the long period of his lordship's enjoying the emoluments of his office, we are led to consider "the means whereby he got the office." His unmanly desertion of the virtuous cause of Queen Caroline was the principal, though not the only, reason of his rapid promotion. In this instance, he committed an indelible stain upon his integrity for the sake of obtaining patronage and wealth. Let the following passage, dictated by this time-serving lawyer, when he advocated the Princess of Wales' cause against the Douglases, bear us out in the justness of our remarks:

> "However Sir John and Lady Douglas may appear my ostensible accusers, I have *other enemies*, whose ill-will I may have occasion to FEAR, without feeling myself assured that it will be strictly regulated, in its proceedings against me, by the *principles of fairness and justice*!"

Who would suppose that boaster of "fairness and justice," Lord Eldon, one of the most forward of the professed friends of the Princess of Wales, could have proved so heartless and active an oppressor of Queen Caroline? We are forcibly reminded of two passages of Scripture, which powerfully apply to his lordship's desertion from the path of honour in this instance; namely, the 2nd Book of Kings, ch. viii, v. 13,[12] and the 2nd Book of Samuel, ch. xii, v. 7[13] and 8! Lord Eldon not only at that time, however, expressed his decided opinion that other enemies existed, but he afterwards named the very parties, and pointed out with what clearness and facility the offence might have been proved against them! But his lordship soon afterwards *sneaked* into lucrative office, and had something better to do for *himself* than procuring justice for the injured, insulted, and persecuted Princess of Wales! Out upon such blood-suckers of their country, we say, and may their *crying* professions of SINCERITY and CONSCIENTIOUS MOTIVES ever be viewed as the ravings of hypocrisy!

Mr. Canning's ministry proved but of short duration. Soon after his appointment to the premiership, his health began to decline, and within four months he was numbered with the dead. This event took place on the morning of the 8th of August, and his remains were consigned to the tomb prepared to receive them, in Westminster Abbey, followed by a long procession of dukes, lords, and other great personages,—the admirers of his political principles.

In taking an impartial review of Mr. Canning's political career, we cannot help thinking that all his public acts were *aristocratical*, and afforded indubitable proof of his love of place. Like most men who have risen to great eminence, he owed much to chance. He was lucky in the time of his decease, and in the day of his deserting his old friends. To very few has it happened to be supported by a party as long as its support was useful, and to be repudiated by it when its affection would have been injurious. The same men who, as friends, had given him power,—as enemies, conferred on him reputation! But his name is not connected with any great act of legislation. No law will be handed down to posterity protected by his support. After generations will see in him a lamentable proof of prostituted talent, and little or nothing to claim their gratitude. The memorialist may delight in painting the talents he displayed, but the historian will find little to say of the benefits he bestowed. Mr. Canning was very irritable and bold in his manners. He defended his conduct in the House and out of it; that is to say, he made some bitter speeches in parliament, and wrote three challenges, or demands for explanation: one to Mr. Hume, one to Sir Francis Burdett, and one to an anonymous pamphleteer. The author of this pamphlet was Mr. (now Sir John Cam) Hobhouse, though the fact is little known; but, for some unexplained cause, the book was speedily withdrawn from publication. A few having been sold, however, we were fortunate enough to procure one, the following extracts from which may not prove unacceptable to our readers:

"Sir,—I shall address you without ceremony, for you are deserving of none. There is nothing in your station, in your abilities, or in your character, which entitles you to respect. The first is too often the reward of political, and frequently of PRIVATE, crimes. Your talents, such as they are, you have abused; and, as for your character, I know not an individual of any party, or in any class of society, who would not consider the defence of it a paradox. Low as public principle has sunk, *you* are still justly appreciated; and no one is deceived by *qualities*, which, even in their happiest exertions, are not calculated or employed to conciliate esteem.

"To what a state of degradation are we sunk, when a defendant is to be cheered into being a plaintiff; to be applauded when he assaults the sufferings of the oppressed, and arraigns the motives of men of honour and unsullied reputation! You are yourself aware, sir, that in no other assembly in England would you have been allowed to proceed, for an instant, in so gross a violation of all decencies of life as was hazarded by that speech, which found a patient and a pleased audience in the House of Commons. Can there exist in that body,— composed as it undoubtedly is of men, who, in the private relations of life, are distinguished for many good qualities,—an habitual disregard of decency, a contempt for public opinion, an absurd confidence, either individually or in mass, to which, absolving themselves from the rules of common life, they look for protection against the censures of their fellow-citizens? Were it not for such a groundless persuasion, there is not a gentleman (for such a being is not quite extinct in parliament) who would not have thought himself compromised by listening to your insolent attacks upon the national character, and to a flashy declamation, which, from beginning to end, supposed an audience devoid of all taste, judgment, spirit, and humanity.

"I am at a loss, sir, to account for the insulting policy of your colleagues in office, who, though they take their full share with you in the public hatred, are far from being equal competitors for its contempt. Those worthies must have had some motive, deeper than their avowed designs, for entrusting their defence to such 'inept hands.' Were they afraid of your partially redeeming your character by silence? Were they resolved, that if you were yet not enough known, some decisive overt act should reduce you below the ministerial level? Did they suspect, that you were again willing to rebel or betray? How was it that you were selected for the odious and TREACHEROUS task of justifying the rigorous measures of the imbecile, but unfeeling, Sidmouth, directed as they were against the aged, the infirm, the powerless of his own countrymen? How was it that you were required to emerge from your suspected, though prudent, silence, in behalf of him whom you had first insulted by the offer of your alliance, then by your coarse hostility, and, lastly, by the accepted tender of an insidious reconciliation?

"You know, sir, and the world should know, that when your seducer, Pitt, was tired of you, you offered yourself to this silly, vain man, who thought your keeping too dear at the proposed price, and accordingly declined the bargain. You know, and the world may remember, the immediate consequence of this slight of proffered service was your lampoons in parliament, your speeches in the papers,—I forget where they fell, but whether in one or the other, they were equally *unprepared* and opportune; these, and other assaults, manfully directed against those whose forbearance was the sole protection of your audacity, can hardly have slipped through the meshes of the ill-woven memories of your colleagues. Perhaps, then, it was intended to reduce you to irretrievable humiliation, and to fit you for the lowest agency, by making you the loudest encomiast of the most undefensible measure of him whom you have reprobated as the 'most incapable of all ministers, the most inept of all statesmen.' You have kissed the hand that chastised you, and have lost but few opportunities of testifying your FEIGNED REPENTANCE to him who commands you from that eminence, which you were adjudged incapable to occupy, even so as to save the few appearances required from ministerial manners.

"Your submission to Lord Castlereagh, tricked out, as he appears, in those decorations of fortune which might well deceive a vulgar eye, was not surprising: it was the natural deference of meanness to success. But it was not expected, even from your condescension, that the butt of his party, the agent of that department which had, even in these times of peace, with infinite address, contrived to make the executive administration not only hateful but ridiculous, that the very minister who had no character for talents should be defended by him who had shewn himself unequal to the defence of his own. Your reply to those who spoke the language of their constituents, of unprejudiced Englishmen, of human nature itself, and who stepped forward to rescue the parliament from indelible disgrace, was such as is seldom hiccupped up from the Bacchanalian triumph of ministerial majorities.

"What, sir! one of the present cabinet dare to accuse any individual of too *much faith* in common rumour or in proffered information? A member of that cabinet, whose *belief* in the idle, malicious falsehoods of spies, pimps, bullies, and all the abandoned broken characters, whom their promises allured into perjury, has been proved by the verdict of juries, has been recorded in the courts, has been the object of general indignation, and, after having been the cause and excuse of a wanton attack on our liberties, has been judged by the cabinet itself so little qualified for examination that believing parliament has been instructed to indemnify the rogues who told the lies, and the fools who believed them. What! an apologist for the gulled, the gaping Sidmouth, to deprecate the indiscriminating reception of tales and tale-bearers? a defender of him who put his trust in Castles, who employed Oliver, and who, on the faith of atrocious fabrications, of which he was alike the encourager and the dupe, has persecuted and imprisoned, has fettered and fractured, and might have put to death, his fellow-countrymen, even to decimation.

"You tell us, you should have thought yourself '*a dolt and idiot*' to have listened for a moment to complaints against an agent of the home department, a runner of Bow-street, a gaoler's turnkey, or a secretary's secretary. Mighty well, sir! but let a runaway from the hulks, a convicted felon, tell you, that a bankrupt apothecary, a broken-down farmer, and a cobbler, are the centre of a widely-spread conspiracy, have formed and partially executed a plan for razing the kingdom, and for taking the Tower of London,—have provided arms, have published manifestoes; let the same respectable evidence impeach the loyalty of the nobles and gentry in particular districts, and of the lower classes in all; let this single felon assert that he is honest, and the majority of his countrymen are rogues,—you do not think YOURSELF A DOLT AND IDIOT!!! you do not think Lord Sidmouth a dolt and idiot for proceeding, chiefly upon such information, to hang, draw, and quarter the first individuals designated by this credible witness! But whatever you or your colleagues thought, the JURY did think the secretary of the home department a DOLT AND IDIOT, and shewed their opinion by their verdict. I will take leave to observe, that there is this difference between the credulity of such men as Mr. Lambton, and of such ministers as yourself and your colleagues: the former may interpose to save, but the consequence of the latter has been to destroy.

"To brand with the names of 'rebel and traitor' those whom you have been unable to prove rebellious and traitorous, is but in the ordinary course of official perseverance and incorrigible folly; but that you should presume to assail those unfortunate individuals, the victims of your own recorded credulity, by making a mockery of old age and of natural infirmities, which have been occasioned by your own injustice!!—such an outrage upon your audience—how is that to be accounted for? '*The revered and ruptured Ogden!!!*' This mad, this monstrous sally was applauded—was received with roars of laughter! and if there was a confession from some more candid lips, that such allusions were not 'quite in good taste,' an excuse was drawn from the *warmth* of the debate, clear as it was, to those accustomed to your patchwork, that the stupid alliteration was one of the ill-tempered weapons coolly selected from your oratorical armoury.

"The little knot of dependants, who were willing to make common stock and carry themselves to market with you, have become ashamed of the trifling, oscillating buffoon, whom they mistook for the head of a party, and who accepted the first and lowest vacancy that could replace him in the precincts of power. Even the miserable chuck-farthing, Ward, who has learnt from you how to run riot on his apostacy, owns, that he hesitates between the disgrace of 'serving without wages, and of being dismissed without a character.'

"Go on, sir, I pray you; proceed with your pleasantries; light up the dungeon with the flashes of your merriment,—make us familiar, make us pleased, with the anguish of the captive; teach us how to look upon torture and tyranny as agreeable trifles; let whips and manacles become the play-things of parliament; let patriotism and principle be preserved only as vain names, the materials of a jest; and, as you have disturbed the bed of sickness with your unhallowed mirth, hasten, with appropriate mockery, the long foretold approaching *Euthanasia* of the expiring constitution. But confine your efforts to that assembly where they have been so favourably, so thankfully received. You will find no other hearers. You are nothing but on that stage. The clerks, the candles, the heated atmosphere, the mummeries and decorations, the trained, packed paper audience, confused, belated, and jaded into an appetite for the grossest stimulants; these are the preparations indispensable to your exhibition. Thank heaven, however, the House of Commons is not the only tribunal; and it is possible, that, in spite of your extraordinary progress and probable success, there may still be, in this country, a body of men, now *dispersed*, but whom their common interest will ONE DAY COLLECT AND UNITE, FOR THE DEFENCE OF THEIR RIGHTS AND THE PUNISHMENT OF THEIR OPPRESSORS.[14]

"Believe me, sir, not an echo of those shouts of laughter which hailed your jests upon rebellious old age and traitorous disease, not an echo has been lost in the wide circumference of the British islands. Those shouts still ring in our ears; they will never die away as long as the day of retribution is deferred; they will never die away until we are finally extirpated by your triumph, or you are annihilated by our indignation. Do not flatter yourself that, by securing the connivance of parliament, you are safe from all national censure. *Parliament does not represent the feelings of the British nation.* It would be an assault upon the character of this great, this glorious people, to suppose that their representatives were sent to the House of Commons to encourage the playful ferocity of a hardened politician. The nobler portion of the nation are certainly not members of either house: the better educated, the more enlightened, and the more wealthy, at least the more independent, are to be found *without the walls of parliament*. You are (and what ministerial man is not?) an enemy to reform. But you shall be told, sir, that the necessity of reform, and of choosing our representatives from some other classes of society, was never so decidedly shewn as in the reception of your speech. If Mr. Canning was, on a former occasion,[15] applauded for saying, that the constitution of that assembly could not be bad, which '*worked so well in practice*' as to admit of the selection of such men as Mr. Windham and Mr. Horner, I am sure it is to be allowed me to say, that the assembly can have no feelings or opinions, in common with the rest of their countrymen, which would receive, with shouts of approving laughter, such a speech as this of Mr. Canning.

"You cannot be far from the close of your career; for, either we shall be so lost that all your farther efforts will be superfluous, or you will be so resisted as to disable you for ever from all noxious exertion. This, then, may be the time for summing up the evidence, furnished by the unbiassed, uncontradictory witnesses of your life; and for enabling your countrymen to pass the verdict.

"Let him speak who ever knew you in possession of any respectable reputation. The rag you stole from Mr. Sheridan's mantle was always too scanty to cover your nakedness: like all mimics, you caught only the meaner characteristics of your archetype; oratorical, not orator; poetaster, not poet; witling, not wit. You were never the first or best in any one line of action. You might not have been altogether inept or slow in playing second parts, but on no one occasion have you ever evinced that sincerity, either of principle or capacity, which the lowest amongst us are accustomed to require from the pretenders to excellence. Your spirit was rebuked in presence of those accomplished persons whom the followers of all parties recognized as beings of a higher order, and were willing to yield even more deference than their unambitious merit required. The chances of survivorship have left you a great man in these days of little men; but you keep true to the epic rule; you end as you began; power has conferred upon you no dignity,—elevation has not made your posture more erect. The decency of your character consists in its entire conformity to the original conception formed of you in early life. It has borrowed nothing from station, nothing from experience. It becomes you, but would disgrace any other man."

To a person of Mr. Canning's warmth of temper, such a production was felt most acutely; for he could not, with all his ready eloquence and talent, deny the truth of the writer's charges, or the justness of his severe censure. When men find themselves exposed, without the possibility of making out a good defence by argument, however speciously employed, it is no uncommon thing for them to abuse their accusers, by stigmatizing them with the epithets of "SLANDERER," "LIAR," "COWARD," "DOLT," "IDIOT," and similar opprobrious names, which, however, generally fall harmless on the person to whom they are applied, while they recoil, with ten-fold vigour, on the head of him who disgraces himself and his cause by their adoption. Such was precisely the case with Mr. Canning, as the following letters will testif

MR. CANNING'S LETTER.

"Gloucester Lodge, April 10, 1818.

"Sir,—I received early in the last week the copy of your pamphlet, which you (I take for granted) had the attention to send to me.

"Soon after I was informed, on the authority of your publisher, that you had withdrawn the whole impression from him, with a view (as was supposed) of suppressing the publication.

"I since learn, however, that the pamphlet, though not sold, is circulated under blank covers.

"I learn this from (among others) the gentleman to whom the pamphlet has been industriously attributed, but who has voluntarily and absolutely denied to me that he has any knowledge of it or its author.

"To you, sir, whoever you may be, I address myself thus directly, for the purpose of expressing to you my opinion, that,

"You are a liar and a slanderer, and want courage only to be an assassin.

"I have only to add, that no man knows of my writing to you; that I shall maintain the same reserve so long as I have an expectation of hearing from you in your own name; and that I shall not give up that expectation till to-morrow (Saturday) night.

"The same address which brought me your pamphlet will bring any letter safe to my hands.

"I am, sir, your humble servant,
(Signed) "GEO. CANNING."
"N.B. Mr. Ridgway is requested to forward this letter to its destination."

THE AUTHOR'S REPLY,

Addressed to the Editor of the Examiner.

"Sir,—You are requested to insert in your paper the reply of the Right Hon. George Canning to my public remonstrance with that gentleman on the insult he lately dared to offer to the people of England.

"I am agreeably disappointed. After ten days' deliberation, he acknowledges the tribunal, and has determined to plead.

"Whilst his judges are deciding on the merits of his defence, it shall be my care to provide the gentleman with another opportunity of displaying his taste and talents in the protection of his character.

"In the meantime, whilst Mr. Lambton is a 'dolt and an idiot,' I am content to be a 'liar and a slanderer, and an assassin,' according to the same inimitable master of the vulgar tongue.

"I am, sir, your obedient servant,
"The Author of the Letter to the Right Hon. G. Canning."

It was hard indeed for Liberty to have so ready and so ruthless an antagonist as Mr. Canning. This minister was not satisfied with those legitimate and classical weapons he was so well skilled to wield, forgot the days of the "Anti-jacobin," and vociferated against and challenged every one whose pen or voice was raised in opposition to him. Thus, whether squibbing "the Doctor," as Lord Sidmouth was called, fighting my Lord Castlereagh, cutting heartless jokes on poor Mr. Ogden, flatly contradicting Mr. Brougham, swaggering over the Holy Alliance, or quarrelling with the Duke of Wellington, he was in perpetual personal scrapes,—one of the reasons which created for him so much personal interest during the whole of his parliamentary career. No imaginative artist, fresh from reading that career, would sit down to paint him with the broad and deep forehead, the stern, compressed lip, the deeply thoughtful and concentrated air of Napoleon. As little would the idea of his eloquence or ambition call to our recollection the swarth and iron features, the bold and haughty dignity, of Strafford. We cannot fancy in his eye the volumed depth of Richelieu's, the volcanic flash of Mirabeau's, or the offended majesty of Chatham's. We should sketch him from our imagination as we see him identically before us, with a countenance rather marked by intelligence, sentiment, and satire, than meditation, passion, or sternness,—with more of the petulant than the proud, more of the playful than the profound, more of the quick irritability of a lively temperament in its expression, than of the fixed or fiery aspect which belongs to the rarer race of men, whose characters are wrought from the most inflexible and violent materials of human nature. We do not wish to deny that Mr. Canning was an orator, a wit, and a poet. Such talents and accomplishments, however, are not of pre-eminent importance to the situation which he occupied at his death. A premier ought to be the bold opposer of corruption, the solid friend of his sovereign, and the uncompromising champion of the people's rights. He should always remember that the security of the throne arises from the interest which the sovereign possesses in the hearts of his subjects, and that all attempts to stifle their voice, under a sense of grievances, must tend to alienate their affections, and inevitably lead to similar calamities which, in other countries, have been produced by arbitrary and corrupt measures. Whether Mr. Canning was such a statesman, we need only refer to his general vacillating conduct to his superiors in office, and to the return made in 1820, that this gentleman had received from the country, during his public association with government, *two hundred thousand pounds*! Upon the demise of Mr. Canning, a pension was granted, by act of parliament, to the trustees of the family, of three thousand pounds per annum, and his widow, shortly after, created a peeress!

The ensuing motley ministry, headed by Lord Goderich, (late Mr. Robinson) soon exhibited symptoms of its inefficiency to stand against the powerful phalanx of Toryism, then in array to oppose everything like liberty. The philosopher, however, deeply deploring the many vicissitudes, the varying process, through which Opinion has to pass in order to be refined to Truth, but calmly aware that the sense of a people never ultimately retrogrades, might have observed through the clouds which, at this period, dimmed the political horizon, the

F. J. Robinson, 1st Viscount Goderich and 1st Earl of Ripon pictured in later life, as depicted in Lucien Wolf's *Life of the First Marquess of Ripon* (1921).

sun of Liberty darting forth its smiling beams, and exhibiting signs of a speedy victory over the murky enemies of mankind,—the brighter period, when a more enlarged intelligence would necessarily triumph,—when warlike Tory despotism, founded on a feverish desire to keep the people down by the bayonet, would wear out its own harassed existence, and a system of freedom, sanctioned and confirmed by a long previous disposition of thought, would be realized, and the spirit and letter of that solemn compact, made and ratified between the crown and the people in 1688, be finally restored to the country.

No Englishman, who cherishes in his heart a love of freedom, and who is at all conversant with the history of his country from its earliest era down to the period of the revolution, can be insensible of the acquisitions procured at that eventful period,—of the accumulation of strength gained by the popular branch of the constitution, the limitation to the power of the crown, and the extension of the admitted and declared rights of the people. Before the revolution, we were the slaves of kingly despotism, and the House of Commons itself was as much subservient to the tyranny of the throne as the personal liberty of the subject. We have heard much talk about Magna Charta, and the triumph over John at Runnymede, by the people,—who, by the way, had nothing to do with the struggle, for it was the struggle of the barons and the king, the former of whom in their several domains were as despotic to those beneath them as they felt the tyranny of the king they sought to humble. It was the invasion of their own power and possessions by John that fired their resentment and animated their public spirit, and hence ensued Magna Charta. But, with the exception of the single clause that forbids arbitrary and vexatious imprisonment, it scarcely adds, either in spirit or letter, anything to the liberties of the people. Not so, however, with the compact as settled at the revolution,—not so with the Bill of Rights and the Act of Settlement. The prerogative of the crown was by these measures curtailed, and the liberty of the people greatly extended and more clearly defined; the purity of the elective right was provided for, as also the short duration of parliaments, the discretionary power of the crown was prohibited, and standing armies in time of peace declared to be illegal! The pretended right of *suspending* or of carrying into execution the laws, at the pleasure of the crown, was done away with; the levying of money for the use of the crown, by pretence of *prerogative*, without the consent of parliament, was forbidden; the right of the subject to petition the king was established; all elections of members of parliament were declared ought to be free; excessive bail and excessive fines were declared should neither be required nor enforced, nor cruel punishments inflicted; and for amending, strengthening, and preserving the laws, it was declared that parliaments ought to be held frequently. The further wise provisions and legislative enactments of that period are proofs that the liberties and happiness of the nation were the chief objects contemplated by our ancestors.

But as all the wise limitations imposed by the friends of liberty on the power of the crown would be rendered ineffectual and useless, without a pure and freely-elected House of Commons, it had long been the chief design of the Tories to destroy this sacred palladium by bribery and corruption. How fatally they succeeded is well known. Thus all the hazards which our forefathers had incurred, all the treasures which they had expended, and all the blood that was shed to establish the freedom of themselves and their posterity, were rendered useless by Mr. Pitt, the Earl of Liverpool, Lord Castlereagh, Mr. Canning, and their mercenary adherents. When this lamentable state of the power of the Tories is considered, and which had been produced by fifty bitter years of misrule, the difficulty of any other ministry being kept together will be apparent. The cabinet of Lord Goderich was a confused mixture of Whigs and Tories, and as the latter possessed a corrupted House of Commons, it were easy to prophesy which party would gain the ascendency, at least for a time; though it were equally observable, that

> "The PEOPLE, by and by, would be the stronger!"

In the month of September, the House of Commons lost one of its worthiest members in the Right Hon. Lord Archibald Hamilton, who died in the fifty-eighth year of his age, after a long and painful illness. His lordship was more than twenty years the representative of the county of Lanark, and one of his constituents publicly declared, that "the noble lord had conducted himself, throughout that long period, so much to the satisfaction of the county and honour to himself, that he was justly considered the pride of Clydesdale and the glory of Scotland." The name of his lordship was always to be found among those who supported the people's rights. His virtues and his talents placed him at the head of civil and religious liberty; he advocated every measure, both in and out of parliament, which had for its object the welfare of man,—of the meanest peasant as well as of the greatest lord. His affability and kindness of heart secured to him a numerous circle of friends, and his unwearied opposition in parliament to corruption and grants to pamper royal libertines gained for him the proud and inestimable title of PATRIOT.

In November, the unfortunate creditors of the late Duke of York were informed that the assets of his royal highness would not furnish means to pay more than *one shilling* in the pound! We know that the duke, in his dying hours, declared himself solvent. Whether he went out of the world with a falsehood in his heart and on his tongue, whether he was kept in ignorance of his affairs by those around him, or whether his estate had been foully dealt with by his family or others, are points which ought to have been better elucidated. We cordially pity the creditors, many of whom have been more grossly defrauded than in any case which has been punished in the Insolvent Court. The conduct of the royal family and the executors of the Duke of York must have appeared to the public in a very unamiable light; for why was not a thoroughly clear account of everything laid before the creditors? Nothing, however, was said about the duke's jewels and the valuable diamond necklace belonging to his duchess!!! We impute nothing to the executors, Sir Herbert Taylor and Sir Benjamin Stephenson, both, doubtless, honourable men,—good Tory placemen; but if people will not make executorship accounts clear and public to all concerned in them, they are liable to be complained of. The wills and affairs of dead princes are always smuggled over and hushed up; but the creditors surely have a right to demand, because they have an interest in demanding, that the wills and executorship accounts of the royal family should be made as public as those of other individuals.

During the session of parliament this year, Mr. Hume made a motion to repeal one of the odious "Six Acts" against the liberty of the press, which subjected to a stamp-duty those cheap periodical tracts that formed the most powerful instruments against the oppression of Toryism. The treatment which Mr. Hume received on this occasion will ever reflect the greatest disgrace on the *pretended* Whig government and their friends. All those members who had opposed the passing of this act now either purposely absented themselves or advocated its *utility*, and the honourable member for Aberdeen had the mortification to see his good intentions frustrated at a time when he calculated upon certain success.

Independently of the vexatious trouble which this act of Lord Castlereagh's framing caused the booksellers, it was found materially to injure the spreading of knowledge. But it was for this very purpose that it became the law of the land. Lord Castlereagh was aware of the truism, that

"Men, once ignorant, are slaves!"

and consequently, to further his own unconstitutional views, he used every exertion to fetter the press and clap a padlock on the mouth of political knowledge. Wiser and better men, however, knowing that the free education of the people is the surest safeguard to the permanent happiness of the community, have lifted up their voices and given their votes against the subjugation of the Press,—the Leviathan protector of all that is worth living for. "The great mass of British subjects," said the venerable and patriotic Lord Erskine, "have no surer means of being informed of what passes in parliament and in the courts of justice, or of the general transactions of the world, than through cheap publications within their means of purchase; and I desire to express my dissent from that principle and opinion, that the safety of the state, and the happiness of the multitude in the laborious condition of life, may be *best secured by their being kept in ignorance of political controversies and opinions.* I hold, on the contrary, that the government of this country can only continue to be secure while it conducts itself with fidelity and justice, and as all its acts shall, as heretofore, be thoroughly known and understood by all classes of the people." Lord Erskine, however, is not singular in his view of this subject; for every philanthropist cannot but subscribe to the justice and equity of such doctrines. The prohibitory duty, therefore, on political periodicals must be considered as a scheme, emanating from a bad heart and weak head, to favour despotism. That law which requires publishers and printers of newspapers to enter into heavy securities, to answer to the consequences of the remote contingency of a LIBEL,—that is, publishing anything having a *tendency* to bring either house of parliament or his majesty's ministers *into contempt*,—must ever operate perniciously to the cause of freedom. For is it not one of the most sacred duties which a rational being owes to society, to his family, and to himself, to endeavour to "bring into contempt" a government, if it really be contemptible? To what did we owe the wreck of our liberties, at this period, except to the *contempt* into which the preceding cabinets had been brought among the people? Is there an Englishman, possessing a particle of manhood, or breathing the inspirations of his ancestors, who would not blush at the human form, could he witness a being so debased as not to perpetuate the contempt into which public virtue had happily brought the names of Liverpool, Castlereagh, Eldon, Sidmouth, and the whole tribe of Tory locusts that so long fastened upon the vitals of his country? In America, the idea of indicting a man for endeavouring "to bring the government into contempt," would appear ludicrous. The language of the public authorities in America would be, "If the government is not contemptible, it will only gain strength from attacks; if it be contemptible, the citizens have a right to prove it so, and to demand a change: it is their duty to discuss the point, and to settle it by reason, and not to suppress it by indictment." Our readers will acknowledge, that we do not here advocate a doctrine we dare not practice; for we despise the unjustness of the "Six Acts," and will never allow their *unconstitutional* powers to intimidate us in the discharge of our public duty.

On the 29th of January,

1828,

parliament was opened by commission, when the ministry, headed by Lord Goderich, was dissolved. The Duke of Wellington and Mr. Peel succeeded the former premier and secretary of state,—a change that could not possibly afford any satisfaction to the public. Mr. Brougham, in an address to the House of Commons on this subject, said, "Though I entertain the highest opinion of the duke's military genius, still I do not like to see him at the head of the finances of the country, enjoying, as he does, the full and perfect confidence of his sovereign,—enjoying all the patronage of the crown,—enjoying the patronage of the army,—enjoying the patronage of the church,—and, in fact, enjoying almost all the patronage of the state. The noble duke is likewise entrusted with the delicate functions of conveying constant and delicate advice to the ears of his royal master. As a constitutional man, this state of things strikes me as being most *unconstitutional*." Mr. Brougham further added, "I have no fear of slavery being introduced into this country by the power of the sword. The noble duke (of Wellington) may take the army,—he may take the navy,—he may take the mitre, he may take the great seal,—I will make the noble duke a present of them all. Let him come on with his whole force, sword in hand, against the constitution, and the energies of the people of this country would not only beat him, but laugh at his efforts." These were the excellent sentiments of Mr. Brougham, and we wish the noble Lord Chancellor may long continue the undeviating advocate of the people's rights and liberties.

We have now to record the death of the Earl of Liverpool, which took place at his residence, Coome Wood, on the 4th of December, in the fifty-ninth year of his age, regretted by none but those who had feasted on the wealth of our country, under his long unfortunate sway over national affairs.

Could we write as severe as the ministerial qualities of Lord Liverpool were injurious to the British people, what a hideous draught of distortion, both in principle and conduct, should we exhibit! Looking at the insignificant origin of his lordship, and the crooked crags of his political progress, we trace the wily ascent of an intriguing speculator, clinging to his towry height by principles hostile to the constitution of England. His career is marked by a glazy ichor, which, though repulsive to the chaste eye of public virtue, and offensive to the independent feelings of public spirit, will be as memorable as odious. Long after the praises of his lordship's minions shall be buried in oblivion, the iniquity of his deeds will pain the recollection of all good men, while he will be regarded as the favourite model of those who aspire to the ruin of their country. The character of this weak and daring man would not deserve the attention of history, if it were not so fatally united with the misfortunes of our country, which are mainly to be attributed to him and his notoriously wicked and over-bearing junta.

When in the House of Commons in 1793, he (then Mr. Jenkinson) was foremost in opposing the memorable petition for parliamentary reform, brought forward by Mr. (now Earl) Grey, and defended the then existing state of the representation, maintaining, "that the House of Commons, constituted as it was, had answered the end for which it was designed,"—namely, we suppose, to subdue the people!

Upon the assassination of Mr. Perceval in 1812, Lord Liverpool became first lord of the Treasury, by the especial request of the regent. Upon his lordship's advancement to this high and important office, Lord Sidmouth and Mr. Vansittart were announced as new members of the ministry. The first act of Lord Liverpool, or what may be termed his first important measure, was the introduction of a bill to increase the magisterial power in various districts of the country, where the inhabitants were suffering from want of employment. By this bill, such persons were not allowed the use of fire-arms, and forbidden to meet in companies. His lordship here mistook tyranny for justice, and appeared to set at defiance the opinion of the admirable Locke, that "there is a way whereby governments are dissolved, and that is, when the legislature and the prince, or either of them, act contrary to their trust."

Another grievous inroad upon the liberties of the people, during the administration of this puissant lord, was his frequent union of offices diametrically opposite to each other; one of which, appointing the clergy to sit on the judicial bench, must ever be considered as an infringement upon that religion which his lordship considered as "part and parcel of the law of the land." The studies of clergymen were originally designed to fit them for the diffusion of "peace and good-will towards men," and not to form them for the exercise of *temporal* power. We do not mean to say that, when people become clergymen, they are to renounce their rights as men; but this is a widely-different matter from investing them with the power of punishing a delinquent. Christ himself exercised no such functions, but left them to the secular authorities. Why, then, should those who pretend to be the followers of Christ presume to that which their master condemned? Alas! their conduct has too often proved them to be no followers of his; yet Lord Liverpool, well knowing the general vindictiveness and domineering austerity of their hearts, considered them the better fit for the magisterial office, as his intention was to rule by forcing the people into obedience, instead of soothing their irritated minds by a few timely concessions.

For the sake of Christianity itself, we hope to see such an unholy union of spiritual and secular power speedily abolished.

It was also under Lord Liverpool's administration that the most revolting scenes of MILITARY FLOGGING occurred. We might relate numerous instances of this barbarous custom, but one will be sufficient for the purpose of illustration: Three soldiers, (MERE BOYS!) in July, 1817, in company with others, met at the Rose and Crown public-house, Tower Hill, where at length a fight ensued. A court-martial being held, Thomas Hayes, Francis Hayes, and George Staniford were ordered to receive eight hundred lashes each! The execution of this sentence, so disgraceful to a civilized

A military flogging as depicted in G.W.M. Reynolds's novel *The Soldier's Wife*. (*Stephen Basdeo Personal Collection*)

country, was commenced; but after Thomas Hayes (who was only twenty years of age) had received six hundred and seventy-five lashes, the surgeon pronounced his life to be in danger, and he was, therefore, carried away. Francis Hayes, only sixteen years of age, received three hundred and thirty-five lashes; and George Staniford, only seventeen years of age, two hundred lashes!—when both the latter had the remaining part of their sentence commuted, upon condition of their entering a condemned regiment! Thus three of our fellow-creatures, who had the misfortune to be English soldiers, and therefore, of all other men in the world, alone liable to be subjected to a system of refined cruelty, alike distinguished for its cold-blooded atrocity and the utter absence of any reasonable plea for its infliction, were tortured in this *Christian* land as long as nature would bear the anguish, and that, too, before the number of lashes awarded by their unmerciful judges had been inflicted upon their poor backs! Is there a man whose heart retains a spark of feeling,—who has not been hardened by military education and habits,—that does not feel an involuntary shudder, a sickening of the heart, when he learns that three of his countrymen—*free-born Englishmen*, (oh, what a satire has that term become!)—were sentenced to have "the living flesh torn from their backs" by the horrid laceration of the cat-o'-nine-tails, for being guilty of a public-house brawl! In the name of an all-merciful Providence, of what materials are military officers composed that they can endure such disgusting spectacles? We wonder how they have so long dared to set at defiance the indignation of the public, and tempt the just vengeance of heaven! Can they, after witnessing such scenes of unbearable torture,—of worse than Russian barbarity,—return to their wives and families, and eat their food with an appetite? But officers are GENTLEMEN,—*young sprigs of nobility*, in most cases,—and the sufferings of the private soldier may possibly be SPORT TO THEM! We hope, however, to see a law passed to give equal rights to the soldier as to the *brute*, at least; for no man in England, be he whom he may, is permitted to treat a dog as soldiers have been and are even *now* treated. Were all Englishmen punished in the same manner for the offence of brawling and drunkenness, where would the flogging system terminate? Certainly not with the private soldier or the foremast sailor; it would assuredly find its way to their *officers*, to the *noble*, the *bishop*, and the *prince*!!!

Lord Liverpool allowed himself to be a prominent actor in the unprecedented persecutions against the Princess of Wales. Had not his lordship arranged the form of the secret proceedings abroad, and consented to the lavish expenditure of our means to suppress truth in that partial business, both the queen and her daughter might, at this time, have been in the enjoyment of health and happiness. His lordship said publicly, that the prosecution against her majesty in 1820 was "the most embarrassing question which ever perplexed any government." This short declaration spoke volumes; for truth is simple, and requires no adornment of language. At the conclusion of the mock trial of her majesty, there appeared, in the House of Lords, a majority of NINE for the Bill against the queen; yet, under these circumstances, his lordship thought proper to abandon the charges against her majesty! His motives for acting thus, we shall presently explain; but in the mean time we contend that such a proceeding was unconstitutional, and not to be defended on any honourable grounds. If the peers had really voted *conscientiously*, they were entitled to the award from their majority; if they had *not* so voted, then they ought to have been expelled from the House for ever, as well as from all honourable society. Either way, therefore, Lord Liverpool acted wrong, and fully proved the verity of the old adage, "Power usurped is weakness when exposed; conscious of wrong, it is pusillanimous, and prone to flight."

At the period of which we are speaking, certain documents were laid before Lord Liverpool, relative to the bonds and promissory notes entered into so solemnly by certain royal princes; and his lordship was assured that, if the bill of pains and penalties did pass, these disgraceful engagements, together with the attendant circumstances, should immediately meet the public eye. Here then was one of the secret reasons of his lordship's abandoning the infamous bill against the queen!

The following is a true copy of the letter conveying this unwelcome intelligence, and which was delivered into Lord Liverpool's own hand:

"Nov. 6th, 1820.

"My Lord,

"Fearless of your displeasure, I beg to submit my sentiments to your lordship without further ceremony. I am in the possession of a copy of *a certain bond*, upon the execution of which your royal master was the first named, and to whom the largest share was to be advanced. If the bill against the queen *pass*, I will expose the whole transaction to the nation, and that will be sufficient to open the eyes even of the wilfully blind. You know the danger, and may provide against it in some degree. I shall also explain the unhappy consequences attendant upon some of the INJURED persons connected with this transaction.

"I am, my lord,

"Your humble servant,

"&c. &c. &c.

"To the Right Hon. Lord Liverpool."

We here subjoin an exact copy of the bond referred to in this letter:

Know all Men by these presents, that We, George Prince of Wales, Frederick Duke of York, and William Henry Duke of Clarence, all living in the City of Westminster, in the County of Middlesex, are jointly and severally, justly and truly, indebted to John Cator, of Beckenham, in the County of Kent, Esquire, and his Executors, Administrators, and Assigns, in the penal sum of *Sixty Thousand Pounds*, of good and lawful money of Great Britain, well and truly paid to Us, at or before the sealing of these presents. Sealed with our Seals this 16th day of December, in the Twenty-ninth year of the Reign of our Sovereign Lord George the Third, by the Grace of God, King, Defender of the Faith, anno domini 1788.

The condition of the above-written obligation is such, that if the above bounden George Prince of Wales, Frederick Duke of York, and William Henry Duke of Clarence, or any or either of them, or any of their Heirs, Executors, or Administrators, shall well and truly pay, or cause to be paid, unto the above-named John Cator, his Executors, Administrators, or Assigns, the full sum of *Sixty Thousand Pounds* of lawful money of Great Britain, within the space or time of six calendar months next, after any one or either of us, the said George Prince of Wales, Frederick Duke of York, and William Henry Duke of Clarence, shall come to and ascend the Throne of England, together with lawful interest on the same; to be computed from the day that such event shall happen, upon whom, to the time of paying off this obligation, then, and in such case, the same shall become null and void; otherwise to be and remain in full force and virtue.

Signed

George Prince of Wales L.S.

Frederick. L.S.

William Henry. L.S.

To save the exhibition of this bond, as well as several others of a similar description, much to the discredit of the sovereign, Lord Liverpool readily gave his assistance, and thus was *forced* to abandon the bill against the queen.

In 1823, Lord Liverpool said in the House, that "The policy of the British government rested on the principle of the law of nations, which allowed every country to judge how it could best be governed, and what ought to be its institutions." This paragraph in his lordship's speech sufficiently proved him to be an *aristocrat*, in the true sense of the word. The policy of *his* government was, doubtless, to concentrate power in the hands of the rulers, and to *force* the mass of the people to submissive degradation and wretchedness.

In 1825, his lordship was again disturbed by an inquiry into some state arrangements, relative to the mysterious demise of the Princess Charlotte, which had been made in 1817, and to which his lordship had been privy. But he declined all inquiries into this disgraceful subject, in a manner not very consistent with his own honour, or the importance of the question. In 1826, his lordship was once more solicited to receive the information, but he still declined, though he must have been aware of the justness of the claim. As we have fully explained these appeals to his lordship in a former part of our work, we have only considered it necessary to glance at them in this place.

At length this statesman, after serving his king in direct opposition to the interests of the people, fell into the stupor of apoplectic and paralytic disease, and expired as previously stated.

In this year, an inquiry was instituted into the death of the patriot Hampden; and, in order to ascertain, if possible, the sort of wound by which he had been killed, his body was disinterred from Hampden church, Bucks. The exhumation was attended by Lord Nugent, Mr. Denman, and several other gentlemen. The following account of the investigation was given to the public by one of the party:

"After examining the initials and dates on several leaden coffins, we came to the one in question, the plate of which was so corroded, that it crumbled and broke into small pieces on touching it. It was therefore impossible to ascertain the name of the individual it contained. The coffin had originally been enclosed in wood, covered with velvet, a small portion only of which was apparent near the bottom, at the left side, which was not the case with those of a later date, where the initials were very distinct, and the lead more perfect and fresher in appearance. The register stated, that Hampden was interred on the 25th day of June, 1643, and an old document, still in existence, gives a curious and full account of the grand procession on the occasion; we were, therefore, pretty confident that this must be the one in question, having examined all the others in succession. It was lying under the western window, near the tablet erected by him, when living, to the memory of his beloved wife, whose virtues he extols in the most affectionate language. Without positive proof, it was reasonable to suppose that he would be interred near his adored partner, and this being found at her feet, it was unanimously agreed that the lid should be cut open to ascertain the fact, which proved afterwards that we were not mistaken. The parish plumber descended, and commenced cutting across the coffin, then longitudinally, until the whole was sufficiently loosened to roll back, in order to lift off the wooden lid beneath, which was found in such good preservation that it came off nearly entire. Beneath this was another lid of the same material, which was raised without much giving way. The coffin had originally been filled up with sawdust, which was found undisturbed, except the centre, where the abdomen had fallen in. The sawdust was then removed, and the process of examination commenced. Silence reigned. Lord Nugent descended into the grave, and first removed the outer cloth, which was firmly wrapped round the body; then the second and a third, such care having been extended to preserve the body from the worm of corruption. Here a very singular scene presented itself. No regular features were apparent, although the face retained a death-like whiteness, and shewed the various windings of the blood-vessels beneath the skin. The upper row of teeth were perfect, and those that remained in the under jaw, on being taken out and examined, were quite sound. A little beard remained on the lower part of the chin; and the whiskers were strong, and somewhat lighter than his hair, which was a full auburn brown; the upper part of the bridge of the nose still remained elevated; the remainder had given way to the pressure of the cloths, which had been firmly bound round the head. The eyes were but slightly sunk in, and were covered with the same white film which characterized the general appearance of the face. As a difference of opinion existed concerning the indentation in the left shoulder, where it was supposed he had been wounded, it was unanimously agreed upon to raise up the coffin altogether, and place it in the centre of the church, where a more accurate examination might take place. The coffin was extremely heavy; but, by elevating one end with a crow-bar, two strong ropes were adjusted under either end, and thus drawn up by twelve men, in the most careful manner possible. The first operation was, to examine the arms, which nearly retained their original size, and presented a very muscular appearance. On lifting up the right arm, we found that it was dispossessed of its hand. We might, therefore, naturally conjecture that it had been amputated, as the bone presented a perfectly flat appearance, as if sawn off by some very sharp instrument. On searching carefully under the cloths, to our no small astonishment, we found the hand, or rather a number of small bones, enclosed in a separate cloth. For about six inches up the arm, the greater part of the flesh had wasted away, being evidently smaller than the lower part of the left arm, to which the hand was very firmly united, and which presented no symptoms of decay further than the two bones of the fore-finger being loose. Even the nails remained entire, of which we saw no appearance in the cloth containing the remains of the right hand. In order to corroborate or disprove the different statements relative to his having been wounded in the right shoulder, a close examination of each took place. The clavicle of the right shoulder was firmly united in the scapula, nor did there appear any contusion or indentation that evinced symptoms of any wound ever having been inflicted. The left shoulder, on the contrary, was smaller and sunken in, as if the clavicle had been displaced. To remove all doubts, it was judged necessary to remove the arms, which were amputated with a penknife. The socket of the left arm was perfectly white and healthy, and the clavicle firmly united to the scapula, nor was there the least appearance of contusion or wound. The socket of the right shoulder, on the contrary, was of a brownish cast, and the clavicle being found quite loose and disunited from the scapula, proved that dislocation had taken place. The bones, however, were quite perfect. Such dislocation, therefore, must have arisen, either from the force of a ball, or from Colonel Hampden having fallen from his horse, when he lost the power of holding the reins, by reason of his hand having been so dreadfully shattered. The latter, in all probability, was the case, as it would be barely impossible for a ball to pass through the shoulder without some fracture, either of the clavicle or scapula. In order to examine the head and hair, the body was raised up and supported with a shovel; on removing the cloths, which adhered firmly to the back of the head, we found the hair in a complete state of preservation. It was a dark auburn colour, and, according to the custom of the times, was very long,—from five to six inches. It was drawn up and tied round at the top of the head with black thread or silk. The ends had the appearance of having been cut off. On taking hold of the top-knot, it soon gave way, and came off like a wig. Here a singular scene presented itself. The worm of corruption was busily employed; the skull, in some places, being perfectly bare, whilst in others the skin remained nearly entire, upon which we discovered a number of maggots and small red worms on the feed with great activity. This was the only spot where any symptoms of life was apparent, as if the brain contained a vital principle within it, which engendered its own destruction; otherwise, how can we account, after the lapse of nearly two centuries, in finding living creatures preying upon the seat of intellect, when they were no where else to be found, in no other part of the body? He was five feet, nine inches, in height, apparently of great muscular strength, of a vigorous and robust frame; forehead broad and high; the skull altogether well formed, such an one as the imagination would conceive capable of great exploits."

We offer no apology for inserting this very interesting inquiry into the cause of the death of one of England's greatest characters. Such investigations, we consider, possess peculiar interest to the lovers of truth, as well as being calculated to effect much public good. The deaths of many other illustrious individuals are yet involved in mystery, which may probably, at no distant period, be cleared up in the same way as that of Hampden has been. The sudden death of George the Third's next brother, Edward, Duke of York, calls aloud for inquiry; and, though it is impossible to make reparation to the departed duke himself, yet such inquiry might lead to the benefit of his INNOCENT, INJURED, and STILL SURVIVING OFFSPRING.

* * *

The excesses of the court at this period, as usual, were enormous. The man who had sworn to do justice and love mercy proved, by his deportment, that he cared not for either. In defiance of prudence, he continued to revel in gaiety and wantonness, totally regardless of the sorrows of his subjects, whose condition daily became more grievous, and whose petitions were disregarded in proportion to the pressure of their miseries. This man of pleasure exhausted what time he could spare from the indulgence of his passions in the invention of expensive and useless decorations and embellishments to the already gorgeous palaces in which he pleased to reside. He was still unwearied in his monstrous demands from the resources of the people, indefatigable in the accomplishment of all his lascivious pursuits, and deaf to the voice of remonstrance and humanity.

At the commencement of the year

1829,

the Catholics of Ireland exhibited so strong a determination to be emancipated from their long oppression, that the Duke of Wellington and Mr. Peel considered it expedient to pass a bill for their relief. We cordially agree in the principle of removing all civil disabilities from men on account of their religion; but we must nevertheless view the conduct of these two inconsistent ministers with the greatest possible contempt. Headed by the wicked Duke of York, they had frequently declared their fixed determination to oppose any further concessions to the Catholics, for fear of endangering the "established church," and had violently and obstinately opposed their just demands on every ground of right and of expediency! Even during the discussions of the preceding year, both of them had expressed no inclination to desert the principles which they had uniformly defended; yet, strange to say,

ANNO DECIMO

GEORGII IV. REGIS.

An Act for the Relief of His Majesty's Roman Catholic Subjects.   [13th *April* 1829.]

WHEREAS by various Acts of Parliament certain Restraints and Disabilities are imposed on the Roman Catholic Subjects of His Majesty, to which other Subjects of His Majesty are not liable: And whereas it is expedient that such Restraints and Disabilities shall be from henceforth discontinued: And whereas by various Acts certain Oaths and certain Declarations, commonly called the Declaration against Transubstantiation, and the Declaration against Transubstantiation and the Invocation of Saints and the Sacrifice of the Mass, as practised in the Church of Rome, are or may be required to be taken, made, and subscribed by the Subjects of His Majesty, as Qualifications for sitting and voting in Parliament, and for the Enjoyment of certain Offices, Franchises, and Civil Rights: Be it enacted by the King's most Excellent Majesty, by and with the Advice and Consent of the Lords Spiritual and Temporal, and Commons, in this present Parliament assembled, and by the Authority of the same, That from and after the Commencement of this Act all such Parts of the said Acts as require the said Declarations, or either of them, to be made or subscribed by any of His Majesty's Subjects, as a Qualification for sitting and voting in Parliament, or for the Exercise or Enjoyment of any Office, Franchise, or Civil Right, be and the same are (save as herein-after provided and excepted) hereby repealed.

II. And be it enacted, That from and after the Commencement of this Act it shall be lawful for any Person professing the Roman Catholic Religion, being a Peer, or who shall after the Commencement

The Catholic Emancipation Act of 1829.

all of a sudden, their opinions changed, and that which had so long appeared to them as being fraught with the greatest danger received their most zealous advocacy and support!

Amongst the occurrences of this time, we cannot help noticing the pompous enthronement of one of the pretended followers of the meek and lowly Jesus,— the Bishop of London,—which took place in St. Paul's Cathedral, on the 16th of January. The cathedral was filled, at a very early hour, with a crowd of curious people to witness the installation of Dr. Bloomfield. After the parade of being met by the Bishop of Llandaff (Dr. Copleston), the prebends, canons, and other functionaries, the lord mayor, &c., the installation speech was delivered in the following words:—

> "I, Dr. Copleston, of the cathedral church of St. Paul, do induct, instal, and enthrone You, the Right Reverend Father in God, Charles James, *by divine permission* **(or by permission of the Lord Chancellor?)** Bishop of London, into the bishopric and episcopacy of London; and the Lord preserve thy going out and coming in, from this time forth for ever more; and mayest thou remain in justice and sanctity, and adorn the place thou art *delegated to by God*! God is powerful, and may he increase your grace."

How far the bishop was delegated by God, we do not pretend to determine; but fifteen thousand pounds per annum for the *great labours* **attendant upon this office** were not, we think, a matter of indifference to the *pious* **bishop; because such a sum would enable his** right reverend lordship to be "charitable to the poor," as well as to keep his "church in good repair," for which purposes such an immense sum was *originally* **designed.**

In the November of this year, died Thomas Garth, esquire, general in his majesty's service, and colonel of the first regiment of dragoons. This gallant general had the good fortune to render himself agreeable to a certain lady of illustrious birth, by whom, *it was said*, he had one son, who bears the general's name, and who now is a captain in the army. This son was the chief mourner at the funeral of the general, which took place on the 27th of November, at St. Martin's in the Fields. It is, however, very probable, that the mystery of this very extraordinary affair will, ere long, be explained, though it may not redound to the *chastity* of royalty. Many places and pensions have been bestowed to prevent an exposure of the circumstances attending the captain's birth, but we have reason to think that TRUTH will ultimately prevail. *We* could ourselves elucidate this mysterious business, if we deemed it requisite; but, as the matter is now pending in a court of law, it would be improper for us to interfere. In referring to subjects of this nature, we cannot help pitying the imbecility and sorrows of George the Third, which were, doubtless, considerably heightened, though not originally produced, by the delinquencies of his family, both male and female.

In the early part of the year

1830,

the king's health materially declined, though the greatest secrecy prevailed at Windsor upon the subject. His disease, however, progressively increased, and in the latter end of March, he became unable to take his usual exercise in the park. From time to time, the organs of the court pronounced his majesty again in tolerable health, and announced his intention to hold a drawing room at St. James; but at the same time they well knew there was no probability that such an event could take place.

On the 15th of April, the first bulletin was issued, and this official document regularly appeared till the announcement of the royal demise, which was as follows:

> "His majesty expired at a quarter past three o'clock this morning, in the 68th year of his age, and in the eleventh of his reign.—*June 26th, 1830, Windsor Castle.*"

The death was lingering and painful, which is not to be wondered at when we consider what an artificial system of body there was to break up, and to what a magnitude it had grown. The wonder is, considering the life which the king had led in his youth, and the ease and luxury in which he indulged afterwards, that he lasted so long. After the usual ceremony of lying in state had been observed, his majesty was consigned to the royal vault at Windsor, on Thursday, the 15th of July. Immediately after which, the greatest bustle was observed in the apartments occupied at Windsor by the Marchioness of Conyngham, and a general scramble and a rapid packing up of valuables took place.

We have so often had occasion to speak of the actions of George the Fourth, that little remains to be said of his general character. That he was handsome, dressed and lived extravagantly, put on fascinating manners when he wished to gain his point, and had an extraordinary good opinion of himself, are *accomplishments* which we believe he possessed in an eminent degree. But what were such insignificant matters to the country in general, when their possessor owned the basest and most vindictive heart that ever disgraced the human bosom? Would his handsome person atone, in the eyes of doting parents, for the seduction of their daughters? Would his splendid habiliments afford a recompense to his ruined creditors? Would his fascinating manners compensate his injured and cruelly-oppressed wife for the brutal, unmanly, and infamous treatment she received from him? Or would his self-love satisfy the heavily-taxed people, who were compelled to administer to his extravagant demands for finery and baubles? Assuredly not; and such "accomplishments," therefore, only tended to render the actions of his majesty more disgusting in the eyes of the better part of the community. In truth, George the Fourth thought of nothing but his personal ease and comforts. When his mistresses or his friends became troublesome, they were instantly and unceremoniously dismissed, without causing the "first gentleman in the world" the least uneasiness as to their future good or ill fortune. In politics, he leagued himself with the Whigs as long as they served his purpose; but, directly they gave him the least trouble, he disowned their acquaintance. He indulged the follies and vices of his chosen companions, till indulging them longer became irksome. He supported the principles of his family as long as supporting them answered his ends. He consented to the passing of the Catholic Relief Bill on the same principle as he had shaken off poor Mrs. Robinson. Protestantism and Perdita were voted bores, and he therefore took the easiest course to rid himself of both. In the latter years of his life, he disliked public exhibitions, because they gave him trouble, and kept him a few hours from indulging his private passions, which he considered as so much time lost. This is the *true* character of George the Fourth, whatever his minions may say to the contrary.

Passing over many circumstances of dubious import, relative to the departed monarch, we proceed to notice some transactions of an unhappy complexion, and which reflect no small portion of dishonour upon his memory. When the late Duke of York returned from his military education in Prussia, he unfortunately brought with him the prevailing vice of the principal courts of Germany,—that of GAMBLING; and to his inordinate attachment to that ruinous propensity may be attributed the frequent loss of property and personal disgrace he endured. The late monarch, also, was equally addicted to a love of play, and the sum allowed him when he attained his majority soon proved insufficient to supply the natural consequences of that uncontrolled passion and his very lavish expenditure in finery of all kinds.

In consequence of the mutual embarrassments of these royal brothers, they found themselves under the absolute necessity of raising money to discharge some of their most pressing accounts. The prince, in conjunction with the Dukes of York and Clarence, tried every imaginable source in this country, from which it was thought a supply could be raised, sufficient to avert the impending storm that hung over their heads; but all their endeavours failed. As a last resource, the late monarch was advised to attempt a loan in Holland; and Messrs. Bonney and Sunderland, then of George-yard, Lombard-street, were appointed notarial agents for the verification of the bonds; and the late Mr. Thomas Hammersley, of Pall-mall, banker, was to receive the subscriptions, and to pay the dividends thereon to the holders on the joint bonds of the Prince of Wales, the Duke of York, and the Duke of Clarence. The sum intended to be raised was about one million sterling, the greater part of which was subscribed for by foreign houses only, at a price which would have proved very satisfactory if the contract had been faithfully performed. The negotiation for this loan commenced in 1788; but an interruption to its completion was occasioned by the death of Mr. Bonney, the notary. It was ultimately confirmed, to the great loss of those who had so rashly speculated in such a questionable security. The loan was to bear six per cent. interest, and the revenues of their royal highnesses were to be invested in the hands of the late Dukes of Northumberland and Portland, in order to ensure the due payment of interest and principal. A large portion of the money, to the amount of nearly half a million, had been received by the princes when the revolution in France, in 1793, presented an opportunity to resist the payment of those bonds which had been circulated, and even the interest due upon them was refused. During the revolution, some of the holders of these bonds escaped, and arrived in England; and, as their last resource, they made numerous applications to the princes for the interest due to them, if it were not quite convenient to discharge the bonds in full. But the law-advisers of the princes pretended that the present holders were not entitled to the interest, as they presumed the bonâ-fide holders had perished during the troubles in France and Holland; and that, consequently, other claims were not legal. On the part of the claimants, the bonds were produced which they had bought, and their right asserted to claim interest and principal equally as if they had been the original subscribers.

This evasive attempt to resist the just discharge of loans, raised at such great hazards, must ever be considered as an indelible stain upon the characters of the princes concerned. We, however, would acquit the Duke of Clarence from any participation in the *profits* of these bonds; his natural affection for his two elder brothers induced him to add his name to the bonds merely as a further security to their holders; and we doubt not that his present majesty will, if he have not already done so, make all the reparation in his power to the heirs of the original sufferers in these very dishonourable transactions.

The holders of these bonds finding themselves so unjustly treated, M. Martignac, one of the original subscribers to them, made an application to the Court of Chancery, and the affair came on by way of motion. Sir Arthur Pigott, who was then Attorney-General to the Duchy of Cornwall, replied, "that he had never heard of the existence of such bonds; but his own opinion was, that the unhappy condition of France and Holland rendered the *identification* of the bonâ-fide holders almost impossible, even presuming they ever had existed; but the inquiry should be made in the proper quarter!" That inquiry, however, never benefitted the distressed refugees. Sir Arthur Pigott, the legal adviser of the Prince of Wales, might, to please his master, attempt to deny the existence of these nominal securities; yet positive proof against such denial was, that they were actually floating in the "money market," as *common as any other security*, AT THAT VERY TIME! There was, indeed, scarcely a broker on the Exchange who had not some portion of them for sale; and it was an indisputable truth that means, of a disreputable nature, were used to depreciate their value in the money market.

We must not here pass over the suspicious conduct (relative to these bonds) of the then secretary of state for the home department. Under the specious pretext of enforcing the Alien Act, this gentleman caused the whole of these injured claimants to be taken and put on board a vessel in the Thames, which was stated to be ready to sail for Holland. This vessel, however, cast anchor at the Nore, for the professed purpose of waiting to receive the necessary papers from the office of the secretary of state. The heart-rending destiny of the unfortunate victims now only remains to be told. Although no charge was preferred against them, they were thus unceremoniously sent out of the kingdom by the decree of arbitrary power. From the list of twenty-six unfortunate creditors of the princes, fourteen of them were traced to the *guillotine*. The other twelve perished by another concocted plan. The two principal money-lenders, M. Abraham and M. Simeon Boas, of the Hague, were endeavouring to maintain their shattered credit, and actually paid the interest themselves due upon these bonds for two years; but they were finally ruined, and one of the brothers put an end to his existence by a pistol,—the other by poison!

Similar tragical scenes were attendant upon another loan, raised for the princes by M. John James de Beaume, and prepared by Mr. Becknel. The *signed* acknowledgment of the princes was for one hundred thousand pounds, payable to the said De Beaume, and vesting in him the power to divide this bond into shares of one thousand pounds each, by printed copies of the bond, &c. The original bond was deposited, for safety, in the bank of Ransom, Morland, and Hammersley, while an attested copy, as well as the bankers' acknowledgment of their holding such security, were given to De Beaume as a proof of his authority in being the agent of the three English princes. They also gave him a letter of introduction to their correspondent in Paris, M. Perregaux. After considerable difficulty, and after having remitted and paid to the princes two hundred thousand pounds, in money and jewels, M. de Beaume and his associates were apprehended, and charged with treason, for asserting that George the Third of England was King of France!!! These unfortunate men were tried, condemned, and actually executed upon this paltry charge within twenty-four hours after their mock trial! So perished Richard Chaudot, Mestrirer Niette, De Beaume, and Aubert, either for purchasing the shares of the princes' securities, or for negotiating them. Such also was the fate of Viette, a rich jeweller, who had bought largely of the shares from De Beaume.

Would that we could here close the catalogue of black offences against certain individuals; but we are obliged, as honest historians, to refer to the cruel death of Charles Vaucher, a banker in Paris. This gentleman quitted France in 1793, and fixed his residence in England, where he married an English lady. He had been the purchaser of twenty shares of the princes' bond, and, as was naturally to be expected, made application for the interest due thereon. The claim being refused, the injured gentleman applied for legal assistance; but the interest was still rejected, because the bond had not been named in the schedule laid before the commissioners appointed to examine into the extent of the debts of the Prince George! Further application was made; though, instead of obtaining justice, this

William Henry-Cavendish, 3rd Duke of Portland.

unfortunate gentleman received an official order to quit England within the space of four days! Having other affairs to arrange, M. Vaucher petitioned the Duke of Portland (then prime minister) to allow him to remain until his affairs could be arranged; but his petition was refused, and a warrant issued, signed by the duke, directing William Ross and George Higgins, two of his majesty's messengers, to take M. Vaucher into custody till he should be sent out of the country, which was immediately put in force! He was conveyed to Rotterdam, and from thence to Paris, where he was imprisoned. On the 22nd of December, 1795, his trial took place upon similar charges to those of M. de Beaume, and he was soon found guilty, and guillotined!

We could recite many other crimes relative to these bonds; but we think we hear the shocked reader exclaim, "Hold! enough!" Indeed such sickening details can hardly obtain credence in the minds of men, possessed of even the common feelings of our nature. To offer any palliation of such monstrous atrocities would only be an insult to the understandings of all unprejudiced observers of royalty!

At the time of the Prince of Wales' greatest embarrassments, an attempt was made to divert the country into a belief of the honourable intentions of his royal highness by the sale of his racing stud, and some other property. But no sooner had parliament voted sufficient money to relieve the prince from his debts than the turf-establishment was revived in a more ruinous style than ever, the field of dissipation and extravagance enlarged, and fresh debts contracted to an enormous amount, which were not either in his or the nation's power to discharge. Strong doubts were also entertained that the money voted by parliament to this "prodigal son" was not applied to the purpose for which it was granted. Had a private individual so committed himself, he would have become the outcast of his family, while all the virtuous part of the community had instantly avoided him; but in the case of this prince, where the example was ten thousand times more contagious, such a flagrant breach of faith and such base ingratitude hardly received the slightest animadversion! Why should more indulgence have been shewn to this man, whose peculiar duty it was to respect popular favour, and to act in such a manner as to deserve it, and from whose exalted station the public had a right to expect lessons of morality and virtue, than to a private person, whose deviation from their rules only produces partial effects, and can be of no detriment to the community at large. How unjust it is, what an inversion of every fair and honourable principle, to suffer the bauble rank to afford a veil to moral depravity! To protect genius, to reward merit, and to relieve distress, is what *ought* to be the duty of a prince; but when the nation was called on to liquidate immense debts, without a single instance of this kind on record to justify such a perversion of their money, it was perfidy to the public, and not a warranted liberality towards the prince, for any parliament to do so. Such conduct, indeed, would not have been tolerated had not the professed representatives of England (who were the nominees of a haughty and unfeeling aristocracy) put it beyond the remedy of the majority of the people. At the periods to which we now refer, the most disgraceful sums were also voted for the repairs and embellishments of Brighton Pavilion, Windsor Castle, Windsor Cottage, (so called) the Palace at Pimlico, and other fanciful buildings of royalty. The money required for these purposes, be it remembered, was drained from a heavily-oppressed people, whose industry, economy, and honesty were, in the aggregate, without a parallel. But it is a serious fact, that, from the accession of George the Third to the death of George the Fourth, the royal expenditure was ninety-two millions, ninety thousand, eight hundred, and seven pounds! Yet, in this amount, the salaries and official emoluments of the royal dukes are not included from the year 1815. We cannot help contrasting the evil done with the benefits that might have been bestowed by this money. What a fund it had made to lessen the hardships imposed upon the poor!—to mitigate the sufferings of the mechanic!—and to lighten the burdens of the honest citizen! Instead of which, it was expended merely to gratify pride and vice. The delight of doing good was the last sentiment for consideration; and though a vast field was open for the exercise of benevolence, yet the offices of real greatness were always neglected by George the Fourth and the greater part of his family.

* * *

Having now brought our history down to the providential release of England by the death of George the Fourth, we cannot part company with our readers before taking a general survey of the lamentable truths it contains. Authors have too often demeaned themselves by concealing facts, and, instead of being historians of an action, have proved themselves the mere lawyers of a party; they are retained by their principles, and bribed by their interests; their narrations are an opening of their case, and in front of their histories, therefore, ought to be written—"I am for the defendant," or "I am for the plaintiff." With such unworthy writers, we should be ashamed to claim affinity. Our unflinching exposures have been made with no sinister motives; for we have dared to brave prosecutions and persecutions, despising the bribes and defying the hate of the minions of power! Our's is the cause, the righteous cause, of the insulted and harassed classes,—the real productors of the national wealth,—who have so long endured the galling yoke of oppression. The time, however, is now fast approaching when fallacious speeches must yield precedence to solid reasoning, when honest governments must supersede systems of despotism, when vice must be recognized and punished in the case of the prince as well as in that of the peasant; when superior talents must be permitted to occupy superior stations; when individuals, most suited to serve the real interests of the kingdom, will be solicited to guide the helm of state; when all policy, opposed to freedom, will be annihilated; when interested men will be compelled to quit their seats in the councils, and weak men be afraid to venture another trial; when he who has the heart of a coward, or the spirit of a sycophant, will not dare to present himself for the suffrages of a free people! Yes, we repeat, such an era is at hand, and "the people" of England are about to enjoy that liberty and happiness, from which they have unjustly been debarred by the cruel and haughty hand of tyranny. An unjust government, whether professing Whig or Tory principles, will vainly attempt to stop this march of liberty by raising the old bugbear cry of—"Anarchy and confusion will be the consequences of entrusting the people with their political rights and privileges!" Such an unnatural doctrine has been held far too long by the titled and wealthy mortality of our land, who are not contented with enjoying the great advantages of rank and property, whether hereditary or acquired, but seem, by their behaviour, determined to prevent their less-fortunate brethren from tasting the happiness which would arise from a possession of their political rights. The tyrannical nature of such characters, unsatisfied with the elevation which their birth or fortune has given them, wish to trample on their "inferiors," and to force them still lower in the scale of intelligent beings. Contemptible proud men, thus to insult those who minister to their luxuries and their wealth! Such vain conduct, however, will never fail to excite the honest indignation of all who can think and feel, and who are remote from the sphere of corrupting influence. It is not only most highly culpable in a moral view, but extremely dangerous in a political. It arises from the hateful spirit of despotism, and, if not timely checked by the people, must soon become universal. A spirit of this nature would allow no rights to the poor but those which cannot be taken away,—the rights of mere animal nature. Such a spirit hates "the people," and would gladly annihilate all of them but those who administer to pride and luxury, either as menial servants, dependent tradesmen, or mechanics,— or common soldiers, ready to shed the blood of those who might render themselves obnoxious to their lordly tyrants. Notwithstanding such contempt of "the people," however, these mighty of the land think they are entitled to represent them in parliament; yet what can be expected from such proud men but that they should be as servilely mean and obsequious to a minister as they are cruel and unfeeling in their behaviour to the poor of their vicinity? By such behaviour, the ARISTOCRATS attempt to form a little world of their own, where Folly and Vanity reign supreme, but where Virtue, Learning, and Usefulness are alike unknown. The grand secret of its constitution is to claim dignity, distinction, power, and place, exclusively, without the painful labour of deserving either by personal merit, or by services to the commonwealth. They talk and laugh loud, applauding each other's self-complacency, and would not be supposed to cast an eye on the "inferior crowd," whose admiration, nevertheless, they are at the same time courting by every silly effort of pragmatical vanity! Men of this cast pay no more, and frequently not so much, as other people; yet they strangely conceive themselves privileged to treat tradesmen,—certainly respectable when honest, sober, and industrious,—as if they were not of the same flesh and blood with "gentlemen," but to be ranked with the ass and the swine. Such proud pretenders to superiority consider the world was only made for them, while their families and their houses must studiously be kept from plebeian contamination. This aristocratical insolence is also visible even at church,—in the immediate presence of Him who made high and low, rich and poor, and where the gilded and painted ornaments on the walls seem to mock the folly of all human pride. The pew of "the great man" is raised above the others, and furnished with curtains, adorned with linings, and accommodated with cushions. Even those who do not bow at the name of Jesus are yet expected to make their lowly obeisance to the lord in the gallery! However indifferent such mighty persons may feel towards religion, they are still zealous for the church; for this is useful, not only in providing genteely for their poorer relations and dependants, but as an engine to KEEP DOWN THE PEOPLE! The temporalities and splendours of the "established" church endear it to them; but, if it had continued in its primitive state, *when poor fishermen were its bishops*, how differently would they have viewed it!

Against principles so dangerous and hostile to liberty, every friend of his country will not hesitate to shew a determined opposition. The poorer part of mankind,—that is, "the people,"—when they are not blinded by ignorance, in which the "great ones" have always endeavoured to keep them, may safely be entrusted with political power. "The people" have lately been presented with a proof of the selfish motives of these "great ones," which have done wonders in opening their eyes to the degraded condition in which they have so long been held, and the natural consequences of such enlightenment are rapidly being made known in language not to be misunderstood. They begin to view themselves as essential parts of one great body; they are therefore determined to possess an equal portion of political rights, and peaceably possess them; for they are too sensible not to be aware that all violence is not only wrong, but totally unnecessary to accomplish this end. If our exposition of the long-hidden things of darkness, as well as of the characters of their oppressors, should assist in producing this happy consummation, our reward will be ample; we desire no more.

In taking a review of our past pages, the intelligent reader will hardly wonder at the awful complexion the present times have assumed. Every evil has its origin, and, however remote it may be, will ultimately produce its effects. What, then, it may be asked, is the cause of the present unhappy state of England,—of its political struggles and divisions? Have they not been mainly produced by the long-concealed secrets of state, which have, alas! led to the commission of crimes—of murders—that must force the tear of pity from the eye of compassionating humanity?

According to the pure fabric of the British constitution, no nation on the surface of the globe ought to have been more happy, more consolidated in friendly intercourse and good understanding, nor more prosperous and contented, than this country. But, from the time of Queen Anne, the state has been gradually retrograding and divided into two aristocratical parties,—Whigs and Tories,—whose watch-words were principles, (which might be said to be constitutionally attached to opposition or place) but whose struggles have ever been for power. The spirit of party has been said to furnish aliment to the spirit of liberty; and so perhaps it does, but in this way: by first creating the despotism which it is the office of the spirit of liberty to counteract, and, if possible, to overthrow. If there had never been the party of the usurpers and abusers of power, there would have been no occasion for that of the leaguers and reformers. It is of necessity that party spirit must, on the whole, have done more harm than good, since assuredly it has raised more giants than it has yet slain. All party spirit, generally speaking, is injurious. It has been truly denounced by one of the greatest friends of freedom the world has ever seen,—the illustrious Washington,—as "the very worst enemy of popular governments." In his farewell address to the American people, he earnestly warns them against it as the thing from which, of all others, they had most to fear. "It serves always," he tells them, "to distract the public councils and enfeeble the public administration. It agitates the community with ill-founded jealousies and false alarms; kindles the animosity of one class against another; foments, occasionally, riots and insurrections; it opens the door to foreign influence and corruption, which find a facilitated access to the government itself, through the channels of party passions." All party ascendancies have this character in common: that they serve to make the interests of the country subordinate to private ends. It is the established mode with dominant factions to distribute the loaves and fishes among their own adherents exclusively,—they could not, in fact, exist as factions otherwise. Worth and talent are no farther regarded than is necessary for the saving of appearances. The sort of followers whom your party minister delights to honour are those who will stick at nothing, who will stand by a leader through thick and thin, who will never consider the right or wrong of anything, but support whatever their patron supports, and resist to the utmost whenever he gives the word,—men, in short, who are prepared to look only to their own and their party's advantage, without at all caring how the interests of the community at large may be affected by their conduct. Ever since the revolution of 1688, England has never been free from the trammels of some such dominant faction or other; and what have been the consequences? One long course of misgovernment, one unceasing heaping of burdens on the people, and of pensions and sinecures on the aristocracy,—one unvarying round of oppression, plunder, murder, corruption, and extravagance. Whether it was Tory or whether it was Whig that was in power, the result to the people was almost always the same. If the Whigs have, on the whole, been less to blame than their rivals, it is to be remembered, on the other hand, that their opportunities of doing evil have been fewer. However the two parties may differ, or affect to differ, on general principles of government, they have always agreed marvellously on one point, namely: the perfect propriety of making the most of their time while in office, to enrich themselves, their relations, and dependants, at the expense of the nation.[16] Thus, public opinion has long been the opinion of certain coteries, and public men, generally speaking, men neither brought forward by the public, nor for the sake of the public! It has been thought necessary that someone should make such a speech as would "tell well," and procure a round of cheers from the House. If such an individual could be found with a large landed estate and a coronet entailed upon him, so much the better; if not, why he must be sought for elsewhere. A school or college reputation, an able pamphlet, a club or county-meeting oration, pointed him out. The minister, or the great man who wished to be the minister, brought him into parliament: if he failed, he sank into insignificance; if he succeeded, he worked for his master during a certain time, and then became a minister or a great man himself. As for the people, he had nothing whatever to do with them; they returned some jolly 'squire, who feasted them well, or some nabob who purchased their votes. Under such a state of things, cheerfully acquiesced in, we say, it is hardly to be wondered at that what are called "the people" should have been very much plundered and very much despised. Were this base party spirit only banished from among us, were all party badges, watchwords, and distinctions, only discarded for ever, were superior talent and tried integrity but once to become the sole passports to preferment, our social system would then be placed on the very best possible footing. The time of so desirable a consummation, we hope and trust, is not far distant; though we are still in the midst of the manifold evils of which the so-much-lauded party spirit has been the source, and we must necessarily deal with matters as they are. Tory is again contending against Whig for the mastery, and with both the real interests of the people seem, as usual, to form only a secondary consideration. A greater proof of this cannot possibly be offered than in the following extract from a late parliamentary report:

"Mr. Dawson, in reference to the appointment of Lord Durham to be lord privy seal, asked whether any portion of the salary due to the noble lord from the time of his appointment to this period had been paid, or whether he had made any application for the payment of this salary. He wished to know the same with respect to the post-master-general.

"Sir George Warrender said, that when the noble lord had found that his was an efficient public office, he had determined to take the salary. When the duke stated his determination not to take the salary, there was upon the part of the committee the general expression of an opinion that the noble duke, in so doing, would be unfair to the office. The committee communicated to him that he would be doing great injustice to the office.

"Mr. J. Wood corroborated the statement of the honourable baronet, both with respect to the Duke of Richmond and of Lord Durham.

"The Chancellor of the Exchequer said, that Lord Durham had received a regular salary. The Duke of Richmond intended also to receive the whole of his salary. He was sure that every honourable member would agree with him in thinking that it was not proper, because an individual had a large income, that he should refuse his salary. Under these circumstances, he thought that both his noble friends did not judge right."

We can readily anticipate the surprise the public must have felt at the nonsensical and unjust doctrine here broached by the *Whig* Chancellor of the Exchequer. A man in the possession of a large income was doing injustice to an office if he refused to take the salary pertaining to it, though such salary was drained from a heavily-taxed people! But it is really wonderful how much a little acquaintance with office will alter the liberal and patriotic opinions of a man,—even of that boaster of economy and retrenchment, the *honest-looking* Lord Althorpe! When Lord Durham and the Duke of Richmond first accepted place, the public heard much of their high-minded contempt for gain, and were told how purely disinterested were their views on entering the public service. Time, however, proved that money was not altogether so offensive to these patriotic peers, and to avoid doing injustice to their offices, they at length consented (amazing condescension!) to receive their salaries. Such an act of justice *to an office*, which cannot be appreciated by the object, is in very bad taste, considering it is detrimental to the public, who would have felt grateful for a similar regard to its own interests. But the Duke of Richmond's conduct by no means surprised us: he who is only a Tory in disguise was just the man to pretend a contempt for salary before he was in place, and to clutch at it ravenously the moment he got into power. Some persons, when he first spoke of taking no pay, laughed at his unfitness for office, and he was strongly advised to resign, as he got nothing but ridicule for his pains. His grace heeded not this rebuke, but appears to have been actuated by the same feeling as the blind fiddler, who was recommended to begone, as every one laughed at him. "Hold thy peace," said the fiddler, "we shall have their money presently, and then we will laugh at them."

Thus it will be seen that the interests of the people have never been considered by any ministry, however great its pretensions to honesty and patriotism. Added to this lamentable fact, an all-opposing and insuperable obstacle has, for many years, been obtruding itself on the energies of the country,—the embarrassing and overwhelming STATE SECRETS. These have ever formed a paramount consideration with royalty; and, in order to prevent them being made public, the constitution has been openly and shamelessly infringed, morality and honesty set at defiance, and the order of society reversed! The enormous charges entailed on this country, by bribing the parties in possession of these secrets, have been made fully manifest in our preceding pages. Still it had been utterly impossible for ministers to carry on such a ruinous system of peculation and crime, if they had not contrived the corruption of the people's representatives. This was so effectually accomplished by Pitt, Liverpool, Castlereagh, and Sidmouth, that every law they thought proper to propose, and every supply of money they demanded, for whatever iniquitous purpose it might be required, was sure to meet with the ready acquiescence of the House of Commons. Hence the crown became a mighty host of power, perpetually acquiring an accession of purchased adherents, whoever exhibited the greatest readiness to accomplish the unconstitutional purposes of their abandoned employers.

It may here not be improper succinctly to explain of what materials this "host of power" consisted at the death of George the Fourth. Out of the six hundred and fifty-eight who composed the House of Commons, four hundred and eighty-eight, or nearly three-fourths, were returned by the influence or nomination of one hundred and forty-four peers, and one hundred and twenty-three commoners. These patrons, by themselves or their nominees, necessarily determined the decisions of both houses of parliament; and, consequently, engrossed the whole power of the state! In the exercise of this overgrown influence, however, they were happily a little restrained by the operation of public opinion, as prompted by the liberty of the press, and sustained by the trial by jury,—both of which they, in vain, attempted to destroy. This body of boroughmongers, as we have shewn, consisted of two hundred and sixty-seven individuals,—including lords, ladies, commoners, lunatics, and minors! They constituted the oligarchy,—that selfish faction so unhappily familiar to the public of the present day by the name of the "Conservatives," or the "Cumberland Club." Of this faction, so long the keepers of the now-explained secrets of state, the nominal ministers of the crown were, in effect, necessarily the tools or agents. Under such a monstrous system of government, carried on for the exclusive interest of the prevailing faction, the blackest deeds were countenanced by men in power, of the truth of which our volumes will furnish future generations with abundant proof. This usurpation of the whole power of the state by two hundred and sixty-seven persons, however, was not effected suddenly; it was the result of gradual encroachments on the right of suffrage by a succession of the votes of a corrupt and venal House of Commons, commencing with the septennial act, a little more than a century ago. As these two hundred and sixty-seven individuals returned nearly three-fourths of the Lower House, and constituted a majority in the Upper, their influence was supreme in both. To the one hundred and forty-four peers who influenced the House of Commons was added the whole tribe of the unchristianlike and ostentatious bishops, who, almost to a man, voted with the oligarchial members, in hopes of coming in for a share of the "loaves and fishes." From this, it is almost impossible to say which house of parliament was most corrupt of the two. Hence arose the incessant attempts to abridge the rights and liberties of the people, through the forms of the constitution. The independence of parliament became words of contempt to all who knew the secret spring of their automaton movements. But, independent of corruption, another grievous cause of complaint exists in the Upper House. It has been frequently proved that both IDIOTS and LUNATICS have exercised their "hereditary" right of assisting in the making of British laws!!! We also lately observed, in the farewell address of Lord Stanley, *who is heir to a peerage*, the reason assigned to his constituents for withdrawing from the House of Commons was, "the rapid growth of an infirmity under which he has long laboured." That infirmity is deafness; and here arises a curious question: if his lordship's infirmity disqualify him from sitting in a house whose functions are legislatorial, how can he be qualified for a seat in a house which is both *legislatorial* and *judicial*? If his lordship's deafness unfit him to be a maker of laws, how can he, when he becomes a member of the Upper House, be fit for the discharge of the duties both of *legislator* and *judge*,—HEARING, in the latter case, being more indispensable than in the former? How injurious is the doctrine of the legitimate descent of wisdom! A member of the Lower House becomes deaf, like Lord Stanley, or an idiot, like some scores of members who shall be nameless, and therefore unfit for the duties of legislation *there*; but if he happen to be the heir to a peerage, the death of a father makes the deaf to hear, and imbues the idiot with intellect; and he is in a moment fitted not only for *legislatorial* but for judicial functions! How much longer will the people tolerate such "hereditary" privileges? But, even from the dawn of the French revolution, and the lesson which Napoleon gave to tyrants, the oligarchy and the people have maintained a constant and increasing struggle; and the year 1832 has plainly proclaimed to which party the victory will be ultimately awarded.

From such an unconstitutional state of things as we have here briefly described, Englishmen may account for the unjust wars which have overwhelmed them with debt, poverty, and taxes, in order to retard the progress of liberty, and stultify the human intellect. In what a miserable plight did such wars leave this vast island, covered as she once was with the gorgeous mantle of successful agriculture! They left her "with Industry in rags, and Patience in despair: the merchant without a ledger, the shops without a customer, the Exchange deserted, and the Gazette crowded." Let us inquire for what purposes these wars were so obstinately maintained. Were they for the benefit of Europe?—for the happiness of mankind?—for the strengthening of liberty?—for the improvement of politics and philosophy? Alas! no. But, by these long and bloody wars, England has compelled the millions in America to manufacture for themselves, and the greater part of the Continent to do the same, to the manifest injury of our own artizans. Besides this impolicy, the American war, from 1776 to 1782, cost this country two thousand, two hundred, and seventy millions, and a half. The fleet alone, in 1779, created an expense of one hundred and eighty millions. During the crusade against French liberty, our national debt was increased from two hundred millions to nine hundred millions, and the interest from nine to forty-five millions per annum. And what was the object to be obtained by this war? To save Louis the Sixteenth, and to check that spirit of propagandism, announced in the French Chamber, from being formidably maintained and spread by the troops of France. To effect this, England took up arms when Louis the Sixteenth had gone to his ancestors, and when the Republican armies, flushed with victory, and threatened with the guillotine in the event of defeat, were become, from raw recruits, desperate and veteran soldiers. We reserved our defence of the monarch till he had perished on the scaffold,—our defence of the monarchy till the French Republic was declared "a besieged city, and France a vast camp!" Then we commenced a war with allies who were become anxious for peace, and who, in taking our money, reserved it to pay the expense of the campaign they had finished, without any consideration for the violent inclination for fighting which we had just been seized with. This was the policy which Mr.

Pitt asked Mr. Canning if he approved of; this was the policy which Mr. Canning came into parliament to defend, and which he did defend on every occasion, and which he always boasted having defended to his dying day! But it is only a person well acquainted with the House of Commons at this period who could believe that Mr. Canning's defence of such ministerial imbecility received enthusiastic applause! There never was a collection of more glaring contradictions, more gaudy sophisms, than the youthful orator's declamatory harangue. The war was to be pursued because we were victorious; peace was to be refused on account of the successes of the enemy; France was too weak to be respected,—too formidable not to be opposed! As for the sums we were expending, they were insignificant when compared with the objects we had in view. Our ancestors, whose immaculate wisdom Mr. Canning was at that time so fond of citing, would certainly have been astonished to find that those objects were the re-establishment of Spain in its ancient power, and the subjugation of Rome to the authority of the Pope! The heart of any reflecting man must burn within him when he thinks that a sanguinary war was undertaken for the purpose of forcing France out of her undoubted right of choosing her own monarch,—a war which uprooted the very foundation of the English constitution, which declared tyranny eternal, and announced to the people, amidst the thunder of artillery, that, no matter how aggrieved, their only allowable attitude was that of supplication, which, when it told the French reformer of 1793 that his defeat was just, told the British reformer of 1688 his triumphal revolution was treason, forgetting that OUR KING HIMSELF WAS THE CREATURE OF THAT REVOLUTION! After an immense loss of life and treasure, the Bourbons were, for a time, restored to the throne of France, contrary to the wishes of at least nine-tenths of the French people; for the Bourbons had proved themselves incapable of learning Mercy from Misfortune, or Wisdom from Experience. Vindictive in prosperity, servile in defeat, timid in the field, vacillating in the cabinet, their very name had become odious to the ears of a Frenchman, and Napoleon had only to present himself to ensure their precipitate flight. The downfall of that great man, who shed a splendour around royalty unknown to it before, will ever be regretted by the majority of the French people, though British ministers have classed the unhallowed act in the list of their achievements! By the same tyrannical means, a prince was restored to Portugal, who, when his dominions were invaded, his people distracted, his crown in danger, and all that could interest the highest energies of man at issue, left his cause to be combatted by foreigners, and fled, with cowardly precipitation, to claim the shameful protection of Lord Castlereagh and his junta! A wretch was also restored to unhappy Spain, in the person of the "beloved" Ferdinand, who filled his dungeons and fed his rack with the heroic remnant that had braved war, famine, and massacre beneath his banners,—who rewarded Patriotism with a prison, Fidelity with torture, Heroism with the scaffold, and Piety with the inquisition! The royal monster proclaimed his humanity by the number of his death-warrants, and his religious zeal by embroidering petticoats for the blessed virgin! Such were the three dynasties restored by these cruel wars. As to the rest of Europe, how has it been ameliorated?—what solitary benefit have the "deliverers" conferred? If we look back to Lord Castlereagh's treaties of 1814 and 1815, we shall there find that the states of the feeble were given to the powerful, and guarantees made to preserve the institutions of every former tyranny. Saxony, Genoa, Norway, and, above all, unhappy Poland,—that speaking monument of regal murder and "legitimate" robbery, furnish a lamentable illustration of the cruel injustice of these treaties. Italy was also parcelled out to temporizing Austria, and Prussia, after fruitless toil and wreathless triumphs, was mocked with the promise of a visionary constitution; while England was left, eaten by the cancer of an incurable debt, exhausted by poor rates, supporting a "civil" list of near a million and a half annually, guarded by an unconstitutional standing army, misrepresented by the House of Commons, mocked with a military peace, and girt with the fortifications of a war establishment!!! This, frightful as the picture may appear, is but an outline of the miseries that have been produced by our long and sanguinary wars, undertaken to protect the monster of legitimacy, and to crush the rising liberties of an enlightened people! These are the "ACHIEVEMENTS" for which the Duke of Wellington received his title and his enormous wealth, and for which he unblushingly claims the *gratitude* of Englishmen!!!

While all this misery was being accomplished abroad, how were our ministers employed at home? Why, in feeding the bloated mammoth of sinecure, in weighing the farthings of some poor clerk's salary, in preparing Ireland for a garrison, and England for a poor-house,—in furnishing means for their spendthrift master to erect Chinese palaces, to decorate dragoons with his "tasteful" inventions, to purchase gold and silver baubles, and to load his mistresses and his minions with the produce of the people's industry! We had also, at this period, a "saint" in the Exchequer, who studied Scripture for some purpose: the famishing people cried out for *bread*, and the pious Vansittart gave them *stones*! But the idea that a man like Vansittart should entail a debt of above four hundred millions of pounds on the country; the idea that "the least, the meanest" of the Pitt tribe should make the House of Commons vote that the Bank note, worth twenty worn shillings, was as valuable as the guinea worth twenty-seven good ones, will hardly be credited by future generations. The weakest man that ever held office under a crown may well boast that he reduced the parliament of England to the lowest degradation, to the most abject servility, that a public assembly of gentlemen was ever trodden to. Yet, strange as it must appear, it was for such services that this same Vansittart was created—a lord!! Lord Bexley was consequently sent to the "Upper House," as a proof of the high approbation in which his talents were held by his admiring master! In that situation, he has since zealously exerted himself to preserve every existing abuse, and his ill-acquired title has ever figured in the list of those who vote against the people.

To keep up such an iniquitous state of affairs, it was deemed necessary to persecute those who struggled to bring back the constitution to its original principles. Hence the employment of spies and informers; hence systematic massacre, imprisonment, and cruelty; hence the regular manufacture of forged seditious placards for the purpose of affording a pretext for the military execution against the reformers at Manchester and elsewhere; and hence, for such atrocities could happen under no other system upon earth, the murders, the cold-blooded murders, recorded in our preceding pages.

Even the most superficial observer must be convinced that our country has long been gradually degenerating from its greatness, that the most fictitious and speculative means have uniformly been devised to prop her exchequer, and that the most plausible, though, to many, unintelligible, pleas advanced for introducing new taxes and new laws of an arbitrary description, tending to abridge the civil liberties and paralyze the energies of the people. These, however, have eventually failed of producing their desired end. Despotism, and the total thraldom of the mind, Providence will never allow to be the destiny of generous and noble-minded Englishmen,—at least for any length of time. An arbitrary use of power naturally leads to extremes, and these extremes eventually to a crisis, opening the door of dissatisfaction and inquiry, where a stand must be made, rescinding every possibility either of proceeding or of retreating. Is not such our present political situation? And whence, let us again inquire, arises this state of affairs? Surely not to be ascribed to a turbulent disposition or a moral degeneracy of the working classes. It is the grossest deceit and hypocrisy, not to say the most audacious and ungrateful calumny, to stigmatize them with such opprobrium; for never were any people more injured, more oppressed, nor more insulted, than were the tax-payers of England during the last two reigns! Ministers have too long imposed upon the credulity of the timid, by describing every riotous proceeding as the natural consequence of the progress of liberal opinions. The excesses of a few rioters, who most probably knew not the extent of the mischief they were doing, ought not to be attributed to the people generally. Such accusations are a gross libel on the peaceable spirit of Englishmen, and are only used by corrupt and designing men to raise an alarm against liberty; for mischief of this kind may be attributed, with more certainty, to the cowardice, folly, and wickedness of certain public functionaries, liberally paid to prevent such disgraceful exhibitions. But the "church and state" men have never failed to turn riots to the illustration of their own injurious theory. "See!" cry they, exulting over the scene, "the effects of power in the hands of the people!" Yet the people,—that is, the grand mass of the community,—were not at all concerned in effecting the mischief, for who beside such libellers would call an assemblage of all the refuse of society—the people? The first irregularities at Bristol, for instance, might have been suppressed by the slightest exertion of manly spirit; or, indeed, that destructive riot had never commenced but for the headstrong or cowardly, (we hardly know which to call it) conduct of Sir Charles Wetherell, who openly declared that he would insult the Bristol people with his detested person, "if a cannon forced his entrance!" Did not the Tories, then, we ask, both create and feed the riots at Bristol, for the purpose of frightening the people from reform? The people at large, we say, ought not to be blamed for such events; the whole of the culpability belongs to the aiders and abettors of them, and the appointed ministers of the law, in whom the people trust, but have mostly been deceived. This blame, however, has always been laid to the people, while all men of arbitrary principles rejoice at the calamity, as an auspicious event, confirming all their theories, and justifying their practice! But these have been some of the murderous means employed to augment and continue the political torpor of the people of England for the last sixty years. When any appeal to the people was in agitation on the subject of liberty, it was sufficient for Pitt, Liverpool, Castlereagh, Canning, Sidmouth, or any of their minions, to exclaim, "Remember the riots!" and the intended measure was sure to be relinquished immediately, when these despotic ministers chuckled over the success of their scheme, as though they had gained the most splendid victory. The excesses of the French revolution in 1793 were peculiarly grateful to the friends of tyranny in England. While the patriot wept, the factor of despotism triumphantly shouted, "Here is another instance of the people's unfitness to possess power, and the mischievous effects of excessive liberty!" Every art which ingenuity could practise, and influence assist in its operation, was exerted to vilify and misrepresent the real design of the French revolution. From this moment, persecutions were vigorously commenced against patriotism, and it became sedition to hint at parliamentary reform,—the root of the people's grievances. Never, since the expulsion of the Stuarts, were such vigorous laws enforced,—never before did Pitt so exult in the downfall of liberty. He and his followers no longer skulked, no longer walked in masquerade. They boasted of their principles, and claimed the honour of being the only friends to law, order, and religion! They talked of the English laws being too lenient for the punishment of sedition, and the acts consequently introduced for its more effectual suppression were made agreeable to the most refined notions of despotism. The clergy now stood forward in their pulpits, and preached, not the word of God, but that doctrine which led the nearest way to promotion, while many other needy and avaricious men wrote in favour of an arbitrary government. Thus fear in the well-meaning, self-interest in the knavish, and systematic subtlety among the state-secret keepers, caused a general uproar in favour of principles and practices at variance with constitutional liberty, and invested the reigning prince and his mother with all but absolute power. How zealously they took advantage of this state of alarm, our volumes fully explain. The friends of humanity, however, have now cause to rejoice that the film of deception is rapidly disappearing from before the eyes of the people, and that such panic fears, servile sycophantism, and artful bigotry, can no longer prevail over cool reason and liberal philanthropy. Such a feverish delirium has passed away, and sober sense perceives the necessity of destroying the destructive power which held so baneful a sway over English liberty during the last two reigns.

Let our readers also not forget the part which the "established church" acted during this long period of misrule. How many of its ministers sacrificed principle and honesty for the pleasure of basking in the sunshine of the vicious court! Gold was the only god they worshipped, and the political creed of tyrants the only testament they read. Ministerial imbecility could always reckon upon their "holy" services, and, in proportion to the callousness and hypocrisy displayed, they were rewarded with bishopricks, deaneries, and other such well-paid offices,—the duties of which they allowed their poorer brethren to perform at wages something less than a common labourer. It is indeed hardly to be credited that in haughty England, who held up her episcopal head so pompously during the reigns of which we are speaking,—in this very country which groaned, and is still groaning, beneath the overwhelming expenses of keeping up a church establishment,—that the real "labourers in the vineyard" were paid so scantily, that their wages, in thousands of instances, did not amount to those of a journeyman mechanic! Yes, in the very heart of this metropolis were to be found men, on whom the fond and foolish ambition of their parents had been exhausted in bringing them up in this profession, who possessed learning and intellectual refinement, starving in back attics, in filthy courts and alleys. This miserable state of the working clergy was not confined to London alone. In many parts of this country (Wales in particular) it was no uncommon thing for a clergyman, with seven children, to do duty for two parishes, at only ten pounds a year each! And we ourselves are acquainted with a gentleman, sixty-four years of age, who was in the church more than forty years, receiving no sort of promotion during the whole of that long period, because he entertained what are termed "liberal principles," and who has lately been obliged to retire from his scanty pittance, and throw himself on the generosity of his friends for a living in his old age.

Let us now take a glance at the drones of the hive,—the men who have ever shewn a peculiar readiness to make themselves a promotion-ladder out of the wreck of their country's liberties. The income of an Archbishop of Canterbury, exclusive of patronage and other valuable emoluments, is thirty thousand pounds. Most of the bishops are also paid, if not quite so extravagantly, in a degree amply sufficient to keep his grace in countenance. Many beneficed clergymen, particularly the younger sons and brothers of our aristocracy, who are not dignitaries of the church, by holding a plurality of livings, drain the country of incomes, varying from five thousand to twelve thousand pounds a year each. And yet these men neither distinguish themselves (although, as in every large class of society, there are honourable and favourable exceptions) either for their grace, learning, or piety,—the only qualification which they possess being the son, brother, nephew, or cousin of a peer, or commoner possessed of parliamentary influence.

A very able article lately appeared in "Blackwood's Magazine," setting forth the abuses here alluded to in such a clear and bold manner, that we cannot refrain from making the following extract from it:

> "The trusts of the church are admitted to be, and used as, patronage in the most vulgar and corrupt sense of the term; and the minister of state who bestows them regularly does it to enrich his connexions, reward his adherents, or bribe his opponents. Why is this man made a bishop? He has been tutor in one noble family or is connected by blood with another, or he enjoys the patronage of some polluted female favourite of royalty, or he is the near relative of a minister, or at the nod of the premier, or he has been a traitor to the church in a matter affecting her existence. Why is this man made a dean? He has married a relative of the home secretary, or he is a turn-coat, who has joined the enemies of the church in the destruction of her securities, or it is necessary to preserve some powerful family from going into the opposition.

Why is this stripling invested with an important dignity in the church? He is an illegitimate son of a member of the royal family, or he is the same to some nobleman, or he belongs to a family, which in consideration of it will give the ministry a certain number of votes in parliament. And why is this man endowed with a valuable benefice? He has potent interest, or it will prevent him from giving farther opposition to measures for injuring the church, or he has voted at an election for a ministerial candidate, or his connexions have much electioneering influence, or he is a political tool of the ministry. At the contest for the university of Oxford, which expelled Sir Robert Peel, it was generally asserted, that certain members of the ministry used every effort to gain votes for him by offers of church preferment; or, in other words, they used the property of the church as bribes to induce the clergy to support the assailant of her securities against the defender of them. After the carrying of the catholic question, the preferments, which fell into the hands of some of the apostate bishops or their connexions, proved that these men had been bought with their own property to turn their sacrilegious hands upon her. The disposal of what is called church patronage in this manner is not the exception, but the rule; it is not a matter of secrecy, or one that escapes public observation; it is looked on as a thing of course; and so far has this monstrous abuse been sanctified by custom, that while no one expects to see a vacancy in the church filled according to its merit, the filling of it in the most profligate way scarcely provokes reprobation.

"Let us now look at those appointments in the church which are not in the hands of government. A great number of livings are private property. On what principle are they disposed of? The owners fill them without the least regard for qualification; they practically give them to their relations while yet in the womb or the cradle, and these relatives enter into orders from no other reason than to enjoy them as private fortunes; or clergymen and others buy such livings solely for private benefit. In the appointment of curates, those are chosen who are cheapest, the least formidable as rivals, and, in consequence, the most disqualified; care for the interests of the church is out of the question.

"Then in the general appointment of the functionaries of the church, whether it rest with the government or individuals, qualification is disregarded. These are some of the inevitable consequences:—1st. The office of clergyman is sought by the very last people who ought to receive it. However brainless or profligate a youth may be, he still must enter into holy orders, because his friends have property or interest in the church; perhaps they select him for it in preference to his brothers, because he happens to be the dunce of the family. 2ndly. The system directly operates, not only to keep ability and piety at the lowest point amidst the clergy, but to render that portion of them which may be forced into orders useless to the church. 3rdly. The clergy and laity are separated from and arranged against each other. The minister has no interest in conciliating, preserving, and increasing the flock; its favour cannot benefit, and its hostility cannot injure, him. To give all this the most comprehensive powers of mischief, almost any man may, so far as concerns ability and character, gain admission into holy orders. A clergyman may be destitute of religious feelings, he may be grossly immoral, he may discharge his duties in the most incompetent manner, and lose his flock; he may do almost anything short of legal crime, and still he will neither forfeit his living, nor draw on himself any punishment."

All unbiased individuals must acknowledge the likeness of the picture here drawn, notwithstanding the high Tory quarter from which it is painted. We are willing to acknowledge that these abuses have been practised ever since the unholy alliance between church and state; but they were certainly carried to a greater extent in the last two reigns than previously known. The whole church-system, indeed, presented this anomalous, inconsistent, but distinguishing feature: while the country was drained for its support, the actual working clergy, as we have shewn, were paid as the most degraded parish hacks; when the enormous revenue which the system produced, and which was amply sufficient to support the whole, by a proper equalization, in comfort and respectability, was swallowed up by a few court-sycophants, who were pampered by the very excess produced by the starvation and degradation of their less fortunate (or more conscientious?) brethren! Little serious amendment in the particulars here complained of, however, can be reasonably expected, till this all-corrupting and derogatory alliance of God and mammon shall be severed; for never have we so much cause for fear as when the enemies of public freedom are concealed under the garb of sanctity. The spiritual peers themselves seem fully determined to hasten this "consummation so devoutly to be wished;" for they must have but little foresight if they cannot see that their mad opposition to the wishes of a united and determined people will, ere long, bring their already dilapidated building about their own ears.

Every person who will not abjectly resign his common understanding, and will bend his mind to investigate, IMPARTIALLY, what has been passing ever since the landing of Queen Charlotte upon our shores, must be satisfied of the bitter provocations which the British public have received,—the indignation arising from which has now burst forth, never to subside till some reparation be made. There are appointed limits to every evil; there are periods when things must reach their utmost boundary; when even forbearance becomes a crime. Such has been the issue of the long-concealed mysteries of state. Englishmen, we trust, will no more tolerate tyrannous power, murderous injustice, and oppressive enactments. The march of intellect has proclaimed her inquisitorial privileges; the enlightened understanding of the people of 1832 have discovered, to the utter dismay of tyranny, that no satisfactory reason can be assigned for the enormous load of taxation with which they have so long been oppressed. The discovery is now made, that there is no justice for the poor man, or man of inferior grade; but that all enactments have been scrupulously made in favour of the rich and the great. Impunity has been their privilege, while the mass of the community were forced to subscribe to the bitter penalty. Times have been, we are sorry to say, when even MURDER, if committed by rank, might be glossed over by a privy council, while the poor man, agonized by the reflections of his own accusing mind, was coldly, and even with asperity, consigned to the gallows! The lady of rank,—even of the *highest*,—might have an illegitimate offspring, and secretly hide her shame by consigning it to an asylum; but the poor woman, who had strayed from the path of virtue, through poverty, must be confronted with the moralizing, austere, brow-beating, clerical magistrate, reproached for her unfortunate lapse from rectitude, and be committed to the treadmill! Such an unequal administration of justice, we repeat, has been; but God grant that it may never occur again!

The present emancipation of the human mind from ignorance and vassalage, through the medium of dauntless and cheap publications, has discovered to all classes of the community that the administration of our national affairs have never been satisfactorily explained; that all has been artifice and delusion; that the rulers of the country have assumed to themselves an extraordinary stretch of power,—a power above law,—employing the country's revenues in enriching themselves, corrupting the sources of justice, and plotting schemes against the happiness of mankind generally. Hence, the people, weary of their burdens, with no prospect presented to them of having their condition ameliorated by their rulers, and disgusted with those who have so constantly deluded and insulted them, have at last been goaded into the exhibition of a determined spirit no longer to submit their privileges and their liberties to such a state of misrule. They have, indeed, as if with one accord, protested against all further fraud, imposition, and slavery. They are determined to have a parliament of their own selecting, and to demand that the principles and legitimate rights of the British constitution be restored to their pristine vigour.

It may here be proper to inquire, "Who and what are they that have so long opposed the just rights of the people?" Is there a member of the House of Lords who has been elevated to the peerage for the last sixty years and upwards, excepting some few individuals in the army and navy, who does not owe his wealth and title to his weight, interest, and exertions to further and perpetuate the corruption of the House of Commons, or for some courtly servility or secret crime committed to pamper the self-love, or to gratify the vindictive feelings, of their royal patrons? Let the facts recorded in our volumes supply the answer. The PEOPLE, however, are not now to be blinded with the glitter of nobility, or their ears startled by the pompous-sounding title of "My lord." They will rather view such ennobled characters in the light of enemies to their country, and pensioners on their industry. They have exhibited themselves as a proud, arbitrary, and selfish faction, leagued against the spirit of liberty, and anxious for nothing but their own individual aggrandizement. But as all unconstitutional power, sooner or later, is sure to over-reach itself, they have, by their exactions, frauds, and galling oppressions, sown the seeds of their own destruction. The people of England are naturally of an easy and contented disposition; but even their inherent generosity will not brook being treated exactly like the subjects of Russian Nicholas,—the assassin of the gallant Poles!

In recurring to the period of Queen Charlotte's tyranny, the enlightened mind must feel petrified at the callous delinquency displayed by her ministers. It is indeed hardly to be credited, that she should have found men,—we will not say *English-men*, because some were of another country,—so congenial to her own views and sentiments. To paint this German princess and her adherents in their proper colours would be impossible; but every crime and enormity was sanctioned in her reign (for George the Third was a mere cypher in the affairs of state) that crime and enormity can be supposed to comprehend; spoliation, murder, incest, espionage, sanguinary plottings, the most inhuman outrages, persecution, and oppression were of common occurrence. Who, we ask, was the secret contriver, aider, and abettor of most of the ills Queen Caroline endured? Who pocketted enormous sums from the illegal sale of cadetships? Who made unfair use of government information to speculate in the funds for the sake of "filthy lucre?" Who indulged in improper intimacies with that wholesale inventor of taxes, William Pitt? Who conceived some of the diabolical plots, executed, too fatally executed, against the holders of her favourite prince's bonds? And who wrote, as well as commanded to be written, such tender, comforting, and promising letters to the late Dr. Croft, just before and immediately after the execution of that cold-blooded deed,—the murder of Princess Charlotte? The answers will easily be supplied by the intelligent reader. But let us hope the day of retribution is fast approaching, when Justice will preside at the examination of all the circumstances attending that most unnatural act,—the foulest, blackest crime "that ever yet this land was guilty of." Had the secret actions of Queen Charlotte been generally known in her life, she would have appeared the basest and most abandoned of women; but the deception and shew of virtue which she so artfully practised made people think her the most amiable of queens. Had she not have shielded her myrmidons from exposure, they would, long ago, have appeared to the public eye as a class of beings of the basest and most odious description. Impeachment had followed impeachment, and the law would have denounced them as men who had violated every principle of honour, of humanity, and of Christianity!

Some of our readers may probably view these reproaches as unmerited aspersions, or hateful invectives, proceeding from a vindictive, malignant, and democratic spirit, and their author deserving to be anathematized as the most execrable of the human race. But Truth, irrefragable Truth, is our defence; she has now burst her bonds, and will no longer be prevented, by the threats of power, from boldly speaking out! Common observation, indeed, might have ascertained that the unnatural and usurped power, which so long controlled the destinies of this country, was of a *foreign* character, and totally at variance with the constitution and chartered rights of Englishmen! Did not Junius expose the illegality of this power? and did not the noble-minded Chatham remonstrate against it? But though Tyranny and Corruption trembled to their very centres at the attacks of these champions of liberty, the base fabricks remained unimpaired till the death of their mistress,—the puissant Charlotte of Mecklenburgh Strelitz!

We come now more immediately to the consideration of those political transactions that ensued when the final incapacity of George the Third to discharge the duties of his sovereignty was made known. At this period, Queen Charlotte, in collusion with her hopeful son, the Prince of Wales, came into full power, which she exercised with a spirit truly in accordance with her restless ambition and mercenary desires. A system of despotism, veiled under the specious garb of piety and the country's safety, was immediately put in force; and new taxes levied under various pretences, but in reality for the purpose of bestowing wealth on her zealous adherents. Indeed, in every proposition of the "devourers of the public wealth," for increasing the amount of "SECRET-SERVICE MONEY," a zealous abettor was always found in the queen. German craft is never at a loss for deceptive plans, nor is German prejudice easily pacified. No machinations were too hideous, nor too infamous, when suggested by the one to gratify the other. If the queen and her son had gained what they strenuously endeavoured to obtain—ABSOLUTE POWER—who would not have justly felt alarm, not merely for the liberties of his country, but for his own individual safety? The proscriptions of the Roman Decemviri and the more recent and horrible cruelties of the French Robespierre are appalling instances of what people CAN DO when armed with absolute power. Had these guardians of the British public, therefore, but succeeded in obtaining such power, to what lengths they would have gone may be estimated by the crimes they actually did commit and countenance without it! Where would the voice of mercy have prevailed on them to sheath the sword of persecution? Their ministers, by distorting the constitution from its original meaning, presumed to tear Englishmen from the bosom of their families, without any assigned cause, loading them with irons, and immolating them in damp and dreary dungeons! Some actually died, horrible as the fact may appear, under this treatment, while the survivors were released without any investigation, without any trial whatever,—nay, without their even being made acquainted with the nature of the suspected offence,—and denied the slightest redress for their cruel injuries! Considering, we say, that such monstrous injustice was practised, it is not too much to suppose that, with absolute power, the same parties would have erected the triangle at the Royal Exchange and at the Mews! We might then have expected to see Englishmen running naked through the streets of London, with caps of burning pitch upon their heads, and blood streaming from their lacerated bodies, or observed them hanging on the lamp-posts, or before their burning dwellings! Did not these horrors actually take place in Ireland in the years 1797 and 1798, when the tyrannical Castlereagh held a public situation in that betrayed, forlorn, and persecuted country? At the very time these atrocities were committed in Ireland, spies, informers, executioners, and all the refuse of society, were employed as the principal instruments of Castlereagh's government; and when Queen Charlotte and her son made that Hibernian monster minister of this country, Castle, Oliver, and Edwards, with many other such wretches, shared the smiles and favours of himself and his colleagues.

The history of Caroline of Brunswick, in whose unhappy fate every person possessed of Christian feeling and principle must be interested, also fully evinces the hateful passions of Queen Charlotte's heart. That victim of a detestable conspiracy was the object of a sanguinary determination from the moment she so unhappily came over to this kingdom. Queen Charlotte, finding herself then defeated in the ambitious desire she had always cherished, that one of her own relations should be the future queen of England, became this noble-minded woman's most uncompromising and inveterate enemy. Into the highest favour and most unlimited confidence, her majesty now received the abandoned Lady Jersey, though she *pretended*, with so much austerity, to preserve the unsullied PURITY OF HER COURT; but this pretension was only made the better to impose upon the country, and to effect the destruction of the guiltless and unoffending niece of the king her husband! Her majesty, however, did not live to see such a wicked scheme accomplished.

When the husband of the unfortunate Caroline attained, by the death of his father, to regal authority, surrounded by the titled hirelings of his own creation and the dependants on his bounty, he judged the opportunity peculiarly favourable to the final ruin of his long-persecuted consort. Every plot, therefore, that could be devised by a servile ministry and a corrupt parliament, was put into active operation for the purpose of depriving her of those constitutional rights which the demise of George the Third had entitled her to expect. The Duke of York stipulated with the king that, in the event of a divorce being granted, his majesty *should not marry again*,—otherwise, he threatened to take part with Queen Caroline! So much for the consistency, love of duty, and purity of motive, which the duke boasted in the House of Lords as solely actuating him in the line of conduct he had followed in opposing the queen!

The injurious reports which ministers circulated regarding Queen Caroline's conduct rendered it impossible for her majesty to remain abroad, even if she had so wished; for they presumed to treat her as the most abandoned of the human race, and therefore it became necessary for any virtuous woman, thus publicly accused, to appear in person, and assert her innocence. In the whole management of the ensuing "trial" against this ill-fated queen, justice, feeling, honour, and common sense were all equally outraged! What was the tribunal before which her majesty was called? How was it constituted? Who sat there "to administer even-handed justice?" The ministers who brought forward the charges against their queen, the officers of the king's household, two of the king's brothers, with many other *noble* persons closely connected with the court, who held places and pensions at its will, and looked up to it for new honours, for patronage, for wealth, and for power! Were such people, then, calculated to administer justice? Justice, indeed! Was the refusing a list even of the names of the witnesses impartial justice? Was it impartial British justice, when the ministers of the king sat as judges, jurors, and accusers? Like triple-headed monsters, did they not, in that joint capacity, most profligately bribe, clothe, feed, house, and amuse a horde of discarded miscreant Italian servants? Was the instructing, drilling, marshalling, living, and conversing *all* together of these wretches, who were watched and kept under lock and key by these Cerberi, an example of the impartiality of British justice? Was the permitting the witnesses instantly to return to their den and communicate all their evidence to those who had not been before the House of Lords another proof of the impartiality of what is commonly termed "the highest court of judicature of the first nation in Europe?" Was the treating her majesty as guilty before her trial a fair specimen of the beauty of this court? Monstrous profanation of terms! Was ever common sense so insulted? Was justice ever so outraged? Were those iniquitous proceedings an evidence of that

> "Justice, by nothing biassed or inclined,
> Deaf to persuasion, to temptation blind;
> Determined without favour, and the laws
> O'erlook the parties to decide the cause?"

When the law-officers of the crown declared, that "there existed no grounds upon which legal proceedings could be instituted," two obvious and distinct paths were open to ministers. They had their election to advise, either that her majesty should return to this country with all the honours and constitutional privileges belonging to her high station, or else that she should be prevailed upon to establish her court abroad. Yet ministers determined to deviate into a dark and crooked path. They did not venture openly to advise that the queen should return; and yet, as if determined that she should come to this country, they took care to render it impossible for her to remain abroad! Was not the name of the noble-minded Caroline insultingly excluded from the Liturgy? And what reason was assigned for so unjustifiable a proceeding? The Archbishop of Canterbury and other church pluralists gave this: "If any defiled name should there be inserted, the principles of morality would be invaded, the foundations of religion would be sapped, and the destruction of our constitution must inevitably follow!" Now, even allowing the queen to have been the abandoned character represented by her hireling enemies,—nay, more, had she been a MURDERESS,—these impudent and canting hypocrites need not have searched far for a precedent to prove her eligibility for a place in the Liturgy! Were Henry the Eighth, Queen Mary, Charles the Second and his queen, James the Second and his queen, all pure and undefiled? But the place-hunting clergy need not have gone out of their own generation for an example of infamy. What were Queen Charlotte, George the Fourth, the Duke of York, or, though last, not least in the VIRTUES of his family, the *undefiled* Ernest of Cumberland? Our volumes fully explain what they were! and yet their names graced the Liturgy, as the Attorney-General has declared that the words "Royal Family" comprehend *all* the individuals of the royal family. But it may be objected that the names of York and Cumberland were not *specifically* mentioned in the days of Queen Caroline's persecutions. Well, then, the Prince of Wales' name, at least, did figure in our Prayer Book, and was he "pure and undefiled?" The *pious* sons of the church formally prayed that "God would endue him with his holy spirit," &c.; but it did not appear, by his actions, that their prayers produced the least effect. When he became king, he was prayed for, "to be endued with heavenly gifts, to incline to the will of God, and walk in his ways." Did his infamous conduct to his wife, and his living in open adultery with the Marchioness of Conyngham and others, qualify him for a place in the prayers of the church, as "pure and undefiled?" If ministers, therefore, consented to deprive the queen of this dignity, because of her imputed immorality, might it not have proved a precedent against George the Fourth himself? The lawyers, even Lord Eldon, if it had suited his purpose, might have afterwards cited the case of Caroline as a case in point, while the country could not refuse to dethrone the king on the same plea as they had dethroned the queen, more particularly as it was so easy a matter to prove the gross adultery and immorality of George the Fourth; for his derelictions from virtue were as notorious as the sun at noon-day. Would to heaven, we say, that a king might have been dethroned for immoral conduct, as the world had not then been so cursed with their atrocious deeds. When at foreign courts, her majesty justly claimed the honours pertaining to her exalted rank, but was insultingly told that she was not known as a queen! Thus subjected, *untried and unheard*, to every indignity which could only have followed upon proof and condemnation, her majesty had no alternative left but to return to England, and boldly face her mean-spirited and unmanly enemies. Had her title been proclaimed, had foreign courts been instructed to receive her with the honours due to a queen of England, her continuing to remain abroad would not have worn the appearance of shrinking from the defence of her reputation,—a fear to which she was utterly a stranger. Her noble soul scorned danger; for a braver heart than her's never beat in human breast. But her husband's ministers rendered her absence from this country incompatible with her honour; they *forced* her to return, and they, and they alone, were responsible for all the mischief that might have ensued to the country from such an unavoidable step on the part of the queen. No one, we think, will doubt that the most serious mischief would have occurred, if these men had persisted in their headlong career. But, *like all cowards*, when they found the danger hovering over their *own* heads, they shrunk from the contest, and took refuge in a timely retreat!

Nothing in the whole history of human suffering could equal the wrongs of her majesty. With respect to the bill of Pains and Penalties, the various records of persecution may be searched in vain for a case so foul, so false, so full of premeditated and disciplined perjury,—the inquest on Sellis was JUSTICE when *compared* with this, though the hand of Lord Ellenborough may be traced in both. The mock "trial" of Caroline, Queen of England, we say, cannot be matched for rancour, cruelty, for monstrous and unnatural malignity. There never was a case at all like it: it is without an example in history, and can never become a precedent; for future generations will read it with pity and with horror. The foul charges preferred against the queen by the lowest of the low were disproved by noblemen of the first consideration, by ladies of the highest rank and of the most unblemished honour, by gentlemen of family, of education, and integrity, and by distinguished and gallant soldiers. The evidence of such respectable characters as these present a picture of her majesty which future generations will admire and venerate. But it is impossible that impartial and discerning Englishmen should believe that the "Bill of Pains and Penalties," nominally aimed against the queen, had not, for its main objects, the doing away with trial by jury and the liberty of the press, and, on their ruins, to establish a system of absolute despotism. Whether these effects were originally foreseen and intended by the sagacious projectors of that wicked measure, is a matter of little importance; it is quite obvious that such would have been its consequences. The place-loving Lord Eldon, however, tried hard to make people believe that bills of Pains and Penalties were then "part and parcel" of the constitution of the kingdom. But a trial of such an indescribably infamous description was never before attempted; and even if it had been, Lord Eldon, as a good chancellor, ought to have declared against it, instead of attempting to defend and perpetuate it. With overbearing oligarchs, any sort of precedent was deemed sufficient; and it is rather wonderful that they did not, by the help of precedent, endeavour to re-establish the Star Chamber! If they had succeeded in such a point, the first of the kind attempted in modern times, the faction would, doubtless, have considered themselves authorised, whenever it had suited their views, to proceed by a bill of Pains and Penalties against any obnoxious individual, instead of going before a common jury! To establish such a monstrous system, we repeat, was one of the real, though disguised, objects of ministers, in the prosecution of Queen Caroline; for they perceived the progress of political knowledge, and felt alarmed lest they should lose their arbitrary authority, if they could not adopt some such tyrannical measure to frighten the people into obedience. It was the glorious majesty of the press that bravely defeated such infamous machinations against liberty, for which future generations will have cause to venerate and worship it.

The queen, however, was most grievously slandered and ill-treated by the Tory portion of public writers. Nothing, indeed, could have been more villanous than the charges which blackened the columns of certain newspapers,—journals that, in their general colouring, were too foul and too dark to obtain belief. Well remunerated by government, the scurrilous editors of such libels against female majesty appeared to exult in the pain they inflicted; so long as they satisfied the hateful revenge of their abandoned employers, their end was answered. However much such prostitution of talent is to be lamented, there was yet a worse crime committed by the enemies of Queen Caroline. The ministers of the "established" church scrupled not to take part against her, and, instead of confining themselves to the exposition of the mild and forbearing doctrines of the Christian religion, not unfrequently indulged their wicked disloyalty by delivering the most foul and blasphemous denunciations against their queen, even from the pulpit! This, of course, could only be done with a view of pleasing those who had "rich livings" to reward their misplaced zeal. One of these contemptible *reverends*, by the name of Blacow, was so violent against her majesty, that the queen's law-advisers thought it right to punish his impertinence by an action, in the Court of King's Bench, for a malicious libel, which was contained in a sermon preached by him in St. Mark's Church, Liverpool, and which was afterwards published in the shape of a pamphlet. The jury having found the reverend defendant guilty, the following sentence was passed upon him by the presiding judge:

> "The defendant," Mr. Justice Bailey said, "had been convicted of a libel, contained in a sermon preached by him. He was a clergyman, and had uttered the libel within the church. It was, he rejoiced to say, a rare instance of so sacred a place being corrupted to such purposes (?). Of all other places, the house of God, where charity and brotherly love alone should be inculcated, was the last which should be made a theatre for attacks upon the characters of

living persons. Every man had enough to do to look to his own character, and it was not necessary to go abroad and make ourselves inquisitors into those of others. This libel was uttered at a time, and upon a subject, upon which there was no great unanimity of thinking, and was therefore, in its nature, calculated to excite far other feelings than such as ought to be indulged in within an edifice devoted to God. The defendant had exercised a most wise discretion to-day, in the line of conduct which he had adopted; and the court had reason to believe that, looking back to his past conduct, he felt contrition for what he had already done. Under all these circumstances, the court having taken the whole matter into their consideration, did order and adjudge that, for this offence, the defendant was to pay to the king a fine of one hundred pounds, be imprisoned in the King's Bench Prison for six months, and, at the end of that time, give securities for his good behaviour for five years, himself in five hundred pounds, and two sureties in one hundred pounds each, and to be further imprisoned until these sureties are perfected.

Thus foiled in patronizing clergymen and public writers to vilify their queen, as well as being compelled to abandon the "Bill of Pains and Penalties," ministers began to feel alarmed lest her majesty should publish an exposition of those state secrets and crimes, which she had so frequently threatened. A more certain plan, therefore, to rid themselves and their abandoned king from this dread of certain disgrace, if not of entire ruin, was now secretly put in force; and her majesty was devoted to a premature end, as we have before explained. One thing, however, we have forgotten to mention in our account of that period, which is this: Lord P——, one of the then ministers, and who is now a member of the *Whig* government, was fatally correct in FORETELLING the death of this injured woman; for he very incautiously said, in a letter to a friend, "The Queen will be dead in less than fourteen days!" The letter containing this fatal prediction is now in being; but we could not prevail upon its possessor to allow us to publish a copy of it.

If we have been too prolix in our account or too severe in our remarks respecting our late basely-treated queen, we hope our readers will excuse us. We certainly might say much more, but the subject being one of importance to history, we could not reconcile it with our duty to say less. We are sure every generous-minded Briton will lament, with us, the untimely end of her majesty. Alas! that the page of history should be darkened by such foul transactions as Truth has obliged us to record! Thousands and tens of thousands of the hard-earned money of the tax-payers of this kingdom, with the pledge of peerages to add to the "illustrious dignity" of the House of Lords, were presented to the persons who effected these diabolical acts of atrocity. The money might possibly have been paid; but, in one or two instances, the perpetrators of these sanguinary deeds became too remorse-stricken to wait for the honours of nobility, and made their exit from the world by committing suicide!

The public must have been frequently surprised at the number of persons, of obscure origin, who, without having either distinguished themselves in the world by their talents, or conferred the least benefit upon their country, were ennobled, loaded with wealth, and received into favour, by the profligate George the Fourth. But the following anecdotes, among many others that might be adduced, will explain to our readers the secret causes of such advancement.

*   *   *

Mr. William Knighton was a surgeon, and in his professional capacity attended Sir John M'Mahon (whose numerous villanies we have before set forth) in his last illness, and immediately upon his decease took possession of all his papers, and carried them away, under pretence that M'Mahon had given them to him. When the prince's *grief* had a little subsided, he went for these papers, but, to his great surprise and consternation, found all the drawers empty! He sent for Mr. Knighton, and asked him about the matter. "Yes," said Knighton, "M'Mahon gave them to me!" "But you mean, of course, to restore them?" "Yes, certainly; but only upon a proper remuneration." "Oh!" said the regent, "I always *meant* to give you M'Mahon's place!" Nor could he do less, since he then

Sir Benjamin Bloomfield.

had made himself master, not only of the *private secrets*, but *public ones* also, which were of the greatest possible consequence. The Duchess of Gloucester was present at this dialogue between her brother the Prince Regent and Mr. Knighton. Our informant had this account from her royal highness' own lips, who also added, "And so my poor brother is obliged to keep this viper about him!" But the ministers said, "The prince may entrust his future secretary with his *private* affairs, but his *public* ones belong to us alone, as keepers of his conscience." Mr. Knighton, however, was compensated for this "loss of secrets" by receiving the *honour* of knighthood. He was also employed to deliver a certain titled lady of an illegitimate child, in Hanover-square, and his faithfulness, in keeping this secret from the public, was rewarded by making him a present of the house, most elegantly furnished, in which the disgraceful affair took place!!! Sir William Knighton had likewise a thousand pounds per annum for his professional attendance on the king!!!

*   *   *

Sir Benjamin Bloomfield, who was some time private secretary to his late majesty, also acquired place and wealth by possessing himself of his master's private transactions. This gentleman was sent from Windsor, by George the Fourth, to the

Earl of Liverpool with a large bill for diamonds due to Messrs. Rundell & Co., and for money to pay it. The bill was so large (seventy thousand pounds) that the prime minister *insisted* upon knowing who these diamonds were for. Sir Benjamin very reluctantly confessed that they had been purchased for Lady Conyngham! Lord Liverpool instantly took Bloomfield with him in his own carriage to Windsor, and requested an audience of the king. His lordship, much to his credit, emphatically told his majesty that Sir B. Bloomfield must resign, or he himself would. The king was so enraged with his secretary for informing the earl of these particulars, that he struck Bloomfield a violent blow, when the mortified knight quickly asked, "Who poisoned the Princess Charlotte?" It was owing to this circumstance that Bloomfield was sent as ambassador to Sweden, into *honourable* exile, and, to soothe his wounded pride and prevent his exposure of certain infamous transactions, in which he himself had acted a very prominent part, he was shortly after created—a Lord!!! A good round sum of money was also given him to hush up the matter. We cannot help admiring the conduct of Lord Liverpool in this instance,—the only one, that we are acquainted with, which deserved the thanks of his country; for his lordship boldly refused to pay for the aforesaid diamonds without the consent of parliament, which the king, for shame, could not agree to!

* * *

The Duke of Wellington, who has been frequently termed the mushroom duke, obtained his wealth and titles for exposing the brave army of England to unnecessary dangers and hardships. The position which he chose for that army at Waterloo would have assuredly proved its entire destruction, if it had not been for the treachery of Field Marshal Grouchy, one of Napoleon's generals! But the Wellesley family were in possession of the STATE-SECRETS, and it was therefore deemed prudent to shower wealth and honours upon the whole family.

* * *

Mr. Conant, the chief magistrate of Bow-street, was knighted for conducting the secret investigation against the Princess of Wales in 1813.

* * *

The Marquis of Conyngham, it is well known, obtained his title through the prostitution of his wife to the libertine George the Fourth. The baneful influence which this designing woman exercised over his majesty, to the very last moments of his life, is a deplorable fact, which not only proved mischievous to the best interests of the country, but will for ever brand the name of her contemptible husband with derision and disgust. This shameless mistress stood as the fountain of emolument and preferment, and she took every advantage of that situation to promote the aggrandizement of her family. The indulgent country, however, would hardly have found fault with this second, Mrs. Clarke, had not, in some instances, the very laws of the constitution been infringed, and the domestic policy of the country become endangered, by the effects of her improper influence, which, as it was *secret*, was fraught with the greater injury. Had the marchioness confined herself to benefitting her own family, the mischief would not have been so deplorable; but when the highest offices in the church were bestowed on persons scarcely before heard of,—when political parties rose and fell, and ministers were created and deposed, to gratify the ambition of a prostitute,—then the palace of the king appeared as if surrounded by some pestilential air, and every honourable person avoided the court as alike fatal to private property and public virtue. Thus the entrance to Windsor Castle became, as it were, hermetically sealed, by the "lusty enchantress" within, to all but her favoured minions! The court of George the Fourth certainly differed from that of Charles the Second, although the number and reputation of their several mistresses were nearly the same in favour and character; but George the Fourth had no confiscations to confer on the instruments of his pleasure, and therefore took care to rob the country of gold to make up such deficiency. The reigns of these two monarchs, dissimilar as they might be in some respects, nevertheless possessed this resemblance: that an illegitimate progeny of royalty were thrust forward to the contempt of all decency, and proved a heavy tax on the forbearance of virtuous society. The wicked George the Fourth, as we have been very credibly informed, gave the Marchioness of Conyngham more than half a million of money, as well as bestowing many titles to gratify her insatiable ambition. We really have no words to express our abhorrence of such proceedings!

* * *

Towards the close of George the Fourth's wicked career, he pretended to be very much attached to the drama, and that accomplished and fascinating actress, Miss Chester, was therefore engaged as READER to his majesty. Sir Thomas Lawrence, at that time engaged in taking a portrait of this lady, as well as one of the king, was entrusted with the delicate negotiation. A meeting was soon obtained, and a kind of excuse adopted to have Miss Chester near the king's person, as "PRIVATE READER," at an annual salary of six hundred pounds! Thus was another beauty added to the royal establishment, and her name emblazoned in the "red book" of the country's burdens. For the kind attentions this lady bestowed on the "polished" monarch, she has lately been admitted to that refuge for royal mistresses, titled dames, and pensioned members of the aristocracy—Hampton-Court Palace! Without disputing Miss Chester's claims to be maintained at the public expense among the noble drones there domiciled, it is not without something like disgust and indignation that we view one of our most ancient kingly edifices, built by the liberality of the nation, and at this moment supported by the public purse, being converted into an asylum of this description. Englishmen are thus taxed to support the paramours, and minions of royalty in ease and luxury! But we need not confine our indignation to this one royal residence; for is not Bushy Park within a mile of

Hampton, where the progeny of an actress kept at that place form now a portion of our *noble* aristocracy? We do not charge these unworthy doings exclusively on the Tories; for, alas! the Grey Whigs seem to be treading very closely in the footsteps of their predecessors in office, by tolerating such royal doings, as well as filling their own pockets and that of their families.

* * *

From such disreputable means of acquiring title and wealth, England has long been imposed on, and the ancient nobility of the country degraded. Any pre-eminent degree of merit, if exercised for the country's benefit, was sure to render its possessor a certain object of George the Fourth's vengeance. His private court, therefore, found their best security in their want of virtue. By a voluntary submission to the tyrant's caprices, they retained the *high privilege* of his smile and favour, and built the bulwark of their safety on their *own personal insignificance!* And yet, strange as the infatuation may appear, these very creatures fancied their nature had undergone a real metamorphosis by his majesty granting them a title; they considered themselves refined by a kind of chemical process, sublimed by the sunshine of royal favour, and thus separated from the dross and the dregs of ordinary humanity,—from that humanity of which the mass of mankind partake, and which, contemptible as it may seem to upstart lords, is the same with the prince upon the throne and the beggar upon the dunghill. But from such proud characters, we may trace the present contempt in which nobility is almost universally held. The great endeavour of George the Fourth's favourites has been to keep "the people" at a distance, lest their own *purer* nature should be contaminated by plebeian society; and the first lesson they teach their offspring is, not to revere God, but to maintain their own dignity in the scale of being! To men of such principles, the king had only to make his wishes known, however monstrous and unjust they might be, and they were immediately, and, in too many cases, *fatally* executed. Under such a government as that of the last sixty years and upwards, it was fortunate indeed to escape notice,— to creep through the vale of obscurity, and to die in old age, without the prison, the pointed steel, or the poisoned cup! From a vigorous mind, in every way calculated to find pleasure and honourable employment in noble and virtuous actions, George the Fourth degenerated into a monster, delighting in baubles and in a wantonness of wickedness that produced the most flagitious habits, and which rendered him the most despicable man in the whole circle of society; yet he was designated "the most accomplished gentleman of the age!!!" We are aware that he was surrounded with flatterers and sycophants, who wished to gratify their *own* avarice and pride by extending *his* tyrannical power; but ought such a mean excuse to be urged in extenuation of his crimes? A man, like him, endowed with nature's choicest gifts, both of mind and body, which were farther heightened by the most liberal education, should have spurned such minions from his presence, and kept company with none but the virtuous and the patriotic. Away, then, with that vindication of George the Fourth's unjust deeds, which would fix the stigma of crimes, prompted by his *own* love of sensuality, to the "advice of evil counsellors!" Evil counsellors would not have dared to present him the cup of flattery, if he had not shewn himself so greedily desirous of swallowing its contents. Let every friend of man and of his country, then, guard against two similar reigns of horror, and defy, as we do, fines and imprisonment, in attempting, by every lawful and rational means, to push back the gigantic strides of tyranny, whether in a king or an overbearing ministry. Even now we are cursed with a power, generated by Queen Charlotte and the late king, her son, which is trying, by every scheme of ingenuity and desperation, to bring back its former unjust, intolerant, and corrupt ascendency, both in church and state; but who is there that can contemplate the possibility of such a state of affairs occurring again, without feelings of horror? What man in the possession of his senses but would exclaim against the national misfortune of having another Pitt, a Liverpool, a Londonderry, a Canning, or a Wellington, in power? Awful, however, as the havoc appears which these men have made, the country need not yet give itself up to despair. We believe that there is a fund of vigour in the empire that may stand experiments, the least of which would shake the sickly frames of other empires to dissolution. There is probably no dominion on earth that has within itself so strong a repulsion of injury, or so vivid and rapid a spring and force of restoration. Its strength is renewed like that of the young eagle; and it is this very faculty of self-restoration that has so long allowed the empire to hold together, notwithstanding the infinite speculations, tamperings, absurdities, and crimes of men in power, under the guidance of Queen Charlotte and George the Fourth. Yet is it right that England should be kept merely above bankruptcy, while she has the original power of being the first, most vigorous, richest, and happiest portion of the world? Where does the earth contain a people so palpably marked out for superiority in all the means of private and public enjoyment of affluence, influence, and security? The most industrious, strong-minded, and fully-educated population of the world inhabit her island. She has the finest opportunities for commerce, the most indefatigable and sagacious efforts and contrivances for every necessity and luxury of mankind; inexhaustible mines of the most valuable minerals, and almost the exclusive possession of the most valuable of them all,—COAL; a singularly healthy and genial climate, where the human form naturally shapes itself into the most complete beauty and vigour; a situation the most happily fixed by Providence for a great people destined to influence Europe,—close enough to the Continent to watch every movement, and influence the good or peril of every kingdom of it from Russia to Turkey, and yet secured from the sudden shocks and casualties of European war by the Channel, of all defences, the cheapest, the most permanent, and the most impregnable!

When these immense and enviable advantages are compared with the present state of England, heavy indeed must the sins of our rulers appear! But a new class and character of hostility is now happily starting up to oppose further inroads upon our liberties, and the question will speedily be brought to a decision, not between the obsolete and formal parties of the two houses of parliament, but between the Treasury bench and the delegates of "the people,"—that people itself shewing a bold and virtuous character, commissioning its representatives with a voice of authority, and exhibiting a rigid determination to see that their duty is done, unexampled in the history of Britain! This is the kind of spirit that has long been wanted, and we look to it as the sure cure for the decaying vitality of the constitution. We are no advocates for a revolution brought about by popular passion, by the vulgar artifice of vulgar demi-gods, by the itinerant inflammation of pretended patriotism; but the present state of public feeling appeals not to the ambition of the democrat, to the baseness of the incendiary, the sordidness of the plunderer, or the fury of the assassin. There is nothing in it but the natural expression of honourable minds, disdaining to look calmly upon injustice, extortion, and royal profligacy, whether practised by Whig or Tory, and however sanctioned by time. The people are indignant at the callous venality of public men, and feel themselves insulted by the open spoil which bloated sinecurists and state-secret keepers have so long committed upon the honest gains of society. They cannot see the necessity of that strangling burthen of taxes which makes industry as poor as idleness, and they shrink from the view of their withering effect on the freedom and prosperity of England. The people who observe matters in this light are not the wild haters of all governments, nor the sullen conspirators against the peace of mankind; but the father of the industrious family, the man of genius, honesty, and virtue, the sincere patriot, are those who now feel themselves compelled to come from their willing obscurity into the front rank of public care, to raise up their voices, till now never heard beyond the study or the fireside, and demand that the House of Commons shall at last throw off its fetters, scorn the indolence, meanness, and venality of the Upper House, knowing no impulse but its duty, no patronage but that of public gratitude, and no party but its country! Such feelings are so just, that they have become universal, and so universal, that they have become IRRESISTIBLE! The minister, be he Whig or Tory, must yield to them, or he instantly descends from his power. All candidates for public distinction will thus be compelled to discover that the most prudent choice, as well as the most manly, generous, and principled, is to side with the country. Then may we hope to see sinecures extinguished; the obnoxious patronage of government destroyed; every superfluous expense of the public service rent away; the enormous salaries of ministers and the feeders on the civil list reduced; the annuities to ministerial aunts, cousins, and connexions of more dubious kinds, on the pension list, unsparingly expunged; which, by disburthening the nation of unnecessary taxes, will enable the Englishman to live by his labour. If these things may be done by the Russell reform bill, it will be only by a circuitous process. But England has no time to wait. What must be done at last cannot be done too speedily. The truth is, that the nation is disgusted with the insolent extravagance of the Grey cabinet, which utters the most zealous declarations of economy and withdrawal of taxes, while the people remain unrelieved of a single impost. They observe a premier lavish of the public money on his own family, while a Chancellor of the Exchequer starts up, and sapiently condemns certain members of the Whig government for refusing their salaries! Thus the old Tory system is still attempted to be perpetuated, under the banners of the Whigs; the tax-gatherer makes his appearance with undiminished demands;

the necessaries of life increase in price as they decrease in excellence; every thing, in short, that man eats, drinks, or wears, loads him with an additional tax, paralyzing his industry, and overwhelming him in poverty.

Every candid and impartial observer will acknowledge that the public voice is not raised against government itself, nor against the many admirable institutions of this country; but against the perversions of government; against unconstitutional and wicked rulers; against abuses of trust, office, and authority; against impositions and corruptions pervading every department of the state, which have been reduced to system, and teem with every species of fraud, tyranny, and oppression; against the Star Chamber of Toryism; against the misappropriation of unnecessary, extortionate, and oppressive imposts; against despotic enactments; against fictitious prosecutions and arbitrary imprisonments; against the perversions of law and the decrees of political judges; against spies and hireling ruffians, suborned to deprive the subject of his liberty, aided by the corrupt practices of heart-hardened clerical and other magistrates; against packed juries, and the artful construction of libel; against the iniquitous forms and delays of the chancery and other courts;—against these, we say, and all such violations of the chartered rights of Britons, is that voice proclaiming its DETERMINATION TO BE FREE!—to be masters of their own wealth, their own industry, their own personal security, and their own liberties! The people of England will no longer be swayed by those upstart peers which George the Fourth created. What claims have such state-pensioners on public confidence? Why should sensible men give up their judgments to a selfish and hypocritical faction of—Lords? What better, in the name of heaven, are they than the rest of human creatures?

> "Remove their swelling epithets, thick laid
> As varnish on a harlot's cheek; the rest,
> Thin sown with ought of profit or delight,
> Will far be found unworthy."

It is, indeed, idle to suppose that the present highly-enlightened inhabitants of this country can be thwarted from their wishes by the vote of such men; for almost all the ancient nobility are with the people. Englishmen, we repeat, care not for the vote of time-serving lords, for the prayers of worldly-minded bishops, or for the tears and vehement gestures of ex-chancellors! The people have resolved to redeem the constitution from their polluting hands. The pupils of those who have brought the country to its present impoverished state by their misrule, during the last two reigns of vice and profligacy, will seek in vain for the support of the people of 1832! A different form of government is now dawning upon us, and the Tories have "fallen, for ever fallen!" Murder, we trust, will now no longer be committed with impunity by rank; exactions, weighing down a people's existence, will cease; the needy will no longer be required to pamper the insatiable avarice and voluptuousness of the great; a system of pure justice in the administration of national affairs will rectify those abuses which have for so many years ingulphed the kingdom in misery. If the people do but prove true to themselves, nothing can now prevent their emancipation from the thraldom of that overgrown power, by which they have cruelly been enslaved. Yet the disease has been so long accumulating, that it still lies deep, and will require both energy and skill to eradicate it. They must, therefore, be upon their guard against the machinations of their wily enemies, who will magnify every little ebullition of public feeling into an attempt to overturn the existing institutions of the country. Sensible men, and true friends to the constitution, and therefore to the king, who forms so considerable a part of it, will understand the Tory cry of "See the effects of power in the hands of the people!" and will not be led into a fear of some future evil, from popular commotion, by such an attempt to divert them from their constitutional rights. In this respect, vigilance is highly necessary to protect them from the secret depredations of their former artful tyrants, who are ever on the alert to regain their lost power. Let the people, then, avoid all riots, tumults, and popular commotions, with the utmost care, and preserve peace, good order, and security to all ranks of society. True patriots will be careful to discourage everything which tends to destroy these natural fruits of a free constitution, not only because whatever tends to destroy them tends to destroy all human happiness, but also because even an accidental outrage in popular assemblies and proceedings, as we have before shewn, is used by the enemies of freedom to discredit the cause of liberty. By the utmost attention to the preservation of the public peace, Englishmen will defeat the malicious designs of servile courtiers; but, whatever may happen, they will not desert the cause of humanity. Through a dread of licentiousness, they will not forsake the standard of liberty. It is the part of fools to fall upon Scylla in striving to avoid Charybdis. Who would wish to see restored the despotic sway of Queen Charlotte and George the Fourth, through the fear of a few transient outrages being committed by the excitation of a long-insulted people? Both these extremes are despotic while they last; but the former is a torrent that would rush its headlong course for ever, if it met not a barrier sufficiently strong to resist its power, while the latter may be compared to a spring flood, that covers the meadows to-day, and disappears on the morrow. The learned and eloquent Dr. Price has a passage so applicable to this subject, that our readers must excuse our introducing it. This humane philosopher observes,

> "Licentiousness and despotism are more nearly allied than is commonly imagined. They are both alike inconsistent with liberty, and the true end of government; nor is there any other difference between them than that one is the licentiousness of great men, and the other the licentiousness of little men; or that by one, the persons and property of a people are subject to outrage and invasion from a king or a lawless body of grandees; and that by the other, they are subject to the like outrage from a lawless mob. In avoiding one of these evils, mankind have often run into the other. But all well-constituted governments guard equally against both. Indeed, of the two, the last is, on several accounts, the least to be dreaded, and has done the least mischief. It may be truly said, if licentiousness has destroyed its thousands, despotism has destroyed its millions. The former having little power, and no system

to support it, necessarily finds its own remedy; and a people soon get out of the tumult and anarchy attending it. But a despotism, wearing a form of government, and being armed with its force, is an evil not to be conquered without dreadful struggles. It goes on from age to age, debasing the human faculties, levelling all distinctions, and preying on the rights and blessings of society. It deserves to be added, that in a state disturbed by licentiousness, there is an animation which is favourable to the human mind, and puts it upon exerting its powers; but in a state habituated to despotism, all is still and torpid. A dark and savage tyranny stifles every effort of genius, and the mind loses all its spirit and dignity."

Mr. Bailey, of Nottingham, an independent writer of great talent, has well defined the causes of political convulsions, and the line of conduct to be pursued by "the people" in times of great excitement. In that gentleman's "Discourse on Revolutions," he says,

"That the progress of civilization may be retarded in states, by the measures of governments, cannot be doubted. That the tendencies towards disturbance in states, which inevitably await on advancing civilization, may be restrained in their development by a politic or resolute government, even whilst its policy is anomalous to the spirit of the age, can as little be doubted. But what, it may be fairly asked, is in reality gained by this procedure? The principle of revolution is not annihilated, the nature of social man is not altered, the impetus of knowledge is not weakened, the momentum of public opinion is not broken! After everything is done which cunning or tyranny can suggest, to avert the day of demand and concession, IT WILL ARRIVE, when demand will be made in a voice of thunder by an infuriated populace, and concession, of the most humiliating description, be granted by an abject sovereign!

"As fires longest pent up in obscurity at length burst out with the most resistless fury, so revolutions longest deferred are attended, in their crisis, with the most terrible consequences. Were the rulers of nations actuated by a spirit of sound wisdom, those dreadful convulsions could never arise in states, on account of social rights, which, after causing the death of thousands of the citizens, and desolating towns and provinces, leave palaces in ruins, and thrones vacant.

"Revolution ought always to be the work of the government, not of the people, except through the expression of public opinion. This is the only species of power which the people can beneficially employ for the redress of grievances,—at least, in old states, where a long indulgence in habits of venality and corruption by the government, and a widely-extended ramification of interests springing therefrom, and pervading all classes of the community, must create a strong disposition in favour of the existing order of things among large masses of the citizens. Physical force ought never to be employed for the correction of social evils, until every species of negative resistance has been proved to be unavailing.

"When despotism has arrived at that state of audacious temerity, that it makes a mockery of suffering, and tramples on remonstrances, sacrificing alike the property, the persons, and consciences of men to its ungovernable lust of dominion, it is justifiable to arraign such tyrants at the tribunal of nature, that so their impotence may be exposed, and their crimes punished."

Let us hope, therefore, that Englishmen, in freeing themselves from despotism, will studiously avoid such scenes as lately took place at Bristol. Britons should recollect that a determined and virtuous people can do anything and everything by firmness and quietness; but all violence defeats its own ends, and gives advantage to our enemies. A thorough reform in church and state MUST take place; a crisis is at hand, and those who wish to see England escape a trial of misery and blood will heartily wish, and openly and resolutely demand, to see a change of that long system, under which Corruption has thickened round the high, while Poverty and Taxation have smitten the low. A longer delay to remedy these evils may unhappily irritate the people into a spirit of vengeance, which the tears of Lord Eldon, the bullying of the Marquis of Londonderry, the professions of a Whig ministry, the intrigues of German women, or the threatenings of Wellington's bayonet law would vainly attempt to oppose! Sullen visions are now upon the clouds, to which place-hunters and renegades are afraid to lift their terrified eyes. But if they tremble at those visions, what will be their fate when they ripen into substance, and let loose their thunders upon the heads of the enemies of our country? May the necessity for such vengeance be obviated by a timely concession to the constitutional demands of an enlightened people is our sincere prayer!

THE END.

Printed by W. H. Stevenson, 5, Whiskin Street, Clerkenwell.

Notes

Notes to the Introduction to The Secret History of the Court of England by Rachael Gillibrand

1. Anon, 'ART. VI. - Secret History of the Court of England from the Accession of George III to the Death of George IV; including, amongst all other important Matters, full Particulars of the Mysterious Death of the Princess Charlotte ', *The Quarterly Review*; 61: 112 (1838), 425-427 (p. 426).
2. The offence of criminal libel was only formally abolished in 2010 when modern 'hate crime' legislation rendered criminal libel null and void, although libel had not been prosecuted as a criminal case since at least the 1840s.
3. W.J. Thoms, 'Lady Anne Hamilton's Secret History', *Notes and Queries*, 5: 8 (1877), 227.
4. Anon, 'ART. VI – Secret History', p. 426.
5. Anon, 'Secret History of The Court of England', *The Monthly Magazine*, 26:153 (Sep. 1838), 257-265 (p. 265).
6. K. D. Reynolds [online], 'Hamilton, Lady Anne (1766–1846), Courtier', in *Oxford Dictionary of National Biography* (Sep. 2004), accessed 28 February 2021. Available at: www.oxforddnb.com.
7. Anon, 'ART. VI – Secret History', p. 426.
8. K. D. Reynolds [online], 'Serres [née Wilmot], Olivia [alias Princess Olive of Cumberland] (1772–1835), Royal Impostor', in *Oxford Dictionary of National Biography* (Sep. 2004), accessed 28 February 2021. Available at: www.oxforddnb.com
9. Anon, 'Secret History of The Court of England', p. 265.

Notes to The Secret History of the Court of England – Volume 1

1. *Members of Parliament—SB.*
2. When the inquest was held, the razor was found on some drawers in the room; but it was placed there by a Bow-street officer, by mistake,—at least, so it was reported. We, however, consider even the very partial evidence published in the "Morning Post" quite sufficient to prove that poor Sellis had nothing to do with the razor himself. Some one else must have thrown it "two yards from the bed." The murdered man could not possibly have so exerted himself after the infliction of such a severe wound!
3. Whatever our readers may think of this jumble of words, we assure them it is *verbatim* from the ORIGINAL affidavit, which is WITHOUT POINTS, as lawyers consider such matters unnecessary.
4. The Duke of Sussex excused himself from taking part in the proceedings against the queen on the plea of being so nearly related to her majesty. When this was stated in the House of Lords, the Duke of York said, "My lords, I have as much

reason, and, *heaven knows*, I would as anxiously desire as my royal relative to absent myself from these proceedings; but when I have a DUTY imposed upon me, of *such magnitude as the present*, I should be *ashamed* to offer such an EXCUSE!" It is astonishing how any man, who had *outraged virtue* and violated HIS DUTY in a thousand ways, could, unblushingly, thus insult the English nation!

Volume Two

1. *Avater* is the Hindoo expression for a divinity assuming the human form, and residing on earth.
2. Mr. Denman has since been created "Sir Thomas," and, at the period of our writing this, holds the office of attorney-general. On the 21st of May, 1832, Lord Stormont brought forward a motion in the House of Commons relative to a general crusade against the press, for what his lordship pleased to term "infamous, obscene, and scandalous libels." It must ever be gratifying to patriots when public men openly confess their errors; and we are, therefore, most happy to record the following extract from Sir Thomas Denman's speech, delivered on the above occasion, relative to the prosecution upon which we have so freely commented: "In May, 1822, he (Sir Thomas Denman) first sat as common-sergeant, and was called upon to try a case of most atrocious libel in 'The Republican:' it contained a summing up of all the blasphemies which had ever been promulgated in that paper, and direct incitements to insurrection. The prosecution was instituted by a constitutional association, which thought the attorney-general was negligent of his duty; but he believed that that association obtained but little credit for thus undertaking his functions. There were two aldermen upon the bench, one of whom thought that two years' imprisonment was the least that could be awarded as a punishment, while the other thought that one year would be sufficient. The middle course was pursued, and the man was sentenced to *eighteen* months' imprisonment. Though this was the *mildest* punishment which had been awarded on any case of a similar description at that time, yet he (the attorney-general) had been held up to odium as a cruel judge. The public, it was clear, had reaped no benefit whatever, and he (the attorney-general) had experienced some pain during the whole of the eighteen months that that man was in prison; for he felt a strong disinclination to proceed against any man who was fairly stating his opinions. The young man was twenty-one years of age, and what he was doing was certainly mischievous; *but when his imprisonment expired, he could assure the House that it was to himself a great comfort.* The liberty of the press was established in this country, and that alone was enough to induce people to publish those opinions; and that liberty would make him extremely cautious of prosecuting merely for opinion. During periods of public excitement, the classes from which juries were taken gave no encouragement to prosecutions, and if only one juryman stood out upon a case, the prosecution was obliged to be dropped. He, therefore, except some very atrocious circumstances should occur, did not think it expedient to proceed. In striking special juries, it was impossible to go into the heart of society, and act as spies in families to ascertain the sentiments of jurymen. *It was necessary to submit to a great deal, lest by legal proceedings bad should be made worse.* Prosecutions against the press were better left alone." The last sentence of this speech contains advice which we hope to see *practised* by all future attorney-generals. In the case of Sir Thomas Denman, however, it is only adopted through *necessity*;

for he freely confesses his wish to prosecute, if he could only insure the verdict of a jury! It is, indeed, a gratifying truth, that attorney-generals cannot controul the decisions of juries; and it is well for the people of England that they cannot. Were it otherwise, the press would soon become worse than useless, and every independent writer speedily be consigned to a prison. We cannot, consequently, join Sir Thomas Denman in his lamentation; and we regret that a gentleman of such lofty pretensions to liberality and patriotism should have tarnished his fame by thus exposing himself to the censure of his countrymen. While upon this subject, we would give a word of advice to Lord Stormont. His lordship has been described as a young man of considerable natural abilities, which have been highly improved by a liberal education. How, then, can he be so blind to the spirit of the present age as to suppose himself capable of restoring the very worst part of Toryism,—that of undermining the glorious LIBERTY OF THE PRESS? His noble father (who was educated in the Pitt school of politics) may have impressed him with an idea of its practicability; but the people are now changed, the age is changed, and we warn him not to expose himself to the disgust of the English people, by making futile attempts to destroy the grand palladium of national liberty. As well, indeed, might he essay to execute Herod's commands to slay the innocents, as to restore, by such means, the absolute power which the Tories so unfortunately exercised during the last two reigns!

3. *The Duke of Bassano was Napoleon's private secretary—SB.*

4. The following is a translation of the letter above referred to: "Rocheford, 13th July, 1815. Your Royal Highness, A victim to the factions which distract my country, and to the enmity of the greatest powers of Europe, I have terminated my political career, and I come, like Themistocles, to throw myself upon the hospitality of the British people. I put myself under the protection of their laws, which I claim from your royal highness, as the most powerful, the most constant, and the most generous of my enemies. Napoleon."

5. However tyrannical the orders of Lord Castlereagh might have been, we cannot help remarking on the petty pleasure Sir Hudson took in executing them, even to the very letter. It was this kind of conduct in Napoleon's jailer that gave rise to the following distich: "Sir Hudson Lowe, Sir Hudson Lowe,By name, and ah! BY NATURE SO!" Napoleon himself said of this governor, "I have had to do with men of all countries; I never saw any who had so bad a physiognomy, and a more execrable conversation. He writes with the intention of being amicable. That is a contrast to the ignoble vexations that are daily imagined. There is something sinister in all this." Without contradicting the repeated asseverations of Sir Hudson Lowe, that he only acted according to instructions, we must say, that any man of honour should rather have resigned his office than have executed them; for they were not only unnecessary to the security of Napoleon, but they were also ILLEGAL. But Sir Hudson did not possess moral courage; he was captious and mistrustful, and was not at all calculated for the delicate offices he had to perform; he created his own fears, and lost his understanding in endeavouring to foresee misfortune. Count Lascases thus writes of him: "The noble-minded English beside us," says the Count, "as well as those who merely visited the island, used to say that our treatment would experience a great and blessed change when the new governor appeared, &c. &c. This new Messiah at length came; but, gracious God!—the

word escapes involuntarily from my pen,—it was an executioner, a *gens-d'arme*, whom they had sent. On his appearance, every thing assumed a dark and gloomy aspect; every appearance of external respect, and all the forms prescribed by a due regard to decency, which had hitherto been observed, at once disappeared; every day since has been to us a day of greater pain and more insulting treatment; he has narrowed still farther the boundaries prescribed to us, and even endeavoured to interfere with our domestic economy; he has strictly interdicted all intercourse with the natives, and even prohibited all society with officers of his own nation; he has ordered our residence to be surrounded with ditches and palisades; he has increased the number of soldiers, and endeavoured to make prisons within prisons; he has surrounded us with objects of affright, and reduced us to close custody. The emperor remains almost always in his prison, and no longer leaves his apartment. The few audiences which he has given to that officer have been highly disagreeable and oppressive to him; he has put an end to them, and determined not to see the governor any more. 'I had just grounds,' he observed, 'to complain of the Admiral, though he had at least a heart; but this man has not even a vestige of the character of an Englishman, he is nothing but a low Sicilian *sbirro*.' Sir Hudson Lowe pleads the instructions of his minister in justification of himself, with respect to all these complaints; if this justification is well founded, his instructions are most barbarous; but he can bear witness, at the same time, that he endeavours to carry them into execution in a barbarous manner."

6. Sir Hudson Lowe is, doubtless, the person here alluded to by the emperor; but he would not have dared to act as he did if such tyrannical and unfeeling conduct had been against Lord Castlereagh's approbation.
7. Particularly his eloquent and manly "Appeal to the Parliament of Great Britain, on the case of the Emperor Napoleon."
8. Plutarch assigns him three different deaths; but Livy tells us, that Hannibal drank poison, which he always carried about with him, in case he should be taken by surprise.
9. More particularly the affair of the bondholders. His lordship also strenuously exerted himself to prevent any public inquiry into the cruel death of the Princess Charlotte.
10. The treatment and death of Napoleon, the funeral of the late queen, the conduct of the ministers and soldiers on that occasion, the murders at Cumberland Gate, the dismissal of Sir Robert Wilson for an attempt to stop the scene of bloodshed, formed but a portion of the black catalogue of their misdeeds.
11. From William Cowper's *The Task*—SB.
12. *2 Kings 8: 13: 'But what is your servant—a dog, that he should do this gross thing?'*—SB.
13. *2 Samuel 12: 7: 'Then Nathan said to David, "You are the man! Thus says the LORD God of Israel: 'I anointed you king over Israel, and I delivered you from the hand of Saul'*—SB.
14. How well has part of this prediction been fulfilled by the people of 1832! May the rest be speedily accomplished!
15. See motion for a new writ for the Borough of St. Mawes, in the room of Francis Horner, esq., deceased.
16. How lamentably is this fact illustrated by the present Whig minister,—the *disinterested* Earl Grey,—who has added to the burdens of his country, by places and pensions to his own family alone, more than sixty-two thousand pounds annually!!!